Food, Nutrition, and the Young Child

FIFTH EDITION

Jeannette Brakhane Endres
Southern Illinois University, Carbondale

Robert E. Rockwell
Southern Illinois University, Edwardsville

Cynthia Gurdian Mense
Saint Louis University, St. Louis, Missouri

PEARSON

Merrill
Prentice Hall

Upper Saddle River, New Jersey
Columbus, Ohio

Library of Congress Cataloging-in-Publication Data

Endres, Jeannette Brakhane.

   Food, nutrition, and the young child / Jeannette Brakhane Endres, Cynthia Gurdian Mense,
Robert E. Rockwell.—5th ed.

      p. ; cm.

Includes bibliographical references and index.

   ISBN 0-13-098485-X

   1. Children—Nutrition. 2. Infants—Nutrition. 3. Day care cneters—Food service.
4. Nursery schools—Food service.

   [DNLM: 1. Child Nutrition. 2. Dietary Services. 3. Infant Nutrition. 4. Nutrition—
education. WS 115 E56f 2003] I. Rockwell, Robert E. II. Mense, Cynthia Gurdian.
III. Title

   RJ206.E63 2004

   613.2'083—dc22

                                                                              2003022956

Vice President and Executive Publisher: Jeffery W. Johnston
Publisher: Kevin M. Davis
Development Editor: Christina Tawney
Editorial Assistant: Autumn Crisp
Production Editor: Sheryl Glicker Langner
Production Coordination: Emily Hatteberg, Carlisle Publishers Services
Design Coordinator: Diane C. Lorenzo
Photo Coordinator: Cynthia Cassidy
Cover Designer: Linda Sorrells-Smith
Cover image: Corbis
Production Manager: Laura Messerly
Director of Marketing: Ann Castel Davis
Marketing Manager: Amy June
Marketing Coordinator: Tyra Poole

This book was set in Palatino by Carlisle Communications, Ltd. It was printed and bound by
R. R. Donnelley & Sons Company. The cover was printed by Coral Graphics.

Photo Credits: Cynthia Cassidy, p. 2; U.S. Department of Agriculture, p. 4; Pearson Learning, p. 33; USDA Photo by:
Ken Hammond, pp. 44, 164, 226, 244; PH College, p. 46; John Paul Endress/Silver Burdett Ginn, pp. 59, 316; Scott
Cunningham/Merrill, pp. 76, 128; Robert E. Rockwell, p. 82; Shirley Zeiberg/PH College, pp. 88, 114; Courtesy of
Medela, p. 91; Cynthia Cassidy/Merrill, pp. 93, 129, 143, 152, 211, 282; Michal Heron/ PH College, p. 102; Teri
Stratford/PH College, p. 103; Roy Ramsey/PH College, pp. 120, 306; Laima Druskis/PH College, p. 122; George
Dodson/PH College, p. 127; C. Traficante/PH College , p. 145; Todd Yarrington/Merrill, pp. 157, 194; Anne
Vega/Merrill, pp. 166, 181, 268, 288, 289, 290, 301, 308; Cynthia Mense, pp. 182, 183; Dan Floss/Merrill, p. 195;
Anthony Magnacca/Merrill, p. 202; Tom Watson/Merrill, p. 209; Peter Buckley/PH College, p. 221.

Pearson Education Ltd.
Pearson Education Singapore Pte. Ltd.
Pearson Education Canada, Ltd.
Pearson Education—Japan

Pearson Education Australia Pty. Limited
Pearson Education North Asia Ltd.
Pearson Educación de Mexico, S.A. de C.V.
Pearson Education Malaysia Pte. Ltd.

PEARSON
Merrill
Prentice Hall

10 9 8 7 6 5 4 3 2 1
ISBN: 0-13-098485-X

To
Alicia Christina, Teri Lynn, Robert Joel, Amanda Sue, Kathryn Lee, Michael Wayne,
August Alvaro, and Maria Gabriella

Preface

The purpose of *Food, Nutrition, and the Young Child* is to provide an easy-to-read book about food and nutrition as it applies to the care of the child from birth through 8 years of age. It provides ways to integrate food and nutrition into the early childhood setting.

FEATURES AND NEW TO THE FIFTH EDITION OF *FOOD, NUTRITION, AND THE YOUNG CHILD*

The book begins with basic nutrition principles in Chapter 1. Chapter 2 applies the principles of food and nutrition, and the food and nutrient standards and guidelines, to everyday life for the teacher.

The book specifically addresses the child who is cared for in home day care, preschool, or full–day-care centers with emphasis on protecting the child's health by providing the tools to assure the teacher and parents that the child is growing and developing normally. The text addresses the role of the child-care facility in helping mothers achieve their goal of exclusive and/or long-term breastfeeding as well as contributing to establishing breastfeeding as a cultural norm.

The text incorporates national standards and policies from renowned organizations such as the Centers for Disease Control and Prevention, the American Dietetic Association, the American Academy of Pediatrics, and the National Resource Center for Health and Safety in Child Care.

Since the last edition there has been increasing evidence that our nation's children stand to be the heaviest generation. This text addresses promotion of healthful eating behaviors and physical activity patterns and identifies policies that contribute to wellness and prevent the secular trend toward obesity. We have incorporated the newest physical activity guidelines for infants and toddlers as well as young children.

Benefits for professors and students include an easy-to-read text that covers the newest information for infants, toddlers, preschoolers, and young children on: what foods to provide; when to provide the foods; how to encourage a nutritious food intake; how to arrange the eating situation to facilitate learning activities; what food and nutrition problems are seen in each age group; and strategies for involving parents.

Chapter 1 includes updated basic information on energy and nutrients. It introduces folic acid and neural tube defects and offers a cautionary note on use of herbal remedies. Helpful tools in this chapter include body mass index (BMI) calculations, dietary analysis programs, and physical activities to help teachers understand energy balance.

Chapter 2 includes Web sites from which to access tools to assess food and nutrient intakes. It introduces the Activity Pyramid for children and Dietary Reference Intakes (DRI) for assessing nutrient intake. In addition, it provides information about the benefits and cautions of physical activity, and dietary implications of childhood disorders.

Chapter 3 introduces the Centers for Disease Control and Prevention's new growth charts. It also updates breastfeeding information, including:

Strategies for maintaining breast milk supply
The role of the care provider in promoting breastfeeding
Tool for assessing a mother's intention to breastfeed exclusively
Care and handling of breast milk
Identification of policies that promote and protect breastfeeding

Chapter 3 also provides the top ten bottle feeding practices to avoid and advice on how to read a baby like a book. It is in this chapter that an infant feeding policy is discussed. Expanded sections are included on the promotion of healthful feeding behaviors, on early childhood caries and the American Academy of Pediatric Dentistry Guidelines Child-Care Settings, and on reflux and reflux disease. This chapter also incorporates the National Resource Center for Health and Safety in Child Care's nutrition standards.

Chapters 4, 5, and 6 provide updated information about eating patterns recommended for children using the new Food Guide Pyramid for Young Children. These chapters incorporate the new Dietary Reference Intakes, Adequate Intakes, and Acceptable Macronutrient Distribution into diets of toddlers, preschoolers, and young children.

A new standard allowing a wider acceptable fat range for each age group and a new recommendation for fiber intake are included, as well as the American Academy of Pediatrics' new recommendations on television viewing and the Centers for Disease Control's new growth charts and BMI for children over age 2. These chapters also include obesity prevention strategies for the young child, incorporation of National Resource Center for Health and Safety in Child Care's nutrition standards, and a listing of model policies that promote nutrition and physical fitness in the child-care center.

New physical activity guidelines are given for 1 hour or more per day.

Chapter 7 has been expanded to include more than how to prepare the menu and now includes new standards and guidelines for food served to young children. It also provides an overview of community programs that address child health and nutrition issues and an expanded food safety section, including references to on-line assistance.

Chapter 8 explores a variety of programmatic approaches used in early childhood programs.

Chapter 9, the final chapter, presents new strategies for involving parents and teachers as partners in nutrition education.

METHOD OF RESEARCH

The text is up-to-date, reflecting numerous new research publications from professional journals, industry, and governmental agencies. Of particular interest is the inclusion of the new Dietary Reference Intakes (DRI) and more emphasis on physical activity, along with sound nutrition practices. The importance of breastfeeding is further emphasized to ensure that centers caring for infants take every available measure to assist breastfeeding mothers. The authors have tested the concepts presented in the book in day-care and preschool centers. They have visited centers and consulted with teachers who have read the material presented.

ACKNOWLEDGMENTS

We wish to acknowledge the efforts of those who helped in the research, diet analysis, and preparation of the fifth edition of *Food, Nutrition, and the Young Child*. We wish to thank Christina Gray who worked on updating basic nutrition. Sharon Barter, researcher at Southern Illinois University–Carbondale, calculated dietary data and designed table after table. Her critical review was also appreciated.

The newest author, C.G.M., would like to thank Anne Muren for babysitting her children, and the faculty and staff at Saint Louis University, for many resources, tips, and impromptu babysitting. Thanks to Patricia Hoffman, Tara O'Shaugnessy, Ana Lewis, and her husband, Jim Mense, for reviewing chapters. Thanks to Carrie Bosch and Cindy Linneman for their attention to detail and help with numerous tables.

We are also grateful to the reviewers: Linda Aiken, Southwestern Community College; Linda Herring, Itawamba Community College; Sally Fogg Jennings, St. Louis Community College; Barbara Lohse Knous, University of Wisconsin-Stout; Joanne Spaide, University of Northern Iowa; Barbara Wiita, University of Akron; John Worobey, Rutgers University; and Jessie Zola, Milwaukee Area Technical College.

J. B. E.; R. E. R.; C. G. M.

Educator Learning Center:
An Invaluable Online Resource

Merrill Education and the Association for Supervision and Curriculum Development (ASCD) invite you to take advantage of a new online resource, one that provides access to the top research and proven strategies associated with ASCD and Merrill—the Educator Learning Center. At **www.EducatorLearningCenter.com** you will find resources that will enhance your students' understanding of course topics and of current educational issues, in addition to being invaluable for further research.

HOW THE EDUCATOR LEARNING CENTER WILL HELP YOUR STUDENTS BECOME BETTER TEACHERS

With the combined resources of Merrill Education and ASCD, you and your students will find a wealth of tools and materials to better prepare them for the classroom.

Research

- More than 600 articles from the ASCD journal *Educational Leadership* discuss everyday issues faced by practicing teachers.
- A direct link on the site to Research Navigator™ gives students access to many of the leading education journals, as well as extensive content detailing the research process.
- Excerpts from Merrill Education texts give your students insights on important topics of instructional methods, diverse populations, assessment, classroom management, technology, and refining classroom practice.

Classroom Practice

- Hundreds of lesson plans and teaching strategies are categorized by content area and age range.
- Case studies and classroom video footage provide virtual field experience for student reflection.
- Computer simulations and other electronic tools keep your students abreast of today's classrooms and current technologies.

LOOK INTO THE VALUE OF EDUCATOR LEARNING CENTER YOURSELF

Preview the value of this educational environment by visiting **www.EducatorLearningCenter.com** and clicking on "Demo." For a free 4-month subscription to the Educator Learning Center in conjunction with this text, simply contact your Merrill/Prentice Hall sales representative.

Discover the Companion Website
Accompanying This Book

THE PRENTICE HALL COMPANION WEBSITE:
A VIRTUAL LEARNING ENVIRONMENT

Technology is a constantly growing and changing aspect of our field that is creating a need for content and resources. To address this emerging need, Prentice Hall has developed an online learning environment for students and professors alike—Companion Websites—to support our textbooks.

In creating a Companion Website, our goal is to build on and enhance what the textbook already offers. For this reason, the content for each user-friendly website is organized by topic and provides the professor and student with a variety of meaningful resources. Common features of a Companion Website include:

For the Professor—

Every Companion Website integrates **Syllabus Manager**™, an online syllabus creation and management utility.

- **Syllabus Manager**™ provides you, the instructor, with an easy, step-by-step process to create and revise syllabi, with direct links into Companion Website and other online content without having to learn HTML.
- Students may logon to your syllabus during any study session. All they need to know is the web address for the Companion Website and the password you've assigned to your syllabus.
- After you have created a syllabus using **Syllabus Manager**™, students may enter the syllabus for their course section from any point in the Companion Website.
- Clicking on a date, the student is shown the list of activities for the assignment. The activities for each assignment are linked directly to actual content, saving time for students.

- Adding assignments consists of clicking on the desired due date, then filling in the details of the assignment—name of the assignment, instructions, and whether or not it is a one-time or repeating assignment.
- In addition, links to other activities can be created easily. If the activity is online, a URL can be entered in the space provided, and it will be linked automatically in the final syllabus.
- Your completed syllabus is hosted on our servers, allowing convenient updates from any computer on the Internet. Changes you make to your syllabus are immediately available to your students at their next logon.

For the Student—

- **Introduction**—General information about the topic and how it will be covered in the website.
- **Web Links**—A variety of websites related to topic areas.
- **Timely Articles**—Links to online articles that enable you to become more aware of important issues in early childhood.
- **Learn by Doing**—Put concepts into action, participate in activities, examine strategies, and more.
- **Visit a School**—Visit a school's website to see concepts, theories, and strategies in action.
- **For Teachers/Practitioners**—Access information you will need to know as an educator, including information on materials, activities, and lessons.
- **Current Policies and Standards**—Find out the latest early childhood policies from the government and various organizations, and view state, federal, and curriculum standards.
- **Resources and Organizations**—Discover tools to help you plan your classroom or center and organizations to provide current information and standards for each topic.
- **Electronic Bluebook**—Paperless method of completing homework or essays assigned by a professor. Finished work can be sent to the professor via email.
- **Message Board**—Virtual bulletin board to post and respond to questions and comments from a national audience.

To take advantage of these and other resources, please visit the *Food, Nutrition, and the Young Child,* Fifth Edition, Companion Website at

www.prenhall.com/endres

Brief Contents

Contents

4 The Toddler (1 to 3 Years)   120

Note: Every effort has been made to provide accurate and current Internet information in this book. However, the Internet and information posted on it are constantly changing, and it is inevitable that some of the Internet addresses listed in this textbook will change.

1

Nutrition: What Is It?

LEARNING OBJECTIVES

Students will be able to:
- Discuss why the study of food and nutrition is important for the teacher.
- Describe factors that influence food and nutrient intake.
- List the basic nutrients, their functions, and dietary sources for nutrients.
- Calculate ideal body weight and determine body mass index.
- Give the positive and negative aspects of using dietary supplements.

Before we can discuss the details of early childhood nutrition, it is important to understand what nutrition means to you, personally. This first chapter will be an overview of the basic concepts of food and nutrition. In the following chapters we will discuss how nutrition affects children.

The media is continually bombarding us with the latest craze or research in food and nutrition, including the newest diets, supplements, and the latest research on what food is "good" or "bad." It is no wonder that the public is confused. Many times parents turn to teachers and nutrition specialists for advice on what information is accurate. For this reason, factual information about food and nutrition is an essential part of the early childhood curriculum and should be understood by all teachers. A basic knowledge of food and nutrition is outlined in Chapters 1 and 2. A greater understanding of basic nutrition principles will not only prepare you to help others understand nutrition more clearly but will also give insight for your daily food selection and will help you have the energy and right combination of nutrients necessary to meet the demands of your profession. In addition, you will be providing a good role model for parents and children.

Nutrition can be defined as all the processes by which a child or adult consumes, digests, absorbs, transports, and uses food substances, and excretes end products as waste. In general, nutrition is the science of food and how it is used by the body. **Nutrients** are substances found in food that must be supplied to the body. When you eat food, your body takes in the nutrients it needs in order to live, grow, maintain good health, and have energy for work and play. Eating a diet with variety and balance can provide those essential nutrients needed for optimal health.

Most people do not eat for nourishment alone; if we did our diets would be very similar. Instead people make nutritional choices based on social, economic, cultural, and psychological factors.

FACTORS THAT INFLUENCE FOOD AND NUTRITION INTAKE

Social

When is the last time you went to an event or social gathering where food was not a factor? Food has a key role in our social lives. We have come to expect food to be a critical part of celebrations, social gatherings, and events. What would happen if

Food: An important part of celebrations

you could no longer get popcorn at the movie theater? Or eat hot dogs at a baseball game? Can you imagine going to a Christmas party without some holiday treat? The food industry has developed foods for every holiday and social event. In fact, we sometimes look forward to the foods more than the holiday or event itself.

It is important to eat a wide variety of foods in order to obtain the nutrients essential for good health. However, if a person or family has very little money to spend on food, overall nutrition and health *may* decline. There is no doubt that the cost of living has an impact on food purchasing. Economic constraints can limit the amount and type of food some individuals or families can afford. These constraints are more apparent in today's culture due to the increasing number of single parent households.

Economic

Some families with limited economic resources may not be able to purchase a variety of foods. Convenience or "instant" foods become a regular part of their diet. Low-income families without adequate transportation may have access only to small grocery stores with limited food selections. In some cases, low-income families may not even have the facilities to cook or store foods. Many times we take for granted the convenience of having functioning stoves, microwaves, freezers, refrigerators, and a variety of cooking utensils.

Convenience foods are prepackaged foods that can be prepared quickly and easily with three steps or less, for example, microwave dinners.

Families may have more difficulty acquiring all the necessary nutrients if only a limited number of foods are consumed. When both parents work outside the home, often they can afford to purchase a wide variety of foods but because of time constraints they buy convenience foods or foods from fast-food restaurants. Food purchased at some restaurants can adequately meet nutritional needs, but families may repeatedly choose to eat only a few selected items from fast-food restaurants, like cheeseburgers and french fries. The nutrient intake may be limited if foods are not selected carefully to contain variety and balance.

> **Ethnic**   Of or relating to a sizable group of people sharing a common and distinctive racial, national, religious, linguistic, or cultural heritage.

Food variety is limited when fast-food restaurants become a routine. The variety of nutritious foods can be limited because of economic constraints and distorted food preferences. Although healthy foods as a whole are not more costly, reliance on convenience foods takes up a large portion of the food dollar, as families grow accustomed to not having to cook.

> **Cultural**   The totality of socially transmitted behavior patterns, arts, beliefs, institutions, and all other products of human work and thought.
>
> *Source:* From *The American Heritage® Dictionary of the English Language,* fourth edition, by Houghton Mifflin Company. Copyright © 2000 by Houghton Mifflin Company.

Cultural

There are very few activities that are as instinctive as eating, and even fewer activities that have such an impact on us psychologically, physiologically, and spiritually. America has long described itself as a melting pot. The culinary pot has absorbed the cultures of millions of immigrants from hundreds of ethnic backgrounds that have settled here. Cultural preferences influence what we eat as the population demographics change. Examining the nutrition attributes of a number of ethnic diets will help you understand that no single cuisine is either completely healthful or unhealthful. About 25% of restaurants in the United States have an ethnic theme, giving consumers choices from Mexican, Italian, German, Asian, and many other foods that can be eaten not only at restaurants but also prepared at home. The population in Canada and the United States is continually changing. According to the 2000 census data, the population of Hispanic or Latinos in the United States has increased 60%, and the African American population has increased 16% since the 1990 census (Table 1.1). School classrooms will reflect the increase in diversity in the United

Table 1.1   Census 2000: Population by race and Hispanic/Latino status

Total Population	Race alone (numbers in millions)	Percent
White alone	194.6	69.1
Black or African American	36.4	13.0
Hispanic or Latino (any race)	35.3	12.5
American Indian and Alaskan Native	4.1	1.5
Asian	11.8	4.2
Native Hawaiian and other Pacific Islander	0.9	0.3
Some other race	18.6	6.6

Source: Based on Census 2000 data available at http://www.census.gov/prod/cen2000/dp1/2kh00.pdf.

States, and an understanding of the cultural and religious differences in food consumption and preparation can enrich the lives of all the children.

Some of the differences in the diets within the United States occur due to the effect that immigrants have had on the region in which they settled. The first large group of settlers from Europe (English, Irish, French, and German) brought many food traditions that have made up traditional American home cooking. Since these immigrants tended to settle in regions that resembled their homeland, they were able to grow many of their familiar foods and incorporate them into the American diet. The European American plates typically were centered on a sizable portion of meat arranged with vegetables and potatoes in separate portions on the plate. The large meat portion is still seen in many popular restaurants today; however, portion sizes of all foods have gradually become larger.

Hispanics.   According to the census data, Hispanics may become the nation's largest minority group by 2005, surpassing blacks. The Hispanic diet is rich in a variety of foods. This cuisine has been influenced by Columbian, Spanish, French, and American culture. Complex carbohydrates—corn and corn by-products, beans, rice, and breads—comprise the typical Hispanic diet. The typical Mexican diet contains adequate amounts of protein in forms of beans, eggs, shellfish, fish, and a variety of meats, such as pork, poultry, beef, and goat. Because of the extensive use of frying as a method of cooking, the Mexican diet can be high in fat [1]. The acclimation to the American diet has moderately increased milk, vegetable, and fruit intake. But this acclimation has also increased the intake of salad dressings, margarine, and high-sugar drinks while decreasing traditional consumption of complex carbohydrates like beans and rice.

African.   The African culture has influenced our eating habits, especially in the southern part of the United States. Involuntary immigrants to the New World, people from Africa struggled to survive under harsh conditions. Their ability to adapt to new food sources and new conditions became a lasting influence on today's American cuisine. The "soul food" of today gets its roots from the regional cuisine of the South. Southern cooking is often characterized as being pan fried, greasy, and overcooked. This description is often incorrect—common characteristics of this cuisine include pots of cooked vegetables, stews, and rice. Frying is also common, as well as the addition of fatback, bacon, and other seasoning to add flavor to recipes. Other typical kinds of Southern food are cornbread, pork products, biscuits, sorghum, collards, black-eyed peas, okra, sweet potatoes, peanuts, and melons.

Asian.   Chinese immigrants introduced a more vegetable-centered diet to American cuisine beginning in the middle of the 19th century. Chinese workers brought food preparation methods that tended to preserve nutrients. They added a variety of sauces and seasonings, such as gingerroot, scallions, garlic, rice wine, and sesame seeds. Their diet of fresh vegetables, minimal amounts of meat (mainly pork and fish), and moderate fat has slowly influenced the eating habits of the United States. Rice and wheat noodles are core to the Chinese diet. Many of these traditional foods have been preserved in the American culture; however, most North American restaurants' versions of Chinese cuisine, whether Szechuan, Mandarin, or Cantonese, are not authentic.

Italian.   This cuisine varies depending on the area of Italy from which the settler originated. Settlers from Northern Italy brought over dishes high in meat, cheese, and dairy products, whereas Southern Italians brought over meals richer in grains, vegetables, dried beans, and fish. Pasta is the heart of the Italian diet. Italians eat six times more pasta than do North Americans. Most of the foods found in American Italian restaurants resemble that of Northern Italy, including veal, cheese, pesto, and cream sauces. Pizza, a Southern Italian food, has become one of the most popular foods in the American diet. However, American pizza differs greatly from the thin-crusted pizza with tomato, basil, and mozzarella cheese typically eaten in Italy.

Many other cuisines have influenced the American diet of today, and different regions of the country will have different ethnic groups. American cuisine will continue to change. When teachers understand the differences in cultural diets and their regional effects, the cultural aspects of the diets can be incorporated into the educational curriculum of the preschool centers.

Religion

The United States has a variety of different faiths within its borders. The religions in the United States with the most members are Christianity (76.5%), Judaism (1.3%), Islam (0.5%), Buddhism (0.5%), and Hinduism (0.4%) [2]. The religious customs may be summarized, but variations exist in the interpretation of many of the customs. Other religions that have special dietary customs are included in Table 1.2.

Some religions have specific foods that are part of the customs and some that are prohibited by religious law. The most common are Jewish customs that are observed in varying degrees in this country by Orthodox, Conservative, or Reform denominations. Jewish law (the laws of kashrut) includes not only specific foods to be eaten but also how the food is to be prepared. Foods such as animals and agriculture products must be kosher in order to be eaten. Milk and meat products cannot be eaten together nor can they be prepared together (Box 1.1).

> **Kosher**   A kosher animal is one that is ruminant (chews its cud) and has split hooves (leaving out camels and pigs). In order to be kosher a trained person (schochet) must slaughter an animal or bird according to Jewish law (Shechita).

There are many different cultural, religious, and ethnic customs that play a role in the way Americans eat. Chapter 7 describes the Seven Steps to Successful Ethnic Meals, and the American Diabetes Association and American Dietetic Association have published a series on practices, customs, and holidays related to various ethnic groups [3].

Emotional

Eating for reasons other than hunger or appetite can be described as emotional eating. Hunger is the need for food to fuel the body. Appetite is the psychological and sensory reaction to food that looks and smells good. Appetite may also be a

Table 1.2   Religious dietary customs

	Prohibited or strongly discouraged	Avoided by most devout	Restrictions on some types of foods and when they are eaten	Special dietary practices
Buddhist		Most meats, including fish and shellfish	Avoidance of eggs and dairy on some occasions	Practice fasting and moderation in eating
Eastern Orthodox			Restrictions to meat, eggs, dairy, and fish on some occasions	Practice fasting
Jewish	Pork, shellfish, or meat and dairy at the same time		Some avoidance to meat, eggs, dairy, fish, and leavened foods (foods using yeast as leavening agent) on some occasions	Practice fasting and ritual slaughter of animals (kosher)
Hindu	Beef and pork, drinking alcohol			Practice fasting
Mormon (LDS)	Caffeine and alcohol			Practice fasting one day per month and moderation in eating
Roman Catholic			Avoidance of meat during certain occasions	Practice fasting
Seventh Day Adventist	Pork, shellfish, alcohol, coffee, tea	Fish	Avoidance of eggs and dairy on some occasions	Practice moderation in eating
Moslem	Pork, alcohol	Coffee and tea	Avoidance of all meat on occasion	Practice fasting and moderation in eating, ritual slaughter of animals

---

Box 1.1   Why not mix milk and meat?—*Rabbi Mordechai Becher*

"This prohibition against meat and milk also serves to remind us where our food comes from. The meat is from a dead animal, the milk from a living animal. 'Do not cook a kid in it's mother's milk'—beware that obtaining meat necessitates death, obtaining milk requires life. These are foods that have their origin in living creatures and keeping them separate makes us aware of their source."

Source: http://www.ohr.org.il/special/misc/kosher.htm.

conditioned response to food, such as eating because it is noon (which is an external cue) instead of because we are hungry (internal cue).

Most people at some time have turned to food for a quick pick-me-up, relaxation, solace, or out of sheer boredom. Emotions can greatly affect the food choices we make on a daily basis. Someone may come home from work and grab a snack to help relax. A bowl of ice cream may comfort the lonely on a Saturday night. These eating behaviors result as our mind's way of coping with emotion. Eating can also be a person's way of controlling a situation. This can result in restricting or overeating of food, which can lead to eating disorders.

Almost every parent believes at some time that a child exhibits eating problems. This occurs when the child refuses to eat a food, eats too many "sweets," or does not seem to eat enough food. In many cases, eating behavior is a way for children to assert their individuality. A child may have a temper tantrum if the family runs out of a favorite cereal. Another child learns that refusing to eat will usually upset the family and may even result in a reward, a "bribe," for improved behavior. Most of these situations are short-lived and have few consequences. Psychologists often disagree about the cause and cure of eating whims expressed by children, but whatever the cause, psychological aspects of food consumption that originate in early childhood often continue throughout life.

Parents or teachers often pass on to children their concepts or ideas about food and dieting. Abramovitz and Birch [4] studied 5-year-old girls' perceptions of dieting. The study indicated that girls who had mothers who dieted were more than twice as likely to have ideas about dieting when compared to mothers who didn't diet. This study suggested that mothers' weight-control attempts may influence their young daughters' ideas, beliefs, and concepts about dieting. The same may hold true for any child's role model or teacher. Dislikes, attitudes, and beliefs about food can be passed on from teachers to children.

BASIC NUTRIENTS AND USES IN THE BODY

Nutrients are chemical substances that are found in foods. They are used in your body to build, maintain, and repair tissues. Nutrients give you the energy you need to perform the daily activities of living. Foods may contain a few or many nutrients, and each nutrient has specific uses in the body. The body requires six nutrient classes to ensure adequate nutritional status and to maintain good health. These classes are further defined in the following text.

| carbohydrates | protein | fat |
| vitamins | minerals | water |

The human body is made from the nutrients it gets from food and drinks. On average, body weight is 60% water, 20% fat, and 20% of the weight is a combination of mostly protein plus carbohydrates, vitamins, and minerals. Foods do not contain the same nutrients or equal amounts of any one nutrient, so it is important

---

Box 1.2   The mighty calorie

Kilocalories, or "calories," are a way of measuring the amount of potential energy in a foodstuff. A calorie is the basic unit for measuring the energy that will raise the temperature of 1 gram of water 1 degree centigrade. One calorie is a very small amount of energy compared with what the human body needs each day; therefore, the term kilocalorie (kcal) is used. A kilocalorie represents a unit that stands for 1,000 times as much energy as a calorie represents. "Calories" are actually kilocalories. The proper shortened form of kilocalorie is Calorie, spelled with a capital C. The common usage is calorie for kilocalorie.

---

to understand that a variety of foods can provide the combination of nutrients to promote optimal health.

The primary function of some nutrients is to provide energy in the form of **kilocalories** or "calories" (Box 1.2). Carbohydrates, protein, and fat provide energy and are measured in terms of calories.

Other nutrients enable the body to grow new cells and tissues. Essential nutrients are important for children while they grow. Nutrients are used for the repair of injured tissue for people of any age. Vitamins, minerals, and water help regulate metabolic processes, including energy metabolism, but do not provide energy. Nutrients also function as part of tissue, as biochemical compounds, or as regulators of body functions.

CARBOHYDRATES

Carbohydrates supply energy and are the body's main source of fuel and come in different sizes. Simple sugars, like glucose, galactose, and fructose, are called **monosaccharides** because they contain one single unit. **Disaccharides,** such as sucrose, lactose, and maltose, contain two saccharides or two simple sugars linked together (Table 1.3). The more complex forms of carbohydrates, or starches, con-

Table 1.3   Composition of carbohydrates

Carbohydrate	Composition
Monosaccharides: One sugar unit	
Fructose	One unit fructose
Glucose	One unit glucose
Galactose	One unit galactose
Disaccharides: Two sugar units linked	
Sucrose (table sugar)	Glucose + fructose
Lactose (milk sugar)	Glucose + galactose
Maltose (malt sugar)	Glucose + glucose
Polysaccharides: Many linked units	
Complex carbohydrates	Many monosaccharide units linked together

tain many units of sugar and are called **polysaccharides.** Breads and cereals, fruits and vegetables, dairy products, and legumes contain complex carbohydrates.

Monosaccharides and disaccharides make up about half of the total digestible carbohydrate intake. These are found in fruits (sucrose, glucose, fructose, pentoses) and milk (lactose). Sugars in soft drinks, candies, jams, jellies, and sweet desserts are composed mainly from sucrose and high-fructose corn syrup.

Complex carbohydrates, which constitute the other half of digestible carbohydrate intake, are starches found predominantly in cereal grains and their products (flour, bread, rice, corn, oats, and barley), potatoes, legumes, and a few other vegetables. Carbohydrates are converted to glucose in the digestive processes before being absorbed and used as a readily available supply of energy. Carbohydrates should make up 45% to 65% of total daily calories [5].

Carbohydrates function primarily as a source of readily available energy, since only a relatively small amount can be stored in the liver and muscle tissues (as glycogen). According to the Institute of Medicine, *both children and adults should consume at least 130 grams of carbohydrates each day* [5]. These carbohydrates should come from the carbohydrates found in unsweetened dairy products, whole grains, vegetables, and fruits. Carbohydrates provide four calories per gram. Carbohydrates serve other vital roles besides being used for energy. In conjunction with proteins, they are used in the formation of antibodies and in the formation and maintenance of cartilage and bones (as well as the fluid that lubricates the joints between them). In addition, some carbohydrates act as body regulators or contribute to the structure of certain cells. Carbohydrates not used immediately for energy are stored temporarily as glycogen in the liver and muscles or converted into and stored as fat.

Sources

The carbohydrate most frequently seen on the table is sugar, or sucrose, a disaccharide. However, the carbohydrate found most frequently in grains, legumes, fruits, and vegetables is starch, or polysaccharide, a more complex form of carbohydrate. Polysaccharides take longer to be broken down by the digestive system when compared with sucrose and high-fructose corn syrup (disaccharides). High-fructose corn syrup is used commercially in soft drinks, baked products, and table syrup and has replaced sucrose (table sugar) in many commercial products. Carbohydrates from grains and legumes are the world's primary source of food, vital to the survival of populations in many countries.

Fiber is considered an indigestible carbohydrate. Dietary fibers are mainly indigestible complex carbohydrates in plant cell walls (cellulose, hemicellulose, and pectin) and a variety of gums, mucilages, and algal polysaccharides. Fiber is either soluble or insoluble. Soluble fiber acts like a gel, and insoluble fiber adds bulk to or softens stool. Insoluble fiber, such as bran, helps move material through the intestinal tract through a process called peristalsis. Soluble fiber found in fruits, vegetables, and oats provides bulk to the stools and may affect the development of certain diseases. Determining the dietary fiber content of common foods can help in consuming the recommended amount of fiber (Table 1.4). Approximately 25 to 38 grams of fiber per day is recommended for adult women and men respectively.

Table 1.4 Dietary fiber in selected foods

Product	Serving size	Dietary fiber (g)
Fruits		
Apple, raw w/skin	1 medium fruit	3.7
Blackberries, raw	1/2 c	3.8
Prunes, canned	1/3 c	2.9
Banana, raw	1/2 medium	1.4
Blueberries, raw	3/4 c	2.9
Figs, dried	1 medium	2.3
Mangoes, raw	1 medium	3.7
Pears, canned	1/2 c	2.0
Papaya, raw	1 medium	5.5
Raisins	1/4 c	1.5
Red raspberries, canned	1/2 c	4.2
Strawberries, raw	3/4 c	3.0
Vegetables		
Brussels sprouts, cooked	1/2 c	2.0
Carrots	1 medium	1.8
Celery	Raw 7.5″ stalk	.7
Corn, cooked	1/2 c	2.3
Corn, creamed, canned	1/2 c	1.5
Okra, frozen, cooked	1/2 c	2.6
Peas, green, young, canned	1/2 c	4.4
Pumpkin, canned	3/4 c	5.3
Squash, winter, cooked (acorn)	3/4 c	6.8
Turnip, green, frozen	1/2 c	1.6
Legumes and Nuts		
Beans, butter, cooked	1/2 c	6.6
Beans, kidney, canned	1/2 c	4.5
Beans, pinto, cooked	1/2 c	7.4
Peas, black-eyed, cooked	1/2 c	4.1
Beans, white, cooked	1/2 c	5.6
Peanut butter, creamy	2 Tbsp	1.9
Almonds, dry roasted	1/4 c	4.1
Peanuts, dry roasted	1/4 c	2.9
Soybeans, roasted	1/4 c	7.6
Breads and Cereals		
Bread, pumpernickel	1 slice	1.7
Bread, whole wheat	1 slice	1.9
Wheaties	1 c	3.0
Wheat Chex	2/3 c	2.2

Source: U.S. Department of Agriculture, Agricultural Research Service. 2002. USDA Nutrient Database for Standard Reference, Release 15, Nutrient Data Laboratory Home Page available at http://www.nal.usda.gov/fnic/foodcomp.

After age 50 the recommendation is 21 grams (g) for women and 30 g for men [5]. The average intake in the United States is closer to 16 g a day. The use of fiber in the diet has been advocated for children to reduce constipation and in the older person to decrease the incidence of atherosclerosis, coronary and aortic disease, appendicitis, disease of the colon, and diabetes. The health claims for a high-fiber diet look promising but are still under investigation. A high-fiber diet causes larger stools and more frequent bowel movements. Foods high in fiber include bran, whole-grain breads and cereals, most fruits and vegetables, nuts, and legumes (Table 1.4). As we increase fiber in the diet, we must increase fluid intake since insoluble fiber absorbs fluid from the intestines.

Sugar Substitutes.   Humans naturally have an appetite for foods that are sweet. Excessive consumption of sugar with a decrease in physical activity can lead to weight gain. Consumers have sought sugar substitutes as low-calorie alternatives to their favorite sweet foods. Sugar substitutes are many times sweeter than sugar, so it takes much less to create the same sweetness. There are four approved sugar substitutes on the market: saccharin, aspartame, acesulfame-K, and sucralose.

Saccharin was discovered in 1879, and it is 300 times sweeter than sugar. It has remained on the market and continues to have a large appeal as a tabletop sweetener. Saccharin has a longer shelf life and is stable at high temperatures, which makes it a good option for baked goods. Saccharin can be made rather inexpensively and is typically less expensive than other sugar alternatives, but has a bitter aftertaste. In the past there has been research with rats linking saccharin intake to cancer, particularly bladder cancer; however the American Medical Association, the American Cancer Society, and the American Dietetic Association agree that saccharin use is acceptable [6]. It is sold under the brand name Sweet' N Low®.

Aspartame was approved for extensive testing in 1981 and is 180 times sweeter than sugar. It is composed of two amino acids linked by a methyl grouping. It is typically used in beverages, desserts, breakfast cereals, chewing gum, and as a tabletop sweetener. It is not as heat stable as other low-calorie sweeteners but leaves no bitter aftertaste.

Acesulfame potassium, or acesulfame-K, was first approved in 1988 as a tabletop sweetener. It is 200 times sweeter than sugar. This sweetener is often combined with other sweeteners to sweeten soft drinks, desserts, puddings, candy, and baked goods. It has an excellent shelf life and does not break down when cooked or baked. It is sold under the brand name Sunett™ by Nutrinova, Inc.

Sucralose was approved by the FDA in 1998. It is 600 times sweeter than sugar. It tastes like sugar because it is made from sugar (sucrose) but it cannot be digested so it adds no calories to food. Due to the combination of being heat stable and having a sugar-like taste, sucralose has been added to many products, including juices, diet sodas, and syrups. It is sold under the brand name Splenda®.

Sugar substitutes may take the place of sugar in sweetening power but not in the functional properties of sugar important in cooking and baking. Using sugar substitutes can help to decrease the caloric content of many foods; however, foods using sugar substitutes are not necessarily lower in fat. The important aspect in achieving a healthy weight is the reduction in total caloric value. Sugar substitutes can be a helpful part of an overall weight loss or maintenance program.

Sugar and Disease

The Dietary Guidelines for Americans [6] specifically encourage using sugar in moderation and increasing intake of complex carbohydrates and fiber, such as whole grains, vegetables, and fruits. The Institute of Medicine recommends limiting added sugars to no more than 25% of total calories. Added sugars are those incorporated into foods and beverages during production. Examples include candy, soft drinks, fruit drinks, and pastries. The suggested maximum level comes from evidence that people whose diets are high in added sugars have lower intakes of essential nutrients [5].

There is no substantial evidence that table sugar (sucrose) intake causes hyperactivity in children, obesity, or diabetes [8–9]. Consumption of sugar-containing beverages and foods can lead to weight gain, obesity, and the risk of chronic diseases such as diabetes if the amount of energy consumed is greater than the needs of the body. Consuming sucrose and high-fructose corn syrup can contribute to tooth decay, so it is important to limit intake of sticky carbohydrate foods that feed bacteria in the mouth.

Should sugar be excluded from the diet of a child? The nutrient density of the food in relationship to the total diet must be considered, not just the sugar content. If a food supplies a high proportion of nutrients in relation to the amount of energy, it is a nutrient-dense food; conversely, if it contains a high proportion of energy, or calories, in relation to the amount of nutrients, it is a calorie-dense food. For example, an orange is denser in nutrients than orange juice because it has less sugar and more fiber per ounce compared to a concentrated drink.

A person who requires large amounts of energy because of exercise or growth can consume more foods that are energy-rich or calorie-dense than a person who is sedentary. The quantity of nutrients needed by an individual remains relatively constant for the same age–sex group. Diets for the elderly and for young children, which are relatively low in kilocalories, need to contain nutrient-dense foods unless extra energy is expended.

Nutrient-dense foods Foods that contain a relatively high amount of nutrients compared to their calorie content. For example, whole-grain breads, cereals, rice, beans, pasta, vegetables, and fruits are nutrient-dense foods because they not only contain carbohydrates but also contribute other essential nutrients such as vitamins, minerals, and fiber. In comparison, table sugar, candy bars, donuts, and cookies contain carbohydrate and/or fat without contributing many other essential vitamins and minerals.

PROTEIN

Protein plays an important role in the growth, restoration, and maintenance of body tissues. Protein contains the main structural building blocks in the body. Protein contributes 15% of the total body weight as part of bone and muscle; protein is also an important component of blood, cell membranes, enzymes, and immune factors. The adult guideline for protein is 0.8 g per kilogram (2.2 lb) or 0.36 g per

---

Box 1.3   Calculating protein needs

Body weight in kilograms (amount in pounds/2.2 = amount in kilograms) × 0.8 g. A 130 lb woman needs 47 g of protein per day (130 lbs/2.2 kg = 59 kg) × 0.8 g = 47 g.

---

pound. We can calculate protein needs (Box 1. 3). The consumption of protein in the United States does not appear to be below recommended levels. In fact, persons consume more protein than is needed to meet the daily recommended allowances. Protein provides four calories per gram. The percentage of calories in the daily diet contributed by protein should be from 10% to 35% for the adult [5]. Unlike fat and carbohydrates, the primary function of protein is growth, maintenance and repair of body tissues, regulation of water balance, help in maintenance of the proper acid base balance within the body, and formation of enzymes, antibodies, and hormones. When sufficient carbohydrates and fats are consumed to meet energy needs, excess protein is converted to and stored as fat.

Proteins are made up of different chemical structures known as **amino acids.** All amino acids are necessary for building various body tissues; however, only 10 of the 22 amino acids are considered essential amino acids because the body cannot manufacture them (Table 1.5). The amino acids that are manufactured in the body are identified as nonessential amino acids. The most recently declared amino acid is arginine. Arginine is produced only in limited quantities in the body but was declared essential in 1992.

Sources

Proteins found in many plant foods lack one or more of the essential amino acids, and different plants and legumes have different amounts of amino acids. Plant foods can be combined during the day and provide all the amino acids required

Table 1.5   Essential and nonessential amino acids

Essential	Nonessential
Histidine	Alanine
Isoleucine	Arginine
Leucine	Asparagine
Lysine	Aspartic acid
Methionine	Cysteine
Phenylalanine	Glutamic acid
Threonine	Glutamine
Tryptophan	Glycine
Valine	Proline
	Serine
	Tyrosine

Table 1.6   Foods combined to provide essential amino acids

Combine legumes and grains	Combine legumes and nuts/seeds	Combine grains and nuts/seeds
Rice and beans	Humus (sesame and chickpeas)	Whole-wheat bun with sesame seeds
Peanut butter on whole-wheat bread	Trail mix (peanuts and sunflower seeds)	Rice cakes with peanut butter
Salad with chickpeas and corn bread		Bread sticks rolled with sesame seeds
Vegetarian chili with bread		
Tofu-vegetable stir-fry over rice		

(Table 1.6). Good sources of complete protein include meats, eggs, milk, and soy. Foods that provide high-quality protein are often also high in fat. However, choosing lean cuts of beef, poultry, and pork, as well as fish, skim milk, and soy can provide high-quality protein with only small amounts of fat.

Complementary proteins are formulated from one or more plant sources to form proteins containing all the amino acids necessary to meet human needs. Two or more foods that contain some of the amino acids are combined to form a protein containing all the essential amino acids. A mixture of proteins from grains, legumes, seeds, nuts, and vegetables eaten over the course of the day will complement the amino acid profiles. It is not necessary that complementation of amino acid profiles be precise and eaten at exactly the same time.

FATS

Fat, oils, waxes, and related substances are collectively known as **lipids.** Fat functions to provide energy, or heat, for the body. Gram for gram, fats have more than twice as much energy potential as protein and carbohydrates: supplying 9 kcal/g (29 g = 1 ounce). A healthy body needs fat. Dietary fat supplies a good padding or protection for the liver, heart, and kidneys, the body's vital organs. In addition, lipids comprise an essential part of many body tissues, such as the brain, bone marrow, and cell membranes. Certain vitamins (A, D, E, and K) are soluble only in fatty substances. Before they can be absorbed from the intestinal tract, these vitamins must be incorporated into a tiny droplet containing fat. In summary, lipids (fats) provide (1) an energy reserve, (2) insulation and padding for body organs, (3) a vehicle for the absorption of certain vitamins, (4) essential fatty acids, and (5) a component of certain body tissues.

Fats consist mainly of fatty acids, which can be classified as **saturated** (solid at room temperature) or **unsaturated** (liquid at room temperature) depending on their structure. Unsaturated fatty acids are further subdivided into monounsaturated and

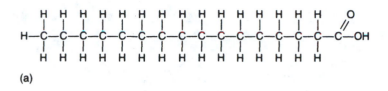

Figure 1.1 Fatty
acid structures:
(a) saturated,
(b) monoun-
saturated, and
(c) polyunsaturated
fatty acids

polyunsaturated fatty acids. Fatty acids have a variety of structures, as shown in Figure 1.1. Foods containing fatty will have all of these fatty acids in various amounts, as shown in Figure 1.2.

The number of carbon atoms in a fatty acid may vary from a few to 20 or more. Note that the number of hydrogen atoms (H) compared to carbon atoms (C) differs among the three fatty acids in Figure 1.1. The fatty acids shown have 16 or 18 carbon atoms and two oxygen atoms (O), but they have different numbers of hydrogen atoms. **Saturated fatty acids** have a maximum number of hydrogen atoms attached to every carbon atom. Therefore, we say that these fatty acids are "saturated" with hydrogen atoms. Saturated fatty acids (Figure 1.1a) are usually solid at room temperature and when refrigerated. The exceptions are some "tree oils" such as palm oil and coconut palm-kernel oil. Other foods containing a high proportion of saturated fatty acids are meats, butterfat, and shortening. Increased intake of saturated fatty acids and dietary cholesterol tends to increase total cholesterol and therefore increase the risk of cardiovascular disease [10].

Monounsaturated fatty acids have one unsaturation where two hydrogen atoms are missing in the middle of the molecule, one from each of two adjoining carbon atoms (Figure 1.1b). Olive oil, peanut oil, and canola oil are good sources of monounsaturated fatty acids.

Polyunsaturated fatty acids (PUFA) (Figure 1.1c) have more than one unsaturation. These fatty acids are found in the oils of vegetable and cereal products, such as soybeans, canola, corn, cottonseed, and safflower. Oils can contain some proportion of all three fatty acids: saturated, monounsaturated, and polyunsaturated. Seafood is an especially rich source of polyunsaturated fatty acids.

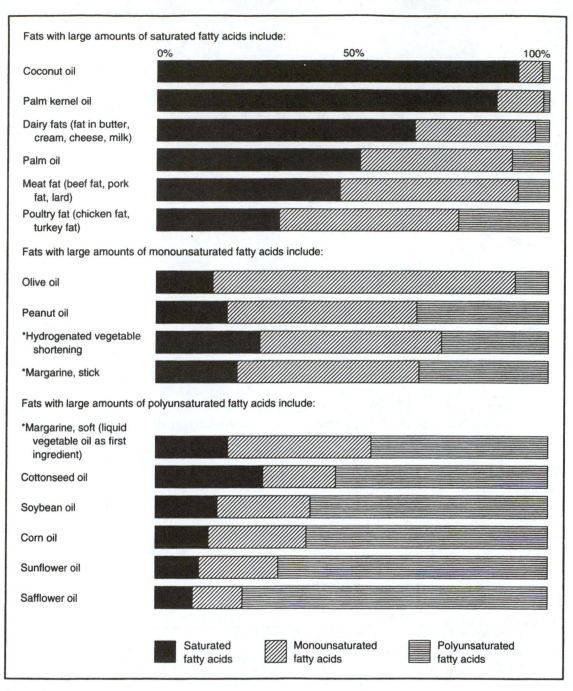

Figure 1.2 Dietary fat and fatty acid proportions
*The amounts of unsaturated fatty acids in these foods vary.
Source: U.S. Department of Agriculture, Human Nutrition Information Service. Preparing foods and planning menus, *Home and Garden Bulletin No. 232–8.*

Trans fatty acids are unsaturated fatty acids formed when vegetable oils are processed and made more solid or into a more stable liquid. This processing is called hydrogenation when manufacturers add hydrogen to oils to make them solid. Trans fatty acids also occur naturally in small amounts in some foods. Trans fatty acids are present in variable amounts in a wide range of foods, including most foods made with partially hydrogenated oils, such as baked goods and fried foods, and some margarine products. Trans fatty acids also occur naturally in low amounts in meats and dairy products.

Scientific reports have confirmed the relationship between trans fat and an increased risk of coronary heart disease. The Food and Drug Administration (FDA) has issued a regulation requiring manufacturers to list trans fatty acids, or trans fat, on the Nutrition Facts panel of foods and some dietary supplements. With this rule, consumers have more information to make healthier food choices that could lower their consumption of trans fat as part of a heart-healthy diet.

Food manufacturers will have to list trans fat on the nutrition label by January 1, 2006. The FDA estimates that by three years after that date, trans fat labeling will have prevented from 600 to 1,200 cases of coronary heart disease, and 250 to 500 deaths each year.

Cholesterol

Cholesterol is a special lipid. It does not contribute energy or calories and unlike fat is not measured in calories. Most of the cholesterol is made in the liver, and the cholesterol eaten is absorbed and carried to the liver. Cholesterol helps carry fat through the blood vessels to various parts of the body where it is needed for energy. Increasing cholesterol in the blood vessels over time will lead to an accumulation of cholesterol in the arteries, developing a build-up of a substance called plaque on the inner walls of the arteries. Plaque narrows the path for blood flow. This narrowing of arteries may increase your risk for blood clots leading to a stroke or heart attack. High blood cholesterol levels are one of the risk factors for heart disease.

Since fat and water (water is a major ingredient of blood) do not mix, cholesterol is carried through the blood in packages or clusters of molecules called lipoprotein, which consists of a cholesterol plus protein. The most commonly known lipoproteins are high-density lipoproteins (HDL) and low-density lipoproteins (LDL). Because of its structure, LDL, the "bad cholesterol," tends to build up (plaque) in the blood vessels as it travels back to the liver. HDL, the "good cholesterol," finds and rescues the LDL and takes it back to the liver. Usually this carrier system works well. In summary, having high levels of LDL cholesterol in the blood is believed to be a risk factor in the development of heart disease. Having high levels of HDL may protect against cardiovascular disease. The more HDL one has, the lower the total cholesterol and, theoretically, the lower the risk of heart disease.

Adults should have knowledge of the normal serum cholesterol values (Table 1.7). Laboratories may provide information not only on serum cholesterol levels, but also on the amount of LDL and HDL cholesterol in the blood. Total serum cholesterol level below 200 milligrams per deciliter (mg/dl) is desirable [11].

Table 1.7   Serum cholesterol values

	Blood cholesterol level (mg/dl)	LDL cholesterol level (mg/dl)	HDL cholesterol level (mg/dl)
Desirable	Adult: < 200 *Children: < 170	Adult: < 100 *Children: < 110	Adult females: 55–60 Adult males: 45–50
Borderline-High	Adults: 200–239 *Children: 170–199	Adults: 100–159 *Children: 110–129	Adult: HDL levels lower than 40 increase risk of heart disease
High	Adults: ≥ 240 *Children: ≥ 200	Adults: ≥ 160 *Children: ≥ 130	*Children HDL values not established

*Classification of total and LDL-cholesterol levels in children and adolescents (ages 2–18) from families with high cholesterol or premature cardiovascular disease.
Sources: Executive Summary of the Third Report of the National Cholesterol Education Program Expert Panel on Detection, Evaluation, and Treatment of High Blood Cholesterol in Adults. *The Journal of the American Medical Association*, May 16, 2001; 285: 2486–2497;
American Academy of Pediatrics Committee on Nutrition. (1998). Cholesterol in Children. *Pediatrics*, *101*(1): 141–147.

Sources of Fat and Recommendations

Fat is a major source of energy for the body and aids in the absorption of essential vitamins. Clogged arteries are the result of lifestyle habits as well as eating too many foods high in fat and cholesterol. Fat and cholesterol are often found together in the diet. Fats are frequently found in our favorite foods for good reason since fat enhances flavor and texture. Because fat is digested more slowly than carbohydrates, the dietary fat makes us feel more satisfied. Fats can be found in both animal and plant foodstuffs, e.g., butter and margarine; whole milk; eggs; oils such as canola, corn, soybean, peanut, and cottonseed; and even in the leanest muscle tissue. Fried foods, including popular snack chips, usually contain fat. Most of the fat eaten in the American diet comes from fats and oils in baked and fried foods, meats, poultry and fish, and full-fat dairy products. Other foods that provide energy from fat include mayonnaise, whipped cream, chocolate, nuts, avocados, and coconut.

Foods high in dietary cholesterol are found only in animal products such as meat, egg yolks, organ meats, whole milk, and high-fat milk products. Recommendations for maintaining or increasing HDL (good cholesterol) blood levels include not smoking, good weight control for height, exercise, and consuming a low-fat diet that does not contain more than 300 mg of cholesterol per day. Reducing saturated fat intake can lower LDL cholesterol levels. Likewise, increasing the intake of fruits and vegetables and low-fat breads and cereals and substituting for foods that are rich in fat, including animal fat (e.g., less meat, butter, milk, and cheese) can lower LDL cholesterol levels. Replace saturated fats with foods that contain high levels of poly and monounsaturated fats like canola oil, olive oil, or a canola-vegetable oil blend. Increasing soluble fiber will also reduce high LDL levels.

Recommended guidelines call for getting 20% to 35% of total calories from fat [5]. Because saturated fat and cholesterol provide no known beneficial role in preventing chronic diseases they are not required at any level in the diet. *Read food labels.* Food labels provide information on the calories from fat, and the amount of

Nutrition Facts

Serving Size ¹/₂ cup (125 g)

Servings about 2.5

Amount Per Serving	
Calories 120	Calories from fat 70

	% Daily Value*
Total Fat 8g	12%
Sat Fat 2g	9%
Cholesterol 10mg	3%
Sodium 800mg	32%
Total Carbohydrate 10g	3%
Dietary Fiber 1g	4%
Sugars 1g	
Protein 3g	12%

Vitamin A 4%	Vitamin C 0%
Calcium 2%	Iron 4%

*Percent Daily Values are based on a 2,000 calorie diet. Your daily values may be higher or lower depending on your calorie needs:

	Calories:	2,000	2,500
Total Fat	Less than	65g	80g
Sat Fat	Less than	20g	25g
Cholesterol	Less than	300mg	300mg
Sodium	Less than	2,400mg	2,400mg
Potassium		3,500mg	3,500mg
Total Carbohydrate		300g	375g
Dietary Fiber		25g	30g

Figure 1.3 Food label showing fat values (cream of chicken soup)

saturated fat and cholesterol in the particular product (Figure 1.3). Avoid foods high in saturated fat and cholesterol content. Manufacturers do not have to list the amount of polyunsaturated or monounsaturated fats in a product. To reduce the risk of heart disease you must not only reduce total fat and saturated fat intake (Table 1.8) but also eliminate cigarette smoking, lower blood pressure, and increase exercise. *Diet alone is not the answer to lowering the risk of heart disease.*

Fat Substitutes

The desire of Americans to reduce fat intake has encouraged manufacturers to market fat substitutes developed through new technology. Many of these substitutes enable food products to taste like fat without real fat. Most fat substitutes are made up

Table 1.8   Food substitutions to lower dietary fat and cholesterol intake

Instead of eating:	Try eating:
Vegetables cooked in butter	Vegetables stir-fried in oil
Croissants	Whole-grain bagels or English muffins
Sour cream	Plain low-fat yogurt
Ice cream	Low-fat ice cream or frozen yogurt
American or cheddar cheese	Low-fat cheese, skim ricotta, or skim mozzarella
Whole or 2% milk	Skim, 1/2%, or 1% milk
Luncheon meats (bologna, salami, pickle loaf), hot dogs	Sliced turkey or chicken, tuna, lean ham, or lean roast beef
Barbecued ribs	Chicken barbecued (without skin)
Heavily marbled beef (sirloin, New York cuts)	Lean beef cuts with all fat removed (flank steak, rump steak, or London broil)
Butter	Reduced calorie margarine
Lard or shortening made from animal fat	All-vegetable shortening
Hydrogenated oils, palm oil, or coconut oil	Canola, sunflower, corn, and safflower oil
Regular salad dressings	Oil plus water and vinegar, reduced-calorie, or fat-free dressings

of starch derivatives, protein derivatives, and engineered fats. Look for these ingredients on many "low fat" or "fat free" labels. Fat substitutes may provide products that are lower in saturated fats; however, the products may be higher in added sugars. Some of the fat substitutes on the market are Stellar, Olean, and Simplesse.

VITAMINS

Vitamins, like minerals, are not energy producing. They are organic and contain carbon compounds; but because they usually are not broken down to carbon dioxide and water (the end products of metabolism), they provide no useful energy. The body cannot manufacture most vitamins, yet vitamins are essential for life and are needed in only small amounts [13–16]. Their role is to regulate biological reactions required for normal metabolism (chemical changes involved in using nutrients for the functioning of the body) of amino acids, fats, and carbohydrates. Vitamins are used to produce energy and synthesize tissues, enzymes, hormones, and other vital compounds. Table 1.9 groups vitamins into those soluble in fat and those soluble in water and provides major functions and sources of vitamins. Vitamins C and E, as well as beta-carotene, are often described as antioxidants, decreasing the risk associated with heart disease. There is still a debate over the protection against heart disease and cancer given by these vitamins [12]. Many "antioxidant" products are marketed with claims that they can help prevent heart disease, cancer, and various other conditions associated with aging without sound medical research backing the claims.

Table 1.9   Major functions and sources of selected vitamins

Vitamin	Function	Sources
Fat-Soluble Vitamins		
Vitamin A	Promotes normal growth of bones, growth and repair of body tissues; bone and tooth formation; vision; antioxidant in the form of beta-carotene	Milk, butter, dairy products, dark green vegetables, yellow-orange fruits and vegetables
Vitamin D	Regulates absorption and use of calcium and phosphorus; aids in building and maintaining bones and teeth	Direct exposure of the skin to sunlight, fortified milk, margarine, eggs, liver, fish
Vitamin E	Protects red blood cells; antioxidant (protects fat-soluble vitamins); stabilizes cell membranes	Vegetable oils, dark green leafy vegetables, nuts, legumes, egg yolks, salad dressings, mayonnaise, wheat germ, whole grains
Vitamin K	Required for synthesis of blood-clotting proteins	Bacterial synthesis in digestive tract, dark green leafy vegetables, liver, milk, grain products, egg yolk
Water-Soluble Vitamins		
Vitamin C (ascorbic acid)	Plays an important role in collagen formation (helps heal wounds, maintains bones and teeth, strengthens blood vessels); antioxidant; strengthens resistance to infection and helps body absorb iron	Citrus fruits and juices, tomatoes, potatoes, dark green vegetables, peppers, lettuce, cantaloupe, strawberries, mangoes, papayas, cauliflower
Vitamin B_1 (thiamin)	Helps enzymes release energy from carbohydrates	Meat, pork, liver, fish, poultry, whole-grain and enriched breads, cereals, legumes, nuts, green leafy vegetables
Vitamin B_2 (riboflavin)	Helps enzymes release energy from carbohydrates, protein and fat; promotes healthy skin and good vision	Milk, cheese, yogurt, enriched breads and cereals, green leafy vegetables, fish, liver, lean meats, yeast
Niacin (nicotinic acid)	Helps enzymes release energy from carbohydrates, protein, and fat; promotes healthy skin, nerves, and digestive system	Yeast, whole grains and enriched breads and cereals, milk, meats, nuts, legumes, peanuts
Folate (folic acid)	Required for red blood cell formation, new cell division, protein metabolism	Dark green leafy vegetables, citrus fruits, enriched grains and cereals, legumes, seeds, melons, yeast, orange juice, asparagus
Vitamin B_6 (pyridoxine)	Required for amino acid metabolism; used in protein and fat metabolism; aids in forming red blood cells and antibodies	Dark green leafy vegetables, whole-grain products, meats, liver, poultry, fish, shellfish, soybeans, wheat germ, fruits
Vitamin B_{12} (cobalamin)	Necessary for normal growth; helps maintain nerve cells and red blood cells; aids in synthesis of genetic materials	Primarily in animal products meat, fish, poultry, liver, eggs, milk and milk products, fortified cereals
Biotin	Coenzyme in energy metabolism; glycogen formation; fat synthesis	Legumes, egg yolks, chocolate, cauliflower, yeast, liver, nuts, milk
Pantothenic acid	Component of coenzyme for energy metabolism	Legumes, whole grains, lean beef, milk, potatoes, yeast, egg yolks, liver, peanuts, tomatoes, broccoli, fish, poultry; small amounts in fruits and vegetables

Fat-Soluble Vitamins

The body retains fat-soluble vitamins A, D, E, and K more readily than water-soluble vitamins. In general, conditions that limit fat intake will limit the consumption of fat-soluble vitamins. No one food contains all the vitamins needed, but eating a wide variety of foods from the basic food groups, including fats and oils, will provide an adequate intake. In the past, vitamins A and D were not available in necessary quantities in the general food supply, and certain foods (for example, fluid milk and other dairy products) were fortified.

Vitamin A is required for bone growth, reproduction, stability of cell membranes, healthy linings of skin and mucous membranes, and visual processes. Vitamin A is essential in preventing night blindness.

The pre-formed sources of vitamin A include animal products such as butter, liver, and whole milk. About half of dietary vitamin A intake comes from animal food sources. Nonfat milk and margarine are often fortified with vitamin A, as are liquid skim, low-fat, and whole milk. Liquid skim and low-fat milk are fortified with the same amount of vitamin A as whole milk, although dry skim milk may not be fortified. The other half of dietary vitamin A comes from fruits and vegetables in the form of provitamin A carotenoids like beta-carotene. Beta-carotene is often referred to as a "precursor" of vitamin A; these precursors are converted in the body to make vitamin A. The use of foods such as dark green, yellow, and orange vegetables—greens, broccoli, and carrots—may play a role in decreasing the incidence of certain cancers. More research into the cancer-fighting mechanisms is needed. **Hypercarotenemia** is caused by very large intakes of beta-carotene resulting in yellow-orange pigmentation of the skin. This condition is not harmful but may be seen in children who consume large amounts of carrots.

Most Americans take in adequate amounts of vitamin A and have large stores of the vitamin in their liver. However, poor vitamin A status has been noted among preschool children who do not eat enough vegetables, the elderly, and low-income groups. Children with severe fat malabsorption, for example, cystic fibrosis, and adults with AIDS or severe intestinal diseases may also show vitamin A deficiency. Vitamin A toxicity may occur when excessive amounts of the vitamin are taken, especially through the use of vitamin supplements.

Vitamin D is sometimes called the sunshine vitamin because it can be obtained from ultraviolet rays in sunlight as well as from food. Generally, if enough sun is available, deficiencies will not occur. An individual who cannot get outside in the sun, as well as rapidly growing infants and children, need a food source of vitamin D. Chapter 3 provides a more detailed discussion of vitamin D requirements and breastfed infants. Vitamin D, also called calciferol, is important in regulating the metabolism of calcium and phosphorus. It helps in absorption of calcium and phosphorus from the intestine so that proper mineralization of the bones and teeth can proceed. Fish-liver oils, egg yolk, liver, cream, fatty fish, and fortified milk and margarine are sources. Growing children who follow strict vegan diets (without milk) risk insufficient vitamin D intake, but selection of fortified soy milk and other foods can ensure an adequate supply. Vitamin D's primary role is to regulate blood calcium levels. Deficiency of vitamin D in infancy will result in rickets, a disease characterized by the softening of bones because of low calcium content, due to lack of sufficient vitamin D to regulate calcium levels. The adult form of this disease is osteomalacia, which is the softening of bones due to low calcium levels. Osteomalacia can result from low calcium or low vitamin D levels.

Vitamin E may reduce the ability of LDL cholesterol to form plaque in artery walls and thereby reduce one of the risk factors of heart disease. Excessive amounts of vitamin E can act as an anticoagulant and increase the risk of bleeding problems for those taking medications such as heparin or warfarin. Eating a diet high in fruits and vegetables, performing regular physical activity, not smoking, and maintaining a healthy body weight are the activities that best protect one against heart disease and cancer. Vitamin E and polyunsaturated fatty acids are present in the same foods, so increasing the amount eaten of one will increase the other. Vitamin E is found in vegetable and seed oils, shortening, egg yolk, margarine, butter, whole grains, and green leafy vegetables.

Vitamin K is vital for blood clotting. Vitamin K also helps form proteins in bone, muscle, and kidneys. Deficiencies are uncommon except in newborn, especially premature, infants, whose intestinal tracts are free of bacteria (a source of the vitamin) and who must rely on maternal stores. Long-term use of antibiotics may also lead to vitamin K deficiency because antibiotics destroy many of the intestinal bacteria needed to produce vitamin K. Vitamin K may influence the effectiveness of medications that are used to reduce blood clotting. Such medicines (heparin or warfarin) are used in patients who have had heart surgery or those who have blood-clotting disorders. The dietary intake of vitamin K-rich foods should remain the same when anticoagulant medication is begun in order to stabilize the effectiveness of the drug. The main sources of vitamin K are intestinal bacteria and foods such as dark green vegetables, fish oils, wheat bran, soybeans, cauliflower, tomatoes, and meats. Toxicity to vitamin K is rarely seen from food intake.

Water-Soluble Vitamins

B vitamins are found in many foods. Because many of the B vitamins are found in combination with one another as well as with other nutrients such as protein and minerals, a deficiency of one B vitamin is rare. There are eight B vitamins: thiamin, riboflavin, niacin, and pantothenic acid. The B vitamins are involved primarily in the energy-releasing function of the body, whereas biotin is used for energy storage, pyridoxine for protein metabolism, and folate and B_{12} for blood manufacturing. Each of the B vitamins is involved in many complex steps in the metabolic processes of the body.

The food sources and major functions of the B vitamins are shown in Table 1.9. In general, the B vitamins associated with releasing energy are needed in larger quantities by persons who have higher energy intakes. B vitamin deficiencies caused by lack of dietary intake are rare today.

Box 1.4   What are neural tube defects (NTDs)?

A neural tube defect is a birth defect occurring in the brain or spinal cord (backbone). NTDs are among the most common of all serious birth defects. The neural tube is the part of the fetus that becomes the spinal cord and brain.

The two major types of NTDs are anencephaly and spina bifida. Anencephaly is the partial or complete absence of the baby's brain. This birth defect causes extensive damage to the fetus, and most of these babies are stillborn or die soon after birth.

Spina bifida occurs when there is an opening of the spine. These babies need to have surgery soon after their birth to close the spine and prevent further damage. They also may need a shunt or a drain to prevent a build-up of spinal fluid in the brain called hydrocephalus. Babies with spina bifida may lack feeling in their legs and later develop problems with walking. In addition, these children may develop problems with their bowel and bladder control. They may also have learning problems, and some may have mental retardation.

Folate deficiency in pregnant women can cause neural tube defects in the fetus (Box 1.4). These defects include spina bifida and anencephaly. Seventy-five percent or more of these defects can be prevented if all women of childbearing age consume at least 400 micrograms (mg) a day.

Another water-soluble vitamin, vitamin C, or ascorbic acid, is found in citrus fruits. Many drink mixes and gelatin products include ascorbic acid in a form chemically identical to the vitamin C found naturally in other foods. Although all water-soluble vitamins can be lost from the diet if the cooking juices are not retained, vitamin C is the most unstable, because it can be destroyed by copper cookware, heat, and especially alkaline solutions. Foods eaten for their water-soluble vitamins should be handled carefully. If possible, vegetables should be steamed to preserve water-soluble vitamins, or the liquid should be used in gravies and soups. Vegetables should be cooked for short periods to retain full nutritional value. Vitamin C is oxidized in the air and lost from food but it also preserves or protects other substances. In this manner, it prevents fruits from turning brown during food processing.

Scurvy, rarely seen today, is the well-known deficiency disease associated with inadequate vitamin C. Vitamin C is believed to be needed for proper functioning of connective tissue, the intercellular cement that holds body tissue together and helps support it. In addition, when taken with iron-rich foods vitamin C facilitates the absorption of iron. Five or more servings of fruits and vegetables per day is thought to be beneficial in preventing cancer and providing sufficient vitamin C intake for healthy people. Most people have little difficulty acquiring enough vitamin C because many foods include ascorbic acid as an ingredient.

Excessive intakes of water-soluble vitamins are excreted in the urine and present little problem of toxicity. However, vitamin C supplements of one gram or more may have adverse consequences in some people [17–18].

MINERALS

A mineral is defined as an inorganic element containing no carbon that remains as ash when food is burned. Minerals cannot be broken down any further. As many as 40 kinds of minerals may exist, but only 17 are known to be essential to human nutrition (Table 1.10).

Minerals comprise only 4% of total body weight. **Macrominerals** are required in relatively large amounts, whereas trace elements, or microminerals, are needed in very small amounts. The macrominerals are calcium, phosphorus, potassium, magnesium, sulfur, sodium, and chlorine. Iron, zinc, selenium, molybdenum, iodine, cobalt, copper, manganese, fluorine, and chromium are **microminerals.**

Mineral functions can be classified as either structural or regulatory. Structural minerals are part of cell tissues or substances. Regulatory minerals help regulate acid-base balance, muscle contractibility, and nerve irritability and also act in the processes of metabolism involving other nutrients.

An important consideration today is whether the increased consumption of processed and refined foods in which the trace element concentrations have been reduced or altered will eventually lead to diseases. No evidence exists that this will be the case.

Calcium. Adequate calcium intake is needed to prevent loss of bone mass. Osteoporosis is related to low calcium intakes. Since human bones reach their maximum mass at about age 25 to 30, children, teenagers, and young adults must get calcium-rich foods throughout these years. Evidence now supports the need for calcium in adults, especially women, who need about as much calcium later in life as they did when they were adolescents [15].

Calcium is the most abundant mineral in the body. Ninety-nine percent of the body's calcium is found in bones and teeth. This mineral makes bones hard and strong and prevents them from breaking, in most cases, when they are subjected to immense force. The remaining percent of calcium is found in body fluids and soft tissues. Calcium in the tissues and fluids acts as a cementing substance, holding cells together, and is used to transmit nerve impulses, to control the movement of substances into and out of cells, and to regulate muscle contractions. Calcium also is used in the blood-clotting mechanism and in the absorption of B_{12}. Factors that make calcium more available to the body include:

- An increased need, for example, pregnancy
- The intake of small amounts of calcium throughout the day
- The presence of lactose (milk sugar in milk)
- Adequate vitamin D in the diet
- Acid conditions in the stomach

Factors that may hinder calcium availability include:

- A high-protein diet may cause calcium to be excreted
- Lack of physical exercise in persons confined to bed

Table 1.10 Major functions and sources of selected minerals

Mineral	Function	Sources
Macrominerals		
Calcium	Strengthens bones and teeth; involved in muscle contraction and relaxation, blood clotting, water balance, nerve function	Milk and milk products, green leafy vegetables, legumes, fortified foods, almonds, fish (with bones), tofu
Phosphorus	Involved in calcification of teeth and bones, acid-base balance, energy metabolism	Meat, poultry, fish, milk, soft drinks, processed foods, whole grains, eggs
Sodium	Promotes acid-base balance, water balance, nerve impulse transmission, muscle activity	Salt, soy sauce, processed foods: cured, canned, pickled, and many prepackaged foods
Potassium	Facilitates many reactions, especially protein synthesis, water balance, nerve transmission, muscle contraction	Meats, milk, fruits, vegetables, grains, legumes
Sulfur	Component of protein; part of biotin, thiamin, insulin	All protein-containing foods
Chloride	Part of stomach acid, acid base balance, water balance	Table salt, soy sauce; processed foods
Magnesium	Involved in protein synthesis, muscle contraction, nerve transmission	Whole grains, nuts, legumes, chocolate, meat, dark green leafy vegetables, seafoods, cocoa
Microminerals		
Iron	Hemoglobin formation, part of myoglobin in muscles; used in energy utilization	Red meats, fish, poultry, shellfish, eggs, legumes, dried fruits, fortified cereals and grains
Iodine	Part of thyroxine, a thyroid hormone that influences growth and metabolism	Iodized salt, seafood, bread
Zinc	Part of insulin and enzymes; vitamin A transport; wound healing; fetus and sperm development; immunity; promotes enzyme activity and metabolism	Protein-containing foods: red meat, seafood, oysters, clams, poultry, eggs, dairy, grains
Selenium	Antioxidant; works with vitamin E; immune system response	Seafood, meats, grains
Manganese	Essential for normal bone development; activates enzymes	Whole grains, legumes, nuts, green leafy vegetables, meat, tea, coffee
Copper	Necessary for formation of hemoglobin; part of energy metabolism enzymes	Organ meats, shellfish, nuts, seeds, legumes, peanut butter, chocolate
Fluoride	Formation of bones and teeth; provides resistance to dental caries	Drinking water (naturally occurring or fluoridated), tea, seafood
Chromium	Enhances effect of insulin; aids in metabolism of carbohydrates and lipids	Mushrooms, dark chocolate, prunes, nuts, asparagus, brewer's yeast, whole grains, vegetable oils
Molybdenum	Aids in oxidation reactions	Legumes, cereals, grains, organ meats
Cobalt	As part of vitamin B_{12}, aids in nerve function and blood formation	Meats, milk, and milk products

- Phytic and oxalic acids, which bind calcium
- Excessive dietary fat that may move calcium through the body too rapidly for absorption

The amount of calcium that a body absorbs depends on the person's age, the presence of vitamin D in the body, the body's need for calcium, and the amount of calcium ingested. Older adults absorb less calcium than younger adults do. Women start to lose calcium around 30 years of age. This process is accelerated in women right before and after menopause. The use of estrogen after menopause seems to slow the bone loss [18]. Low estrogen levels, as seen in postmenopausal women, can lower calcium absorption. Many women take calcium supplements after menopause to maintain calcium levels and to reduce risk of osteoporosis. Supplements of calcium are best absorbed in amounts of 500 mg or less between meals [19].

Phytic and oxalic acids bind to calcium and prevent calcium absorption in the body. Phytic acid, also known as phytates, is present in whole-grain cereals; oxalates (oxalic acid) in foods such as greens, rhubarb, and chocolate. Harmful effects of these substances depend on the quantities consumed. Fortunately, dietary calcium is plentiful, especially in dairy products, compared with the amounts of phytic and oxalic acid.

Osteoporosis and osteomalacia are two bone abnormalities related to calcium. Osteoporosis is a loss in total amount of bone, and osteomalacia is the loss of calcium and phosphorus crystals from the bone. Adequate consumption of foods high in calcium in childhood and adolescence appears to be needed not only for growth and development, but to assure high bone density and greater latitude for maintenance of skeletal integrity in the face of bone loss in later years.

Milk and dairy products are the best sources of calcium. Chocolate milk is a rich source of calcium; it can be low in fat and has been shown not to promote tooth decay, which makes it a good option, especially for children, for increasing variety without decreasing calcium. Other sources of calcium are broccoli, okra, dried beans, and peas, providing much less calcium than milk. One cup of whole milk (8 oz) provides 290 mg of calcium compared with 1/2 cup of broccoli that provides only 21 mg of calcium.

Phosphorus.　Like calcium, phosphorus is found in large amounts in bones and teeth. This mineral gives rigidity to bones and teeth and performs more functions than any other mineral element in normal cell metabolism and functioning. Phosphorus is involved in the metabolism of carbohydrates, protein, and fat. It is part of many enzyme systems and plays an important role in the energy metabolism of muscle.

> **Enzyme**　An **enzyme** is any of several complex proteins that are produced by cells and act as catalysts in specific biochemical reactions. Enzyme systems may include other nutrients or minerals.

Persons generally need to be more concerned about getting enough calcium than phosphorus. Soft drinks are often overlooked as sources of phosphorus, and frequent intake of these beverages can disrupt the body's calcium–phosphorus balance. Consuming large amounts of antacids may interfere with phosphorus absorption and result in phosphorus depletion.

Sources providing the most phosphorus include foods containing calcium and protein such as milk, cheese, meat, and bread. Other sources include breakfast cereals, bran, eggs, nuts, fish, and carbonated beverages.

Sodium.   Sodium is used in foods as a seasoning and a preservative. It is part of ordinary table salt, sodium chloride. The principal element in extracellular fluids, sodium is involved primarily in regulating the acid-base balance in body fluids. Along with potassium, it is important in regulating the body fluid volume. The cells work to keep sodium on the outside of the cell membrane (extracellular) and potassium on the inside (intracellular). If the amount of sodium in the blood changes, the fluid balance of the body is affected.

Many Americans regularly eat more than two teaspoons of salt per day (2400 mg sodium). A safe and adequate supply for adults is less than one teaspoon of salt (1200 mg sodium). The sodium or salt described here is that included in foods as well as the salt added to foods after preparation.

The kidneys conserve sodium, filtering any excess from the blood into the urine. Too much sodium may lead to an increase in blood volume and extra pressure on the arteries, causing the heart to work harder to pump blood and the blood pressure to rise in persons who are particularly sensitive to sodium. Excessive intake of sodium, primarily from table salt (sodium chloride), has been implicated in hypertension (higher blood pressure) but only for those who have been shown to be sensitive to sodium. There is some evidence that excessive consumption of salt-preserved or salt-pickled foods increases the risk of stomach cancer [20]. The Dietary Guidelines for Americans [7] recommends using sodium "in moderation" (Chapter 2).

Sodium is found naturally in greater quantities in animal foods than in plant foods. Cured meats, sausages, canned soups and vegetables, soy sauce, and steak sauces have high sodium content. Up to 75% of the salt in the diet is added to foods by food processors. Check labels for sodium content, try to eat fresh foods in place of processed, or look for reduced sodium alternatives for favorite foods. Because over-the-counter drugs may also be a source of sodium, labels should be read carefully.

Potassium.   Potassium is an essential mineral that maintains intracellular fluid balance. It is a component of lean body tissue. The need for potassium increases during growth of lean tissue. Potassium is lost when the muscle breaks down because of starvation, protein deficiency, or injury. Some of the sudden deaths that occur during states of fasting or in cases of severe vomiting and diarrhea are thought to be the result of heart failure from extensive potassium loss. Nerve and muscle cells are rich in potassium.

Sodium and potassium ions exchange places during nerve transmission and muscle contraction. Therefore, they keep the heart beating regularly. Several studies have shown that groups of people who eat low-potassium diets have an increased incidence of high blood pressure and heart disease. Extreme dieting (liquid-protein diets) may lead to loss of potassium and can cause heart abnormalities. Adults may be warned not to take diuretics, unless under the guidance of a physician, since some of them may cause potassium excretion.

Fruits and vegetables, such as bananas, tomatoes, citrus juices, and potatoes, grains, meats, fish, and poultry, are among the richest sources of potassium. Milk is also a good source of potassium. Following the Food Guide Pyramid (Chapter 2) as recommended in the Dietary Guidelines for Americans as well as consuming the recommended five servings of fruits and vegetables would provide sufficient potassium [7]. Persons taking potassium supplements when prescribed should have regular serum potassium levels evaluated. Potassium toxicity from taking potassium in a supplement form is of greater concern than potassium deficiency. The body needs the other nutrients listed in Table 1.10: magnesium, sulfur, and chloride. Discussion of the specific role of these nutrients is limited since they are found in a wide variety of foods and consumed in adequate amounts to meet the needs of healthy individuals.

Iron. Iron is required in smaller amounts than the minerals previously listed. It is probably one of the most widely known minerals. Certain populations in the United States, including some children, have an iron intake less than the recommended level [16]. Iron deficiency in the United States is prevalent among toddlers, adolescent girls, and women of childbearing age [21]. The cause of iron deficiency is typically inadequate intake of foods containing iron and/or malnutrition. Blood loss is also a cause of iron deficiency.

Iron is found in the blood as part of hemoglobin in red blood cells and myoglobin in muscle tissue. Its best-known task is in providing oxygen to the cells of the body. It is also part of enzyme systems. Iron must be absorbed to be usable. Acids enhance absorption and the presence of vitamin C. When there is a physiological need for iron and when iron is presented in a form called "heme" iron it is absorbed more readily. Iron from meats, fish, and poultry is known as **heme iron.** Nonheme iron is from plants such as vegetables, legumes, and grains. As with calcium, phytic acid, found in bran, binds iron and forms an insoluble complex. At recommended levels of fiber consumption, decreased absorption because of phytates and oxalates is not significant [22]. Fiber may cause food to move through the intestinal tract quickly, reducing the time needed for complete digestion of foods and iron absorption.

Iron-deficiency anemia may be seen in young children after 6 months of age and in adolescents, especially girls. A low iron intake can lead to iron-deficiency anemia, which lowers the blood's oxygen-carrying capacity. Tiredness, weakness, headaches, increased sensitivity to the cold, apathy, and paleness characterize iron deficiency anemia.

Good sources of iron include liver and other organ meats, red meat, whole-grain or enriched and fortified cereals, oysters, clams, dried beans, some fruits, and dark green vegetables. Although the iron from plant sources is poorly absorbed, absorption can be increased by eating a small amount of meat or by eating foods high in vitamin C with the meal.

It is not recommended that you take supplemental iron unless prescribed by a physician after appropriate laboratory tests confirm an iron deficiency. Iron supplements should be kept out of the reach of children, because children can fatally overdose on supplements.

Iodine.   Iodine is necessary for the proper functioning of the thyroid gland; without iodine, the thyroid enlarges to capture what little iodine is available in the blood. This enlargement, or goiter, is seen as a swelling in the neck.

The major source of iodine is iodized salt. Iodized salt is mandatory in Canada; however, iodized salt is used optionally by about 50% of the U.S. population [16]. Although iodized salt costs a penny or two more than the noniodized form, this small investment goes a long way toward preventing goiter, especially when seafood is not eaten frequently. Seafood may have higher concentrations of iodine since marine animals concentrate iodine from seawater. Processed foods may also contain higher levels of iodine due to the addition of iodized salt [16]. Some manufacturers use iodine as a dough conditioner.

Zinc.   Present in every tissue, zinc is essential as a component of enzymes involved in vital metabolic pathways. It is necessary for normal growth, prevention of anemia, general repair of all tissues, and wound healing.

Zinc deficiency has been noted in children, and it appears that regular intake of zinc through diet, particularly during periods of growth and stress, is necessary. Zinc deficiency is characterized by night blindness, poor appetite, delayed healing of cuts, decreased taste and smell, hair loss, susceptibility to infection, and poor growth in children. Zinc toxicity can result from supplementation; therefore, use supplements with care and keep bottles out of reach of children. Sources of zinc include red meats, milk, liver, poultry, eggs, fish, and seafood, especially shellfish.

Selenium.   Selenium is an essential trace mineral in the human body. This nutrient is an important part of antioxidant enzymes that protect cells against the effects of free radicals that are produced during normal oxygen metabolism. The body has developed defenses such as antioxidants to control levels of free radicals because they can damage cells and contribute to the development of some chronic diseases. Selenium is also essential for normal functioning of the immune system and thyroid gland. Selenium deficiency is most commonly seen in parts of China where the selenium content in the soil is low, therefore selenium intake is very low. Selenium deficiency is linked to Keshan Disease. The most common signs of selenium deficiency seen in this disease include an enlarged heart and poor heart function. Food sources of selenium include seafood, kidney, and liver, and to a lesser extent other meats [13]. Other microminerals listed in Table 1.10 are readily available in foods eaten. Deficiency may be seen during chronic or acute illnesses. The reader is encouraged to study the minerals in great detail [13–16, 22].

WATER

Water is one of the most essential nutrients. It is a required part of our diet and without it the body would not be able to survive more than 6 days. Water is crucial for carrying nutrients to the cells in the body and for carrying wastes from the cells. It helps in regulating body temperature and keeps our bodies working more efficiently. It is the body's cooling system; when the body temperature goes up, water is released on the skin as perspiration. Water is also the main part of our blood and tissues. Needless to say, water is an extremely important nutrient.

For a child, the proportion of body surface area to body mass is much larger than for an adult; thus, children need proportionately more fluid; however, infants do not require water since breast milk or formula provides the necessary fluid. The water lost by evaporation from the young child accounts for more than 60% of that needed to maintain the body, compared with 45% for the adult. However, it is difficult to determine how much water a child needs, because surface area, activity, and other foods consumed are all contributing factors. It is important to offer fluids to a child often in order to reduce the risk for dehydration.

Dehydration, or too little water, is a problem worldwide. Adults lose about 48 ounces (1.4 L) of fluid per day through urine, feces, and perspiration. At least this much should be replaced from food and beverages each day. A greater quantity of liquids should be taken frequently in warm weather or during strenuous exercise. Anyone who refuses liquids, is vomiting, or has diarrhea can rapidly become dehydrated. Infants and elderly are especially vulnerable to dehydration. Burns can also cause deadly dehydration, since damaged skin cannot prevent excessive fluid loss.

Water is also important for proper elimination. One of the first factors to be considered when a child or adult complains of constipation is the amount of fluids consumed. A recommended practice is to drink 8 cups of water or liquids per day for a total of 64 ounces.

It is important to drink an adequate amount of water each day

Bottled versus tap water? Why are people getting so excited about water in a bottle? For many people bottled water is a convenient way to drink fluids each day. Americans may choose bottled water because they feel it is safer than regular tap water; others because they think the taste is better. Standards for municipal water supplier (tap water) are enforced by the EPA (Environmental Protection Agency), which requires regular testing and monitoring of the public water supply. However, many municipal water suppliers also add fluoride to tap water to aid in prevention of tooth decay. Most bottled waters do not contain fluoride. The bottled water industry is regulated by the FDA and is forced to meet standards that have a maximum allowable standard of contaminants for bottled water. But the FDA only regulates bottled water sold interstate, across state lines, so individual bottling companies within the state only have to be compliant with state regulations. The answer to the question of which is better is really up to the consumer. There is no definite best choice for water; it is all determined by cost, taste, convenience, and perceived safety by the consumers.

VITAMIN AND HERBAL SUPPLEMENTS

There are few, if any, quick solutions for gaining and maintaining good health. "Popping pills" appears an easy solution for losing weight or making up nutrients missed in dietary intake. However, benefits are largely unproven. Nutrients function together; therefore, an excess intake of one may create a greater need for others. In addition, the use of pills is inappropriate modeling behavior for persons involved with young children. Unless a specific deficiency has been diagnosed in laboratory and clinical tests, the habitual intake of large doses of vitamins and minerals should be discouraged [23]. Dietary supplements come in various forms such as vitamins, minerals, herbals, enzymes, amino acids, and many others.

Dietary supplement Defined by the Dietary Supplement Health and Education Act (DSHEA) as a vitamin, mineral, herb or other botanical, an amino acid, a dietary substance for use by man to supplement the diet by increasing the total dietary intake, or a concentrate, metabolite, constituent or extract. *Source:* Public Law 103–417.

Moderate supplementation that is in the range of the recommended daily values or is at levels that could be eaten in a nutrient-rich diet are recommended for people with increased nutritional need. Some people that may benefit from moderate supplementation are pregnant and breastfeeding women, women with heavy menstrual bleeding, people with severe food restrictions, vegans, children, infants, and the elderly.

Pregnant women may take supplemental folic acid to decrease the risk for neural tube defects in their baby. There may also be a need for increased iron due to higher iron needs during pregnancy. Morning sickness may also increase the need for supplementation of some vitamins and minerals due to decreased food intake secondary to nausea. Breastfeeding women have higher nutritional needs during lactation. Women who have heavier menstrual periods may supplement their diets with iron. Supplements may be recommended for people who severely restrict their diet due to weight loss regimes or eating disorders. If infants have limited access to sunlight they may need supplementation of vitamin D. Since vegans abstain from animal food and dairy products they may need to supplement their diets with vitamin B$_{12}$, and possibly calcium, zinc, and iron. The elderly commonly have inadequate stomach acid and may need supplements of vitamin B$_{12}$. They may also need supplementation of calcium and vitamin D for bone maintenance.

For healthy people eating a varied diet, a single daily dose of a multiple vitamin–mineral supplement containing 100% of the RDAs is not known to be either harmful or beneficial. High-potency vitamin and mineral supplements should be avoided unless prescribed by a physician. These include protein powders, single amino acids, fiber, and lecithin. Many organizations, including the American Dietetic Association [23], recommend no vitamin or mineral supplement for healthy people eating a varied diet.

Phytochemicals.   **Phytochemicals** are plant chemicals. They are not required in the diet but they have certain properties that may reduce the risks associated with heart disease, cancer, osteoporosis, and other chronic diseases in people who consume them regularly. Variety in the diet has its bonuses by providing not only a rich supply of vitamins and minerals but also a supply of phytochemicals. Studies have shown that populations that consume more fruits, vegetables, legumes, and whole grains tend to have lower rates of certain chronic diseases. Researchers continue to look at specific foods and nutrients for the beneficial characteristics or functional properties such as their antioxidant properties. Consume a wide variety of foods, especially vegetables and fruits, instead of specific compounds found in pills. Since scientist are still studying the many healthful properties of whole foods, supplements of phytochemicals are not advised.

Herbal remedies are becoming increasingly popular. There are a variety of herbal supplements that claim to cure a variety of ailments as well as enhance well-being. Herbs have been used for medicinal purposes for thousands of years. Consumers commonly associate herbal supplements as being "safe" because they are "natural." However, just because these products come from natural sources does not necessarily make them safe. Consumers who choose herbal remedies should use them with care. Consult a physician or dietitian before taking herbal products and do your own research. If a supplement claim seems too good to be true, it probably is. Many herbal supplements interact with prescription and over-the-counter drugs. It is very important to know the side effects and interactions a drug, supplement, or herb may have on your body before taking it.

> **Phytochemicals**
>
> For more information on phytochemicals visit the Food and Nutrition Information Center at http://www.nal.usda.gov/fnic/etext/000015.html.

Some nutrients are needed in large quantities and others in smaller quantities. The task of providing nutrients to the body in the amounts necessary to ensure adequate nutritional status may seem overwhelming. However, there are shortcuts to selecting the proper nutrients. Using food guides and standards (Chapter 2) will help in selecting a variety of foods to obtain the nutrients needed for health and life. Because each nutrient is found in a wide variety of foods, eating from a wide variety of foods will increase the likelihood of your diet containing all of the essential nutrients.

ALCOHOL

A review of nutrition would not be complete without a discussion of alcohol and its nutritional effects on the body. Alcohol provides seven kilocalories per gram (kcal/g) but is not considered a carbohydrate, protein, or fat. It is a drug. Alcohol is not digested. It is absorbed quickly throughout the length of the gastrointestinal tract, including the stomach. It is water-soluble and disperses throughout the body fluids.

The American Heart Association recommends limited alcohol intake in order to reduce the risk for heart disease [11]. Alcohol is a source of empty calories, and high intakes can increase the risk for obesity as well as hypertriglyceridemia (high levels of triglycerides). If an individual chooses to consume alcohol, intake should be limited to two drinks per day for men and one drink per day for women [24]. Avoid alcoholic beverages when pregnant [24].

Children do not consume alcohol; however, it is important to remember that nutrition concerns for young children begin during the prenatal period. You may be caring for children with fetal alcohol syndrome (FAS), a result of over-consumption of alcohol during pregnancy [24]. Poor fetal and infant growth, physical deformities (especially facial features), limited hand–eye coordination, and mental retardation characterize children with FAS. The effects from alcohol exposure during pregnancy can vary depending on the amounts of alcohol consumed, but may include irreversible behavioral and learning disabilities as well as growth retardation in children. No amount of alcohol has been found to be absolutely safe during pregnancy [24].

ENERGY

Energy is the ability to do work. Energy is required to sustain the functions of the body such as physical work, maintenance, respiration, and circulation. Energy comes from the foods eaten and is released in the body to yield the chemical energy needed to sustain metabolism, nerve transmissions, respiration, circulation, and physical work. Heat that is produced during this process is used to maintain body temperature. Dietary intake and energy expenditure makes up energy balance. Imbalances between intake and expenditure result in gains or losses of body components such as fat. Imbalances result in changes in body weight. In the United States more people are overweight or obese, in positive energy balance, than underweight or in negative energy balance. Thirty-three percent of the U.S. population is considered overweight and more than 30% are obese.

Sources of energy

Carbohydrate: 4 calories/gram
Protein: 4 calories/gram
Fat: 9 calories/gram
Alcohol: 7 calories/gram

Energy is measured in calories. Foods you eat provide energy through carbohydrates, protein, and fat. Each gram of fat provides more than two times the energy supplied by carbohydrate or protein. Alcohol, although not a nutrient, supplies seven calories per gram. If energy intake is above or below that which is required by the body over a period of time, the child or adult will gain or lose body weight. Overweight and obesity is a major health problem in the United States.

Are You Overweight?

If one exercises regularly and eats in moderation, energy balance is maintained. When overweight or obesity occurs, the person has either taken in too many calories or exercised too little. One indication of excess fat stores in the body is when an individual weighs more than the standard. A standard developed to indicate if weight for height puts you at risk for chronic diseases is the body mass index (BMI). No longer do most health professionals use height and weight tables to determine the best weight and the caloric needs of individuals. BMI is calculated using the formula shown in Box 1.5. Note that the female in the example is overweight and at some risk for developing chronic diseases. Interpretation and risk according to BMI score can be found in Table 1.11. There are calculators online that help calculate BMI: http://www.cdc.gov/nccdphp/dnpa/bmi/calc-bmi.htm or http://www.nhlbisupport.com/bmi/bmicalc.htm. BMI does not take into account muscle mass or frame size, so some discretion should be used when calculating BMI. The same formula is used for men and women. A BMI greater than 25 may or may not be due to increases in body fat. For example, professional athletes may be lean and muscular, with little body fat, yet they may

---

Box 1.5   Calculating BMI for adults

BMI = [Weight in pounds ÷ Height in inches ÷ Height in inches] × 703

Fractions and ounces must be entered as decimal values.

Example: A 160-lb 67-in.-tall person

BMI = [160 pounds divided by 67 inches, divided by 67 inches] × 703 = 25.1

Table 1.11   BMI interpretation and risk

Range	Interpretation	Risk*
Below 18.5	Underweight	The lower the BMI, the greater the risk
18.6–24.9	Normal	Very low risk
25.0–29.9	Overweight	Some risk
30.0–45.4	Obese	Moderate to high risk
Greater than 45.5	Morbid obesity	Very high risk

*BMI is a reliable indicator of total body fat, which is related to the risk of disease and death. The score is valid for both men and women but it does have limits. Limits are: It may overestimate body fat in athletes and others who have a muscular build, and it may underestimate body fat in older persons and others who have lost muscle mass.
Source: National Institutes for Health: http://www.nhlbisupport.com/bmi/bmicalc.htm.

Table 1.12   Selected energy (calories) requirements

Dietary guidelines issued by the Institute of Medicine estimate the daily energy requirements, in calories, for people age 30 and of various heights, weights, and levels of activity.

	Sedentary (Calories)	Active (Calories)
Five-feet-one-inch, 98 to 132 pounds		
Women	1,688 to 1,834	2,104 to 2,290
Men	1,919 to 2,167	2,104 to 2,290
Five-feet-five, up to 150 pounds		
Women	1,816 to 1,982	2,267 to 2,477
Men	2,068 to 2,349	2,490 to 2,842
Five-feet-nine, 125 to 169 pounds		
Women	1,948 to 2,134	2,434 to 2,670
Men	2,222 to 2,538	2,683 to 3,078
Six-feet-one, 139 to 188 pounds		
Women	2,083 to 2,290	2,605 to 2,869
Men	2,382 to 2,736	2,883 to 3,325

Source: Institute of Medicine. (2002). *Dietary Reference Intakes for Energy, Carbohydrates, Fiber, Fat, Protein and Amino Acids (Macronutrients).* Washington, DC: National Academy Press.

weigh more than individuals with the same height because of their muscle mass regardless of BMI.

BMI is age and gender specific for children. Because BMI changes substantially as children get older, BMI-for-age is the measure used for children ages 2 to 20 years. Health professionals plot BMI-for-age on growth charts (Chapter 2). A discussion of the BMI table and childhood obesity will also be covered in Chapter 5.

The amount of energy needed for physical activity can vary greatly and is under your control. This amount can vary depending on activity. The energy balance of an individual depends on his/her dietary energy intake and energy expenditure. Judge what you should eat by the amount of exercise or activity performed each day. The adult should strive to exercise 60 minutes per day. Food intake should be regulated so that the adult is not overweight. Using the Food Guide Pyramid as a healthy eating pattern and exercising *60 minutes each day* is recommended to decrease BMI to the recommended level. It is more important to keep track of your activity than the calories consumed. If you desire to determine the calories consumed each day, there are dietary analysis Web sites online to help you (Appendix I). Selected daily energy requirements are found in Table 1.12. See Chapter 2 for a discussion of foods to meet the energy and nutrient needs of young children using food guides and standards. For food and nutrition needs of children ages birth through 6 years, see Chapters 3–6.

Figure 1.4 Body shape and fat distribution: android (left) and gynoid (right)
Source: Drawn by student workers, 2000.

Where Is Energy Stored?

If the body receives more energy than it can use for growth, maintenance, and activity, energy is stored as fat. The region where fat is stored affects the risk for weight related health problems (Figure 1.4). People who store body fat in upper body areas are identified as having android obesity or being apple-shaped. Others store body fat in the lower region and are known to have gynoid obesity or being pear-shaped. Excess fat in any region can result in health problems, but each of

> **Box 1.6   Determining waist-to-hip ratio**
>
> 1. Measure around the waist near your navel while standing relaxed.
> 2. Measure around the hips over the buttocks, where they are largest.
> 3. Divide the waist measurement by the hip measurement to determine your waist to hip ratio.
>
> *Example:*
> Waist = 28 in.
> Hips = 40 in.
> 28 ÷ 40 = less than 1
> Waist = 39 in.
> Hips = 37 in.
> 39 ÷ 37 = more than 1

these areas, whether lower or upper, has its unique health risks. You can determine body shape using a simple formula (Box 1.6).

Android (upper body) obesity occurs when waist to hip ratio is greater than 1. This body type is typically characteristic in males. A waist to hip ratio of more than 1.0 in men or 0.8 in women can indicate upper body fat storage. This body type is related to heart disease, high blood pressure, and type 2 diabetes. High testosterone levels and increased alcohol intake may increase android obesity.

Gynoid obesity is greater in women due to estrogen's and progesterone's role in encouraging lower-body fat storage. This body type can carry more weight before showing the same health risks as the person with android obesity. Ratios close to or above 1.0 (android) are linked with greater health risk.

SUMMARY

Nutrition is the science of food and how the body uses it. The study of nutrition involves the social, economic, cultural, and emotional factors that affect the intake of food.

- There are six classes of nutrients with specialized functions in the body.
- Carbohydrate, protein, and fat are major nutrients that have specific functions but also supply heat, or energy, to the body.
- Each of the nutrients is found in a wide variety of foods. Therefore, the wider the variety of foods one eats, the more likely the diet will contain all essential nutrients.
- HDL and LDL cholesterol are related to heart disease and may be altered by diet, blood pressure, smoking, and exercise.
- Consider activity when calculating energy needs. Increasing exercise may allow for an intake of more food.

- Alcohol contributes 7 kcal/g. Alcohol consumption may have detrimental effects on the fetus.
- Supplementing the diet with large amounts of vitamins, minerals, phyto-chemicals, and herbs is not advisable. Megadoses of specific nutrients should be prescribed only after appropriate clinical and laboratory tests confirm the need.
- Applying the basic principles of nutrition to your personal diet provides experience in learning what factors to evaluate in diets of children.
- Practicing good nutrition principles helps teachers to be good role models for parents and children.

DISCUSSION QUESTIONS

1. Describe the nature, functions, and use of the essential nutrients.
2. List and describe an ethnic group not included in the text that influences your center activities. How might you include characteristics of the ethnic groups into the food and educational program?
3. Which nutrients supply energy to the body, and which one supplies energy most efficiently?
4. In addition to the specific nutrients found in foods, which other factors must be considered when the subject of nutrition is studied?
5. What are the consequences of exceeding nutrient requirements?
6. Why should you as a teacher practice the principles of good nutrition?
7. What is the role of alcohol in the diet? What are some negative effects of adult alcohol consumption?
8. Should I be concerned about the amount and kind of fat in my diet?
9. Why is water so important in the daily diet?
10. Are recommendations for vitamins the same for children as for adults? Why or why not?

REFERENCES

1. Pillsbury, R. (1998). *No foreign food: The American diet in time and place.* Boulder, CO: Westview Press.
2. Largest religious groups in the United States of America. Retrieved January 20, 2002 from http://www.adherents.com/ rel_USA.html, accessed Jan. 20, 2002.
3. American Dietetic Association and American Diabetes Association, Inc. (1995–1998). *Ethnic and regional food practices: A series.* Chicago, IL: Author.
4. Abramovitz, B.A., & Birch, L.L. (2000). Five-year-old girls' ideas about dieting are predicted by their mothers' dieting. *Journal of American Dietetic Association, 100,* 1157–1163.
5. Food and Nutrition Board, Institutes of Medicine. (2002). *Dietary Reference Intakes for energy, carbohydrates, fiber, fat, protein, and amino acids (macronutrients).* Washington, DC: National Academy Press.

6. U.S. Department of Agriculture and U.S. Department of Health and Human Services. *Nutrition and your health: Dietary guidelines for Americans* (5th ed.). Washington, DC: U.S. Government Printing Office.

7. Henkel J. (1999). Sugar substitutes: Americans opt for sweetness and lite. *FDA Consumer, 33*(6), 12–16.

8. Coulston, A., & Johnson, R. (2002). Sugar and sugars: Myths and realities. *Journal of American Dietetic Association 102,* 351–353.

9. Wolraich, M. L., & Lindgren, S. (1994). Effects of diets high in sucrose or aspartame on the behavior and cognitive performance of children. *New England Journal of Medicine, 330,* 301–307.

10. Lauber, R.P., & Sheard, N. E. (2001). The American Heart Association dietary guidelines for 2000: A summary report. *Nutrition Reviews, 59*(9), 298–306.

11. Executive summary of the third report of the National Cholesterol Education Program (NCEP) expert panel on detection, evaluation, and treatment of high blood cholesterol in adults (adult treatment panel III; 2001). *Journal of the American Medical Association, 285*(19), 2486–2497.

12. Meydani, M., & Meisler, J. C. (1997). A closer look at vitamin E. Can this antioxidant prevent chronic diseases? *Postgraduate Medicine, 102*(2), 199–201, 206–7.

13. Food and Nutrition Board, Institutes of Medicine. (2000). *Dietary Reference Intakes for vitamin C, vitamin E, selenium, and carotenoids.* Washington, DC: National Academy Press.

14. Food and Nutrition Board, Institutes of Medicine. (1998). *Dietary Reference Intakes for thiamin, riboflavin, niacin, vitamin B_6, folate, vitamin B_{12}, panothenic acid, biotin, and choline.* Washington DC: National Academy Press.

15. Food and Nutrition Board, Institutes of Medicine. (1997). *Dietary Reference Intakes for calcium, phosphorus, magnesium, vitamin D, and flouride.* Washington, DC: National Academy Press.

16. Food and Nutrition Board, Institutes of Medicine. (2001). *Dietary Reference Intakes for vitamin A, vitamin K, arsenic, boron, chromium, copper, iodine, iron, manganese, molybdeum, nickel, silicon, vanadium, and zinc.* Washington, DC: National Academy Press.

17. Levine, M., Rumsey, S.C., Daruwala, R., Park, J., & Wang, Y. (1999). Criteria and recommendations for vitamin C intake. *Journal of American Medical Association, 281*(15), 1415–1423.

18. National Institutes of Health (NIH; 2000, March 27–29). Osteoporosis prevention, diagnosis, and therapy. *NIH Consensus Statement, 17*(1), 1–36.

19. National Institutes of Health (NIH; 1994, June 6–8). Optimal calcium intake. *NIH Consensus Statement, 12*(4), 1–31.

20. Joossens, J. V., Hill, M. J., & Elliot, P. (1996). Dietary salt, nitrate, and stomach cancer mortality in 24 countries. *International Journal of Epidemiology, 25*(3), 494–502.

21. Looker, A., Dallman, P., Carroll, M. (1997). Prevalence of iron deficiency in the United States. *Journal of the American Medical Association, 277,* 973–976.

22. Whitney, E. N., Cataldo, C. B., & Rolfes, S. R. (2002). *Understanding Normal and Clinical Nutrition* (6th ed.). St. Paul, MN: West Publishing.

23. American Dietetic Association. (1987). Recommendations concerning supplement usage: ADA statement. *Journal of American Dietic Association, 87,* 1342–1343.

24. Schydlower, M., et al. (1993). Committee on substance abuse and committee on children with disabilities, fetal alcohol syndrome, and fetal alcohol effects. *Pediatrics, 91*(5), 1004–1006.

2

Foods for Health

LEARNING OBJECTIVES

Students will be able to:
- Describe and use tools to promote health and prevent disease:
  - Dietary Guidelines for Americans
  - Food Guide Pyramid
  - Food Labeling
  - Dietary Reference Intake (DRI)
- Describe the benefits and cautions of physical activity.
- Describe the dietary implications of conditions seen in childhood:
  - obesity and overweight
  - diabetes
  - iron deficiency anemia
  - lead poisoning
  - immune compromised
  - asthma/allergies

Chapter 1 included the basic components of nutrition. This chapter presents food and nutrient guides and recommendations used to assess dietary intake. Frequently occurring medical conditions are included that may be seen in the childhood population, including their description, prevalence, and dietary implications. The purpose of the review of diseases and other health care conditions is to help the teacher become familiar with the child and review the best practices for assisting children with the conditions.

The Western world is plagued with chronic diseases, for example, heart disease, cancer, stroke, and diabetes. Usually we associate these diseases with the aging population. Chronic diseases are really lifestyle-related and take 20 to 30 years to emerge. The indiscretions of today can result in tomorrow's chronic diseases. Diet and physical activity patterns of the young will affect their health in future years.

Children across the country are flunking healthy eating. Some of the most troubling indicators reveal that:

- Only 2% of youth meet all the recommendations of the Food Guide Pyramid; 16% do not meet any recommendation [1].
- Less than 15% of school children eat the recommended servings of fruit; less than 20% eat the recommended servings of vegetables; about 25% eat the recommended servings of grains, and only 30% consume the recommended milk group servings on any given day [2].
- Only 16% of school children meet the guideline for saturated fat on any given day [2].
- Teenagers today drink twice as much carbonated soda as milk [3] and only 19% of girls ages 9 to 19 meet the recommended intakes for calcium [4, 5].

Choose a variety of foods, including five servings of fruits and vegetables

The habits that lead to high fat and low vegetable, fruit, grain, and milk intake are begun in the early years. Food intake and physical activity behaviors must be addressed prior to the middle and high school years. Parents and teachers can influence intakes of children. For example, mothers who drink milk tend to have children who also drink milk [6]. Teachers play a major role in shaping good lifestyle habits by

1. planning and eating meals based upon the Food Guide Pyramid.
2. providing opportunities for physical activity for the child within the program.
3. demonstrating as role models regular physical activity at home and within the preschool environment.
4. incorporating food activities into meals and as components of the educational curriculum.
5. encouraging parents to set examples for children by exercising regularly and eating meals based upon the Food Guide Pyramid.

GUIDELINES FOR FOOD INTAKE

Guides and standards have been developed to help understand food and nutrient intake and assess adequacy of the dietary intake. A tool to promote overall health is the Dietary Guidelines for Americans 2000. A tool that examines whole foods is the Food Guide Pyramid. Using these tools can help balance food intake and physical activity. There are a variety of foods from which to choose in most developed countries. However, children and adults do not always make wise choices, and these guides can help.

Figure 2.1   Dietary Guidelines for Americans

Dietary Guidelines for Americans

The Dietary Guidelines (http://www.nal.usda.gov/fnic) can help promote health and reduce the risk of chronic diseases such as heart disease, certain cancers, diabetes, stroke, and osteoporosis. These diseases are leading causes of death and disabilities among Americans.

The Dietary Guidelines for Americans state:

- Let the Pyramid guide your food choices.
- Choose a variety of grains daily, especially whole grains.
- Choose a variety of fruits and vegetables daily.
- Choose a diet that is low in saturated fat and cholesterol and moderate in total fat.
- Choose beverages and foods to moderate your intake of sugars.
- Choose and prepare foods with less salt.
- Keep food safe to eat.

The Guidelines use three messages, the ABCs (Figure 2.1). Each has a message that is easy to remember.

Aim for Fitness stresses the need for a healthy weight by being physically active each day. Do moderate physical activity daily, and make physical activity part of your routine. Newer information recommends 60 minutes of physical activity daily for adults *and* children [7]. Enjoy regular physical activities with children. Pay attention to serving sizes. Sensible portion sizes as well as physical activity are keys to healthy weight.

Build a Healthy Base means letting the Food Guide Pyramid (Figure 2.2) direct your food choices. Choose a variety of grain products daily, especially whole grains; choose a variety of fruits and vegetables daily. In addition to choosing a variety of foods, keep food safe to eat. Chapter 7 includes ways to keep food safe at home and in the child-care center, during preparation, and when serving and cleaning up, as well as during food activities within the educational curriculum.

Choose Sensibly includes choosing a diet that is low in saturated fat and cholesterol and moderate in total fat; choose beverages and foods to moderate your intake of sugars; choose and prepare foods with less salt. Teachers should be commended for emphasizing milk intake for the very young child. Data indicate that young children do receive sufficient foods high in calcium; however, this intake does not continue into the teenage years when calcium intake is very important. There has been a decrease in milk consumption after the preschool years due, in part, to the switch to sweetened (sugar or high-fructose corn syrup) beverages [8].

Vending machines are often in child-care centers ostensibly for teachers and parents. Be an advocate at your child's school to include milk, flavored or white, in vending machines. Set an example by eating fruits, vegetables, whole grains and, yes, by drinking milk every day so that the children in your care as well as your own children can see you set the example of choosing sensibly.

As an adult, consider your habits. When shopping for butters or margarine, limit use of the solid fats, such as butter and hard margarine, choose vegetable oils as a substitute. Try fat-free or low-fat milk products, fat-free or low-fat salad dressings, mayonnaise spreads, lean red meats, and poultry. Eat cooked dry beans and peas and fish more often without added fat. Try low-sodium bouillon. Use labels to help choose foods lower in total fat. Try to limit fat in general and in servings of vegetables, grains, and dairy products to no more than 5 grams per serving. To keep sodium intake moderate, choose and prepare foods with less salt or salty flavorings. Use fruits, vegetables, or wine to flavor meats. The alcohol in wine will evaporate when used to marinate meats if cooked to the proper temperature. If you choose to drink alcoholic beverages, limit intake to one drink a day for women or two a day for men.

The Food Guide Pyramid

The Pyramid (http://www.nal.usda.gov:8001/py/pmap.htm) is an outline of what to eat each day. It's not a rigid prescription, but a general guide with options for choosing a healthful diet. The Pyramid calls for eating a variety of foods to get the nutrients and the right amount of energy to maintain or improve your weight.

The Pyramid illustrates the research-based food guidance system developed by USDA and supported by the Department of Health and Human Services (DHHS). It goes beyond the old "basic four food groups" to help put the Dietary Guidelines

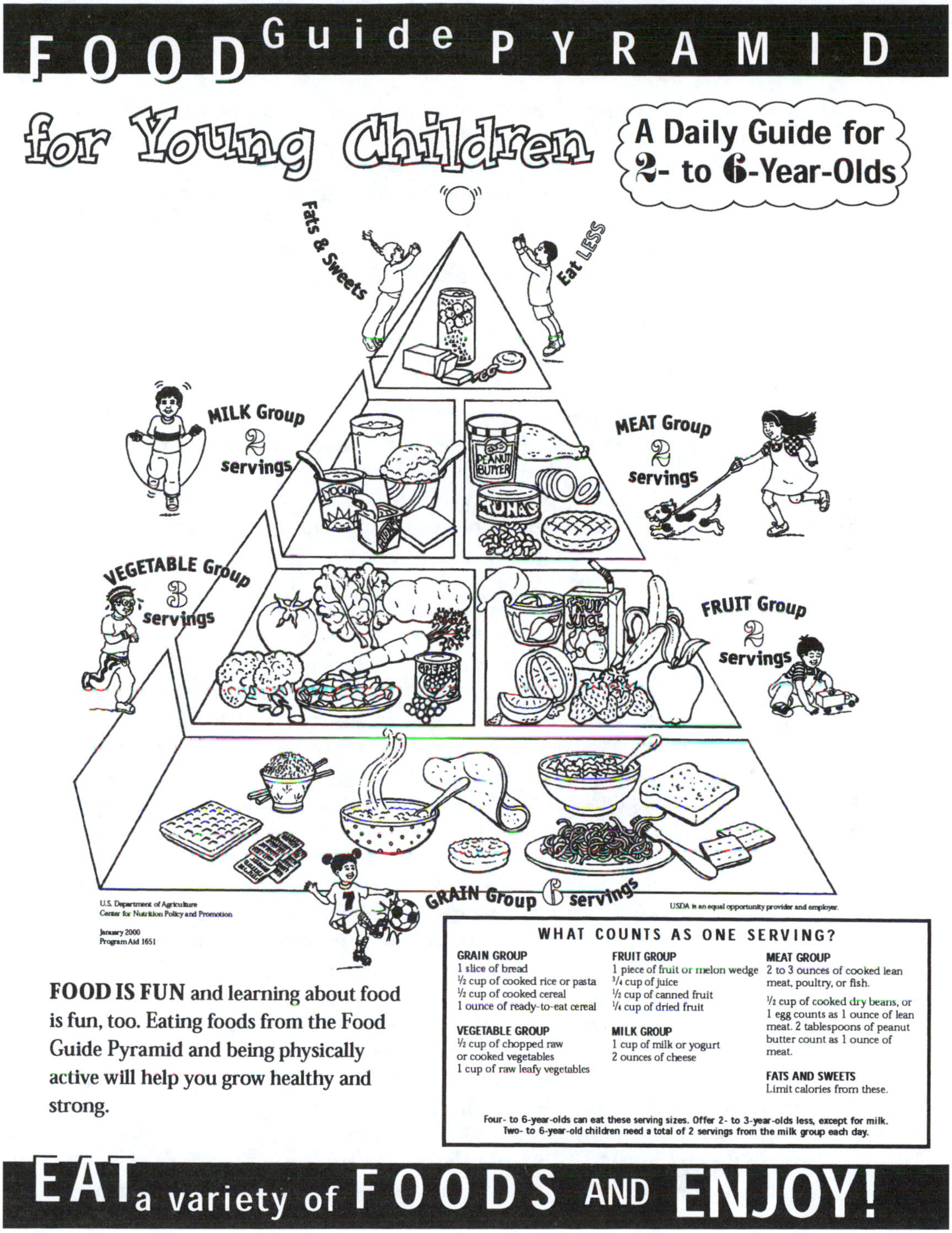

FOOD Guide PYRAMID

for Young Children

A Daily Guide for 2- to 6-Year-Olds

Fats & Sweets — Eat LESS

MILK Group
2 servings

MEAT Group
2 servings

VEGETABLE Group
3 servings

FRUIT Group
2 servings

PEANUT BUTTER

TUNA

GREAT

FRUIT JUICE

GRAIN Group 6 servings

U.S. Department of Agriculture
Center for Nutrition Policy and Promotion

January 2000
Program Aid 1651

USDA is an equal opportunity provider and employer.

FOOD IS FUN and learning about food is fun, too. Eating foods from the Food Guide Pyramid and being physically active will help you grow healthy and strong.

WHAT COUNTS AS ONE SERVING?

GRAIN GROUP
1 slice of bread
½ cup of cooked rice or pasta
½ cup of cooked cereal
1 ounce of ready-to-eat cereal

VEGETABLE GROUP
½ cup of chopped raw or cooked vegetables
1 cup of raw leafy vegetables

FRUIT GROUP
1 piece of fruit or melon wedge
¾ cup of juice
½ cup of canned fruit
¼ cup of dried fruit

MILK GROUP
1 cup of milk or yogurt
2 ounces of cheese

MEAT GROUP
2 to 3 ounces of cooked lean meat, poultry, or fish.

½ cup of cooked dry beans, or 1 egg counts as 1 ounce of lean meat. 2 tablespoons of peanut butter count as 1 ounce of meat.

FATS AND SWEETS
Limit calories from these.

Four- to 6-year-olds can eat these serving sizes. Offer 2- to 3-year-olds less, except for milk. Two- to 6-year-old children need a total of 2 servings from the milk group each day.

EAT a variety of FOODS AND ENJOY!

Figure 2.2   Food Guide Pyramid for Young Children

49

into action. The Pyramid is based on USDA's research on what foods Americans eat, what nutrients are in these foods, and how to make the best food choices for you. The Pyramid will help you choose what and how much to eat from each food group to get the nutrients you need and not too many calories, or too much fat, saturated fat, cholesterol, sugar, sodium, or alcohol. The Pyramid focuses on fat because American diets are too high in fat. Following the Pyramid will help keep intake of total fat and saturated fat low. A diet lower in fat will reduce the health risks associated with certain diseases and help maintain a healthy weight.

The Pyramid visually emphasizes foods from the five major food groups. Each of these food groups provides some, but not all, of the nutrients. Foods in one group can't replace those in another. No one food group is more important than another. Fat and sugars are concentrated in foods from the Pyramid tip—fats, oils, and sweets. These foods supply calories, but little or no vitamins and minerals. By using these foods sparingly, you can have a diet that supplies needed vitamins and minerals without excess calories. When choosing foods for a healthful diet, consider the fat and added sugars in choices from the food groups, as well as the fats, oils, and sweets from the pyramid tip. In general, foods that come from animals (full-fat dairy and meats) are naturally higher in fat than foods that come from plants. But there are many low-fat dairy and lean meat choices available, and these foods can be prepared in ways that lower dietary fat.

Fruits, vegetables, and grain products are naturally low in fat. But many popular items are prepared with fat (e.g., French-fried potatoes, pastries, or croissants), making them high-fat choices. It's the added fat and sugars that provide calories with few vitamins and minerals. Most of the added sugars in the typical American diet come from foods in the Pyramid tip—soft drinks, candy, jams, jellies, syrups, and table sugar.

The Food Guide Pyramid for Young Children does not differ greatly from the general Food Guide Pyramid. It is the guide used for children ages 2 to 6 years old. Prior to this age other guides for the younger child are more appropriate (see Chapter 3). Serving sizes are at the lower end compared to the adult pyramid. For example, only 6 servings of the grain group are recommended instead of the 6 to 11 recommendation in the adult pyramid. Resources are available that help teachers teach children to enjoy healthful eating, along with physical activity, from the early years when children begin to make their desires known. There are no bad foods, only bad diets, and bad diets contribute to poor health outcomes, including childhood obesity. The Food Guide Pyramid shows how everybody can make food choices for a healthful diet. We have developed a daily menu using the minimum number of servings with the recommended serving sizes from the Food Guide Pyramid that may be provided to a 5 year old (Table 2.1). After 5 to 6 years of age, the serving size for the child will probably be the same as allowed for the adult. The calculation, weight (lbs) $\times$ 40.9 kcal, can approximate the child's energy needs.

Healthy Eating Recommendations
(http://www.usda.gov/cnpp/KidsPyra/PyrBook.pdf)

Portion Sizes. Encourage a wide variety of foods for a healthy diet, keeping the portions in line with the recommended amount (Figure 2.3). Most of the

Table 2.1 Sample Menu Compared to Food Guide Pyramid

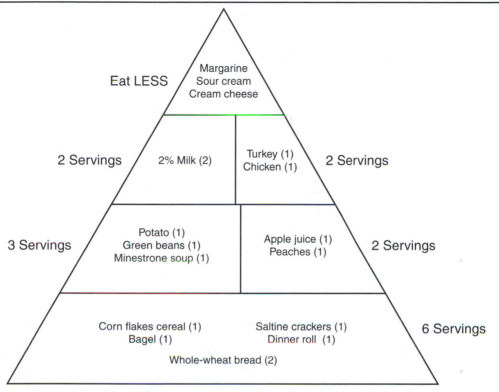

Eat LESS
Margarine
Sour cream
Cream cheese

2 Servings — 2% Milk (2) | Turkey (1) Chicken (1) — 2 Servings

3 Servings — Potato (1) Green beans (1) Minestrone soup (1) | Apple juice (1) Peaches (1) — 2 Servings

Corn flakes cereal (1) Bagel (1) | Saltine crackers (1) Dinner roll (1) — 6 Servings
Whole-wheat bread (2)

( ) indicates the number of Food Guide Pyramid servings for the amount of food consumed

Breakfast	Snack	Lunch	Dinner
Corn Flakes (1 oz = 1 Grain) **Whole Wheat Toast** (1 slice = 1 Grain) **Margarine 1 tsp** **2% Milk** (1/2 c = 1/2 Dairy)	**Bagel** (1/2 = 1 Grain) **Cream Cheese 1 tsp** **2% Milk** (1/2 c = 1/2 Dairy)	**Turkey** (2 oz = 1 Meat*) **Whole-Wheat Bread** (1 slices = 1 Grain) **Minestrone Soup with Beans** (1 c = 1 Vegetable) **Saltine Crackers** (1 oz = 1 Grain) **Canned Peaches** (1/2 c = 1 Fruit) **2% Milk** (1 c = 1 Dairy)	**Roasted Chicken Breast-No Skin** (2 1/2 oz = 1 Meat*) **Green Beans** (1/2 c = 1 Vegetable) **Baked Potato** (1 small = 1 Vegetable) **Dinner Roll** (1 medium = 1 Grain) **Margarine 2 tsp** **Sour Cream 2 tsp** **Apple Juice** (3/4 c = 1 Fruit)

*2 servings of meat for a total of 4 1/2 oz

Grain Group: 6 servings
- 1 slice of bread
- 1/2 cup of cooked rice or pasta
- 1/2 cup of cooked cereal
- 1 ounce of ready-to-eat cereal

Fruit Group
- 1 piece of fruit or melon wedge
- 3/4 cup of juice
- 1/2 cup of canned fruit
- 1/4 cup of dried fruit

Meat Group
- 2 to 3 ounces of cooked lean meat, poultry, or fish
- 1/2 cup of cooked dry beans or 1 egg counts as 1 ounce of lean meat. 2 tablespoons of peanut butter counts as 1 ounce of meat

Vegetable Group
- 1/2 cup of chopped raw or cooked vegetables
- 1 cup of raw leafy vegetables

Milk Group
- 1 cup of milk or yogurt
- 2 ounces of cheese

Fats and Sweets
- Limit calories from these

Figure 2.3   What counts as one serving?*

*Four- to 6-year-olds can eat these serving sizes. Offer 2- to 3-year-olds less, except for milk. Two- to 6-year-olds need a total of two servings from the milk group each day.

Source: USDA Center for Nutrition and Policy Promotion, January 2000, Program Aid 1651.

Box 2.1   Child-sized servings

Children 2 to 3 years of age need the same variety of foods as 4- to 6-year-olds but may need fewer calories. Offer them smaller amounts.

- A good estimate of a serving for a 2- to 3-year-old child is about 2/3 of what counts as a regular adult Food Guide Pyramid serving. The adult servings are generally 1/2 cup fruit or vegetable, 3/4 cup of juice, 1 slice of bread, 2 to 3 ounces of cooked lean meat, poultry, or fish.
- Two- to 6-year-old children need a total of 2 servings from the milk group each day.
- Younger children often eat smaller portions. Offering smaller servings and allowing them to ask for more satisfies their hunger, does not waste food, and may curtail excessive intake.
- By the time children are 4 to 5 years old, they may eat amounts that count as regular Food Guide Pyramid servings eaten by teachers. However, smaller servings are indicated in the Child Nutrition Program guidelines that most child-care centers follow (see Chapter 7).
- Let the child take small "try me" portions, 1 or 2 tablespoons, and let children ask for more.

---

portion sizes received in restaurants, including child-sized portions, are larger than recommended. Help children choose child-sized servings that are recommended (Box 2.1).

Be Patient.   Young children may not be interested in trying new foods. Offer a new food more than once. The food may be accepted when it becomes more familiar to your child.

Be a Planner.   Most young children need a snack or two in addition to three regular daily meals.

- Check to ensure that the center is offering foods from three or more of the five major food groups for breakfast and lunch.
- Offer foods from four or more of the five major food groups for the "main meal."
- Plan the teaching schedules so snacks are not served too close to mealtime, and offer foods from two or more of the five major food groups.

Be a Good Role Model. What you do can mean more than what you say. Children learn from you about how and what to eat.
- Eat meals with the children.
- Try new foods and new ways of preparing them with your children and encourage the food service staff to prepare dark green leafy vegetables, deep-yellow vegetables, fruits, and whole-grain products.
- Walk, run, and play with children; don't just sit on the sidelines.

Be Adventurous. Coordinate with food service staff and young children to choose a new vegetable or fruit, from two or three choices, for a weekly "try-a-new-food-day." (See Chapter 7.)

Be Creative. Encourage your child to invent a new snack or sandwich from three or four healthful ingredients you provide. Try a new bread or whole-grain cracker. Talk about what food groups the new snack includes and why it tastes good. Is the snack smooth, crunchy, sweet, juicy, chewy, or colorful? (See Chapters 8 and 9 for snack ideas.)

Fat and Sugar Tips.
- Choose lower fat foods from the food groups.
- Go easy on fats and sugars added to foods in cooking or at the table—butter, margarine, gravy, salad dressing, sugar, and jelly.
- Choose fewer foods that are high in sugars—candy, sweet desserts, and soft drinks.

NUTRIENT STANDARDS

Food Labeling

Nutrition Facts, Nutrient Content Descriptor, Health Claims, and Ingredient Lists are part of the Food Labels in the United States. Nutrition information became mandatory with enactment of the Nutrition Labeling and Education Act (NLEA). According to NLEA, nutrition labels must appear on most products except for meat and poultry, restaurant foods, ready-to-eat foods prepared on site (e.g., supermarket deli items), and foods of low nutrient content (e.g., spices, coffee, and tea). Nutrient information on many raw foods, fruits and vegetables, fresh fish, meat, and poultry are still provided on a voluntary basis through a point-of-purchase program encouraged by the USDA and FDA.

Nutrition facts help consumers follow a healthful diet that meets the Dietary Guidelines by comparing nutrient content of similar products. Product nutrient

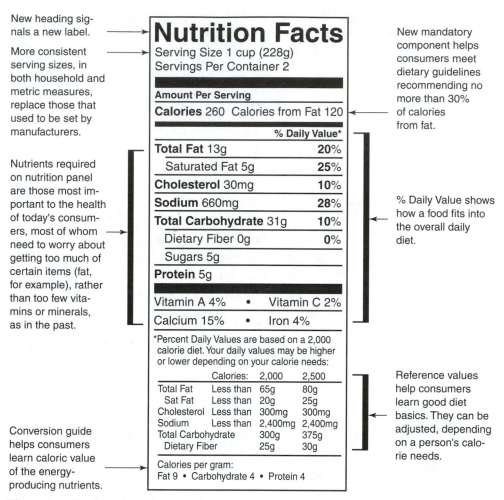

New heading signals a new label.

More consistent serving sizes, in both household and metric measures, replace those that used to be set by manufacturers.

Nutrients required on nutrition panel are those most important to the health of today's consumers, most of whom need to worry about getting too much of certain items (fat, for example), rather than too few vitamins or minerals, as in the past.

Conversion guide helps consumers learn caloric value of the energy-producing nutrients.

New mandatory component helps consumers meet dietary guidelines recommending no more than 30% of calories from fat.

% Daily Value shows how a food fits into the overall daily diet.

Reference values help consumers learn good diet basics. They can be adjusted, depending on a person's calorie needs.

Nutrition Facts
Serving Size 1 cup (228g)
Servings Per Container 2

Amount Per Serving

Calories 260   Calories from Fat 120

% Daily Value*

Total Fat 13g	20%
Saturated Fat 5g	25%
Cholesterol 30mg	10%
Sodium 660mg	28%
Total Carbohydrate 31g	10%
Dietary Fiber 0g	0%
Sugars 5g	
Protein 5g	

Vitamin A 4%	•	Vitamin C 2%
Calcium 15%	•	Iron 4%

*Percent Daily Values are based on a 2,000 calorie diet. Your daily values may be higher or lower depending on your calorie needs:

	Calories:	2,000	2,500
Total Fat	Less than	65g	80g
Sat Fat	Less than	20g	25g
Cholesterol	Less than	300mg	300mg
Sodium	Less than	2,400mg	2,400mg
Total Carbohydrate		300g	375g
Dietary Fiber		25g	30g

Calories per gram:
Fat 9 • Carbohydrate 4 • Protein 4

Figure 2.4   Explanation of a food label

information is provided for standardized serving sizes, which are set by the government according to commonly consumed amounts. In addition to calories, total fat, protein, sodium, and total carbohydrate, labels include information on calories from fat, saturated fat, cholesterol, sodium, dietary fiber, and sugars to emphasize the role of nutrients in preventing chronic diseases. Except for these nutrients that must be listed on the food label, manufacturers may disclose others (e.g. monounsaturated fat and potassium) for which a Daily Value (DV) has been established. Appendix II includes the Daily Values used for the labels. Daily Values are not required levels of nutrients but reference points derived from comparison of the products' nutrient content to recommended amounts of intake. Diets of 2000 and 2500 calories are used to calculate Percent Daily Values included on labels; consumers may refer to Percent DVs for insight on what is in their diet and what it needs to be. (See Figure 2.4.)

In some circumstance, variations in the format of the nutrition panel are allowed. Some are mandatory. For example, the labels of foods for children under 2 (except infant formula, which has special labeling rules under the Infant Formula Act of 1980) may not carry information about saturated fat, polyunsaturated fat, monounsaturated fat, cholesterol, calories from fat, or calories from saturated fat. The reason for this is to prevent parents from wrongly assuming that infants and toddlers should restrict their fat intake, when in fact they should not. Fat is important during these years for adequate growth and development.

Nutrient content descriptors and health claims follow rigid and consistent regulations set for all food products by the NLEA (Box 2.2). Food labels may include nutrient content descriptors (e.g., low fat) and health claims (e.g., good source of dietary fiber). Terms describing levels of nutrients in food or health claim statements can be used on food packages only when products meet specific government requirements for nutrient content. Nutrient content descriptive terms include *free, low, good source, high, lean,* and *extra lean.* Comparative terms such as *reduced, less, light,* and *more* are also used to describe differences between nutrient content of regular and nutritionally altered products. Health claims for diet–disease relationships include:

- calcium and reduced risk of osteoporosis;
- dietary fat and increased risk for cancer;
- dietary saturated fat and cholesterol and an increased risk of coronary heart disease;
- fiber-containing grain products and a reduced risk of cancer;
- fruits and vegetables and a reduced risk of cancer;
- fruits, vegetables, and grain products containing soluble fiber and a reduced risk for coronary heart disease;
- sodium and an increased risk of hypertension;
- folic acid during pregnancy and a reduced risk of neural tube defects;
- sugar alcohols and dental caries (eating of foods high in sugar and starches may promote tooth decay—sugarless candies made with certain sugar alcohols do not);
- dietary soluble fiber, such as that found in whole oats and psyllium seed husk, and coronary heart disease; and
- soy protein in a diet low in saturated fat and cholesterol may help to reduce the risk of coronary heart disease.

There are many examples of heath claims on labels of products such as cereal (Figure 2.5). Beware of health claims for supplements (Box 2.2) that do not require strict government approval.

Ingredients list indicates the contents of the product in the order of their prominence by weight and has to follow product standardization and food additive guidelines. Teachers must check all labels for ingredients if a child has been diagnosed with a specific food allergy. Depending on the agency that regulates a product, these guidelines may be set by the USDA or FDA. Product standardization dictates what standard ingredients must be in the product and what ingredients may be added

Figure 2.5   Health claims
Source: Health Claims. (1997). *FDA Consumer, 31*(3), 24.

Box 2.2   FDA regulation of health claims

Federal law allows for certain claims to be made in the labeling of food and supplements. These include claims approved by the Food and Drug Administration that show a strong link, based on scientific evidence, between a food substance and a disease or health condition. These approved claims can state only that a food substance *reduces the risk* of certain health problems—not that it can *treat* or *cure* a disease. Two examples of *approved* claims are: "The vitamin folic acid may reduce the risk of neural tube defect-affected pregnancies," and "Calcium may reduce the risk of the bone disease osteoporosis."

Dietary supplements also may carry claims in their labeling that describe the effect of a substance in maintaining the body's normal structure or function, as long as the claims don't imply the product treats or cures a disease. The FDA does not review or authorize these claims. An example of such a claim is, "Product B promotes healthy joints and bones." When a dietary supplement is promoted with a claim like this, the claim must be accompanied with the disclaimer, "This statement has not been evaluated by the Food and Drug Administration. This product is not intended to diagnose, treat, cure, or prevent disease."

To learn more about the kinds of labeling claims that can be made for foods and dietary supplements, see http://www.cfsan.fda.gov/~dms/hclaims.html.

(e.g., no product can be called peanut butter if it does not contain 90% peanuts). In regulated products, ingredients are listed in order of weight predominance. Terms "natural" and "no preservatives" have set specific meanings. For example, according to FDA regulations "natural" products have no artificial flavor, no coloring and/or synthetic ingredients, and no chemical preservatives. Similarly, products with "no preservatives" do not include antioxidants or antimicrobials. If additives account for less than 2% of total product weight, they may be grouped under a general title (e.g., flavorings). Ingredient and additive guidelines may not ensure that the product is free of a specific food allergen.

Dietary Reference Intakes (DRI)

The tools discussed in the preceding section—the Dietary Guidelines for Americans, the Food Guide Pyramid, and Food Labels—help you look primarily at food intake and provide a method to measure whether food choices promote health and prevent disease. DRI is a generic term that includes tools or standards used to evaluate nutrients in the diet, especially for groups such as child-care centers, group homes, or schools.

To ensure that the best possible diet has been planned for groups of individuals or for the menus served in preschool or child-care facilities, dietitians often rely not only on food guides but also on nutrient standards. They compare the nutrients calculated from foods on the menu with the appropriate nutrient standard. Although food guides answer the question: "Am I getting enough of the right foods?" the **Dietary Reference Intakes** (DRIs) best answer the question, "Are the diets or menus providing groups of children with the nutrients needed to meet their needs?" Nutrient analysis can further determine if the choices from the Food Guide Pyramid are meeting the nutrient needs. A pattern for a preschooler was presented in Table 2.1. The nutrients have been calculated for these foods (Figure 2.6). Note that at least 130 g of carbohydrate is included and the allowance for dietary fat for children is between the recommended 25% to 40% of the calories from fat [7].

You can use the computer analysis programs, listed in Appendix I, online to analyze the nutrient values of food intake. When all the foods are recorded for a day or several days, nutrients can be calculated and the nutrient amounts can be compared to a nutrient standard. As of this writing, there were several programs that provided the information to use; some programs are easier to use than others. Use the services of a registered dietitian to ensure the site is reputable, or consider the following:

Definitions of Nutrient Standards

EAR Estimated Average Requirement is the intake value that meets the estimated nutrient needs of 50% of individuals in a specific life-stage and gender group.

RDA Recommended Dietary Allowances is the nutrient intake that meets the nutrient needs of almost all (97–98%) individuals.

AI Adequate Intake is used to evaluate nutrient intake when there is insufficient scientific evidence to establish an EAR.

UL Tolerable Upper Intake Level is the maximum level of daily nutrient intake that is unlikely to pose health risks to almost all of the individuals in the group for whom it is designed.

Nutrient Analysis

Calories	1468				
% Kcal from protein	21%	Protein (g)	78	Dietary Fiber (g)	16
% Kcal from carbohydrate	54%	Carbohydrate (g)	198	Cholesterol (mg)	159
% Kcal from Fat	26%	Fat (g)	42		
		Sat. Fat (g)	14		

Figure 2.6   Energy and nutrients calculated from the daily meal pattern for a 5-year-old (based on Table 2.1)

- There is little or no advertising. Don't use a program that immediately offers advice on weight reduction methods or herbal use; the program probably wants to sell a diet product. There should be no reason to provide an e-mail address. If the program insists you enter your e-mail address, use one of the free services to establish an e-mail address. Beware of spam mail.
- The source of the nutrient information is the USDA or other governmental nutrient databases.
- Foods can be entered by meal. Even if final analysis is not by meal, entering by meal helps keep track of what has been entered.
- Includes a way to enter foods not in database. For example, the composition of a Tofutti® frozen nondairy product can be entered using the nutrition label.
- Provides, minimally, energy, protein, fat, carbohydrate, calcium, iron, and vitamins A, C, D, E values and calculates the percentage of total calories from protein, fat, and carbohydrate.
- Compares food to a standard. If the program compares intake to the Food Group Pyramid, check what is included. For example, some programs count potato chips as a vegetable and bacon as a meat instead of fat.
- May relate diet to physical activity patterns but should not promote exercise programs or equipment.

BENEFITS AND CAUTIONS OF PHYSICAL ACTIVITY

With the increase in incidence of obesity, teachers are becoming concerned about energy balance as it affects not only energy intake but also energy expenditure. Physical activity helps children and adults: expend energy and increase muscle and bone strength; increase lean muscle mass and decrease body fat; maintain weight; and enhance psychological well-being. Physical inactivity is considered a risk factor for developing coronary artery disease and increases the risk of stroke, obesity, high blood pressure, low HDL cholesterol levels, and diabetes. The American Heart Association [13] recommends a daily combination of moderate and vigorous physical activity for both children and adults. Persons of all ages should include physical activity in a comprehensive program of health promotion and disease prevention and should in-

Most children get all the exercise they need during play.

crease their habitual physical activity to a level appropriate to their capacities, needs, and interests. All children age 5 and older should participate in at least 30 minutes of enjoyable, moderate-intensity activities every day, and a minimum of 30 minutes of vigorous physical activity at least 3 to 4 days each week, to achieve cardiovascular fitness [14]. Adults and children should therefore allow a total of 60 minutes per day for physical activity whether at school or home.

Physical activity A wide variety of movements, including activities that involve the large skeletal muscles that promote health and well-being.

Positive energy balance (greater energy or caloric intake compared with calories expended or used) produces weight gain in excess of needs. Needs of the body include primarily growth, development, repair of tissue, and physical activity. The teacher can be instrumental in increasing exercise by increasing the physical activities in the child-care center and therefore increasing the young child's energy expen-

Exercise Planned or structured activities that maintain or improve physical fitness.

diture. As the problem of obesity is more widely recognized, parents may pressure teachers to modify a child's dietary intake and physical activity patterns.

Caution regarding preschool exercise programs comes from both the early childhood and the health care professions. Exercise programs at too early an age put infants and young children in inappropriate learning situations as well as expose them to the risk of physical and/or psychological damage. Most children can get all the exercise they need by doing what they do naturally as they use their senses and movements to explore their world [15].

The American Academy of Pediatrics [16], after a 2-year study of preschool programs, concluded that infant exercise programs do nothing to improve a baby's physical fitness. The Academy advises general play until age 6. Exercise programs geared to children under age 3 do not enhance the development of the healthy child. Structured exercise programs do not belong in the early childhood curriculum. Teachers should provide a physical environment that provides freedom of movement and exploration. Specific recommendations for physical fitness activity for each age group are provided in other chapters.

The teacher can effectively promote physical activity in young children by:

- recognizing developmentally appropriate motor skills (see Chapters 3–6)
- providing opportunities for physical activity
- encouraging children to participate in activity
- being a positive role model
- supervising children to ensure safety

The Activity Pyramid (Figure 2.7), like the Food Guide Pyramid, can be used as a tool to motivate children and teachers to engage in physical activity. A printable copy of the Activity Pyramid is available at http://muextension.missouri.edu/xplor/hesguide/foodnut/gh1800.htm and could be posted in the classroom. There are recommendations for physical activity [17] for the toddler and preschooler and these are presented in Chapters 3–6.

FREQUENTLY ENCOUNTERED FOOD- AND NUTRITION-RELATED PROBLEMS

Making wise food and physical activity choices is always important when caring for healthy young children. The diagnoses of certain nutrition-related diseases or conditions may require you to modify some food and/or physical activity practices. Some of the disorders include obesity and overweight, diabetes, iron deficiency anemia, lead poisoning, immune compromised conditions, asthma, and food allergies.

Some of the nutrition issues related to the most frequently addressed diseases and disabilities seen in the pediatric population are presented with a brief description and the teacher's role in addressing the issues. Other nutrition-related problems and dietary implications are also addressed in each age-specific chapter. Pediatricians, local health departments, or registered dietitians can help in assessing and managing the food and nutrition needs of children (http://www.eatright.org).

Obesity

Definition.   **Obesity** is defined as the presence of excess adipose (fatty) tissue. The term "overweight" is a milder degree of excess fat. In the past, centers have used height and weight measurements to determine if a child was overweight. Today height and weight measurements are used to calculate body mass index

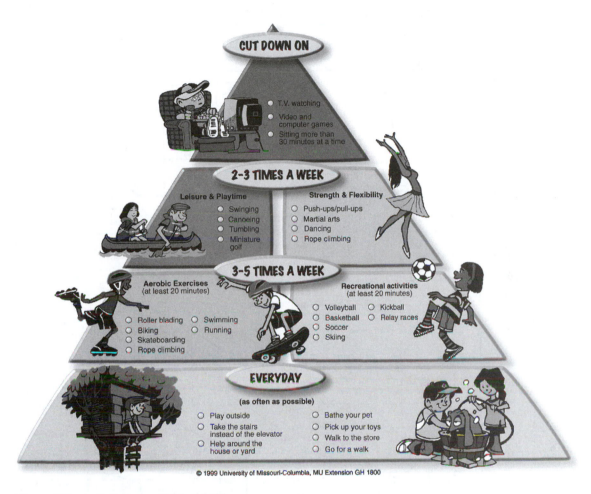

Figure 2.7 Activity pyramid for children
Source: "Children's Activity Pyramid," MU Extension publication GH1800, University of Missouri, Columbia, MO. Used with permission.

(BMI). Center staff will need to learn to calculate BMI by using the formula (see Box 2.3, p. 64) or use online Web calculators for children (http://www.keepkidshealthy.com/welcome/bmicalculator.html). In either case, calculate BMI by determining height and weight of the child. Complete the calculations with the formula or online. Once the number for the BMI is found, compare the number to the chart for the girls or boys (Figures 2.8a and b).

BMI is commonly used to classify children who are overweight or at risk of becoming overweight. **Overweight** is usually defined as the child with a body mass index that is above the 95th percentile for age. A body mass index that is above the 85th percentile for age puts the child at risk of becoming overweight.

Prevalence
The number of individuals with a specific condition divided by the total number of individuals within that population. For example, the number of obese individuals divided by total number of individuals (obese and nonobese) within that population.

2 to 20 years: Girls
Body mass index-for-age percentiles

NAME _____

RECORD # _____

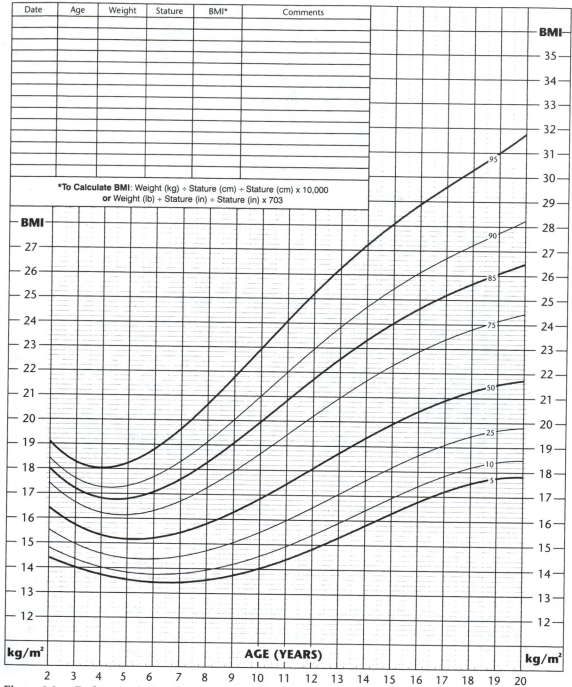

To Calculate BMI: Weight (kg) ÷ Stature (cm) ÷ Stature (cm) x 10,000
or Weight (lb) ÷ Stature (in) ÷ Stature (in) x 703

Date	Age	Weight	Stature	BMI*	Comments

Figure 2.8a   Body mass index-for-age percentiles, girls

Source: Developed by the National Center for Health Statistics in collaboration with the National Center for Chronic Disease Prevention and Health Promotion. (2000). Available at http://www.cdc.gov/growthcharts.

2 to 20 years: Boys
Body mass index-for-age percentiles

NAME _____

RECORD # _____

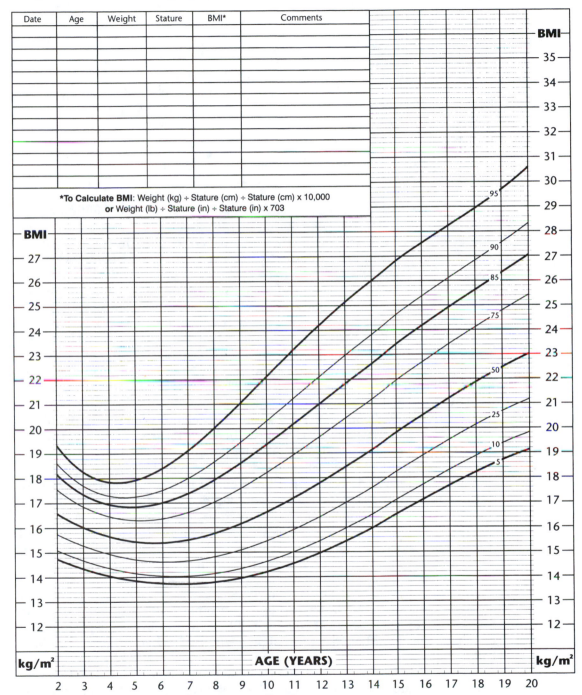

Date	Age	Weight	Stature	BMI*	Comments

*To Calculate BMI: Weight (kg) ÷ Stature (cm) ÷ Stature (cm) x 10,000
or Weight (lb) ÷ Stature (in) ÷ Stature (in) x 703

Figure 2.8b   Body mass index-for-age percentiles, boys
Source: Developed by the National Center for Health Statistics in collaboration with the National Center for Chronic Disease Prevention and Health Promotion. (2000). Available at http://www.cdc.gov/growthcharts.

Box 2.3   Calculating BMI for a child

Calculating BMI

 BMI = [Weight in pounds ÷ Height in inches ÷ Height in inches] × 703

Fractions and ounces must be entered as decimal values.

Example: A 33-lb 4-oz child is 37 5/8 in. tall

BMI = 33.25 pounds ÷ 37.625 inches ÷ 37.625 inches × 703 = **16.5**

Each of the BMI-for-age charts contains a series of curved lines indicating specific percentiles. BMI decreases during the preschool years, then increases into adulthood. The percentile curves show this pattern of growth. For example, the BMI for a boy may increase from 18 to 21 between the ages of 4 and 9 years, yet both values place the BMI at the 95th percentile BMI-for-age.

The data for the BMI for overweight children aged 2 to 17 were adapted from the guidelines by the National Center for Chronic Disease Prevention and Health Promotion (CDC) at http://www.cdc.gov/nccdphp/dnpa/bmi/bmi-for-age.htm.

An obesity epidemic within the U.S. population is vividly portrayed by the fact that in 1991, only 4 of 45 states that reported data had obesity rates of 15% to 19% and none had rates greater than 20%. By the year 2000, all of the 50 states except Colorado had rates of 15% or greater, with 22 of the 50 states having obesity rates as high or higher than 20% [18].

The percentage of young people who are overweight has more than doubled in the last 30 years. An estimated 13% of children 6 to 11 years, and 14% of adolescents 12 to 19 years, are overweight. This represents a 6% to 9% increase from the overweight estimates in the 1980s [19]. Because obese children are likely to become obese adults, increased obesity prevention efforts targeting children in the early years is important. Obesity is not a benign condition for children, or one that they are likely to outgrow. Approximately 60% of overweight 5- to 10-year-old children already have one associated biochemical or clinical cardiovascular risk factor, such as hyperlipidemia (increased fat levels), elevated blood pressure, or increased insulin levels, while 25% have two or more risk factors [20].

Dietary Intervention.   Obese children younger than 2 years should be referred to a pediatric obesity program for appropriate treatment [21]. Individuals who are trained in obesity management for young children may be in a better position than child-care teachers to help parents. Children who are 2 to 7 years old with a BMI of 85th–94th percentiles should be encouraged to maintain weight and if there are complications related to obesity, refer the child to a health care provider for evaluation. Intervention should be related to the cause of obesity. Most researchers agree that poor dietary habits, increased consumption of calorie-dense foods, and fewer opportunities for physical activity contribute to the problem of obesity. There is also the genetic predisposition to obesity, that is, if one or more parents are obese, the child is more likely to be obese.

Whatever the cause, the treatment is centered on achieving healthy eating and physical activity behaviors rather than obtaining ideal body weight. Healthy lifestyles can be addressed in the child-care centers. The time spent watching television, learning on the computer, and playing video games can be tempered with physical activity and lower-calorie snacks.

When an overweight child comes to the center, the first step is to determine if, upon initial interview, parents recognize or express concern for the child's overweight condition. Parents' knowledge and concern for the child's overweight status will determine what action the teacher should take. Parents should indicate if a registered dietitian or other health care professional is following the child. Assuming that there is a health professional involved, the second step is to study the plan of action agreed upon by parents and health professional to see if certain actions can be taken at the center level. If no health professional is involved, suggest that the child be referred to a pediatric obesity program through a child health clinic or the Special Supplemental Nutrition Program for Women, Infants, and Children (WIC) discussed in Chapter 7. The third step is to put the action plan into practice with specific behavior-change goals and objectives to achieve at home as well as at the center. Parents and teachers should agree on and establish desired outcomes according to the plan and identify points of progress. The teachers should inform the parents and health professional on the progress and continually update the child's plans. See Chapter 5 for a more detailed review of obesity and intervention strategies.

Issues to consider when caring for children who are overweight are their tendency to eat more and move less than their counterparts. The teacher can observe the amount of food eaten and physical activity level and assess what can be modified to either decrease over-intake and/or increase physical activity. In general, it is best to increase physical activity, rather than restricting intake. Even at a very young age, children often feel uncomfortable about participating in physical activities. If applicable, encourage increased participation in more physical activities that will continue into the adult years. Keep in mind that children should participate in physical activity at least one hour each day, and it is important that the teacher also participate in the physical activities.

Diabetes

Definition.   High levels of blood glucose resulting from defects in insulin secretion by the pancreas, insulin action, or both characterize **diabetes.** Cells in the human pancreas produce insulin, a hormone that allows the body to convert blood sugar to energy. The type 1, or insulin dependent, diabetes occurs when insulin-producing cells are not present or not functioning. Type 1 may be described as **juvenile,** or **juvenile-onset diabetes.** While type 1 is usually diagnosed before the age of 30, it can occur at any age. Children with type 1 diabetes must replace insulin on a regular basis with insulin injections in order to sustain their life. Insulin helps the body convert the food eaten to energy. What and when a child eats becomes important since the food and the insulin supply must be coordinated.

Type 2, also called adult-onset diabetes, occurs when the body still produces some insulin, but either produces insufficient amounts or the insulin that is produced is not utilized effectively. Type 2 or non-insulin dependent diabetes is the most common form of diabetes, affecting 90% of those with the disease. Today, more children are being diagnosed with type 2 diabetes. Oral medications, rather than injections, are used to reduce insulin resistance and consequently make the body's own insulin more effective.

Prevalence.   The Centers for Disease Control and Prevention (CDC) estimate that 17 million Americans suffer from the disease, with 11.1 million people diagnosed and 5.9 million people undiagnosed [22]. American Indian/Alaska Natives, and Non-Hispanic blacks are more likely to develop the condition than other ethnic groups. The percentage of adults with diabetes is greatest among those aged 65 to 74 years (21.6%). Compared with adults, there are fewer cases of childhood diabetes but the prevalence is rising. Approximately one in every 400 to 500 children and adolescents has type 1 diabetes, and data indicate that type 2 diabetes is becoming more common among American Indian, African American, and Hispanic/Latino children.

Obesity is an established risk factor for non-insulin-dependent diabetes, the most common type of diabetes. In fact, a dramatic increase in diabetes has been seen with increased relative weight. Prevalence of diabetes is about three times higher in people whose weight is 40% above the desirable weight for their sex and height than in those at or below desirable weight. In addition, the longer one is obese the greater the chance of developing diabetes. Therefore, childhood obesity that persists into adulthood may predispose the child to later onset of diabetes [23]. Although we are seeing more cases of diabetes in the preschool centers, the peak incidence of type 1 in youth occurs between 10 to 12 years in girls, and 12 to 14 in boys; however, cases in children as young as 4 years of age have been documented.

The epidemic of obesity and the low level of physical activity among young people, as well as exposure to diabetes in utero, may be major contributors to the increase of type 2 diabetes during childhood and adolescence. Current statistics have indicated that children and adolescents diagnosed with type 2 diabetes were generally between 10 and 19 years old, obese, insulin-resistant, and had a strong family history for type 2 diabetes.

Intervention.   The best dietary advice for a child with diabetes is a balanced diet, choosing foods from the Food Guide Pyramid that are low in fat and sugar, moderate in amounts of protein, and high in complex carbohydrates (beans, vegetables, and grains). In general, children with diabetes should eat about the same number of calories each day, eat meals and snacks around the same time each day, and never skip meals. The meal pattern will depend on the type of insulin given as well as individual requirements. Parents can help the teacher recognize symptoms of low blood sugar.

According to the American Diabetes Association [24] a diabetes care plan must exist to address the specific needs of the child and provide specific instructions. The health professional in conjunction with parents and the center director develop this plan so that all factors at home and center are considered (Box 2.4).

Box 2.4   Center requirements for care of a child with diabetes

---

1. Immediate availability to treatment of hypoglycemia without the necessity for the child to be without direct supervision by a knowledgeable adult and without the necessity for the child to travel long distances to obtain such treatment
2. An adult and back-up adult trained to be able to: perform finger-sticks and record results; take appropriate actions to bring glucose levels within desirable target ranges; test urine for ketones, and respond to results accordingly
3. An adult and back-up adult trained to administer glucagon
4. A location in the school to provide privacy during testing and insulin administration
5. An adult and back-up adult who will know the child's schedule for meals and snacks and who will also work with the parents to adjust feedings according to school schedule of events and physical activity routines
6. Training to all adults providing education/care for the child on the symptoms and treatment of hypo/hyperglycemia, and other emergency procedures
7. Permission for the child to see school medical personnel upon request
8. Permission for the child to snack anywhere, including the classroom or the school bus, if necessary; permission to use the rest room and access to fluids, as often as necessary
9. Permission of excused absence for monitoring of diabetes management
10. Appropriate location for insulin and glucagon storage

The preschool child is usually unable to perform diabetes tasks independently. By 4 years of age, children may be expected to generally cooperate in diabetes tasks. Preschool age children with diabetes often need frequent blood glucose tests because they have not yet learned to recognize symptoms of hypoglycemia, or can't tell others when they are feeling "low." Note that young children with diabetes can go through the same fussy eating phases as other children. As much as possible keep the food service procedures the same for all children, and foods low in fat and sugar should be served to all children.

Elementary school children should be expected to cooperate in all diabetes tasks at school. By age 8 years, most children are able to perform their own finger-stick blood glucose tests with supervision. Take cues from the child and parent on how to handle the child with diabetes. Also, help the child to fit diabetes care into the school schedule rather than adjusting the schedule to accommodate diabetes care.

Iron Deficiency Anemia

Definition and Prevalence.   Anemia (iron deficiency) is one of the most common nutritional deficiencies in the world [25]. Iron deficiency in children is associated with developmental delays and behavioral disturbances. Iron deficiency anemia is characterized by low hemoglobin (Hb) concentration or a low hematocrit (Hct) level. Lower

Anemia
The Centers for Disease Control and Prevention defines anemia as Hb < 11.0 g/dL for children 1 to less than 2 years; Hb < 11.1 g/dL for children 2 to less than 5 years; and Hct < 33% for children 1 to less than 5 years.

Source: Center for Disease Prevention. (1998). *Pediatric Nutrition Surveillance, 1997 Full Report.* Atlanta, GA: U.S. Department of Health and Human Services, Center for Disease Control and Prevention.

than normal Hb values indicate a diminished production of hemoglobin resulting from insufficient iron, usually due to inadequate oral intake.

Prevalence data indicate that 18% of children have anemia. Rates have been higher in black (24.6%), American Indian/Alaskan Native (18.6%), and Hispanic children (18.4%); they are lower in Asian/Pacific Islander (15.1%) and white children (15.2%). Overall prevalence of anemia in children less than 2 years has declined by 1% since 1989. However, a 3.6% increase has been observed in black children [26].

Dietary intervention.   Breastfeeding provides infants with iron that is well absorbed. The breastfeeding mother provides iron in a readily available form to the infant. Children who are breastfed do not need other iron supplementation up to 4 months of age [27]. Non-iron-fortified milk (e.g., cow's milk, goat's milk, and soymilk) should not be given to children less than 12 months of age. Iron-fortified formulas must be used in non-breastfed infants; low-birth-weight infants will require increased supplementation starting at 1 month of age and continuing until 12 months after birth [27].

Three tablespoons of iron-fortified cereal can be mixed with formula, breast milk, or water to provide the recommended amount of iron after 4 months and up to 4 years of age. Iron rich foods—meats, fish, poultry, raisins, dried fruits, sweet potatoes, lima beans, kidney beans, chili beans, pinto beans, green peas, peanut butter, enriched cereals and breads—should be included in children's diets. However, iron from these foods (non-heme) is not absorbed as well as iron found in animal foods (heme).

Conditions such as chronic infection/inflammation, bleeding disorders, and drug therapy may increase iron requirements. In such cases, supplements from ferrous sulfate, ferrous gluconate, and ferrous ascorbate are used to supplement the diet. Vitamin C taken with high iron foods or supplements increases bioavailability.

Lead Poisoning

Definition and prevalence.   **Lead poisoning** can damage a young child's developing brain, causing learning and behavioral disabilities. CDC has established 10 mcg/d or higher of blood-lead levels as exceeding acceptable standards [28]. Lead poisoning is associated with poor school performance and there is persuasive evidence of lead's damage to intellectual functioning at even lower blood-lead levels [29].

Almost one million American children under the age of 6 (approximately 4% of children in that age group) have dangerously high levels of lead in their blood, making lead poisoning one of the most widespread childhood diseases. This problem is most severe among families that live in older housing units: Sixteen percent of low-income children and 21% of African American children who live in older housing have elevated lead levels [30]. In 1978, 14.8 million American children suffered from lead poisoning in the United States. Since then, children's blood-lead levels have declined more than 80% due to the elimination of lead from house paint, gasoline, and food and beverage cans [31]. Lead has been significantly reduced in industrial emissions, drinking water, consumer goods, hazardous waste sites, and other sources. However, 27% of the nation's housing units (25.5 million units) still contain lead paint hazards. The most common cause of lead exposure for young children is lead paint in older housing.

Intervention. There are several ways to reduce a child's exposure to lead poisoning. Know the sources of lead: peeling or chipping paint in homes or centers built before 1978, dust from sanding or removing old paint and wallpaper, food stored in glazed pottery and ceramic ware or stored in open cans. Have children wash their hands and face after play outside and before eating. Clean all pacifiers each time they fall on the floor. Wash children's toys often. Wash fruits and vegetables before cooking or eating. Wash all countertops before preparing food. Children age 6 months to 6 years in high-risk areas should be assessed each year for possible lead contamination.

Health officials agree that the primary dietary recommendations include [32]:

- Providing foods that contain good sources of protein, iron, calcium, and vitamins A and C daily;
- Providing meals on regular schedules, including snacks to help children maintain a full stomach;
- Limit high-fat and greasy foods in a daily diet (for children over 2 years of age);
- Do not store food in open cans, pottery, pewter, or lead crystal.

Human Immunodeficiency Virus (HIV)

Definition and Prevalence. **Human immunodeficiency virus (HIV)** is an infection that attacks and wears down the immune system resulting in increased sensitivity to infection. HIV is transmitted primarily by exposure to contaminated body fluids; however, most children are infected through perinatal transmission. **Acquired immunodeficiency syndrome (AIDS)** is used to describe someone who is HIV positive and no longer has enough cells that protect the body from infection. HIV positive individuals may have one or more opportunistic infections (infections that the human body normally fights off easily). Initially the child can be without symptoms, followed by an onset of serious opportunistic infections. Due to having a compromised immune system, there is a rapid progression from multiple disease infections to death. Due to increased availability of antiretroviral drug therapies, infected children may remain asymptomatic and immunologically intact for many years.

According to the CDC, 12,969 cases of AIDS in infants, children, and adolescents have been reported since 1982. Most children become HIV infected through perinatal transmission from an infected mother. According to CDC data in 1999, HIV is the fourth leading cause of death in women ages 35 to 44 years, and the tenth leading cause of death in children ages 5 to 9 years in the United States [33].

Dietary intervention.   Of the clinical problems related to the management of HIV infection in children, malnutrition and growth failure are among the most challenging. The consequences of malnutrition in children are potentially more devastating than those for adults. Children should be monitored for dehydration, energy, and protein intake. Most HIV-related hospital admissions are due to dehydration. Risk factors for malnutrition in children infected with HIV include low weight and height for age, low protein stores, and low energy intake; these children may have delayed growth. Working with the health professionals, teachers can identify the barriers to adequate nutrition so that strategies are implemented to help child and family overcome the obstacles [34–36].

Providing food that is safe is especially important when the child has a compromised immune system. Some foods such as cold cuts (lunchmeat products), soft cheeses, and hot dogs, as well as sprouts, should be excluded from the infected child's diet, unless these foods are cooked thoroughly. All food should be prepared and served under safe conditions, keeping hot food hot and cold food cold (see Chapter 7).

Prior to antiretroviral therapy, many children with HIV suffered from significant developmental setbacks and were unable to function normally in the classroom. The American Academy of Pediatrics (AAP) [37] recommends that schools communicate with health professionals to monitor children with HIV, and provide them with the drug therapies they need, as well as access to special education and other related services if their disease progresses.

Asthma

Definition and prevalence.   **Asthma** is a chronic inflammatory disease of the airways that results from interactions among inflammatory cells, mediators, and other airway cells and tissues. Common symptoms include episodic or chronic wheeze, cough, and breathlessness. In the United States, asthma affects approximately 15 million persons; an estimated 4.8 million cases are children [38]. Fifty to 80% of children with asthma develop symptoms before the age of 5, while the most common cause of asthmatic symptoms in this age group is viral respiratory infection [39].

Asthma is frequently underdiagnosed in children younger than 5 years who may then not receive adequate therapy. On the other hand, wheeze and cough are also symptoms of other medical conditions, thus caution is needed to prevent unnecessary prolonging of antiinflammatory therapy with corticosteroids. Long-term administration of the latter can affect nutritional status and growth. Therefore, decisions to initiate such therapy must derive from carefully weighing possible long-term effects of inadequately controlled asthma versus possible adverse effects of therapy given over prolonged periods. Preliminary studies suggest that when childhood asthma is well controlled, risk for more serious asthma or irreversible obstruction in later years decreases [40].

Dietary Intervention.   Food-triggered asthma is very rare among asthmatic individuals. There is evidence that common food allergens (milk, eggs, peanuts, tree nuts, soy, wheat, fish, and shellfish) and food additives such as sulfites and sulfiting agents may trigger asthma in a small number of people. Suspected to trigger asthma, although scientific evaluations have not been conclusive, are also the following: tatrazine, a food coloring; preservatives such as benzoates, BHA, BHT, nitrates, and nitrites; monosodium glutamate (MSG). Avoiding or eliminating foods and additives thought to be allergenic is the best way to prevent food-induced asthma in asthmatic children. Meals should include foods high in calcium, potassium, zinc, vitamin D, and nonallergenic protein sources to counteract side effects of anti-inflammatory therapy on nutritional status. Use of supplements of these nutrients may be considered for the child.

Food Allergies

Definition, Prevalence and Diagnosis.   Allergies are defined as a condition where protein content of foods (antigen) triggers an immune system reaction in persons allergic to these foods. Presence of immunological characteristics (i.e., immunoglobulin E, antibody production, and release of cellular chemicals that cause allergy symptoms) help distinguish food allergies from other types of food sensitivities. Food sensitivities are intolerances (e.g., lactose intolerance), metabolic disorders (e.g., Phenylketonuria), and idiosyncratic reactions like those to food additives and preservatives (e.g., sulfite-induced asthma). To illustrate the difference, a lactose intolerant person may experience non-life-threatening symptoms such as bloating and diarrhea when milk is ingested. However, a drop of milk can be fatal for somebody with a true food allergy to milk.

Allergies are the sixth leading cause of chronic disease in the United States, costing the health care system $18 billion annually [41]. Virtually any food can cause an allergic reaction. Over 160 foods that can cause allergic reactions have been identified but the following 8 are the most common: peanuts, tree nuts, milk, eggs, soy, fish, shellfish, and wheat. Peanut, tree nut, fish, and shellfish allergies are rarely outgrown. Peanut or tree nut allergies affect approximately 3 million Americans and cause the most severe food-induced allergic reaction [42]. It is impossible to assure a parent that the child-care center will be free of peanuts or peanut residue.

Upon exposure to an offending food, onset and severity of symptoms varies from person to person. Clinical symptoms may occur alone or in combination and include sneezing, runny nose, shortness of breath, skin rashes, hives, eczema, diarrhea, and vomiting. In the worst case scenario individuals may experience anaphylaxis, a life-threatening reaction that begins within minutes; emergency treatment with epinephrine is usually administered to prevent death.

True food allergies affect less than 2% of the population and are most prevalent in infants and young children (4–8%). However, prospective studies have demonstrated that approximately 85% of confirmed symptoms are absent by 3 years of age. The ability to develop a food allergy is inherited and risk increases in presence of family history and/or other types of allergies (e.g., asthma).

Misunderstanding of food allergy can result in unnecessary food restrictions or can become life threatening. Therefore, a thorough evaluation by a board-certified allergist should be recommended to distinguish food allergy from other medical disorders. Diagnostic steps include: thorough medical history to identify the suspected food; amount eaten to cause a reaction; amount of time between food consumption and development of symptoms; frequency of reaction; and other detailed information from a complete physical examination and laboratory tests.

Dietary Intervention. In contrast to environmental allergies (e.g., allergy to pollen), no drug therapy is available to treat or alter the long-term course of a food allergy. Elimination of the offending food (allergen) is so far the only proven therapy. Food and Drug Administration guidelines on food biotechnology and food allergy are set for manufacturers to ensure that foods posing a potential risk to allergic individuals are properly labeled.

Diets where single foods are systematically eliminated (i.e., elimination diets) should be developed according to the child's ability to tolerate the offending food(s) and the need to avoid nutritional deficiencies; ease of following the diet regimen needs to be considered. Teachers of children with a food allergy need to know the forms of food to be avoided, identify listed and "hidden" allergens on food labels, and be able to select alternative food sources for nutrients. Breastfeeding may reduce the risk of food allergies and is recommended for infants from families with history of allergies. Infants who are breastfed are less likely to be exposed to foreign proteins that cause food allergies. Antibodies and other components of human milk [43] also protect them. See Chapters 3 and 4 for further discussion of allergies.

SUMMARY

- Basic principles of a healthy diet include the concepts of variety, moderation, and balance.
- Follow the Dietary Guidelines for Americans to obtain the foods and nutrients needed every day.
- Use the Food Guide Pyramid to select a wide variety of foods, consuming more servings from the base of the Pyramid and fewer servings from the top of the Pyramid.
- Teachers can emphasize variety in meals by insisting on including an abundance of vegetables, fruits, and whole grains. No single food supplies all nutrients, and a healthy diet needs to include a variety of foods from the five major food groups.
- Along with variety, the diet should incorporate appropriate portion sizes of foods from the Pyramid.
- Weight can be maintained or improved through moderate food intake, such as limiting fat and sugar as well as controlling the portion sizes.
- Labeling is a valuable tool for indicating serving sizes and making food choices that meet the Food Guide Pyramid.
- Balance the foods provided for the child with physical activity to maintain a healthy weight [44]. Physical activity along with age and sex of the child determine the amount of food needed. Use the Activity Pyramid.
- Structured exercise programs must be done in the context of play and routine activities.

- Modified diets due to special conditions, for example, obesity, diabetes, iron deficiency anemia, lead poisoning, immune-related diseases, asthma, and allergies can include variety, moderation, and balance.

DISCUSSION QUESTIONS

1. List the Dietary Guidelines for Americans 2000, and apply the guidelines to you and a child in your care.
2. What is the purpose of the Food Guide Pyramid and how might the child-care center use the Pyramid?
3. What does physical activity have to do with food intake?
4. Discuss structured exercise and physical activity programs for children under age 6. What differences exist and why?
5. Pick three labels from similar products and identify the nutrients in each. Which product is nutritionally superior?
6. Describe a label you have seen that makes or relates to a health claim.
7. Because obesity will be seen in most child-care centers in the United States, identify tools you might use in diagnosing the problem.
8. Calculate the BMI for a 3-year-old and 5-year-old in your center. Is the child overweight?
9. Why should you be familiar with the nutrition-related diseases seen in children?

REFERENCES

1. Munoz, K.A., Krebs-Smith, S., Ballard-Barbash, R., & Cleveland, L.E. (1997). Food intakes of U.S. children and adolescents compared with recommendations. *Pediatrics, 100,* 323–329. Errata: *Pediatrics, 101*(5), 952–953.
2. Gleason, P., & Suitor, C. (January 2001). *Changes in children's diets: 1989–91 to 1994–96.* U.S. Department of Agriculture, Food, and Nutrition Service. Report No. CN-01-CD2. Retrieved September 13, 2002, from http://www.fns.usda.gov/oane/MENU/Published/CNP/FILES/Changes.pdf
3. U.S. Department of Agriculture, Agricultural Research Service. *Food and nutrient intakes by children 1994–1996, 1998.* Retrieved December 15, 1998, from http://www.barc.usda.gov/bhnrc/foodsurvey/home.htm
4. U.S. Department of Health and Human Services. *Healthy people 2010: Understanding and improving health.* Conference Edition. Retrieved February 15, 2000, from http://www.health.gov/healthypeople/
5. U.S. Department of Health and Human Services, National Center for Health Statistics. (1994). *The third national health and nutrition examination survey 1988–1994.* Hyattsville, MD: Author.
6. Johnson, R.K., Panely, C.V., & Wang, M.Q. (2000). Associations between the milk mothers drink and the milk consumed by their school-aged children. *Family Economic and Nutrition Review, 13,* 27–36.
7. Food and Nutrition Board, Institutes of Medicine. (2002). *Dietary Reference Intakes for energy, carbohydrates, fiber, fat, protein, and amino acids (macronutrients).*

Washington, DC: National Academy Press.

8. Harnack, L., Stang, J., & Story, M. (1999). Soft drink consumption among U.S. children and adolescents: Nutritional consequences. *Journal of the American Dietetic Association 99*, 436–441.

9. Food and Nutrition Board, Institutes of Medicine. (2002). *Dietary Reference Intakes for vitamin C, vitamin E, selenium and carotenoids.* Washington, DC: National Academy Press.

10. Food and Nutrition Board, Institutes of Medicine. (1998). *Dietary Reference Intakes for thiamin, riboflavin, niacin, vitamin B_6, folate, vitamin B_{12}, panothenic acid, biotin, and choline.* Washington, DC: National Academy Press.

11. Food and Nutrition Board, Institutes of Medicine. (1997). *Dietary Reference Intakes for calcium, phosphorus, magnesium, vitamin D, and flouride.* Washington, DC: National Academy Press.

12. Food and Nutrition Board, Institutes of Medicine. (2001). *Dietary Reference Intakes for vitamin A, vitamin K, arsenic, boron, chromium, copper, iodine, iron, manganese, molybdeum, nickel, silicon, vanadium, and zinc.* Washington, DC: National Academy Press.

13. American Heart Association. (1996). Fletcher et al. Statement on exercise: Benefits and recommendations for physical activity programs for all Americans. *Circulation, 94*, 857–862.

14. American Heart Association. (n.d.). Scientific Position. *Exercise (physical activity) and children.* Retrieved May 3, 2002, from http://www.americanheart.org/presenter.jhtml?identifier=4596

15. Elkind, D. (1987). *Miseducation: Preschoolers at risk* (p. 13). New York: Knopf.

16. American Academy of Pediatrics, Committee on Sports Medicine and Fitness. (2000). Physical fitness and the schools. *Pediatrics, 105*, 1156–1157.

17. Food and Nutrition Board, Institutes of Medicine. (1998). *Dietary Reference Intakes for energy, carbohydrate, fiber, fat, fatty acids, cholesterol, protein, and amino acids (macronutrients).* Washington, DC: National Academy Press.

18. National Center for Chronic Disease Prevention and Health Promotion. (n.d.) *Obesity trends: Prevalence of obesity among U.S. adults, region and state.* Center for Disease Control and Prevention. Retrieved October 7, 2002, from http://www.cdc.gov/nccdphp/dnpa/obesity/trend/prev_reg.htm

19. National Center for Health Statistics. (1999). *Prevalence of overweight among children and adolescents.* Center for Disease Control and Prevention. Retrieved October 24, 2001, from http://www.cdc.gov/nchs/products/pubs/pubd/hestats/over99fig1.htm

20. Freedman, D.S., Dietz, W.H., Srinivasan, S.R., & Berenson, G.S. (1999). The relation of overweight to cardiovascular risk factors among children and adolescents: The Bogalusa Heart Study. *Pediatrics, 103*, 1175–1182.

21. Barlow, S.E., & Dietz, W.H. (1998) Obesity evaluation and treatment: Expert committee recommendations. *Pediatrics, 102(3)*, e29. Retrieved October 8, 2002, from http://www.pediatrics.org/cgi/content/full/102/3/e29

22. Centers for Disease Control and Prevention. (2000). *National diabetes fact sheet: General information and national estimates on diabetes in the United States, 2000.* Atlanta, GA: U.S. Department of Health and Human Services. Retrieved October 8, 2002, from http://www.cdc.gov/diabetes/pubs/factsheet.htm#citation

23. American Diabetes Association. (1996). *Diabetes 1996 Vital Statistics* (p. 25). Alexandria, VA: American Diabetes Association.

24. American Diabetes Association. (2002). Care of children with diabetes in the school and day care setting. *Diabetes Care, 25 (Supplement 1)*, s122–s126.

25. DeMaeyer, E.M. (1989). *Preventing and controlling iron deficiency anemia through primary health care: A guide for health administrators and program managers.* Geneva, Switzerland: World Health Organization.

26. Center for Disease Control and Prevention. (1998). *Pediatric nutrition surveillance, 1997 full report.* Atlanta, GA: Department of Health and Human Services.

27. Centers for Disease Control and Prevention. (1998). Recommendations to prevent and control iron deficiency in the United States. *Morbidity and Mortality Weekly Review, 47,* RR-3.

28. Centers for Disease Control and Prevention. (1991). *Preventing lead poisoning in young children: A statement by the Centers for Disease Control, October 1991.* Atlanta, GA: U.S. Department of Health and Human Services.

29. Schwartz, J. (1994). Low-level lead exposure and children's IQ: A meta-analysis and search for threshold. *Environmental Research, 65,* 42–55.

30. Centers for Disease Control and Prevention. (1997). Update: blood lead levels—United States, 1991–1994. *Morbidity and Mortality Weekly Review, 46(26),* 607.

31. American Academy of Pediatrics. (1998). Screening for elevated blood lead levels. *Pediatrics, 101(6),* 1072–1078.

32. Endres, J. Montgomery, J., & Welch, P. (2002). Lead poison prevention: A comparative review of brochures. *Journal of Environmental Health, 64(6),* 20–25.

33. Centers for Disease Control and Prevention, National Center for HIV, STD, and TB Prevention. (2000). Estimated number of adult/adolescent AIDS cases by sex, exposure category, and year of diagnosis, United States. *HIV/AIDS Surveillance Report, 12(2),* 1–48.

34. Miller, T.L., Easley, K.A., Zhang, W. (2001). Maternal and infant factors associated with failure to thrive in children with vertically transmitted human immunodeficiency virus-1 infection: The prospective, P^2C^2 Human Immunodeficiency Virus multicenter study. *Pediatrics, 108(6),* 1287–1296.

35. Miller, T.L., Evans, S.J., Orav, E.J., McIntosh, K., & Winter, H.S. (1993). Growth and body composition in children infected with the human immunodeficiency virus-1. *American Journal of Clinical Nutrition, 57,* 588–592.

36. Nicholas, S.W., Leung, J., & Fennoy, I. (1991). Guidelines for nutritional support of HIV infected child. *Journal of Pediatrics, 119,* 59–62.

37. American Academy of Pediatrics. (2000). Education of children with human immunodeficiency virus infection. *Pediatrics, 105(6),* 1358–1360.

38. Adams, P.F., & Marano, M.A. (1995). Current estimates from the National Health Interview Survey, 1994. *Vital Health Statistics 10,* 94.

39. National Institutes of Health. (July 1997). Clinical Practice Guidelines. *Expert panel report 2: Guidelines for the diagnosis and management of asthma.* NIH publication No. 97-4051.

40. Agertoft, L., & Pedersen, S. (1994). Effects of long-term treatment with an inhaled corticosteroid on growth and pulmonary function in asthmatic children. *Respiratory Medicine, 88,* 373–381.

41. American Academy of Allergy, Asthma and Immunology. *The Allergy Report: Science-based findings on the diagnosis and treatment of allergic disorders, 1996–2001.* Retrieved October 1, 2002, from http://www.aaaai.org/ar/volume1.pdf

42. Sicherer, S.H., Munoz-Furlong, A., & Burks, A.W. (1999). Prevalence of peanut and tree nut allergy in the United States determined by a random digit dial telephone survey. *Journal of Allergy and Clinical Immunology, 103,* 559–562.

43. Chandra, R.K. (1997). Food hypersensitivities and allergic disease: A selective review. *American Journal of Clinical Nutrition, 66 (suppl),* 526S–529S.

44. International Food Information Council Foundation; U.S. Department of Agriculture; Food Marketing Institute. (1996). *The Food Guide Pyramid: Your Personal Guide to Healthful Eating.* Washington, DC: U.S. Department of Agriculture, Center for Nutrition Policy and Promotion.

3

The Infant
(Birth to 12 Months)

LEARNING OBJECTIVES

Students will be able to:
- Identify tools used to evaluate nutritional status.
- Describe the unique components of breast milk that give it distinct advantages over infant formula.
- Recognize the role of nutrition in conception, pregnancy, and lactation.
- Identify practices that promote and support breastfeeding.
- Describe infant formulas and safe preparation techniques.
- Discuss signs of readiness and appropriate choices for solid foods during the first year.
- Describe strategies to promote healthy eating behaviors.
- Evaluate infants' dietary intake and related feeding and eating skills.
- Discuss common nutrition concerns during birth to 4 months and 4 to 12 months.
- Identify policies that promote nutrition and physical activity during infancy in the child-care center.

Some of you may have yet to hold and feed babies, while some of you will have extensive experience in caring for babies, maybe your own. In either case, this chapter presents recommendations for infant nutritional needs, enabling you to provide the best infant care. To further extend your knowledge, consult the recommended references and resources identified throughout the chapter for an in-depth study of growth, development, nutritional needs, feeding practices, and common nutritional problems of infants. In addition, knowing your local health department nutritionist or registered dietitian will help you access resources and establish a referral contact for parents.

GROWTH AND PHYSICAL DEVELOPMENT

Children will never grow so rapidly as during the first year. Normal infants will double their weight by 5 months and triple their weight by their first birthday. However, newborn infants must rely upon parents or caregivers for all physical, social, and emotional needs, with crying as the main form of communication. When these basic needs are met on a timely and consistent basis, infants build the trust necessary to bond with parents or caregivers.

At birth, normal infants are able to coordinate sucking and swallowing to take in nourishment when offered. Aside from crying, their ability to communicate hunger is limited to subtle cues like blinking eyes, scooting, and putting a fist in their mouth. They cannot lift their head or roll over, or in any other way signal for food. If these early cues are ignored, babies will progress to crying as a late indication of hunger and may be harder to satisfy.

Infants attain developmental milestones in a predetermined sequential order [1]. As gross motor and fine motor skills develop, infants' responses to stimuli become more complex. Muscles grow stronger and eventually allow them to sit upright by 4 to 6 months of age. Infants can now signal their interest in food by looking at the food and attempting to grab the food. In addition, crying is easier to distinguish as a cry of pain, hunger, discomfort, fatigue, boredom, or simple tension discharge.

By 8 months of age children are finger-feeding and eating from a spoon. Within a few more months they will improve chewing skills, hold a bottle or cup, drink from a cup, hold a spoon, and attempt to feed themselves. Supporting a child's natural progression to independent feeding will produce a child willing to try new foods and willing to eat when hungry.

Critical Periods of Development

As infants grow, the caregiver may note critical periods when they develop new oral, adaptive, and gross motor skills. Table 3.1 summarizes normal feeding development during these critical periods from infancy through 1 year of age. Infants' feeding skills can be observed and compared to the standard. There is a wide variation in when children will achieve certain developmental milestones. Therefore, a thorough assessment by a pediatrician is needed to determine true delays.

> Telling parents how the milestones relate to feeding will help parents recognize when it is time to progress to more independent feeding and perhaps avoid feeding battles.

The physical development and skills mastered in each critical period impact food intake. At birth the sucking reflex is used to obtain nourishment from a nipple. Not until about 6 months of age does the sucking motion become modified enough for infants to accept semisolid food from a spoon and allow drinking from a cup. Also, the large muscles of the body assist infants in sitting upright.

By 7 to 9 months, infants' chewing becomes more refined and they are able to sit erect. Increased physical independence is possible with free hand movement, and grasping objects with thumb and forefinger. These are all signs that infants are ready to participate in feeding by using the spoon, finger-feeding, and holding a cup.

By 9 to 12 months infants will play peek-a-boo and explore foods with eyes, hands, and mouth. They will transfer objects from one hand to the other and begin cruising, crawling, and walking. Infants are ready to participate in family meals for short periods of time.

Tools and Techniques for Health Assessment

Measure infants routinely during the first year to determine if growth is occurring at a healthy rate. The measures of length, weight, and head circumference provide a reliable indication of how infants are growing compared to infants in the reference

Table 3.1 Stages of development for infants*

Stage	Physical	Nutritional	Intellectual
Fetal: Conception to birth	Development of anatomic characteristics followed by growth and elaboration of all systems	Receives nourishment via placenta; maternal weight gain first trimester 1 to 2 kg with 0.4 kg per week gain for remainder of pregnancy	Brain grows to about 25% of adult size
Newborn: Birth to 10 days	Average weight—3.4 kg; average height—50 cm; average HC†—35 cm; has large head, round face and chest, prominent abdomen, and short extremities; loses weight	Seeks source of nourishment by rooting reflex from bottle or breast, consuming colostrum or prepared formula	Brain growth continues; coordination of senses and motor functions begins
Infancy I: 10 days to 2 months	Regains birthweight; sitting height equal to 57% of body length; rapid growth of head and body	Continues to nurse mature breast milk or formula; not developmentally ready for solid food (orally or physiologically, e.g., renal solute load)	Inspection of surroundings begins; differentiation of self from others
Infancy II: 3 to 5 months	Doubles birthweight; increases length; posterior fontanel closes; deciduous teeth begin erupting	Continues to be nourished by breast milk or formula; iron stores begin to be depleted	Attention span increases; hand-eye coordination begins
Infancy III: 6 to 9 months	Subcutaneous fat reaches peak by 9 months; closure of anterior fontanel by 9 months	Oral mechanism ready to accept solid food; cereal introduced first in a very thin consistency; consistency thickened, as tolerated; new foods introduced, as tolerated	Imitation of others begins; understands a few words
Infancy IV: 10 to 12 months	Triples birthweight; average HC† of 47 cm equals chest circumference; 6 to 8 teeth present	Tooth eruption progresses; tolerated transition from pureed to chopped foods; formula or breast milk recommended until end of the first year	First words; concept of object permanence develops; brain weight now about 75% of adult's

*This chart provides the health professional with a standard tool for assessing feeding levels.
†HC = Head circumference.

(continued)

Table 3.1   (Continued)

Stage	Oral/Motor	Speech and Language	Social/Behavioral
Fetal: Conception to birth	Embryological development of oral structures: lips, tongue, hard palate, soft palate, peripheral muscles		
Newborn: Birth to 10 days	Rooting reflex; gag reflex; sucking (flexor tone in neonate); suckling, phasic bite reflex; palmomental reflex; smooth coordination of sucking, swallowing, breathing	Birth cry; cry becomes longer; strong, rhythmical breathing	
Infancy I: 10 days to 2 months	Suckling, phasic bite reflex, palmomental reflex continue	Smiles; visually localizes speaker; breath stream lengthens; coos (vowel sounds); uses special cry for hunger	Regards face; eye contact; smiles
Infancy II: 3 to 5 months	Suckling; cup-drinking; spoon-feeding begins; phasic bite reflex develops to munching	Controls breath stream; varies pitch; vocalizes vowel sounds (nonimitative); begins to babble (consonant sounds); responds to name	Laughs aloud; responds to talking
Infancy III: 6 to 9 months	Sucking; cup-drinking continues; more refined spoon-feeding; chewing	Recognizes some familiar names; plays peek-a-boo, pat-a-cake; stops at "no"; gestures to some familiar words or requests (come, bye-bye, up); babbles imitatively	Differentiates family members; fearful of strangers
Infancy IV: 10 to 12 months	Sucking, cup-drinking, spoon-feeding, and chewing continue	Follows simple verbal requests (put that down); understands simple questions (where?); attends to speech; gestures appropriately; first words (mama, dada, bye-bye)	Plays peek-a-boo and pat-a-cake

Table 3.1 (Continued)

Stage	Gross Motor	Fine Motor	Reflex
Fetal: Conception to birth		Sucks thumb in utero	
Newborn: Birth to 10 *days*	Flexed-adducted posture	Grasp reflex; palmomental reflex; inserts thumb when hand is brought to mouth	Sucking, rooting, gagging, asymmetrical tonic neck reflex (ATNR) present; moro and tonic labyrinthine reflexes emerge
Infancy I: 10 *days to* 2 *months*	Flexed-abducted posture emerges; head extension in prone (60° at 3 months); head lag when pulled to sitting; midline positioning of head begins in supine; forearm propping	Grasp reflex continues; hands often open; ulnar side of hand strongest; mouthing of fingers and mutual fingering	Rooting (3 months) and sucking (2 to 5 months) disappear; phasic bite reflex present
Infancy II: 3 *to 5* *months*	Extended-abducted posture emerges; extended arm position in prone; rolls prone to supine and back; head erect in supported sitting (6 months); sits propping on arms	Raking fingers; immediate approach and grasp on site, then eyes and hands combine in joint action; radial fingers begin to dominate	Grasp reflex disappears (4 to 6 months) and moro disappears (5 to 6 months); tonic labyrinthine disappears (6 months); symmetrical topic neck reflex (STNR) emerges at 6 months
Infancy III: 6 *to 9* *months*	Rotational patterns emerge; sits erect with hands free; reerects self in sitting and comes to sitting independently; pivots on stomach; pulls to standing; crawls on stomach	One hand approach to objects; transfers objects; thumb begins to move toward forefinger	Protective extension forward in upper extremities begins (9 to 10 months); phasic bite develops to munching
Infancy IV: 10 *to 12* *months*	Independent mobility by crawling (9 months), creeping (12 months), or walking (12 to 15 months); pivots on hips in sitting; walks holding onto furniture	Finer adjustment of digits; inferior-pincer grasp; pokes with forefinger; beginning of voluntary release and neat pincer grasp with slight extension of wrist (10 to 11 months)	Protective extension sidewards in upper extremities begins at 7 months; STNR disappears (8 to 12 months); tilting responses in sitting begin at 7 and 8 months.

Source: Modified from Harvey-Smith, M., et al. (1982). *Feeding Management of a Child with a Handicap: A Guide for Professionals.* Memphis: University of Tennessee Center for the Health Sciences.

Care providers measure length of infant

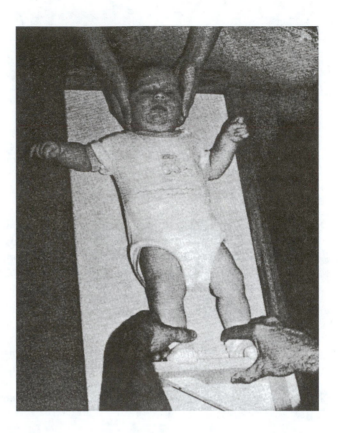

"Well-child visits" refers to a visit with a physician or qualified health provider, for the purpose of observing the child's growth and development, providing guidance, and administering immunizations. Visits are not planned in response to an illness. During the first year of life the American Academy of Pediatrics recommends several basic well-child visits; one soon after birth and then once every 2 months.

population. From birth to 1 year of age, average infants increase their weight by 200%, length by 55%, and head circumference by 40%. Infants can be measured at the center or the parents can provide measurements obtained through regularly scheduled well-child visits at 8 weeks, 4 months, 6 months, 9 months, and 12 months conducted by a physician or health professional.

Measuring.   To obtain length, infants are measured while lying down in a recumbent position. National growth chart standards until age 2 are based on recumbent length, ideally measured on a table with an immovable headpiece and movable foot piece. A measuring tape (preferably graduated in millimeters and nonstretchable) runs along the table's length. Two people are needed to steady the head and stretch out the legs.

Measure the child's weight using a beam-balanced scale with nondetachable weights. Undress children down to as little clothing as possible for measuring each month. Balance the scale before each weighing.

Head size can be measured using a nonstretchable tape measure with a notch. Slip the tape over the head and place it across the forehead, above the ears on both sides, and around the largest part of the back of the head; then move up or down slightly to obtain the maximum circumference. Infants' heads are disproportionately larger than their bodies. Expect a steady growth as brain size nearly doubles by the year's end. A head size that progresses steadily is a healthy indication of brain growth. When head size lags behind or starts out small and continues to falter, a doctor's referral is necessary.

Center staff taking the measurements must follow proper techniques for measurement and plotting growth on reference charts. Mistakes will lead to misinterpretation of health status. To ensure competency, have staff use the Centers for Disease Control and Prevention's (CDC) self-directed, interactive training modules for users of the pediatric growth charts at the following Web address: http://www.cdc.gov/nccdphp/dnpa/growthcharts/training/modules/index.htm.

Growth Charts.   The National Center for Health Statistics, NCHS, in collaboration with the CDC, developed the standards for growth assessment, which draw from a wide sample of breastfed, formula fed, and racially and ethnically diverse populations. Train any staff working with children to use these assessment tools. Sample growth charts are included in Appendix IV. To access a printable version of the charts go to http://www.cdc.gov/growthcharts/.

Each chart contains a series of curved lines, numbered to show selected percentiles. These refer to the rank of this measurement compared to a hypothetical group of 100 children. If a child's weight is taken and a mark is placed on the 95th percentile of weight for length (Figure 3.1), it means that only 5 children among 100 of the corresponding age and sex can be expected to have a weight for length greater than that recorded and that 95 can be expected to have a weight for length less than that recorded.

Interpreting.   An individual child's growth can be tracked on a growth chart. Measurements are plotted based on age or another index. For normal children, several measurements over several months will reveal a somewhat smooth pattern of growth. Measurements that appear below the 25th or above the 90th percentile are in the normal range but must be judged against previous and subsequent measurements and genetic and environmental factors that affect infants. If the child's growth pattern plots above the 95th percentile or below the 5th percentile, you may want to check the accuracy of the measurements and discuss recent illness or change in appetite with the parents. Rapid changes are less likely to be significant when they occur between the 25th and the 75th percentile. Growth occurs in starts and stops, and is affected by many factors. Therefore, plotting a single value has little relevance and must not be used to diagnose problems. Table 3.2 shows weight and length at the 50th percentile as children grow each month.

Growth rates also differ based on mode of feeding. Breastfed infants grow vigorously during the first three months, and then begin a slow and steady growth velocity with lower total energy intakes than formula-fed infants. In fact, some

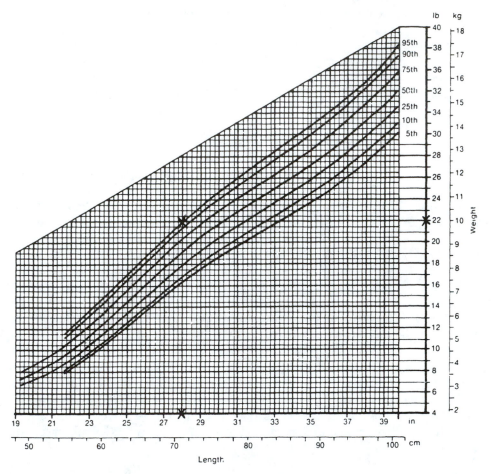

Figure 3.1   Girls' growth chart from birth to 36 months showing weight for length at 95th percentile.
Source: U.S. Department of Health, Education, and Welfare, National Center for Health Statistics. (1979).

breastfed infants may appear to have faltering growth after the first three months [2, 3] when compared to formula-fed infants. However, the current growth charts include a larger sample of breastfed infants to correct for this problem. Refer concerned parents to their pediatrician.

Laboratory Measurements.   Infants are more susceptible to nutrient deficiencies and environmental hazards due to their rapidly growing state and their immature systems. For infants, the most common laboratory tests screen their blood for low iron levels and excessive lead levels. Either condition can affect brain development. Low iron levels precede iron deficiency and iron deficiency anemia; which are discussed in detail later in the chapter.

Table 3.2   Lengths and weights at 50th percentile for various ages

	Girls	Boys	Girls	Boys
Age	Length in inches	Length	Weight in pounds	Weight
1 month	21 3/4	21	8 3/4	8
3 months	24	23	13	12 1/4
6 months	26	25 1/2	17 1/2	15 1/2
9 months	28	27 1/2	20 1/4	18 1/2
12 months	29 1/2	29	22 1/4	20 1/2
18 months	32	31	25 1/2	24 1/4
24 months	34 1/4	33 1/2	28	26 1/4

Source: National Center for Health Statistics in Collaboration with National Center for Chronic Disease Prevention and Health Promotion. (2000). April 20, 2001, revision. Available at http://www.cdc.gov/growthcharts.

The American Academy of Pediatrics (AAP) recommends that babies be screened for lead exposure by 9 to 12 months of age and again at 24 months of age when blood lead levels peak. Even ingesting small amounts of lead dust from the fingertips can elevate lead levels when repeated over time, so identifying and eliminating the source of lead is essential. Address lead poisoning prevention strategies (introduced in Chapter 2) with parents when their children are 3 to 6 months of age and again at 1 year of age.

Early and periodic screening for iron deficiency and elevated blood lead-levels can prevent and augment damage to the brain. The day-care center that promotes these screenings participates in public health promotion for the children under their care.

> Lead can be found in drinking water obtained from lead pipes. Never use standing water. Rather, allow the water to run cool from the faucet to let the standing water pass. Also, hot water may retain more lead.

Dietary Assessment.   Dietary assessment during the first year can provide valuable information. Beyond assessing the quantity of food eaten and comparing it to the standard, a skilled interviewer can obtain information about daily routines and early feeding patterns, and determine the nature of the feeding relationship. Breastfed infants can be assessed for feeding frequency, duration, stool patterns, and number of wet diapers. Formula preparation techniques can be assessed for proper dilution and sanitation. Various techniques can be used, including a diet history, 24-hour recall, food frequency, and 3-day food record. The right form will prompt the interviewer to ask the right questions. The form in Appendix V is designed to capture key issues of concern for the 0- to 6- and 7- to 11-month-old. When problems or concerns arise, a referral to the local community nutritionist or registered dietitian can help parents improve their family's diet.

> Abnormal data from any one measure alone does not indicate malnutrition. The measures described must be coupled with other medical, laboratory, and dietary indexes before the parents or care provider should become concerned.

MATERNAL NUTRITION NEEDS

The fetus relies on the mother for nutrition even before pregnancy. Women who enter pregnancy undernourished increase their likelihood of having a baby with neural tube defects or low birth weight. Low birth weight infants weigh less than 5.5 lbs at birth and have more difficulty adjusting to life outside the womb, and more difficulty resisting illness and death. Neural tube defects and low birth weight are preventable through good nutrition. Therefore, we will address maternal nutrient needs assuming the child's caregiver serves mothers indirectly through care of the child, and will have a chance to promote healthy maternal behaviors and disseminate information and resources to parents.

Preconception

Women who are in an optimal state of nutrition at the point of conception will have the necessary nutrients immediately available to the growing fetus during the critical first weeks of pregnancy and well before the pregnancy is known. Folic acid in particular is known for preventing neural tube defects, but it must be present before pregnancy and during the first few weeks; the recommended amount is 400 μg a day. Conversely, women who are underweight, smoke, and have a diet low in key nutrients such as iron and folate at conception and during pregnancy will reduce the potential health of their infant and increase the likelihood of having a low birth weight infant [4, 5].

Pregnancy

Health behaviors during pregnancy impact the health of infants. Pregnancy prepares mothers for the demands of labor and recovery, as well as the nutrient demands of lactation. Prepregnancy weight and weight gain during pregnancy are two of the most important determinants of a pregnancy's outcome. The National Academies' Institute of Medicine (IOM) guidelines for pregnancy weight gain are based on prepregnancy body mass index or BMI. Adult BMI calculations were discussed in Chapter 2. Women with a normal BMI need to gain 25 to 35 pounds. Underweight women need to gain 28 to 40 pounds, and overweight women need to gain 15 to 25 pounds. Obese women need to gain at least 15 pounds.

Harmful Substances During Pregnancy.   Alcohol is not safe during pregnancy. In addition, illegal drugs are not compatible with a healthy pregnancy. Smoking during pregnancy is related to low birth weight, even when women gain the recommended amount of weight. Smoking limits the amount of oxygen and nutrients available to the growing fetus. It is never too late to quit. Resources for women who wish to quit smoking are available from the local chapter of the American Lung Association at http://www.lungusa.org/ffs/.

Herbal and botanical supplements and alternative remedies are growing in popularity. However, the safety of using such products during pregnancy must be evaluated. For the latest information regarding the safety of herbals and botanicals during pregnancy, go to the Federal Drug Administration Web site, http://vm.cfsan.fda.gov/~dms/aems.html.

Resources.   Information on diet, nutrient needs, and lactation is available from your local WIC program (Appendix VI) and your local March of Dimes. Also, the National Women's Health Information Center's Web page provides current, reliable, and commercial-free health information at http://www.4woman.gov/.

Diet.   There are no special foods for pregnancy; nevertheless, pregnant women are considered to be at high risk for food-borne illnesses such as Listeria and exposure to mercury, two health concerns discussed in Chapter 7. Eating healthy foods during pregnancy supplies the fetus with all the nutrients needed for growth and development. The average additional calories per trimester are 96/day in the first trimester, 265/day second trimester, and 430/day for third trimester [5]. Overweight and obese women can improve the nutrient density of their diet by choosing lower fat, no sugar added, and whole food varieties of each food group while meeting minimum weight gain recommendations. Underweight women need to consume extra calories to reach their ideal weight for a healthy pregnancy. They can obtain extra energy by choosing whole-milk dairy products and using medium- to high-fat meats. In either case, the Food Guide Pyramid remains useful for determining food choices and serving size (see Chapter 2). Additional servings of dairy foods, grains, fruits, and vegetables as well as meat, fish, and beans will increase nutrient density of the diet and provide the necessary nutrients and energy stores for a healthy baby and the lactation period.

Other recommendations for pregnant women include taking a low-dose iron supplement, and 600 μg of folic acid [6]. Other vitamins and minerals may be required for special needs based upon women's nutrition and health status. Registered dietitians can help pregnant women develop a plan to meet individual nutrient needs, manage high-risk pregnancies, or cope with common discomforts of pregnancy.

Lactation

When women produce breast milk, they allow their body to naturally complete the cycle of birth. Completing this cycle bestows its own benefits to mothers [7, 8]. There is an immediate benefit of enhanced recovery from delivery compared to nonbreastfeeding counterparts: less postpartum bleeding and the womb recovers to normal size sooner. This is followed by increased initial weight loss, temporary cessation of menstruation, and increased sense of well-being aided by a gradual shift in hormonal balance. In the long term there is enhanced resistance from breast cancer, ovarian cancer, and enhanced bone density with greater effects related to longer duration of breastfeeding. Meanwhile, infants receive nutrients and disease resistant properties for optimal growth and development. In the end, breastfeeding women and children emerge from the first year of life with many exclusive health benefits.

Most women can produce enough milk to support infant growth. Caloric needs vary depending on maternal BMI and are not less than 1800 kcal/day for most women,

Mother breastfeeds infant

and can reach up to 2700 calories per day at 6 months [5, 9]. The process of lactation has been reviewed by experts and the following is generally agreed upon [5, 9]:

- Milk volume is regulated by milk removal and is generally not influenced by an increase in calories or fluids.
- Minerals in breast milk can be drawn from body stores to remain constant. The negative impact of a low-mineral diet will be limited to the mother.
- Vitamin content of breast milk depends upon women's current vitamin intake and stores.

Restrictive Eating Patterns.   Lactating women, following restrictive eating patterns such as very low calorie, vegan, or vegetarian diets that eliminate entire food groups, need corrective measures to improve their intake. Be sure to refer these mothers to a registered dietitian for help meeting all of their nutrient requirements.

For mothers who worry about food sensitivities being passed through their breast milk, refer to the section on Food Reactions and Allergies later in this chapter.

When Breastfeeding Is Contraindicated.   Although breastfeeding is strongly recommended, it is not appropriate for babies whose mothers use street drugs such as cocaine, "ecstasy," PCP, or marijuana; whose mothers consume more than minimal amounts of alcohol; whose mothers receive certain therapeutic or diagnostic agents such as radioactive elements and cancer chemotherapy. Women who are HIV-positive can transmit the virus to their infants through their breast milk, unless it is treated [10]. Do not assume that drugs safe during pregnancy will be safe during lactation because different pathways are involved. Women should ask their physician or pharmacist before taking any medicines or herbal remedies. An additional resource regarding the transfer of drugs into breast milk is the American Academy of Pediatrics (AAP) statement available at http://www.aap.org/policy/0063.html.

Maintaining Breast Milk Supply.   The most common challenge for lactating mothers returning to work is maintaining their breast milk supply during separation from their infant. Drinking at least 6 to 8 glasses of liquid per day is recommended for all adults, yet there is little evidence that increasing fluid intake much above 32 ounces per day actually increases milk production [11, 12]. Mothers produce about 3 to 3 1/2 cups of milk per day (750–800 ml/day). Breast milk production is stimulated by breast milk removal. Babies are the most efficient at breast milk removal so frequent nursing is key. Extra milk removal directly after feedings or between feedings stimulates milk production as well.

For mothers returning to full-time work, the most common solution is an electric double pump made by a recognized hospital-grade pump manufacturer. Electric pumps are faster, and a pump with double flanges reduces the pumping time when both breasts are pumped at the same time. However, using a manual pump for an occasional bottle can meet some women's needs. Mothers can avoid buying the wrong pump by considering all aspects of pumping during separation before purchase. Hospital-grade pumps are available from about $150 to $200 or more. In some states the WIC program covers the cost of breast pumps. Locate your local WIC program by typing in WIC at the federal Web-site search engine at http://www.Nutrition.gov.

Providing a breast pump rental program through the center makes higher quality expensive pumps available to more women and may prolong breastfeeding. Including a breast pump rental station at your day care provides a practical service and promotes breastfeeding as the cultural norm without appearing to show a preference for breastfeeding mothers and babies. For information on becoming a pump rental station contact breast pump manufacturers at http://www.breastpump.com/.

In addition to selecting the best pump to meet her needs, a new mom can try the following strategies to promote a generous breast milk supply:

- Maintain plenty of skin-to-skin contact with her infant.
- Continue night feedings to promote the release of breast-milk production hormones.

Box 3.1   Intention to breastfeed questionnaire

This questionnaire was developed to assess your intent to breastfeed and use or avoid formula supplements. Please answer the following questions by circling

Yes (Y)/ No (N)/Unsure (U)

1. **Y/N/U**   I want to exclusively breastfeed my baby.
2. **Y/N/U**   It is important to me to avoid use of formula supplements.
3. **Y/N/U**   It is important to me to avoid using pacifiers.
4. **Y/N/U**   I plan to delay the introduction of solid foods until my infant is 6 months old because it may interfere with breastfeeding.
5. **Y/N/U**   I plan to pump breast milk at work.
6. **Y/N/U**   I also plan to pump breast milk on the weekend so that I can build up a good back-up supply.
7. **Y/N/U**   I can leave work early if my baby runs out of milk.
8. **Y/N/U**   I would like a phone call at work to notify me if my breast milk supply is running low.
9. **Y/N/U**   I plan to breastfeed as long as it is convenient for me and my baby; if I run out of milk please use a bottle of formula, which I have supplied.
10. **Y/N/U**   I would like a phone call before you give my baby formula.

- Delay the use of formula supplements for as long as possible and solids for at least 6 months, as they interfere with breast milk supply.
- Complete the Intention to Breastfeed Questionnaire in Box 3.1 or have a written statement based on the same information to give to the center.
- Purchase or rent a pump designed to meet individual needs.
- For each bottle, add an additional 5–10 minute double pumping session between or directly after nursing if a formula supplement is used. Even if very little milk is immediately produced, extra pumping to remove milk will stimulate milk production.
- Contact the hospital's Lactation Consultant or contact La Leche League (LLL) at http://www.lalecheleague.org/m2m_home_intro.html or in your local phone book.
- Consider part-time/flexible work schedule to improve success at long-term breastfeeding.

Resources and Support Groups.   Most large communities will have various support networks for breastfeeding mothers. Check out the local LLL and county health department, community hospital, or WIC program for more information and resources. A comprehensive guide for breastfeeding mothers was developed by the AAP and is available at http://www.aap.org/family/brstguid.htm. For simple educational handouts and pamphlets on breastfeeding, it is best to avoid commercial resources provided by baby food/formula companies; instead, try your state or local health department.

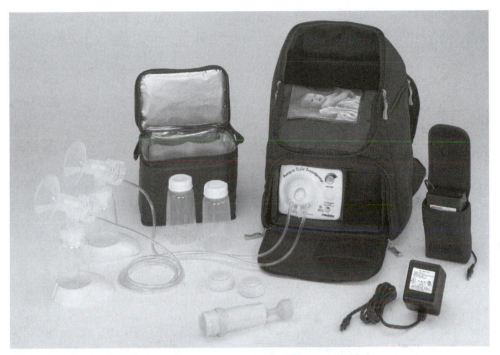

A hospital grade electric breast pump can extract milk from both breasts at once, compared to a hand pump which is used on one breast at a time

INFANT FEEDING RECOMMENDATIONS

Breastfeeding and Human Milk

Human milk should no longer be considered merely a food with some antibodies, but rather, a collection of biologically active protective agents that also provides nutritional support.

Newburg [13]

Breast milk provides a shield against a hostile environment. Scientists are just beginning to discover additional disease-fighting components of breast milk. Most research has looked at antibodies, but scientists have quickly learned that the nature of breast milk is complex. So far we know that breast milk builds brain cells, soothes the intestines, provides long-term disease and allergy resistance, and may prevent adult obesity and death from SIDS. Some examples of new functions being investigated include the following [13]:

- Breast milk supports the optimal development of body systems such as the brain, digestive tract, and the immune system.

- Some breast milk sugars and carbohydrates act as decoys for harmful bacteria, viruses, and pathogens, while some promote overgrowth of beneficial microflora.
- Antibodies protect intestines from pathogens looking to bind to cell walls and inhibit growth of harmful microorganisms.
- Hormones regulate growth and stimulate development of the immune system.

These protective factors appear to work together, providing several layers of protection before and during recovery from acute and chronic illness.

Several major players in health care have issued statements declaring the superiority of breast milk [14–17]. Also, National Health Objectives for Breastfeeding aim for 75% initiation, 50% at 6 months, and 25% until 1 year of age. Currently 69.5% of infants are breastfed at birth and 32.5% continue breastfeeding at 6 months of age, representing the highest incidence of breastfeeding recorded to date [18]. However, the rates are lower in some low-income populations and only a small percent are still breastfeeding until 1 year or longer. Perhaps the most prominent organization to issue a pro breast feeding statement is the American Academy of Pediatrics, which recommend exclusive breastfeeding for 6 months with continued breastfeeding for 1 year or longer. The AAP offered this clarification [16]: *From birth to about 6 months of age, breastmilk alone meets all the nutrient needs for most healthy infants, with the exception of some low-birth weight infants who will need supplemental iron and certain populations of dark-skinned infants who experience low sunlight exposure and therefore need supplemental vitamin D.*

Supporting and Protecting Breastfeeding.   Providing a quiet spot to breastfeed infants need not be complicated. Simply placing a swivel rocking chair in a dimly lit nursery or corner office can provide enough privacy for most women. Rooms for pumping at the day care are unnecessary; instead, encourage mothers to nurse while at the center. Breast milk production is stimulated to a greater degree when there is skin-to-skin contact, so promote as many nursing encounters as possible, especially in the early months. This practice has the added benefit of establishing a comforting routine for a smooth morning departure and a relaxing drive home.

Breastfeeding mothers will appreciate your efforts to recognize and reinforce the special breastfeeding relationship. For example, when mother's budding toddler plays with a doll and puts it in a nursing position, talk to the child about nursing and avoid offering a toy bottle. Including storybooks about breastfed babies and their mommies is also supportive. Check out the La Leche League Web site for children's books at http://www.lalecheleague.org.

Care and Handling.   Breast milk is a living fluid that requires special handling. Mothers should strive to keep at least a day's supply of fresh unfrozen milk divided into usual servings size (2–4 oz) ready for consumption. Also a 1 to 2 day supply of frozen breast milk is needed for a back-up supply. Freeze in 1 to 2 oz servings for easy defrost and to avoid waste. When transporting breast milk, keep it cold in a cooler bag.

Guidance for the care provider includes the following:

- Accept pumped breast milk in clearly labeled (nonfading) bottles with flat sealing disks that form an airtight seal. Do not put nipples on the bottles because they interfere with an airtight seal.
- Recommend using frosted opaque bottles and do not use clear hard plastic bottles that are polycarbonate and may contaminate milk with plastics residue when heated.
- If plastic bags are used, double bag and store in a hard container to avoid contamination from nicks and tears in the bag.
- Label all bottles and bags with the child's name and date pumped, so as not to give breast milk to the wrong baby, and potentially expose infants to infections (including HIV–AIDS virus) via the breast milk.
- Check refrigerators or freezers used to store formula or breast milk for a consistently safe temperature range of 40 degrees Fahrenheit or colder for the refrigerator and zero degrees or colder for the freezer. Place a thermometer in each compartment. Use refrigerated breast milk first and within 48 hours.
- Frozen breast milk will last at least 3 months (some experts say 3–6 months) in a properly cooled freezer with a separate door from the refrigerator. When using frozen breast milk, rotate and use the oldest first, thaw under cold running water or in the refrigerator, and use within 24 hours. For tips on handling breast milk and decreasing risk for contamination in the child-care center, access the USDA Web site at http://www.fns.usda.gov/tn/Resources/feeding_infants.html for the document "Feeding Infants: A Guide for Use in Child Nutrition Programs."

Common Feeding Patterns of Breastfed Infants.   The nature of the breastfeeding relationship seems to promote certain beneficial food behaviors in breastfed infants. Infants of breastfeeding mothers are able to regulate their own

Breast milk is properly stored in bottles with caps and no nipples

intake, while their mothers tend to exhibit less controlling behaviors on their food intake [19].

Breastfed infants will indicate their desire to nurse 8 to 12 times in 24 hours. Crying is a late indicator of hunger. Feed infants when early cues of hunger such as scooting, eye blinking, or alertness are displayed. End feedings when signs of satiety like turning from the nipple and losing interest in nursing are displayed.

Within the first 6 to 12 weeks infants experience growth spurts, characterized by fussiness, increased interest in nursing, and taking more milk than expected. This change in contentment is temporary and should not be interpreted as a sign to supplement with formula. See tips for maintaining breast milk supply under the Lactation section of this chapter. Advise mothers who are upset to take a day off to cuddle up with baby and nurse through the growth spurt.

Care providers have a crucial role in ensuring breastfeeding success. They must alert nursing moms to changes in their baby's appetite because it may signal a need for more breast milk or consideration of a formula supplement. Again, the breastfeeding mothers' supplement use questionnaire, Box 3.1, will help devise a plan for these times.

Counting diapers is the most reliable method of assessing breast milk intake. A breastfed baby produces about 6 to 8 wet-soaked diapers in a 24-hour period, and several stools per day. Breast milk stools have their own "normal" quality. They have a very mild odor, a yellow or orange color, and may have a seedy texture somewhat like cottage cheese or pea soup. Older breastfed infants will develop a unique stooling pattern that may be less than once a day. Exclusively breastfed infants rarely suffer from constipation since breastmilk is a natural laxative.

Complementary Foods and Supplements.   Research shows that solid foods are unnecessary for exclusively breastfeeding infants in the first 6 months of life and do not improve growth [20]. Before this age, solid food does not complement the diet, growth is not enhanced, and there are not fewer night feedings, or fewer day feedings, and there is no improvement in sleeping through the night [3, 19]. Begin a gradual introduction to solid foods after 6 months of age. Solid foods complement the diet when they do not interfere with normal growth. This process is detailed later in the chapter under Solid Foods.

Vitamin D.   Infants rely on sunshine to synthesize the vitamin D needed to support bone growth. Providing routine exposure to sunlight 15 to 20 minutes a day outdoors or near a sunny window is essential. For breastfed babies who do not get routine exposure to sunlight, pediatricians can recommend a supplement to meet their DRI requirement of 5 µg of vitamin D (DRIs were introduced in Chapter 2 and listed in Appendix III) [21]. Certain at-risk infants, including those whose mothers are vitamin D deficient or those with low sunlight exposure or those with low iron stores, will need a vitamin D supplement [16].

> All babies need their daily "sunshine vitamin." Plan daily outdoor activities or time in front of a sunny window as a routine, equaling 15 to 20 minutes a day.

Iron. Exclusively breastfeed full-term infants readily absorb about 50% of the iron in breast milk, making supplementation unnecessary in healthy infants less than 6 months of age. Include iron-fortified foods as part of breastfed infants' diets at about 6 months of age. Consider a daily low-dose oral iron supplement if these foods are rejected. The DRI is 11 mg/day for 7 to 12 month olds. Iron deficiency anemia is discussed later in this chapter under Nutrition Related Health Concerns.

Fluoride. Assess fluoride needs in breastfed infants after 6 months of age. Fluoride is usually not needed unless the water supply is severely depleted to < 0.3 ppm [16].

Formula Supplementation. Formula supplementation decreases breastfeeding duration and impairs mineral absorption from breast milk, thereby decreasing its nutritional value. Also, formula supplementation decreases breast milk supply by reducing breast stimulation. The effects are more negative with earlier introduction: The sooner a formula supplement is introduced, the sooner breastfeeding may end [16, 22]. To maintain an adequate breast milk supply, advise mothers to try the strategies suggested earlier in this chapter under Maintaining Breast Milk Supply.

Introducing a formula supplement is not guaranteed to ruin breastfeeding, however mothers' satisfaction with day care can be related to their success at achieving breastfeeding goals. In particular, exclusive breastfeeding can be a difficult goal to achieve for women returning to full-time work. Identifying mothers who desire exclusive breastfeeding will help you discern which mothers want additional support. To help you in this task, a form designed to determine a mothers' intention to breastfeed is included in Box 3.1. The care provider plays an active role in managing the breast milk supply by maintaining good communication with mothers and taking care to properly handle the breast milk as described earlier.

> Seek mothers' approval for use of formula supplements and, if given permission, time supplemental usage carefully so as not to interfere with the breastfeeding anticipated upon their return to the center.

Weaning. In addition to the disease resistance and superior nutritional properties of breastmilk, extended breastfeeding imparts psychological benefits for mothers and children. Weaning remains a matter of personal choice. However, as scientific evidence mounts regarding the benefits of longer duration of breastfeeding, experts have backed away from recommending a specific age for weaning. As understanding and acceptance of breastfeeding increases, expect a behavioral shift toward extended nursing. For infants weaned from the breast prior to 1 year, cow's milk is not an adequate substitute; instead, use iron-fortified formula.

> For the comfort of mothers and to reduce stress on infants, recommend gradual weaning taking place over several days or weeks. Tips on weaning are available on the La Leche League Web site at http://www.lalecheleague.org.

Breast Milk Substitutes

If breast milk is unavailable from the mother or a human milk bank, the AAP Committee on Nutrition recommends that all nonbreastfed or partially breastfed infants receive iron-fortified commercially prepared formula from birth to 12 months of age [23]. Infant formulas supply the main nutrients in breast milk. Breast milk is estimated to have over 300 known ingredients; formula is manufactured with about 50 nutrients and cannot be made with human factors. The nutritional content of all commercial infant formulas is regulated by the FDA and guided by the AAP Committee on Nutrition. Healthy, normal infants consuming iron-fortified formula will need no supplements except flouride; and then only if flouride is not available in the water supply. Substitutes such as low-iron formula, goats' milk, or evaporated milk are inadequate.

As a care provider you will most certainly encounter parents who believe that the iron in formula is causing a host of problems ranging from spitting up to constipation and diarrhea or general fussiness and colic. Yet data linking iron formulas to common infant feeding complaints are lacking [23]. Infants with low iron stores will risk impaired brain growth and development, as well as anemia.

Parents should supply their own formula in ready-to-feed factory-sealed cans or in cans of powder or concentrate to be prepared on site. If parents insist on using a low-iron formula (less than 4 mg/l), require a doctor's note indicating the length of time the child should spend on low-iron formula.

Now that we have established that nonbreastfed infants require commercially prepared iron fortified formula, let's consider the types of formula available. Cow's-milk–based formulas are the most common choice of formula for nonbreastfed babies. The main difference in basic nutrient composition is that breast milk has 7% protein while cow's milk has 20% protein and must be adjusted to suit human needs. Furthermore, the protein balance is constant and cannot adjust with growth like breast milk.

Soy Protein Formulas.   Soy protein formulas are recommended when cow's milk formulas or breast milk are not used. They are considered a safe alternative, yet they offer no distinct advantages over breast milk or cow's milk formulas, including the prevention of allergic disease or colic, or in supplementing the diet of breastfeeding infants [24]. Soy formulas are appropriate for infants with galactosemia or hereditary lactase deficiency. Soy formulas are also effective in treating gastroenteritis in infants with documented lactose intolerance.

Hydrolyzed Formulas.   Approximately 10% of the population is allergic to the intact protein in cow's milk and soy-protein–based formulas. If breast milk is unavailable for these infants, hypoallergenic formula will benefit the majority, and is recommended. Extensively hydrolyzed and free amino-acid–based formulas are intended for infants who have significant malabsorption due to disease or protracted diarrhea, and should not be confused with partially hydrolyzed formulas [25]. Hydrolyzed formulas are not a cure for colic, sleeplessness, or irritability.

Lactose-Free Formulas. Lactose-free formulas and sugar-free formulas were once a common treatment for diarrhea, but clinical evidence regarding their effectiveness is lacking. For short-term mild to moderate diarrhea, oral rehydration therapy (e.g., Pedialyte, Kaolectrolyte fluid replacements for infants) can be followed by a return to full strength formula [26]. Lactose-free formula can be fed to infants with lactase deficiency, but because it contains trace lactose, this solution is not appropriate for infants with galactosemia.

Weaning and Follow-Up Formulas. As formula companies develop new strategies to compete for the parent's dollar, the idea of marketing a formula to older infants was launched. The packaging and pricing of these formulas may be misleading, so advise parents to be cautious in making the switch by first calculating the actual cost per ounce, not a can-for-can price. Since the AAP and the Food and Drug Administration assure the nutrient content of all commercially available infant formulas, there is no medical reason to switch to a follow-up or weaning formula for healthy infants [26].

Cow's Milk. The AAP does not recommend using cow's milk (whole, 2%, or skim) before the age of 1 year, due to the low levels of linoleic acid, iron, vitamin C, and the offending renal load from too much protein sodium and potassium. This also applies to breastfed infants who can continue to avoid cow's milk through the second year of life as long as breast milk provides a substantial part of the diet [26].

Goat's Milk. Goat's milk may be easier to digest for some infants but the inadequate amounts of iron, folate, and vitamin D make it a poor choice for a formula base. However, canned goat's milk is available with the missing nutrients added and may be prescribed by some physicians.

Health Food Milks. Health food milks are not appropriate for infants [27]. There have been at least two reported cases of "severe nutritional deficiencies" caused by consumption of health food milks by children under two. Health food milks labeled as "milk" are not milk's nutritional equivalent. They are often inadequate in calcium, protein, and vitamins, which are abundant in formula, and breast milk.

Fruit Juice. Pure 100% fruit juice does not offer any benefits beyond fresh fruit. If it is used, pour it into a cup and limit it to 4 to 6 ounces per day served as part of a meal or snack. Continue to offer fruits on a daily basis. If juice intake begins before solids or is made readily available, the child may reduce breast milk or formula intake. The effect is similar to the effect of early introduction of solid foods; it compromises the nutrient density of the diet. The child who is allowed to roam with a bottle, box, or sippy-cup of juice risks severe tooth decay. The prolonged exposure will decay the teeth. In addition, unpasteurized fruit juice is not a safe choice for children, including infants [28].

The nonformula choices (cow's milk, goat's milk, or other health food milks or juice) mentioned are not adequate substitutes for breast milk. Do not use these non-formula items for infants under 1 year of age, without considerable documentation from a pediatrician.

Formula Preparation. Safe formula preparation begins with a safe water source. To determine the safety of your water supply, call the Environmental Protection Agency at 1-800-426-4791. If using tap water, allow water to run cool for about 2 minutes and use only cool tap water. If you are depending on well water, use nitrate-free bottled water and consult a physician regarding a fluoride supplement.

When preparing formulas from concentrate or powder, carefully follow the instructions on the formula can. Have parents supply their own formula; if the center provides it, use factory-sealed cans [29]. If parents request different concentrations, obtain instructions from the physician, including specific directions to reach desired concentration and duration of the change. Discard any leftover formula [29].

Common Feeding Patterns of Formula Fed Infants. From birth to 6 months, infants increasingly consume larger amounts of formula. Anticipate formula intake for normal, healthy infants to average about 20 to 24 oz/day at 6 weeks and to reach an average peak of about 32 to 36 oz/day at 6 months. The peak will begin to descend after the introduction of solid food at about 6 months of age. The amount will slowly begin decreasing to about 24 oz/day at 12 months. However, keep in mind that the day-to-day intake will vary with the influence of growth spurts and periods of nongrowth [30].

In collaboration with the American Academy of Pediatrics and the American Public Health Association, The National Resource Center for Health and Safety in Child Care has developed National Health and Safety Performance Standards: Guidelines for Out-of-Home Child Care Programs. Throughout our text their nutrition and safety standards are cited. The complete set of standards, guidelines with rationale, are available at http://www.nrc.uchsc.edu/.

INFANT FEEDING POLICY

So much of infants' world is centered on their feeding experiences that attention to the mechanics of feeding are essential to providing good care in the first year. Children in day care will be subjected to the feeding styles of all the individuals who feed them. It makes sense for the center to have an infant feeding policy and to educate all staff in its implementation. The policies should cover safety and sanitation in feeding and address the following issues:

- Who will feed the baby and when? (Limit the number of caregivers bottle feeding young infants.)
- How will new foods be introduced?
- What foods will be offered?

- How many infants will be spoon-fed by one person at the same time? (Try to limit to not more than three to limit risk of cross contamination.)
- Where will the baby be fed?
- What accommodations will be made for parents to feed their babies?
- What type of individual record keeping will be done?

Base policies on research and avoid arbitrary rules. Cited throughout this text are research-based recommendations from established nutrition authorities such as the American Dietetic Association, the American Academy of Pediatrics' Committee on Nutrition, and the National Resource Center for Health and Safety in Child Care [31]. Put policies in writing and make them available to parents in a parent handbook that they can share with their primary health care provider and refer to as needed.

Parents come with definite ideas on how, when, and what their babies will be fed. Their methods are usually family traditions, rarely based on scientific evidence, and not always the best for their infant. To promote acceptance of the center feeding policy, explain that policies are intended to ensure the health and well-being of infants through sound nutrition practices.

> Explain the rationale and intent of feeding policies to parents and offer additional references and support materials. If the parent's choices are still not in line with current research evidence, ask them to talk to their pediatrician. If parents continue a practice that is dangerous, consult the center director.

Bottle Warming/Microwave. There has been at least one reported case where a mother put formula into a disposable plastic liner of a baby bottle, sealed the bottle with the rubber nipple, and microwaved it for 1 minute. She removed the bottle from the oven and a few seconds later the liner exploded, resulting in burns to the infant's abdomen and thigh [32]. The bottle stayed cool while the milk was super heated and steam build-up caused the explosion. The American Academy of Family Physicians warns against using the microwave due to uneven heating and the severe burns caused by hot spots.

Many babies will accept formula or breast milk without it being warm. In addition, heating expressed breast milk may compromise its protective properties. But, if desired, the best way to warm a bottle is to simply take the chill off of the bottle by placing it in a container of warm water and letting it stand for a few minutes reaching a lukewarm—not very warm at all—temperature.

Safety and Sanitation. Most large centers will be required to use only cleaned and disinfected bottles and nipples washed in a dishwasher or boiled for 5 minutes prior to filling [29]. However, it is advisable to sterilize all bottles if many of the children in the home or center are suffering from acute infections.

When bottle feeding infants, avoid certain practices. The center director can evaluate the daily routine and check to see that all staff are aware of unsafe practices and follow the established feeding policy. Box 3.2 lists the top ten bottle-feeding practices to avoid.

Box 3.2 Top ten common bottle-feeding practices to avoid	
Bottle-feeding practices to avoid	Rationale
1. Heating bottle in the microwave	Burns
2. Using warm tap water	Lead exposure
3. Putting baby to bed with the bottle	Tooth decay
4. Not keeping filled bottles cold	Bacterial growth
5. Over-diluting formula or over-concentrating formula	Inadequate nutrition
6. Not sterilizing bottles and nipples	Cross-contamination
7. Not verifying the source of water as free of contaminants	Exposure to toxins
8. Adding cereal to the formula bottle, without doctor's note	Ignores developmental needs
9. Adding sweeteners to the formula bottle	May introduce harmful bacteria
10. Not holding the infant for each feeding	Choking risk, extended bottle use

Source: Data compiled from Fein, S. B., and Falci, C.D. (1999). Infant Formula Preparation, Handling, and Related Practices in the United States. *Journal of American Dietetic Association, 99* (10), 1234–1248.

PROMOTING HEALTHFUL EATING BEHAVIORS

Feeding babies has become a well-researched science. More than 20 years ago, Ellyn Satter empowered mothers by proposing a division of responsibility in the child-feeding relationship. Mothers were encouraged to abandon rigid feeding schedules and, instead, listen to their babies and allow them to regulate their own eating.

> *The parents are responsible for the* what, when, *and* where of feeding, *and children are responsible for the* how much *and* whether of eating.

> Ellyn Satter [33]

Since then, this feeding principle has been at the center of researching the feeding relationship. In addition, the health community, government agencies, and the medical community have adopted this principle into their feeding advice [16, 34]. In particular, the National Resource Center for Health and Safety in Child Care has recognized feeding as a relationship and encouraged the dropping of rigid feeding schedules in favor of baby-led feeding that responds to infants' nutritional and emotional needs [29].

The division of responsibility is the underlying principle in feeding infants. You must accept the fact that babies know how much to eat and when to stop. You must learn to read their signals or "cues" correctly so that you can respond appropriately. This will allow the child to take in the right amount of nourishment to accommodate growth spurts, increased appetite, or a change in activity level. Table 3.3 is a guide to reading baby's cues.

Table 3.3   How to read a baby like a book*

"I am hungry"	"I am terribly hungry"	"I am full"	"Too much food, already!"	"I am tired but still hungry"
Awake and alert Eye blinking Turns head to breastfeeding position Moving arms and hands toward mouth	Scooting Lip-smacking noises Crying Fussing Turning from side to side	Turns head away from nipple Pushes bottle away Relaxes body like rag doll, limp body posture Arms, if gently tugged, will fall away from body Open fists Relaxed, sleepy state, falls away from nipple	Pushes away from nipple Fusses, cries Arches back	Falls asleep but still holds on to nipple Fists clenched, arms flexed, pulled in close to body, but asleep; if arm gently tugged away from body, it will spring back to flexed position. (Expect this baby to be ready to feed again after a short rest)

*These are some cues that may indicate stages of hunger and satiety for young infants. Keep in mind that babies are individuals and they may have their own unique signals, too.

Before discussing what to feed infants, stop and emphasize the value of the feeding relationship. The feeding relationship begins with *how* nourishment is offered, not *what*. Do not underestimate your influence as a role model to parents. If you follow these recommendations, parents will witness your success in feeding and, in turn, they will adopt your techniques at home.

Bottle Feeding.   When it is time to feed babies for the first time, remember you are building a relationship and must be open to reading individual feeding cues. Feed the bottle like a breast and begin by using a close supportive hold and focusing attention on the baby. Now, after getting comfortable and identifying hunger cues, offer hungry babies their bottle by lightly touching their lips with the nipple and waiting for them to open up their mouth and "invite" you to put in the nipple. Do not force any uninvited food past their lips! Don't jiggle the bottle or shove it their mouth; you must be patient and allow babies to lead the way. Feeding should provide not only food, but also a feeling of trust, security, and love.

To take a break in feeding, look for a pause in swallowing or signals of satiety, such as turning away from the bottle, to end a feeding. Breastfed infants take smaller amounts of food, so don't expect them to finish an 8-oz bottle. Also, breast milk is a precious fluid, so don't waste it: start out small. Because they practice self-regulation and they usually determine when the feeding ends, most breastfed babies will take smaller, more frequent feedings than formula-fed babies.

Check the nipple for the flow of milk: About 1 drop per second is adequate. Too little and babies will work too hard. Too fast and babies will be overwhelmed by the flow and be unable to coordinate suck and swallow.

Always hold the baby close during feeding

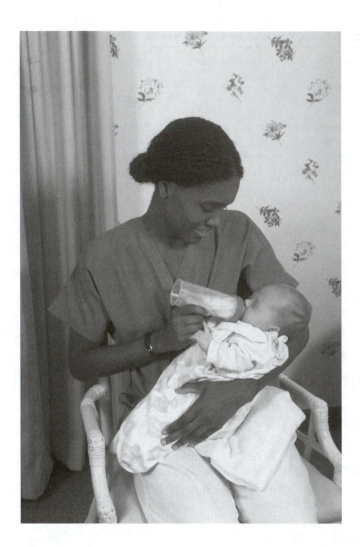

Spoon Feeding.   When babies are ready for solid foods, use a spoon and respond to an invitation to put food in their mouth. Don't press the spoon against their lips waiting for them to open up. Don't coax children to eat: It is not your job to coax them. Your job is to get to know them and respond to their individual attempt to eat and pace the feeding. Make feeding time pleasant and relaxing and avoid talking about positive or negative aspects of the food. Create a warm, supportive, and pleasant environment for the feeding relationship to develop.

Forms of Force Feeding.   Any type of feeding that does not allow infants to share control in feeding is essentially force feeding. It can take many forms. Forcing the last ounce of milk into infants' mouths is common. Propping the bottle is the practice of allowing infants, who are incapable of holding a bottle, to feed unattended.

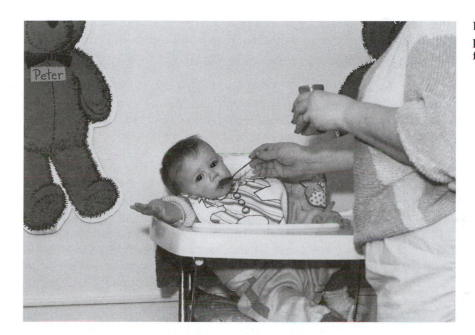

Baby signals care provider to stop feeding

The bottle is propped against a pillow or rolled blanket with the nipple placed in the mouth. However, infants are unable to stop and resume feeding as they desire. Infant feeders are bottles with large openings that allow cereals or pureed foods to pass quickly into the stomach with strong sucking. Their use is not recommended [29]. Infants are unable to gauge fullness or pace feeding with infant feeders because they suck and are expecting liquids. However, the pureed food may leave them overfull. In each of these undesirable instances, the goal has been reduced to simply getting food into the infants with the least amount of human interaction. The opportunity to communicate with each infant is lost. Each of these practices ignores infants' ability to self-regulate feeding and may lay the foundation for disordered eating or obesity.

Feeding Sensitive Babies.   Some infants are more or less sensitive to the surrounding environment when feeding. Observe the baby for signs of discomfort. Many preterm or low-birth weight infants will be sensitive babies when it comes to feeding. They likely entered this world with the unpleasant tubes and needles of an intensive care unit. These sensitive babies are becoming more common as technological advances increase their survival rates. These babies need a quiet room, soft lights, and soothing talk. Feed them in a smooth uninterrupted way. Avoid jerky movement or old techniques for keeping the baby awake such as tickling the feet, because these techniques don't work. The sensitive baby will give subtle cues, which, in time, can be recognized by consistent caregivers. For more resources on feeding preterm or low birth weight infants go to the resource Gaining and Growing: Assuring the Nutritional Care of Preterm Infants online at http://staff.washington.edu/growing/.

Cup Feeding.   Children can approximate lips to the rim of a cup by 5 months and can begin drinking from the cup by 6 months. To minimize spills put no more than 2 to 3 tablespoons in the cup.

Eating With Utensils.   At about 8 to 10 months of age, babies will be interested in using spoons for feeding. Use a spoon with a flat, wide bowl for easier scooping; a dish with sides also makes scooping easier. It is best to place a vinyl or plastic cloth underneath the high chair or to spread papers on the floor.

Solid Food

The introduction of solid food into infants' diets is often seen as a milestone to communicate to grandparents and capture on film. Many parents fall prey to the old advice that feeding the infant cereal will improve sleeping through the night or somehow make their child grow faster. There is no evidence that feeding solids early will enhance growth, reduce the number of night feedings, or make infants sleep through the night [20]. In fact, early introduction of solids may be related to increased allergies and digestive problems [35]. Indeed, for the formula-fed infants, the best time to introduce solids is most accurately determined by assessing their ability to consume foods and communicate interest or disinterest in eating. Direct parents who are anxious for their infants to begin solids to the questions in Box 3.3 to assess individual readiness for solid foods. The center should consider developing this into a handout.

First Foods.   The ideal first food to feed older infants is iron and vitamin-C–fortified rice cereal. The rice is easy to digest, the additional iron is needed at this age, and the addition of vitamin C will enhance the absorption of iron. Mix the cereal with breast milk or formula for added protein and feed with a spoon. Don't use juice to dilute the cereal because juice reduces the protein content of the total

---

Box 3.3   Developmental readiness for solid foods

My baby* is ready for solids when . . .

- He can sit up with support in an upright chair, not the 45°-angled infant feeding chair.
- She uses the muscles in her neck to hold up her head.
- He doesn't slide down in his high chair.
- She opens her mouth to anticipate a bite of food and closes it around the spoon.
- He brings fingers and toys to his mouth.
- She doesn't push out food with her tongue after I spoon it in; she can move it to the back of her mouth.
- He can turn his head away from food he doesn't want.
- She can "invite" a bite of food by opening her mouth.

*Most infants are ready for solids at about 6 months of age.

Table 3.4　Dietary Reference Intakes for selected nutrients for infants 0 to 6 months and 7 to 12 months

Daily Nutrient Needs	0–6 Months*	7–12 Months*
Estimated Energy Requirement, EER	$89 \times$ wt in kg $- 100$	$89 \times$ wt in kg $- 100$
Carbohydrate (g/d)	60	95
Fat (g/d))	31	30†
Protein (g/d)	9.1	**13.5**
Vitamin A (µg/d RE)	400	500
Vitamin D (µg/d)	5	5
Vitamin E (mg/d-TE)	4	5
Vitamin K (µg/d)	2.0	2.5
Vitamin C (mg/d)	40	50
Folate (µg/d)	65	80
Niacin (mg/d NE)	2	4
Riboflavin (mg/d)	0.3	0.4
Thiamin (mg/d)	0.2	0.3
Vitamin B_6 (mg/d)	0.1	0.3
Vitamin B_{12} (µg/d)	0.4	0.5
Calcium (mg/d)	210	270
Phosphorus (mg/d)	100	275
Iodine (µg/d)	110	130
Iron (mg/d)	0.27	**11**
Magnesium (mg/d)	30	75
Zinc (mg/d)	2	**3**

*Weight in lbs $\times$ .454 = weight in kg.

†Recommended Dietary Allowances (RDAs) are in bold type.

Source: Data compiled from *Recommended Dietary Allowances.* (1989). Washington, DC: National Academy Press. Institute of Medicine. (2002). *Dietary Reference Intakes for Energy, Carbohydrate, Fiber, Fat, Fatty Acids, Cholesterol, Protein, and Amino Acids.* Washington, DC: National Academy Press. Institute of Medicine. (1997). *Dietary Reference Intakes for Calcium, Phosphorus, Magnesium, Vitamin D, and Fluoride.* Washington, DC: National Academy Press. Institute of Medicine. (1998). *Dietary Reference Intakes for Thiamin, Riboflavin, Niacin, Vitamin B₆, Folate, Vitamin B₁₂, Pantothenic Acid, Biotin, and Choline.* Washington, DC: National Academy Press. Institute of Medicine. (2000). *Dietary Reference Intakes for Vitamin C, Vitamin E, Selenium, and Carotenoids.* Washington, DC: National Academy Press. Institute of Medicine. (2001). *Dietary Reference Intakes for Vitamin A, Vitamin K, Arsenic, Boron, Chromium, Copper, Iodine, Iron, Manganese, Molybdenum, Nickel, Silicon, Vanadium, and Zinc.* Washington, DC: National Academy Press. These reports may be accessed via http://www.nap.edu.

diet. Introduce new foods one at a time and allow several days between choices, to allow for easier identification of food sensitivities such as rashes. If a rash appears, temporarily avoid the associated food.

You may advance the food texture by varying the amount of liquid added to the cereal. It is important to progress to a lumpy texture before 10 months of age to improve acceptability of differing textures and avoid difficulty in feeding table foods [36]. As infants' skills improve, progress to soft bits of cooked vegetables, soft peeled fruit, and strained baby meats. The DRIs for infants are listed in Table 3.4;

to meet these needs chose foods that add essential nutrients during the first year such as:

- 4–6 months as appropriate: iron-and vitamin-C-fortified infant cereals (start with rice) and mix breast milk or formula, avoid wheat or high-protein cereals, use a spoon to feed a smooth consistency, and increase lumpiness by 8 months
- 6–8 months: (1) strained single-ingredient vegetables and fruits, mashed potatoes, banana, mango, and squash, (2) fruit juice* is not necessary but can be introduced in limited amounts—one 4-oz cup per day
- 7–10 months: (1) peeled soft bits of fruit or cooked vegetables, (2) "O" type cereals or wheat-free cereals for finger feeding, (3) cheese*, chopped into small soft bites, plain yogurt, (4) mashed beans/lentils, (5) small pieces or strips of bread, crackers, pita bread, tortillas, or flat breads; wheat can be introduced to nonallergic infants
- 8–9 months: introduce strained baby meats for an excellent iron source
- 9–12 months: (1) add tender chopped meats, egg yolk cooked†, and fish†, (2) may offer 4–8 oz water/24 hrs after introducing protein-rich solid foods

*Avoid using fresh cheeses such as queso fresco, unpasteurized juices, or honey due to food-borne illness risks.
†Avoid for allergic infants.

> Sometimes, parents will resist progressing in textures because they fear choking. Determine readiness to tolerate thicker textures on an individual basis. Infants who display the skills to grab a hard infant biscuit and chew or gnaw on it are ready for more challenging textures.

Infants unable to achieve this variety of intake may benefit from taking a vitamin-mineral supplement. Also, caregivers can review age-appropriate foods and discuss the feeding relationship. Difficult cases can benefit from additional counseling by a registered dietitian.

> When serving finger foods, don't be tempted to lay the food directly on a clean table; using plates will reduce risk of food-borne illness. Similarly, serve commercial baby food by removing food with a clean spoon into a clean dish; serving directly from the jar risks contamination [29].

Finger Foods. At 6 to 7 months, infants may also be ready for finger foods and will be eager to self-feed. During this time, children are open to many new flavors and picky eaters are in the minority. One positive experience with a food is enough to make it a favorite [37].

How Much Food?   The care provider may need to answer this question to determine the needs for a group, but, as stated earlier, children's intake of food will vary day to day. Table 3.5 is a general guide to food amounts. Still, breastfed infants tend to leave one-fourth of the all nonmilk foods offered to them [2, 3].

Table 3.5   **Guide to amounts of foods for infants to meet Estimated Energy Needs***

Age (months)	Average weight for age† (lbs)	Foods	Approximate Energy Provided
Up to 1	9–10	23 fl oz breast milk or iron-fortified formula	472
2 to 3	10.5–13.2	29 fl oz breast milk or iron-fortified formula	572
4 to 5	12–16	30 fl oz breast milk or iron-fortified formula	596
6 to 7	16–18.5	30 fl oz breast milk or iron-fortified formula 4 Tbsp dry baby cereal 4 Tbsp baby vegetables 1 oz baby fruit juice	668
8 to 9	18–20.2	32 fl oz breast milk or iron-fortified formula 4 Tbsp dry baby cereal 4 Tbsp baby vegetables 3 Tbsp baby fruit or 2 oz baby fruit juice 2 Tbsp strained meat or meat alternate	746
10 to 11	19.5–22	32 fl oz breast milk or iron-fortified formula 4 Tbsp dry baby cereal 6 Tbsp vegetables 4 Tbsp fruit 2 oz fruit juice 3 Tbsp strained meat or meat alternate	817
12	21–23	26 fl oz breast milk or iron-fortified formula 1/2 c dry cereal 8 Tbsp vegetables 4 Tbsp fruit 2 oz fruit juice 2 oz strained meat or meat alternate	844

*This guide is a starting point to assess dietary intake for the average child for variety and amounts of different foods. It may also be used to screen dietary intakes of infants to help identify those with excessive intakes. Growth spurts and activity levels can greatly impact requirements, and a healthy infant may eat more on one day and less on another day.

†Average weight based on 50th percentile on growth charts developed by the Centers for Disease Control and Prevention, National Center for Health Statistics. 2000. Available at http://www.cdc.gov/growthcharts/.

Source: Compiled from Institute of Medicine. (2002). *Dietary Reference Intakes for Energy, Carbohydrate, Fiber, Fat, Fatty Acids, Cholesterol, Protein, and Amino Acids.* This report may be accessed via http://www.nap.edu.

NUTRITION-RELATED HEALTH CONCERNS

During the first year infants begin to make sense of the world and, with proper care, emerge with a sense of trust, enjoyment in eating and a bonded feeling with the caregiver. By achieving oral motor and fine motor feeding skills, infants can participate in satisfying their own hunger. Establishing positive feeding relationships with children is key to a caregiver's success. When health concerns do arise they are often related to the inability to accomplish these developmental milestones (see Table 3.1). Aside from supporting breastfeeding mothers, the care provider may be confronted with questions regarding iron deficiency anemia, lactose intolerance, and food allergies. Perhaps even more common are concerns about constipation, diarrhea, and spitting up or vomiting. Nutrition plays a role in the diagnosis and management of each health concern.

Lack of Breastfeeding

The primary nutrition issue for infants is the lack of breastfeeding. Infants who are formula-fed or wean early miss out on the properties of breast milk that enhance growth, development, and disease resistance. The scientific evidence is clear: when babies are breastfed for a longer duration, their health and well-being will greatly improve [8, 38, 39]. Although the decision to breastfeed is made by parents long before the baby arrives at day care, early weaning from the breast can be postponed or completely avoided if the center creates a supportive environment as described early in this chapter.

Iron Deficiency

Iron deficiency is the most prevalent form of nutrition deficiency in this country. Infants are at an increased risk for iron deficiency due to their rapid growth and need to replenish iron stores from birth. Preterm infants are further at risk. The effects are serious. Children with iron deficiency anemia experience long-term cognitive insults, irreversible developmental delays, and behavior problems [40, 41, 31]. Children with iron deficiency without anemia also have lower test scores and mental and motor delays that may or may not be reversible [31].

Supplementation.   With clinical tests documenting blood iron below recommended levels, iron supplementation may be necessary for any infants less than 6 months of age. The tests for iron sufficiency were described at the beginning of the chapter under Laboratory Measurements. The DRI for iron for young infants, birth to 6 months of age, is .27 mg; for 7- to 12-month-old children it increases to 11 mg [21].

Iron in the Diet.   Nutrition guidelines to prevent iron deficiency include the following:

1. Prolong breastfeeding to 12 months or longer.
2. Use iron-fortified formula after weaning and for infants not breastfed.

3. Delay starting regular cow's milk until 12 months.
4. Introduce infant cereals fortified with iron and vitamin C at about 6 months of age.
5. Include iron-rich and vitamin-C-rich foods during solid food meals. For example, serve iron-fortified cereals/breads or lima beans with orange juice.
6. Give 9- to 12-month-old children iron-rich meat, fish, or poultry along with whole grains, legumes, and beans. Include a vitamin C source with iron-rich foods.

Lactose Intolerance

Lactose is the natural sugar in milk that is digested with the help of an enzyme called lactase. Breast milk has a high concentration of lactose, and full-term infants nearly always tolerate lactose well, even if they are from populations where there is a high prevalence of lactose intolerance among adults. Some mothers with fussy babies may be instructed to avoid all dairy products to reduce lactose in their milk; however, most infants will respond to elimination of cow's milk in their mothers' diets [42]. Removing all dairy products is often unnecessary. When lactose intolerance occurs in infancy, the intolerance is usually temporary, a secondary symptom of illnesses that affect the intestinal lining (mucosa), producing diarrhea. A physician should confirm lactose intolerance before treating with a lactose-free formula. It is normal for some older children to produce less of the enzyme lactase as they grow.

> Lactating mothers of potentially allergic infants can alter their diets to avoid peanuts, treenuts, fish, and shellfish. However, refer lactating mothers to a registered dietitian before they eliminate milk, egg, or entire food groups from their diet.

Food Reactions and Allergies

During the first year of life, infants may show signs of food intolerance or food allergy. Food intolerances may show up as delayed mild reactions affecting the skin, breathing, or the digestive tract. These reactions do not usually indicate a food allergy and may be due to toxins in the food or may be metabolic disorders, or may be unique to that child. True food allergies are estimated to affect about 5 to 6% of the pediatric population [35] and result in an abnormal immune system response to a food protein. The symptoms of a food allergy may include:

- swelling of the face and lips
- itchy watery eyes or skin
- hives or rash
- dry cough, shortness of breath, runny nose, wheezing
- itching of mouth, abdominal pain
- nausea, vomiting, or diarrhea
- severe life-threatening reaction accompanied by a drop in blood pressure (most often caused by peanuts and tree nuts)

Most food allergies will be outgrown within 1 to 4 years of diagnosis, and the odds of outgrowing allergies are better if the food is completely avoided. Peanut, tree nut, and fish/shellfish allergies are rarely outgrown.

Resources
- Food Allergy and Anaphylaxis Network (FAAN)
  Fairfax, Virginia
  Tel: 800-929-4040
  Website: http://foodallergy.org.

This site has many publications with information about shopping, food labels, and food preparation.
- American Dietetic Association
  Chicago, Illinois
  Tel: 800-877-1600, extension 5000
  Website: http://www.eatright.org

Infants with a family history of allergies are more susceptible to allergies. A review of recent studies recommends exclusive breastfeeding of the first 4 to 6 months, prolonged breastfeeding (1 year or longer) for these infants, delayed introduction of certain solid foods and, if formula is used, choosing an extensively hydrolyzed formula [35, 43]. Introduce single-ingredient solids by about 6 months of age. If no symptoms occur, mixed food can be tried. Avoid cow milk and dairy until 1 year of age, delay eggs until age 2, and delay peanuts, tree nuts, and fish until age 3. Following these guidelines may delay symptoms 18 to 60 months.

Allergic children do not "build up a tolerance" for allergic foods. Instead, avoid food allergens completely to avoid allergic insults. A skin test is the best way to determine if a food allergen shows a decreased reaction.

Encourage mothers of potentially allergic infants to breastfeed, because infants are rarely allergic to breast milk. Even though breast milk does contain food allergens, it is still a better choice than formula for allergic infants.

Gastrointestinal Tract Disturbances

Parents often come to care providers complaining that their children are constipated or have diarrhea. The definition, incidence, and treatment of constipation are all subjects of dispute. It is generally agreed that a hard, dry stool passed with straining characterizes constipation, not the frequency of the stool. Some babies may have a stool only three or four times a week. A daily stool is unnecessary.

When solid foods have been introduced, increasing use of whole-grain cereals, fruits, or vegetables may alleviate mild constipation. Check children's current diet, including fluid intake, and modify it with food and additional fluids. With the decreased consumption of milk, other fluids may not be sufficient to meet their needs. If repeated episodes of constipation occur, refer to a health professional and seek appropriate counseling.

Diarrhea.   Diarrhea is the passage of frequent, unformed, or watery stools. The term usually implies a change from the infant's usual stool pattern. Acute diarrhea is frequently brief in duration—1 to 4 days—and represents a problem primarily with water and electrolyte (especially sodium and potassium) balance, which can be serious in infants due to their rapid dehydration. Diarrhea accompanied by a temperature over 101°F, diarrhea accompanied by vomiting that lasts more than 24 hours, or severe diarrhea with stools more than 10 times per day with a large volume of water lost requires immediate medical attention. Always consult a physician. If the infant is dehydrated, the pediatrician will prescribe oral rehydration replacement therapy for water and electrolytes.

If infants are not severely dehydrated, attempt to feed them while treating diarrhea. However, avoid foods that have been recently added to the diet. When mild diarrhea lasts for more than 3 days, focus attention on providing adequate calories and nutrients and on maintaining water balance. Instruct mothers to consult their physician.

GER or GERD.   Spitting up, or regurgitation, is the return of small amounts of food during or immediately after eating. Also know as **gastroesophageal reflux, GER** is a common occurrence in up to 40% of healthy infants. For these infants, weight loss is not a consequence and they can be considered "happy spitters" [44]. Regurgitation peaks at about 4 months and resolves by itself around 8 to 12 months due to the development of muscle tone and the transition to a more solid diet. **Gastroesophageal reflux disease,** or **GERD,** is persistent and has negative consequences for infants. GERD infants share the same symptoms as GER infants, combined with growth failure and/or other complications. For both conditions, GER and GERD, the following conservative measures can be effective [44]:

- Don't hold the bottle too low, allowing air to be swallowed.
- Don't jiggle infants as a soothing technique.
- Avoid using the seated position after feeding.
- Lay infants on their stomach in a prone position. For sleeping in this position, consult a physician.
- Thicken infant formula, if used: 1 tablespoon rice cereal per 1 ounce of formula; feed using a bottle with cross-cut nipple.
- Avoid tight clothing.
- Evaluate every 2 months or withdraw when symptoms subside.

Refer infants who are unresponsive to conservative treatment to their physician for further evaluation. Some serious cases may need medication or surgical procedures [44].

In contrast to GER or GERD, vomiting is a more complete emptying of the stomach, especially when it occurs some time after feeding. Vomiting is common in infancy and is associated with many problems that vary widely in severity. Always consult a physician.

> Parents can be very anxious about regurgitation. Helping them identify the "happy spitter" may reduce their anxiety and improve their acceptance of this normal stage. In addition, advise parents who smoke that tobacco smoke complicates symptoms.

Early Childhood Caries

The use of a bottle as a pacifier may contribute to development of baby bottle tooth decay now referred to as Early Childhood Caries (ECC) [45]. If the disease goes undetected, it can become severe, resulting in pain, infection, growth retardation, and costly complicated treatment [46]. The condition occurs when children's teeth are exposed to carbohydrates for long periods, such as when they fall asleep with the bottle in their mouth or when children sip on a bottle or cup all day long. Sweetened drinks, fruit juices, and formula can all cause caries.

To prevent dental disease in later life, within 6 months from the appearance of the first tooth, children should have an oral health assessment [46]. The first sign of tooth decay is chalky white spots on the teeth. If noted, refer parents to their pediatrician or dentist. Parents are advised to wipe their infants' teeth and oral cavity after each feeding; however, this may be impractical for the care providers. The center can follow recommendations from the American Academy of Pediatric Dentists [47]:

> Many parents could benefit from a hands-on demonstration on infant teeth brushing from a local pediatric dentist or dental hygienist. Learning how to position children for the easiest access to their teeth and ways to gain their cooperation can prove very helpful.

- Don't allow children to fall asleep with a bottle containing milk, formula, fruit juices, or other sweet liquids. Never let children walk with a bottle in their mouth.
- Always make sure pacifiers are clean and never dip them in a sweet liquid.
- Introduce children to a cup as they approach 1 year of age. Eliminate the use of bottles soon after their first birthday.
- Notify parents of any unusual red swollen areas in their child's mouth or any dark spots on their child's tooth so that a parent can consult a dentist.

Obesity

Obesity in infancy should not be an overwhelming concern. The majority of obese infants tend to outgrow their fatness compared to older children [48]. Suggest to concerned parents of normal-weight infants that they follow the positive child feeding practices, introduce a wide variety of healthy foods, and incorporate daily physical activity as described in this chapter under Exercise and Physical Activity. Parents should also avoid passive forms of entertainment for baby, such as computers and television. Refer children with abnormal growth patterns to their pediatrician.

Colic

Colic is experienced by approximately 5 to 8% of infants. It usually shows up at 2 to 6 weeks and is characterized by fussiness, inconsolable crying, and irritability that lasts for 3 or more hours a day and 3 or more days per week. The latest research finds that most symptoms peak at 6 weeks and fade to about 1 hour a day by 3 months. Colic may be a normal part of development [49].

EXERCISE AND PHYSICAL FITNESS FOR INFANTS

The National Association for Sport and Physical Education (NASPE) indicates that exercise for infants doesn't mean baby calisthenics. It means that part of the infant's day should be spent with a care provider or parent who provides systematic opportunities for planned physical activity. These experiences should incorporate a variety of games such as peek-a-boo and pat-a-cake [50].

The National Association for the Education of Young Children suggests the following physical fitness activities for infant center care providers: If you have time, you can play physical fitness games with babies for a minute or two once or twice a day. Move the arms gently in a rhythmic pattern. Make the legs "ride a bike." Firmly holding the baby under the arms, boost the infant slightly above your face so the child can laughingly look down at you. Hold the baby under the arms in a standing position on the lap and dance the child briefly up and down.

Encourage sluggish babies, but don't force them. For example, motivate the sedentary crawler by holding an attractive toy inches in front of the child to see if the child will creep to get it. Don't tease, though, if the baby appears to be frustrated. It seems pompous to call this a "curriculum." These are the things most mothers have done for centuries. But it is part of what people trained as infant workers are shown how to do because all these activities in gentle moderation are good for babies [51]. The following movement skills were observed during a visit to an infant-at-risk program [52]:

- tumbling
- care provider exercising extremities during diaper changing
- doing pull-ups on walker
- scooting, crawling, and climbing up and down an incline board
- pushing bolster
- care providers holding babies by waist or hands, walking them around
- pushing a toy wagon
- care providers encouraging babies to reach out or crawl for objects
- playing with pop-up pets
- squeezing soft animals
- care providers and babies playing pat-a-cake before mirror
- watching overhead mobiles in cribs
- care providers placing babies on tummy, raising them up and down
- care provider and baby rolling ball while seated

Structured exercise programs in infant care centers that serve children age 6 weeks through age 1 are not necessary. An encouraging caregiver and a physical environment that permits freedom of movement and exploration are enough to help infants develop their natural abilities.

Infant interacts with care provider

POLICIES OF THE CENTER

Earlier in this chapter we introduced the concept of a feeding policy as a way to streamline safety and sanitation practices for infants. The center can further contribute to the health and well being of infants by adopting policies that promote, support, and protect breastfeeding. In addition, the policies can establish positive child-feeding practices and promote physical activity. Consider including the components listed as part of the center's policies.

- Include practices that support, promote, and protect breastfeeding.
- Train staff to recognize and be sensitive to individual feeding patterns and focus on developing a feeding relationship.
- Promote daily physical activity by encouraging the infants to achieve motor skills and develop strength for walking.
- No television or videos for infants.

SUMMARY

- Height, weight, head circumference, hemoglobin, and hematocrit, along with dietary intake, are measurements used to evaluate infants' nutritional status.
- A healthy pregnancy outcome begins with attention to health before and during pregnancy.
- Breastfeeding conveys more than nutrition to babies; its disease-fighting properties provide several layers of protection from acute and chronic dis-

ease. Consider breast milk the norm for feeding infants from birth to 12 months of age or longer.

- Exclusive breastfeeding can meet all of an infants' nutritional needs for the first 6 months of life and thereafter with breast milk and complementary foods until 1 year or longer.
- Breast milk production is stimulated by breast milk removal. Frequent nursings promote a good milk supply.
- When breast milk is unavailable, iron-fortified formula given through the first year of life can supply birth to 12-month-old children with all known essential nutrients (except fluoride) without the addition of vitamin and mineral supplements.
- Solid foods are usually introduced when children are developmentally ready to chew, usually at about 6 months of age. Breastfed infants can delay solids until after 6 months of age.
- Although weight gain is the best method to determine whether food intake meets energy and nutrient needs, examining what and when children are eating can help determine any changes needed in food intake.
- Infants can regulate their own intake, deciding whether or not to eat when offered a feeding.
- Some babies will be oversensitive to feeding.
- Use of foods, eating utensils, and the eating situation as educational tools should begin during infancy.
- Iron deficiency anemia, lactose intolerance, food allergies, GERD, and Early Childhood Caries are nutrition-related problems facing parents during their child's infancy.
- Exercise and fitness routines for infants are looked upon as activities that most mothers have done naturally for centuries.
- Policies should be written and communicated to parents by care providers.

DISCUSSION QUESTIONS

1. Do breastfed infants and bottle-fed infants grow at the same rate?
2. How does breastfeeding benefit mothers and children?
3. Name several ways you can help mothers meet their goal of exclusive breastfeeding for the first 6 months. What resources should be available at the center and in the community?
4. What supplemental needs will breastfed infants have?
5. How do mothers' health and diet before and during pregnancy and lactation affect their infants?
6. What are the consequences of introducing solid foods before 4 months of age?
7. What are sources of iron after 6 months of age? What are the consequences of iron deficiency?
8. Consider two nutrition-related problems of infancy. How might these problems be managed?

9. What can care providers do to stimulate movement activities for infants?
10. What role does the physical environment of an infant center play in infant fitness?

REFERENCES

1. Patel, D. R., Pratt, H. D., & Greydanus, D. E. (2002). Pediatric neurodevelopment and sports participation: When are children ready to play sports? *Pediatric Clinics of North America, 49*(3), 505–531, v–vi.
2. Dewey, K. G., Heinig, M. J., Nommsen, L. A., Peerson, J. M., & Lonnerdal, B. (1993). Breast-fed infants are leaner than formula-fed infants at 1 year of age: The DARLING Study. *American Journal of Clinical Nutrition, 57*(2), 140–145.
3. Dewey, K., Heinig, M., Nommsen, L., Peerson, J., & Lonnerdal, B. (1992). Growth of breast-fed and formula-fed infants from 0 to 18 months: The DARLING Study. *Pediatrics, 89*(6), 1035–1041.
4. Susser, M., & Stein, Z. (1994). Timing in prenatal nutrition: A reprise of the Dutch Famine Study. *Nutrition Review, 52*(3), 84–94.
5. Reifsnider, E., & Gill, S. L. (2000). Nutrition for the childbearing years. *Journal of Obstetric, Gynecology, Neonatal Nursing, 29*(1), 43–55.
6. National Academies' Institute of Medicine. (1990). *Nutrition during pregnancy: Weight gain and nutrient supplements.* Washington, DC: National Academy Press, Subcommittee on Nutritional Status and Weight Gain During Pregnancy, Subcommittee on Dietary Intake and Nutrient Supplements During Pregnancy, Committee on Nutritional Status During Pregnancy and Lactation, Food and Nutrition Board.
7. Labbok, M. H. (2001). Effects of breastfeeding on the mother. *Pediatric Clinics of North America, 48*(1), 143–158.
8. Lawrence, R. A. (2000). Breastfeeding: Benefits, risks and alternatives. *Current Opinion in Obstetrics and Gynecology, 12*(6), 519–524.
9. National Academies' Institute of Medicine. (1991). *Nutrition during lactation: Summary, conclusions, and recommendations.* Washington, DC: National Academy Press, Subcommittee on Nutrition During Lactation, Committee on Nutritional Status During Pregnancy and Lactation, Food and Nutrition Board, Institute of Medicine, National Academy of Sciences.
10. United States Breastfeeding Committee. (1998, January). *Working statement on breastfeeding and HIV.* Retrieved June 21, 2002, from www.usbreastfeeding.org/Breastfeeding-and-HIV.html
11. Zembo, C. T. (2002). Breastfeeding. *Obstet Gynecol Clin North Am. 29*(1), 51–76.
12. Dusdieker, L. B., Stumbo, P. J., Booth, B. M., & Wilmoth, R. N. (1990). Prolonged maternal fluid supplementation in breast-feeding. *Pediatrics, 86*(5), 737–740.
13. Newburg, D. S., & Street, J. M. (1997). Bioactive materials in human milk: Milk sugars sweeten the argument for breastfeeding. *Nutrition Today, 32*(5), 191(111).
14. American College of Obstetricians and Gynecologists (ACOG). (July 1, 2000). *ACOG issues guidelines on breastfeeding.* Retrieved January 14, 2003, from http://www.acog.org/from_home/publications/press_releases/nr07-01-00.cfm
15. American Public Health Association (APHA). (January 1, 2001). *APHA supports the health and human services blueprint for action on breastfeeding.* Retrieved January 14, 2003, from http://www.apha.org/legislative/policy/policysearch/index.cfm?fuseaction=search_results

16. American Academy of Pediatrics Work Group on Breastfeeding. (1997). Breastfeeding and the use of human milk. *Pediatrics, 100*(6), 1035–1039.

17. National Association of Pediatric Nurse Practitioners (NAPNAP). (March 2001). *NAPNAP Position statement on breastfeeding.* Retrieved January 14, 2003, from http://www.napnap.org/practice/positions/breastfeeding.html

18. Wright, A. L. (2001). The rise of breastfeeding in the United States. *Pediatric Clinics of North America, 48*(1), 1–12.

19. Spruijt-Metz, D., Lindquist, C. H., Birch, L. L., Fisher, J. O., & Goran, M. I. (2002). Relation between mothers' childfeeding practices and children's adiposity. *American Journal of Clinical Nutrition, 75*(3), 581–586.

20. Dewey, K. G. (2001). Nutrition, growth, and complementary feeding of the breastfed infant. *Pediatric Clinics of North America, 48*(1), 87–104.

21. Institute of Medicine. (2001). *Dietary Reference Intakes for vitamin A, vitamin, K, arsenic, boron, chromium, copper, iodine, iron, manganese, molybdenum, nickel, silicon, vanadium, and zinc.* Food and Nutrition Board. Washington, DC: National Academy Press.

22. Slusser, W., & Powers, N. G. (1997). Breastfeeding update 1: Immunology, nutrition, and advocacy. *Pediatric Review, 18*(4), 111–119.

23. American Academy of Pediatrics Committee on Nutrition. (1999). Iron fortification of infant formulas. *Pediatrics, 104*(1), 119–153.

24. American Academy of Pediatrics Committee on Nutrition. (1998). Soy protein-based formulas: Recommendations for use in infant feeding. *Pediatrics, 101*(1), 148–153.

25. American Academy of Pediatrics Committee on Nutrition. (2000). Hypoallergenic infant formulas. *Pediatrics, 106*(2), 346–153.

26. Lucas, B. (1999). Normal nutrition from infancy through adolescence. In P. Samour, K. Helm, & C. Lang (Eds.), *Handbook of pediatric nutrition* (pp. 99–120). Gaithersburg, MD: Aspen.

27. Carvalho, N. F., Kenney, R. D., Carrington, P. H., & Hall, D. E. (2001). Severe nutritional deficiencies in toddlers resulting from health food milk alternatives. *Pediatrics, 107*(4), e46.

28. American Academy of Pediatrics Committee on Nutrition. (2001). The use and misuse of fruit juice in pediatrics. *Pediatrics, 107*(5), 1210–1213.

29. American Academy of Pediatrics, American Public Health Assocation, and Maternal and Child Health Bureau. (2002, January). *Caring for our children: National health and safety performance standards guidelines for out-of-home child care programs.* Retrieved March 8, 2002, from http://nrc.uchsc.edu/cfoc/index.html

30. Adair, L. S. (1984). The infant's ability to self-regulate caloric intake: A case study. *Journal of the American Dietetic Association, 84*(5), 543–546.

31. Cheng, T. L. (1998). Iron deficiency anemia. *Pediatric Review, 19*(9), 321–322.

32. Puczynski, M. D., & Rademaker, E. (1983). Burn injury related to the improper use of a microwave oven. *Pediatrics, 72*(5), 714–715.

33. Satter, E. M. (1986). The feeding relationship. *Journal of the American Dietetic Association, 86*(3), 352–356.

34. American Dietetic Association. (1999). Position of the American Dietetic Association: Dietary guidance for healthy children aged 2 to 11 years. *Journal of the American Dietetic Association, 99*(1), 93–101.

35. Wood, R. (2002). *Food allergy: From recognition to prevention.* Paper presented at the John's Hopkins' Advances in Pediatrics, Baltimore, Maryland.

36. Northstone, K., Emmett, P., & Nethersole, F. (2001). The effect of age of introduction to lumpy solids on foods eaten and reported feeding difficulties at 6 and 15 months. *Journal of Human Nutrition and Dietetics, 14*(1), 43–54.

37. Birch, L. L. (1999). Development of food preferences. *Annual Review of Nutrition, 19,* 41–62.

38. Davis, M. K. (2001). Breastfeeding and chronic disease in childhood and adolescence. *Pediatric Clinics of North America, 48*(1), 125–141, ix.

39. Haller, C. A., & Simpser, E. (1999). Breastfeeding: 1999 Perspective. *Current Opinion in Pediatrics, 11*(5), 379–383.

40. Picciano, M., McBean, L. D., & Stallings, V. A. (1999). How to grow a healthy child: A conference report. *Nutrition Today, 34*(1), 6–14.

41. Halterman, J. S., Kaczorowski, J. M., Aligne, C. A., Auinger, P., & Szilagyi, P. G. (2001). Iron deficiency and cognitive achievement among school-aged children and adolescents in the United States. *Pediatrics, 107*(6), 1381–1386.

42. Vonlanthen, M. (1998). Lactose intolerance, diarrhea, and allergy. *La Leche League Breastfeeding Abstracts, 2003.*

43. Kleinman, R. E. (2000). Complementary feeding and later health. *Pediatrics, 106*(5), 1287.

44. Orenstein, S. R. (1999). Gastroesophageal reflux. *Pediatrics in Review, 20*(1), 24–27.

45. Caufield, P. W., & Griffen, A. L. (2000). Dental caries: An infectious and transmissible disease. *Pediatric Clinics of North America, 47*(5), 1001–1019, v.

46. Schafer, T. E., & Adair, S. M. (2000). Prevention of dental disease. The role of the pediatrician. *Pediatric Clinics of North America, 47*(5), 1021–1042, v–vi.

47. American Academy of Pediatric Dentistry. (January 1997). *The American Academy of Pediatric Dentistry Guidelines for Child Care Settings.* Retrieved December 2, 2002, from http://www.cd.civ/ncidod/hip/abc/facts02.htm

48. Strauss, R. S. (2002). Childhood obesity. *Pediatric Clinics of North America, 49*(1), 175–201.

49. Barr, R. G. (2002). Changing our understanding of infant colic. Arch Pediatr Adolesc Med, *156*(12), 1172–1174.

50. *NASPE releases first ever physical activity guidelines for infants and toddlers.* (February 6, 2002). Retrieved January 23, 2003, from http://apherd.org/naspe/template.cfm?template=toddlers.html

51. Ideas that work with young children: What is curriculum for infants in family day care (or elsewhere)? (1987). *Young Children 42*(5), 59.

52. Interviews and Observation: Lessie Bates Davis Neighborhood House, East St. Louis, IL.

4

The Toddler (1 to 3 Years)

LEARNING OBJECTIVES

Students will be able to:
- Describe how the physical and psychosocial characteristics of the toddler may affect eating habits.
- Describe the need for dietary guidelines for children and why dietary guidelines for Americans may not meet needs of the 1- to 2-year-old.
- State the nutrients of concern and the related food sources for the toddler.
- Describe the methods used to determine the toddler's energy, fat, and protein requirements.
- Describe the Food Guide Pyramid for children as it relates to the intake of toddlers.
- Describe the care provider's role in promoting healthful eating behaviors and creating a positive atmosphere.
- Describe the management of nutrition-related problems of the toddler.
- Describe obesity prevention strategies for toddlers.

Imagine learning for the first time that you have the power to make things happen, go where you want, and grab everything within your reach. Everything is yours and everyone is there to help you meet your needs! This is the outlook of a toddler. This new awareness of the world brings delightful surprises and anxious moments for caregivers as each new task is mastered. The newfound dexterity, during ages 1 to 3, brings the toddler closer to independence. When it comes to feeding, the desire for independence is natural and eating may become a battleground if food is forced, restricted, or used as a reward. Encouraging the toddler to verbalize hunger and satiety can help satisfy the desire for independence.

GROWTH AND DEVELOPMENT

During the toddler years, the rate of growth declines. After tripling their birth-weight by the end of the first year, toddlers will reach approximately four times their birth weight by age 2. Infants take on the appearance of young children, with an increase of 2.5 to 3.5 inches in height, exceeding the increases in weight gain. It is estimated that at 18 to 24 months for girls and 24 to 30 months for boys, about 50% of adult height has been achieved. However, increase in weight is only beginning. The median weights and heights of children from 1 to 3 years are shown in Table 4.1; the gain in weight is approximately 4.5 to 6.5 pounds per year.

Toddlers eat a variety of foods

Table 4.1   Median weights and heights* of children from 1 to 3 years

Age	Boys' Length (inches)	Girls' Length (inches)	Boys' Weight (lbs)	Girls' Weight (lbs)
12 months	29.7	29.1	22.7	20.9
18 months	32.2	31.6	25.8	24.2
24 months	34.3	33.8	28	26.7
35 months	37.4	37	31.3	30.2

*Measurement of height is taken standing.
Source: National Center for Health Statistics in collaboration with National Center for Chronic Disease Prevention and Health Promotion (CDC). (2000). Growth charts available at http://www.cdc.gov/growthcharts/.

Health Assessment

As discussed in Chapter 3, height, weight, and head circumference recorded over time are some of the best indicators of children's growth. Train staff in the appropriate techniques for measuring toddlers; a training module is available at http://www.cdc.gov/nccdphp/dnpa/growthcharts/training/modules/index.htm.

The CDC/NCHS growth charts discussed in Chapter 3 continue to be the best tool for assessing growth. Complete sets for ages 2 to 5 or 2 to 20 are available at the CDC Web site, http://www.cdc.gov/growthcharts/. Samples are in Appendix IV.

Height.   The CDC/NCHS growth charts for children from birth to 36 months are based on recumbent length and require a toddler to lie down for the measurement

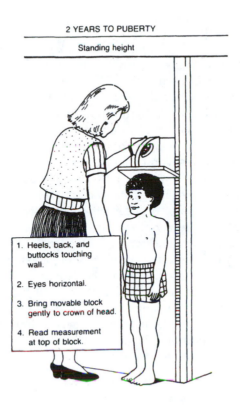

2 YEARS TO PUBERTY

Standing height

1. Heels, back, and buttocks touching wall.

2. Eyes horizontal.

3. Bring movable block gently to crown of head.

4. Read measurement at top of block.

Figure 4.1 Technique for measuring standing height
Source: Reprinted with permission from *Maternal and Child Health Program Manual,* Maternal and Child Health Branch, North Carolina Division of Health Services, 1978, Raleigh, NC.

(see Chapter 3). If children remain in the center through the preschool years, switch to the stature-for-age charts for girls or boys, 2 to 20 years, when standing height becomes routine.

Standing height (or stature) is best measured by a fixed, rather than a free-standing measuring device. Adjust the movable board to contact the top of the head (Figure 4.1). Three measurements should be taken and averaged, when possible.

Weight. Weight is best measured using a beam-balanced scale with nondetachable weights. Remove outer clothing. For serial measurements, the same amount of clothing should be worn at each measuring. Weight may be tracked on the same growth chart started at birth and until 36 months.

Head Circumference. Head circumference is an ongoing assessment of brain growth; measurement techniques were discussed in Chapter 3. Growth from 1 to 2 years is about 5 cm and then continues at 1cm/yr from age 2 to 3.

Interpreting Growth Patterns. What do the measurements, height (length), and weight mean? In referring to the weight and length areas of the chart, a series of measurements at below the 5th or above the 95th percentile should arouse some concern. Low height for age or short stature suggests long-term health insults and stunting. Weight for height, or stature, is useful in determining healthy weight.

After several measurements are taken and plotted, a growth pattern will emerge. If growth appears to: (1) falter, dropping two or more percentiles, for example, from 75% down to the 25%; (2) accelerate, for example, from 75% up to the 95%; (3) remain above the 95th percentile; or (4) linger below the 5th percentile; growth needs further evaluation. However, before making a health referral, the following factors must be taken into consideration: (1) birth weight, (2) nationality, and (3) heights and weights of biological parents. Premature or low birth weight children may take several years to catch up with the children born in the normal range for height and weight. Likewise, height and weight may be strongly influenced by the biological parents, and attention to parental body structure may help determine if the pattern of growth is actually abnormal. Nationality of children may also play a role; certain groups have longer legs and a shorter body structure, whereas others have shorter legs and a longer body structure [1].

When growth patterns fall below reference standards for weight and height during the first 3 years, children are considered to be **failure-to-thrive.** This growth failure may also be combined with a small head circumference. The causes for failure-to-thrive can be due to insults during pregnancy or an underlying medical condition causing inadequate intake, absorption, or utilization of nutrients. If there is no medical condition, it may be related to social or behavioral dysfunction resulting from any of the following:

- neglect
- poverty and family stress
- poor parent–child attachment
- inadequate social support
- inadequate physical space and resources
- economic and cultural considerations

In most cases there is a combination of medical and social factors causing the problem. The most effective treatment is family-centered therapy administered by a team of health professionals including a physician, registered dietitian, public health nurse, and therapist or social worker.

Measurement Errors.   If none of the above factors apply, a child's weight may still vary from month to month due to any of the following:

- faulty measuring equipment
- error in measurement
- recent over- or under-consumption of food
- frequent or recent acute illness (for example, upper respiratory infection or diarrhea)
- chronic illnesses

If none of these conditions exist and losses or gains continue to plot below the 5th percentile, seek a more thorough examination from a health professional. The pediatrician or health care team can help the care provider and parents plan any modification in diet.

Laboratory Measures. Laboratory measures described in Chapter 3 remain relevant and useful for toddlers. Regular screenings for iron deficiency and elevated lead levels can have a significant impact on the health and development of the children as the brain is still growing.

Clinical. Clinical observations include looking at children for a first impression and physical signs of malnutrition. Observe children at play. Healthy children will appear robust with bright eyes and expressions. Malnourished children appear apathetic, depressed, and weak, and will appear thin and somewhat wasted. The most common clinical signs of malnutrition affect the skin, eyes, hair, teeth, gums, and tongue. Look for brown spotted teeth, dull, dry hair that is easily plucked, bleeding gums, bright red colored tongue, and eye drainage. Also look for bowed legs, which may be related to vitamin D rickets, which has been on the rise in certain dark-skinned ethnic groups [2]. Refer parents of children with clinical symptoms to their physician.

Dietary. As discussed in Chapter 3, the diet should be assessed for fluoride in the water source. In addition, assess a toddlers' dietary intake for inclusion of a vitamin D source, calcium, and excessive fruit juice. Look for food behaviors that are associated with Early Childhood Caries (discussed in Chapter 3), such as prolonged use of a bottle. Now is also an ideal time to advise parents to begin regular dental checkups. Sample diet assessment forms for children are included in Appendix V.

Developmental Skills

Achieving independence becomes the main focus of toddlers. This is a time marked with increased independence, with an increased ability to express needs and respond physically in more complex and coordinated ways. The toddlers can run, jump in place, and throw a ball overhead. Fine muscle control also is developing, allowing the children to master such tasks as drinking through a straw, eating with a spoon, and attempting to eat an ice cream cone. Table 4.2 describes developmental abilities that can be expected during the toddler years. These developmental scales provide a quick reference for parents who want to ensure that their children are feeding and eating according to developmental readiness.

Having mastered hand-to-mouth coordination, children are able to feed themselves many foods. Toddlers are still curious babies, and every new object must be handled and explored, probably with the mouth as well as the hands. Any solid or liquid, including poison, becomes an item for exploration and a potential safety hazard. To further help with the process of eating, teeth erupt; the front teeth begin erupting at about 6 months of age, and the molars at about 1 year. All 20 primary (baby) teeth have usually erupted by 2 1/2 to 3 years of age. Often it is believed that children can be given foods to chew only after the teeth have erupted; however, most chewing can be done with the gums while using the cheeks for swallowing.

Table 4.2   Stages of development for toddler years*

Stage	Physical	Nutrition	Intellectual
Toddler I: 1 year	Loses subcutaneous fat. Mild lordosis and protuberant abdomen appear. Eight more teeth erupt.	Growth continues at a rapid pace (physical and brain). Appetite good with bite-size foods tolerated.	More words appear; words combined into phrases and short sentences. Thought can sometimes be substituted for action.
Toddler II: 2 years	Slow but steady gain in height and weight.	Tolerates regular foods well. Growth begins to slow with some decrease in appetite.	Perception of self as distinct from others very prominent; child very assertive.

Stage	Gross Motor	Fine Motor	Oral/Motor
Toddler I: 1 year	Climbs on and off furniture. Sits in a small chair with no lateral support. Walks well and rises to standing without assistance.	Opposition or thumb/forefinger grasp. Wrist extended and deviated to ulnar side for accurate prehension (12–14 months).	More refined cup-drinking (Stage II). Chewing. Refined spoon feeding by 2 years.
Toddler II: 2 years	Runs. Ascends and descends stairs independently. Backs self into a small chair for sitting. Squats in play. Rides and steers a tricycle well.	Gradual progression of one hand grasping with two fingers and the thumb.	By 3 years sucking through straw.

Stage	Speech and Language	Social/Behavioral
Toddler I: 1 year	13–18 months: Rapid receptive growth. Slow expressive development. 18–24 months: The naming stage. Holophrases. Jargoning. Echolalia. Two and three-word phrases.	Eats at table with family. More social and verbal. Negativism emerges.
Toddler II: 2 years	By 2 years, uses 40% sentences. Rapid syntactic development. Early-developing consonants emerge.	Temper tantrums and refusal of food common. Toilet training in process if not already completed.

*This chart provides the health professional with a standard tool for assessing feeding levels.
Source: Modified from Harvey-Smith, M., et al. (1982). *Feeding Management of a Child with a Handicap: A Guide for Professionals.* Memphis: University of Tennessee Center for the Health Sciences.

Toddlers learn to drink through straws

Psychological and Social Characteristics

Another characteristic of this period is sudden changes in mood, from the cooperative child who is a helper to the child who responds with only "No!, No!, No!". Any question beginning with "Do you want . . . " may be answered "No!," including questions regarding food and eating.

The children want and need to become independent and must demonstrate the need for autonomy by doing things alone. Erikson [3] described the situation as autonomy versus shame. Attempting to accomplish tasks beyond toddlers' ability causes frustration and feelings of shame and doubt. Children's skills may outrun judgment, forcing the caregiver to restrain children from dangerous activities. Wanting to help the care provider chop vegetables with a knife instead of breaking them, to pour water from the large rather than small container, and to mix the fruit salad

Young boys shape small portions of dough

or bread dough with a large spoon in a large bowl are examples of how children's curiosity and enthusiasm can be channeled into productive but safe activities.

Just at the time when children are mastering the eating process and when almost all foods can be given directly from the family table, toddlers show a decreased interest in eating. To add to the struggle, newly verbal and expressive toddlers can make known their desire to eat, stop eating, or refuse to eat at all. As growth slows during this period, children gain less than 1/2 pound (0.22 kg) per month as compared to 1 pound (0.45 kg) or more per month during the first 6 months of life. Activity levels will increase as children begin exploring their environment on foot, often making them too busy to stop and eat. In any case, the care provider must support children to grow as individuals and experience the social aspects of eating in a group.

Negativism will begin to fade by age three. Care providers often avoid confrontation by offering the child a choice between two equally acceptable alternatives. When talking to toddlers about acceptable mealtime behaviors try depersonalizing information to help diffuse struggles. Instead of saying " No, you can't do that!" give toddlers information they can use to control their behavior. For instance say " We sit at the table when we eat," "Food stays at the table," "The food on your plate (or spoon, fork) is not for sharing," "Pacifiers are for nap time," "We will eat again when it is snack time," and so on. These phrases give toddlers information to navigate the world.

Toddlers are making the transition from high chair to the dinner table, they can get the food into their mouth but that is no guarantee they will be neat about it! Just

Toddlers may become unenthusiastic about food

as you have discarded the bibs, they begin exploring food with hands and utensils. They also notice your reactions to their behaviors. Although it is entertaining in small doses, you must learn to ignore certain undesirable behaviors. If certain behaviors can make others laugh or draw negative attention, they will become a natural part of eating. It is best to ignore the following behaviors in toddlers:

- spitting and throwing food
- eating semi-liquid foods with their hands
- pushing food onto the floor
- behaviors which do not contribute to a positive meal time

Parents can become anxious about feeding when their babies enter this stage. They need ongoing assurance that their children are progressing normally and information about normal toddler feeding behaviors. However, if growth patterns

The division of responsibility discussed in Chapter 3 continues to be the foundation of a positive feeding relationship. The parent/caregiver offers regular nutritious meals and snacks while toddlers control the decision to eat and when to stop.

slow or exceed normal expectations, discuss concerns with parents and direct them to check with their physician and/or refer them to a registered dietitian.

RECOMMENDED ENERGY AND NUTRIENT NEEDS

As infants become toddlers the need for nutrients to support growth may decline along with the appetite; however, their activity level will increase energy needs. Also, their nutrient requirements for all nutrients except protein will increase as shown in Table 4.3.

Include nutrient-dense choices in menus with adequate calories, protein, and fat. Certain nutrients deserve additional concern because they are often found to be low in toddlers' diets. They are (in order of highest deficit) calcium, iron, vitamin A, zinc, folic acid, and vitamin B_6 [1]. In addition, children may be put at risk when their parents adopt an overzealous approach to fat reduction. This section will discuss these particular nutrients and build on the nutrition information regarding Dietary Reference Intakes (DRIs) and nutrient functions from Chapters 2 and 1, respectively.

Table 4.3   Recommended nutrient intakes for infants 7 to 12 months and toddlers ages 1 to 3

Nutrient	7–12 months	1–3 years
Estimated Energy Requirement (EER) (cal)	676, 743*	992, 1046*
Protein (g/d)	9.1	**13.5**
Fat (AMDR as % of total calories)	–	30–40
Dietary Fiber (g/d)	–	19
Calcium (mg/d)	270	500
Folate (mg/d)	80	**150**
Fluoride (mg/d)	0.5	0.7
Vitamin A (μg/RE/d, as tocopherol)	500	**300**
Vitamin B_6 mg/d	0.3	**0.5**
Vitamin C (mg/d)	50	**15**
Iron (mg/d)	**11**	7
Zinc (mg/d)	**3**	**3**

*EER based on active females followed by males ages 7 to 12 months and 1 to 2 years respectively. All other DRIs based on ages 7 to 12 and 1 to 3. For a complete listing of DRI for nutrients see Appendix III. *Source:* Data compiled from Institute of Medicine. (2002). *Dietary Reference Intakes for Energy, Carbohydrate, Fiber, Fat, Fatty Acids, Cholesterol, Protein, and Amino Acids.* Washington, DC: National Academy Press. Institute of Medicine. 1997. *Dietary Reference Intakes for Calcium, Phosphorus, Magnesium, Vitamin D, and Fluoride.* Washington, DC: National Academy Press. Institute of Medicine. 1998. *Dietary Reference Intakes for Thiamin, Riboflavin, Niacin, Vitamin B_6, Folate, Vitamin B_{12}, Pantothenic Acid, Biotin, and Choline.* Washington, DC: National Academy Press. Institute of Medicine. 2000. *Dietary Reference Intakes for Vitamin C, Vitamin E, Selenium, and Carotenoids.* Washington, DC: National Academy Press. Institute of Medicine. 2001. *Dietary Reference Intakes for Vitamin A, Vitamin K, Arsenic, Boron, Chromium, Copper, Iodine, Iron, Manganese, Molybdenum, Nickel, Silicon, Vanadium, and Zinc.* Washington, DC: National Academy Press. These reports may be accessed via http://www.nap.edu.

Recently the Institute of Medicine released DRIs for fat, protein, and carbohydrates [4] in ranges referred to as Acceptable Macronutrient Distribution Ranges (AMDR). The AMDR allow for day-to-day variations in the intake of healthy individuals and are included for the chapters addressing fat, protein, and calories for children. The new ranges avoid the very low-fat and high-carbohydrate level combinations that have been found to be detrimental to "good" cholesterol levels and allow greater variability in protein intake. No longer do recommendations assume a "one size fits all" approach. Children age 2 and older can begin a gradual transition to the recommended ranges.

Energy

Energy balance in healthy children is achieved when caloric intake and physical activity support expected growth. Any assessment of energy balance in a healthy toddler assumes a moderate physical activity level and therefore the focus is on dietary intake. A diet assessment can identify missing food groups as well as total calories. Toddlers' intake can vary greatly from day to day, so if intake is of concern, average the calories over several days.

As shown in Table 4.3, the Estimated Energy Requirement (EER) for the active 1- to 2-year-old toddlers is 992 calories per day for girls and 1046 calories per day for boys. EER for active girls and boys age 3 are 1395 and 1485 calories per day respectively [4]. Keep in mind, the energy allowance is estimated for four different activity levels. Many children may eat more or less without a loss or gain in weight. For a detailed discussion of activity levels see Chapter 2.

Fat

Fat is an essential component of a healthy diet. During infancy the almost 50% fat content supplied essential nutrients for brain growth and development. The AMDR for fat intake for children ages 1 to 3 is 30% to 40% of total calories from fat [4]. Then after age 2, the toddler can begin a gradual transition from the higher-fat diet of infancy to a more moderate intake. See Box 4.1 for steps to calculate fat grams.

Fat carries fat-soluable vitamins and is needed for ongoing brain development and growth. A fat restrictive diet not only limits growth, but makes for an unpalatable diet. From age 1 to 3 growth needs are still significant and in the normal child obesity is uncommon. Use whole milk products for 1-year-olds and through the second year of life. Then, after age 2 and until age 5, a gradual transition to lower-fat milk may begin.

Protein

The AMDR for protein intake for children 1 to 3 years is 5% to 20% of total calories or about 13 grams per day [4]. An individual

Vegan toddlers will need added sources of fat in the diet such as nut butters, ground seeds, avocados, olives, dates, and dried fruits, all carefully selected to avoid choking and allergy hazards. For a discussion of vegetarian diets and children see Chapter 5.

> **Box 4.1   Steps to calculate fat grams recommendation in a toddler's diet**
>
> For an active 3-year-old boy consuming 1485 cal/day the Acceptable Macronutrient Distribution Range (AMDR) for fat is 30% to 40% of calories.
>
> *To calculate calories from fat:*
>   Multiply 1485 cal by .40 = 594 calories fat
>   Or 1485 cal by .30 = 445 calories fat
>
> *To determine grams of fat:*
>   Divide 594 calories fat by 9 cal/gram = 66 g fat maximum
>   Or 445 calories fat by 9 cal/gram = 49 g fat minimum

calculation of the protein DRI can be determined by using 1.1 grams of protein for each kilogram of body weight. This level allows protein to be used for growth and allows for a greater intake of protein. This age group may have a more difficult time meeting protein standards due to the need for good chewing skills, and if they follow a strict diet due to food allergies or family practices such as vegetarianism.

The recommended amount of protein can be obtained from 2 cups (16 oz) of milk (8 g protein per cup) or 2 oz of meat (7 g protein per 1 oz). In a vegetarian diet 1/2 cup of beans and 2 tablespoons of peanut butter provide a similar amount of protein. Both estimates exclude the protein in vegetables and bread. Most children will not have difficulty obtaining enough protein.

Carbohydrates

Carbohydrates should comprise about 45% to 65% of total calories or about 130 g/day. This AMDR range for carbohydrates must be balanced with AMDRs for protein and fat [4]. Whole grains, fruits, vegetables, and beans provide complex carbohydrates. Simple carbohydrates from added sugars, such as those added to soft drinks, fruit drinks, sweetened foods, or candy should not exceed 25% of total calories. Natural sugars found in fruit and milk are not a concern. See Box 4.2 to calculate grams of added sugars.

Dietary Fiber

After age 3, include a consistent source of fiber in children's diets. Dietary fiber has a positive effect on blood glucose levels and cholesterol levels. It also reduces the risk of coronary heart disease [5]. Increase fiber gradually and accompany with an increase in water or other liquid to avoid distress from too much fiber. A high-fiber diet is usually low-fat. The DRI for fiber is 19 g/d for ages 1 to 3 [4].

Average toddlers gets about 11 g fiber per day [6]. Increase fiber by adding fiber-rich whole grains, bran, whole fruits, dried beans and peas, nut butters,

---

Box 4.2   Steps to calculate grams of added sugar in a toddler's diet

---

For a two-year-old consuming 1046 calories, calories from added sugars should not account for more than 261 calories or 65 grams, or 25% of total calories.

To calculate calories from simple carbohydrates:
Multiply 1046 total calories per day by .25 = 261 calories from added sugar

To determine grams of sugar:
Divide 261 by 4 calories/gram = 65 grams or approximately 2 teaspoons
   (30 gm = about 1 teaspoon of sugar)

---

and vegetables to the diet. Read labels when choosing baked goods and cereals and opt for choices with more fiber per serving. Fiber can be added to home-baked foods by substituting bran, wheat flour, or oats for some of the flour in the recipe.

Calcium

With the development of bones and teeth, calcium becomes crucial. The DRI for calcium in toddlers is 500 mg daily [7]. An 8-oz cup of milk contains approximately 300 mg calcium and is a great start toward meeting the requirement when combined with other foods. For the breastfed toddler, breast milk will supply about 46% of the calcium needs [8], so an addition of two 4-oz servings of milk with meals will meet calcium needs.

Milk, breast milk, and milk products are the main sources of calcium for toddlers, but other sources include dried beans and dark green vegetables. Table 4.4 provides calcium equivalents. It becomes obvious that milk is by far the best source of calcium. Children who do not drink milk will need calcium-containing foods daily. However don't assume that a calcium-fortified juice, or a health food alternative, can take the place of milk, which also provides toddlers with a significant amount of protein and vitamin D. A wide variety of dairy foods can be used in the center to encourage adequate calcium intake.

Iron

Infants use iron stored prior to birth during the first months of life. By age 1, iron stores may be low, particularly if children are given whole milk before 12 months of age or if iron-rich foods were not introduced at 6 months. Recommendations for meeting iron needs before iron stores are depleted are intended to rebuild iron reserves before iron deficiency. Continue to offer iron-rich foods, such as iron-fortified cereals, to toddlers.

Other important iron sources include meat, green vegetables, and enriched or whole-grain products. If meat, fish, or poultry is eaten with vegetables, the absorption

Table 4.4   Calcium equivalents to meet DRI of 500 mg/day

301–500 mg calcium per serving

Evaporated milk, 3/4 c	Orange juice fortified with vitamin C, 1 c
Plain yogurt, low fat, 1 c	Cheese enchilada, 1
Sardines, with bones, 3 oz	Ricotta cheese, part skim, 1/2 c
Fruit yogurt, low fat, 1 c	Pizza, 1/4 of 14″ pie

200–300 mg calcium per serving

Skim milk, 1 c	Chocolate milk, 1 c
Buttermilk, 1 c	Nachos and cheese, 2 oz
Cheese Swiss, 1 oz	Cereal enriched calcium, 1 c
Milk, 2%, 1 c	Cheese cheddar, 1 oz
Soy milk, 1 c*	Soy beans, green 1 c

100–199 mg calcium per serving

Cheese, American process, 1 oz	Soy beans, cooked, 1 c
Cheese, cottage, low fat, 1/2 c	Tofu, processed with calcium sulfate, 4 oz
Macaroni and cheese, 1/2 c	Navy beans, cooked, 1 c
Taco, beef, 1	Great northern beans, cooked, 1 c
Cheeseburger, 1 small	Turnip greens, 1/2 c
Cheese food American, 1 oz	Spinach greens, 1/2 c
Salmon, red with bones, 3 oz	Spaghetti with meatballs and tomato sauce, 1 c
Collards, 1/2 c	Pancakes, 1″–4″ diameter
Pork and beans, 1 c	Baked beans, 1 c
Chick peas, cooked, 1 c	

50–99 mg calcium per serving

Shrimp, canned, 3 oz	Corn bread, 2 1/2 square
Almonds, 1/4 c	Meatloaf, 3 oz
Tortilla, corn, 6″	Brazil nuts, 1/4 c

*Recently soy milks have been fortified with calcium—check labels for 250–300 mg to replace cow's milk.
Source: Based on USDA National Nutrient Database for Standard Reference, Release 15 (August 2002).

Iron and the Vegetarian Diet

A vegetarian diet tends to be high in fiber, and this excessive bulk may interfere with iron absorption. In addition, toddlers are challenged to obtain adequate calories from bulky foods. Vegan toddlers should be weighed and measured routinely to assure adequate weight gain. In addition, iron levels should be checked at least every 6 months. For a discussion regarding the safety of vegetarian diets see Chapter 5.

of iron from the vegetables is enhanced. Consumption of foods high in vitamin C along with iron-rich foods will also help the body absorb iron.

Toddlers requires 7 mg of iron daily [9, 10]. Table 4.5 indicates the quantities of certain foods that children would have to eat to obtain from 1 to 5 mg of iron. Note that only small quantities of formula and infant cereal are required to supply 7 mg of iron.

Table 4.5   Approximate iron equivalents of selected foods

Foods	Iron (1 mg)	Iron (5 mg)
Meat and Meat Alternatives		
Beans, dry (cooked)	>3 Tbsp	1 c
Beef round steak	1.0 oz	5.0 oz
Black walnuts	> 1/4 c	1 1/3 c
Cashews	>3 Tbsp	1 c
Egg yolk, medium	1 1/4 egg yolks	6 1/4 egg yolks
Lentils, dry (cooked)	1/4 c	1 1/4 c
Liver, beef	<1/2 oz	2 oz
Liver, pork	<1/4 oz	<1 oz
Osyters (raw)	1 medium	5 medium
Peanuts, roasted	1/3 c	1 1/2 c
Peas, dry (cooked)	5 Tbsp	>1 1/2 c
Pecans	1/3 c	1 1/2 c
Pork loin chops	1.0 oz	5.0 oz
Tofu, soft	365 oz	16 oz
Bread and Cereals		
Enriched cream of wheat, cooked	1 Tbsp	1/3 c
Enriched bread	1 1/2 slices	7 1/2 slices
Infant cereal (dry)	3/4 to 1 Tbsp	4 to 5 Tbsp
Iron-rich formula	1/3 c	1 1/2 c
Oatmeal (cooked)	2/3 c	3 1/2 c
Ready-to-eat cereal, iron enriched	>2 1/2 tsp	4 1/2 Tbsp
Wheat germ	2 Tbsp	1/2 c + 2 Tbsp
Whole wheat bread	1 1/4 slices	6 1/4 slices
Pasta, enriched	1/2 c	2 1/2 c
Fruits and Vegetables		
Asparagus (canned)	2 1/2 spears	13 spears
Dried apricots	5 medium halves	25 medium halves
Dried prunes	3	15
Oranges, small	2	10
Raisins	3 Tbsp	1 c
Spinach (cooked)	1/4 c	1 1/4 c
Potato (baked)	3/4 c small	3 1/3 small

Source: Based on USDA National Nutrient Database for Standard Reference, Release 15 (August 2002).

Zinc

Zinc is needed for normal growth, bone mineralization, and energy metabolism. Diets with adequate animal protein often contain adequate zinc, which is found in meats. In addition, pumpkins seeds, almonds, peanuts, wheat germ, legumes, and whole-grain cereals provide moderate amounts of zinc. The DRI for zinc is 3 mg/day for children ages 1 to 3 [9, 10]. Two ounces of meat provides 3 to 6 mg zinc. Adding 3 servings of milk and several whole-grain choices will easily provide the 3 mg/day requirement.

Fluoride

Children younger than 3 years of age do not need supplemental fluoride if (1) they brush their teeth and (2) fluoride is present in the drinking water. If fluoride is not present in the water at home or in the center, the child's parents should consult the pediatrician or dentist for recommendations on supplementation. Children are prone to swallow much of the toothpaste used in brushing their teeth. If they brush more than twice a day, this may be at least 1 to 3 mg compared to the adequate intake of .7 mg/day [7].

Vitamin A

Vitamin A is needed for vision, growth of bones, teeth, and skin, and to maintain a healthy immune system. The DRI for vitamin A is 300 μg RE [10] and should be easily obtained from the diet if children continue to breastfeed or eat a wide variety of foods including green and yellow vegetables such as carrots or spinach, fortified margarine, butter, and other fortified dairy products.

Vitamin B_6

Vitamin B_6 is another vitamin closely linked to meat sources as it is stored in the muscle of animals. Whole grains will also provide a moderate amount. Vitamin B_6 is required for carbohydrate, fat, and protein metabolism and plays an important role in synthesis of hemoglobin that carries oxygen in red blood cells. Children ages 1 to 3 will need .5 mg/day [11].

Folate

Folate is essential for DNA synthesis, new cell formation, and normal growth. The DRI for children ages 1 to 3 is 150 μg /day [11]. Folate is found in dark green leafy vegetables, wheat germ, sunflower seeds, cabbage, orange juice, and legumes. Folate-enriched breads and cereals are also an excellent source. Eggs and oranges also provide moderate amounts.

Vitamin C

A balance of all nutrients is important, and a daily source of vitamin C (ascorbic acid) is recommended. The DRI for vitamin C is 15 mg, and is supplied by less than 4 ounces (1/2 cup) of orange or grapefruit juice or foods rich in vitamin C [12].

Supplementation

The toddler's decreased interest in food may lead some parents to consider using a vitamin/mineral supplement. In reality, it is a natural development of this period. By the time the child reaches 1 year of age, an adequate diet can be obtained if a variety of healthy foods are offered. It is generally believed that if the child receives sufficient nourishment from foods, vitamin and mineral supplementation is unnecessary. No particular benefit is seen from a multivitamin and mineral preparation for healthy toddlers. For a complete discussion of supplementation, see Chapter 5.

FOOD NEEDS

Although knowing individual nutrient requirements is important, there is a convenient way to ensure a healthy diet that meets nutrient requirements; the tool used is the Food Guide Pyramid. The Food Guide Pyramid for Young Children, Figure 4.2, was introduced in Chapter 2 and is designed to promote healthy eating and activity in young children ages 2 to 6. The message emphasizes balancing food intake from all food groups with physical activity. Parents and caregivers should rely on the Food Guide Pyramid for Young Children to direct them to healthful food choices and avoid extremes. Table 4.6 specifies the recommended food intake in each food group with average serving sizes for the toddler years. These serving sizes have been derived from the authors observing children eating in day-care and preschool centers.

Using this guide and the Child Care Food Program guidelines (Chapter 7), care providers and parents can plan nutritious meals that meet national recommendations. Additional tips for using the Food Guide Pyramid are available from the USDA at http://www.usda.gov/cnpp or call (202) 512-1800 and ask for pamphlet number 001-000-04665-9.

Grain Group

Six servings from the grain group will provide sugars and starches in the form of carbohydrates, which is used for quick energy in the body and brain. The healthiest choices are enriched, whole grain, contain fiber, and are prepared with little or no added fat or sugar. Nutrient-dense choices include whole grains and are fortified with at least 1 g fiber per serving. Nutrient labels should be compared to select the best choices and incorporate them as staples in the diet.

Choices that tend to be high in fat or simple sugars are cookies, crackers, muffins, doughnuts, cereal bars, granola, pancakes, and french toast sticks. When buying these products, check the label for products that obtain less than 50% of energy from fat or contain minimal amounts of sugar (6–10g or less per ounce for bread products). More and more of these products are becoming available in higher fiber, lower fat, whole-grain versions. Also consider that refined white products, although they may be low in fat and sugar and enriched with B vitamins, are devoid of fiber and trace elements found in whole grains. Rely on more nutrient-dense high-fiber choices for routine foods.

The easiest foods to chew and the easiest to abuse may be from the bread and cereal group. Although children need diets high in carbohydrates, many refined grain

> **High-iron cereals**
>
> If high-iron cereal becomes the only food eaten by a child there is a chance of excessive iron intake. A 1-ounce serving of ready-to-eat iron-fortified cereal may contain as much as 18 mg of iron. This amount exceeds the iron DRI recommendation of 7 mg/d for ages 1–3 years.

FOOD Guide PYRAMID

for Young Children

A Daily Guide for 2- to 6-Year-Olds

Fats & Sweets — Eat LESS

MILK Group — 2 servings

MEAT Group — 2 servings

VEGETABLE Group — 3 servings

FRUIT Group — 2 servings

GRAIN Group — 6 servings

U.S. DEPARTMENT OF AGRICULTURE
CENTER FOR NUTRITION POLICY AND PROMOTION

U.S. Department of Agriculture
Center for Nutrition Policy and Promotion
March 1999
Program Aid 1650

USDA is an equal opportunity provider and employer.

FOOD IS FUN and learning about food is fun, too. Eating foods from the Food Guide Pyramid and being physically active will help you grow healthy and strong.

WHAT COUNTS AS ONE SERVING?

GRAIN GROUP
1 slice of bread
½ cup of cooked rice or pasta
½ cup of cooked cereal
1 ounce of ready-to-eat cereal

VEGETABLE GROUP
½ cup of chopped raw or cooked vegetables
1 cup of raw leafy vegetables

FRUIT GROUP
1 piece of fruit or melon wedge
¾ cup of juice
½ cup of canned fruit
¼ cup of dried fruit

MILK GROUP
1 cup of milk or yogurt
2 ounces of cheese

MEAT GROUP
2 to 3 ounces of cooked lean meat, poultry, or fish.
½ cup of cooked dry beans, or 1 egg counts as 1 ounce of lean meat. 2 tablespoons of peanut butter count as 1 ounce of meat.

FATS AND SWEETS
Limit calories from these.

Four- to 6-year-olds can eat these serving sizes. Offer 2- to 3-year-olds less, except for milk. Two- to 6-year-old children need a total of 2 servings from the milk group each day.

EAT a variety of FOODS AND ENJOY!

Figure 4.2   Food Guide Pyramid for Young Children
Source: U.S. Department of Agriculture Center for Nutrition Policy and Promotion. (January 2000). Program Aid 1652.

Table 4.6   Recommended food intake with older toddler servings based on the Food Guide Pyramid for Young Children*

Food Group	Servings Per Day§	Suggested Serving Size (1 up to 2y)†	Suggested Serving Size (2 up to 3y)‡
Vegetable Group	3	1Tbsp–1/4 c	2Tbsp–1/2 c
Green vegetables	(1)		
Other vegetables	(2)		
Fruit Group	2	1/4 c	1/2 c
Vitamin C source	(1)		
Grain Group	6	1/2 slice	1/2 slice
Bread			
Ready-to-eat cereals, enriched, whole grain			
Cooked cereals: macaroni, pasta, rice		1/4 c, 1/3 oz	1/4 c, 1/3 oz
Milk Group	2	1/2 c	3/4 c
Milk: whole, 2% 1%, 1/2%		(whole milk)	(2% ok)
Cheese (1.5 oz = 1 c milk)			
Meat Group	2	1 oz	1 1/2 oz
Lean meat, fish, poultry, eggs, nut butters (peanut, soynut), nuts (as appropriate)	(2–3 /week)	2 Tbsp (no nuts)	3 Tbsp
Cooked dried beans/peas	(1–2)	1/4c	1/4 c
Fats and Sweets	3 (age 1–2)	1 tsp	
Butter, margarine, oils, mayonnaise	Use Sparingly		1 tsp, small amounts
Soft drinks	(> 2 y)		
Candy, desserts, jelly, sugar			

*Serving sizes based on CACFP meal pattern in Table 7.2.
†Do not limit fat in children under 2, Food Guide Pyramid does not apply.
‡Food Guide Pyramid for Children begins at age 2.
§Allow a minimum serving of 1 Tbsp/year of age for cooked fruits, vegetables, cereals, and pasta until children reach 1/2 c portion size. Additional servings of food may be needed to meet energy requirements of some children.

products come with 50% of energy from fat and excessive amounts of sugar. It is difficult for a care provider to justify these as grain products for use in the center. Figure 4.3 is a guide to reading the food labels to select nutrient-dense cereals, and is based on the nutrient profile of the following nutrient-dense cereals:

- Multi–Bran Chex
- Multigrain Cheerios
- Low Fat Granola without Raisins
- Wheaties
- Shredded Wheat Miniatures
- Raisin Squares Mini-Wheats
- Strawberry Mini-Wheats
- Grapenuts Flakes
- Quaker Oatmeal Squares

Nutrition Facts	Cereals
Serving Size:	1/2 c, 30–50 g
Amount per Serving **Calories**	60–150
Total Carbohydrate **Dietary Fiber** **Sugars*** **Protein**	1–5 <6 g 1–4
Vitamins and Minerals **Iron** **Folate** **Others**	25% daily value 25% of daily value *Look for several vitamins or other minerals at 25% of daily value.*

Figure 4.3   Food label guide for choosing nutrient-dense cereals
*Food choices with greater amounts of sugar than suggested will be more calorie-dense and usually have a lower nutrient density. Use these foods less often and in smaller amounts. When food choices have added fruit or dried fruit to the product expect 5–10 more grams of sugar. Some processed grain products may be fortified to appear more nutritious but they usually do not have more than 1 g fiber per serving. Use these foods less often and in smaller amounts.
Source: Nutrient-dense foods were identified using the USDA National Nutrient Database for Standard Reference, Release 15 (August 2002), and defined by the author.

Cereal grain bars, animal shaped crackers, granola bars, and french toast sticks have found their way onto children's menus. Many of these choices are calorie dense, promote tooth decay, and cannot be relied upon for providing the major nutrients targeted in this food group. It is best to use these items sparingly.

Fruit Group and Vegetable Group

Five servings of fruits and vegetables are the minimum recommended each day. Fruits and vegetables provide the majority of vitamin C and vitamin A in the diet. This group also contributes significant amounts of magnesium and fiber to the diet.

Parents and care providers can act as good role models by eating the recommended quantities of fruits and vegetables per day. Young children when hungry will try a variety of cooked vegetables such as carrots, green beans, and cooked dried beans; young children enjoy even stronger-flavored vegetables—turnips, broccoli, cabbage, and cauliflower. Often children will eat these foods warm or cold, especially if vegetables are not mushy and fruit is not browned. Before the meal, when children are particularly hungry, try placing a stick of cooked vegetable, warm or cold, on each child's tray instead of crackers or bread. You may be surprised to find that children readily accept these foods.

Soft, chopped, or sliced foods are preferred for this age group because they require less chewing and may be used as finger foods. This does not mean that toddlers should be given only chopped or peeled foods. Toddlers approaching the age

> **Box 4.3   Can fruits count as vegetables in a child's diet?**
>
> Children need a good source of vitamin C and vitamin A in their diet. Vitamin C can be found in citrus fruits, papayas, mangoes, peaches, watermelon, kiwi, and strawberries. Vitamin A is abundant in apricots, papayas, pomegranates, mangoes, and cantaloupes. So continue to offer a wide variety of fruits and promote vegetable consumption by eating and enjoying vegetables in front of children.
>
> This and other child nutrition issues are available online or by subscription to the USDA/ARS Children's Nutrition Research Center at http://www.bcm.tmc.edu/cnrc/consumer/archives/fv-interchangeable.htm.

of 2 can hold a piece of fruit or a cooked vegetable. Softer raw foods (such as bananas or ripe pears) may be safer cut in large pieces than small chunks because the child can hold and chew the larger piece. Children should always be closely supervised when eating.

The Food Guide Pyramid for Young Children recommends five different servings of fruits and vegetables each day. Care should be taken to include a vitamin C source daily, a vitamin A source 3 to 4 times per week, and a dark green vegetable daily, if possible. Vitamin A and C sources were reviewed in Chapter 1. To help you meet the five-a-day recommendation for babies and toddlers, the American Dietetic Association has developed specific tips for this age group at http://www.eatright.com/nfs0302.html. Also, see Box 4.3 for tips on providing nutrients from either fruits or vegetables.

Fruit juices are often seen as a great source of nutrients because they can be fortified with vitamin A, vitamin C, and calcium. They should not become a routine replacement for the use of fruit. Juice servings should be limited to 6 to 8 ounces daily. Diets that include 12 oz or more of fruit juices may compromise nutritional content and can result in abdominal pain, bloating, Early Childhood Caries, and malnutrition.

Meat Group

Most parents encourage the consumption of meats and meat products. However, meat alternates such as eggs, beans, peas, and nut butters can also provide a good protein source, especially when taken with a small amount of meat, milk, and cheese or when combined with grain (such as rice or wheat). Two meat servings, 1 oz each, are recommended.

The meat group includes red meats, poultry, fish, dry beans, eggs, and nuts. Peas and beans should be included in the diet at an early age to promote acceptance. When cooked in a soup, these foods are generally well accepted. Use caution when serving nuts, which could become lodged in a child's throat or may produce symptoms in an allergic child. Beans should be cooked until they can be mashed with a fork. Flatulence seems to be less of a problem if beans are served on a regular basis (2 to 3 times per week). It appears that there is a change in the intestinal flora with frequent use of beans. A general rule to follow is 1/4 cup of cooked beans in exchange for 1 ounce of meat.

Today we have a growing concern that some precooked meats may be contaminated with listeria. Selection and preparation of meats such as luncheon meats, hot dogs, and processed meats with regard to food-borne illness is discussed in Chapter 7. However if breaded meat or fish products are used, choose lightly breaded chicken and fish sticks (breaded) prepared in the oven. The best choices are those in which meat makes up more than 50% of the item. Most care providers choose processed meats because of their quick preparation, but read the labels carefully.

Children who are vegetarian at this age do so based on their parent's beliefs or practices. If meats and dairy products are not consumed, the diet can be nutrient deficient. Care must be taken to plan meals that meet nutrient requirements for growth and development. Some vegetarian diets can also be so high in fiber that the diet is unpalatable and caloric deficiencies develop. For a more detailed discussion of vegetarian diets see Chapter 5.

Milk Group

If the toddler is using the bottle, milk consumption may be excessive (over 3 cups per day), threatening iron intake. Recently weaned children may need a reminder to drink milk or eat foods with more calcium. Once children are on cow's milk, stay with whole milk until 24 months of age [6]. The milk group contributes calcium, protein, and many nutrients, but it contains small quantities of iron and vitamin C (see Chapter 1).

Among some toddlers, milk is consumed in large quantities at the expense of other foods, especially if a bottle is taken between meals. Water can be offered when milk intake consistently exceeds 24 ounces (3 cups or 720 ml)/day and limits consumption of other food groups. It is easy for an 18-month-old to drink a lot of milk and then be unwilling to eat other foods. However, if normal weight children consume a varied diet from all food groups it should not become a concern. Often, offering milk with meals is a good strategy for increasing milk intake; however, some religious practices prohibit milk with meals so for those children make accommodations to serve milk in an acceptable manner. Children who prefer to drink other drinks should be offered milk with meals and snacks. Dairy products such as cheese, cottage cheese, and yogurt are substitutes for milk (for calcium equivalents see Table 4.4). If dairy products are not eaten, large quantities of other calcium-containing foods must be included in the diet to ensure adequate amounts of calcium (see end of chapter for the section Lactose Intolerance). If there is allergy to cow's milk protein (see Chapter 3 for more on food allergies), try the following strategies to add calcium to the diet:

- Try flavored milks: malt, strawberry, banana, or chocolate.
- Use dairy in foods and recipes.
- If lactose intolerant try serving small portions of milk and dairy frequently with a meal or snack.
- Choose low-lactose dairy products like yogurt, aged cheeses, cheddar, Colby, Swiss, Parmesan.

Trendy dairy products and vitamin-fortified treats are marketed toward toddlers

- Try lactase drops in the milk.
- Serve calcium-fortified cereals and juices.

Dairy foods with added sugars are not recommended unless additional energy is needed. Some ice creams and puddings have small amounts of calcium compared with caloric value, and thus have limited use in the preschool menu. Yogurt products targeting children tend to be higher in sugar, containing more than 16 grams (4 tsp) in a 4-ounce serving. Manufacturers use a variety of packaging strategies aimed at children (see photo). The fun pictures, cute shapes, and easy-to-use individual serving sizes make these tempting, but don't fall prey to this. Consider these as treats—healthier than candy but still treats. Some sweetened versions may still provide more calcium per ounce than milk. Cream cheese, butter, and margarine cannot be used as milk substitutes. Two cups of milk meets the calcium allowance of 500 mg for the toddler.

Nutritional Contribution of Breast Milk

It's the lucky baby, I feel, who continues to nurse until he's two.

Child Psychiatrist Coello-Novello, US Surgeon General [13]

Why breastfeed a toddler? Breast milk promotes optimal growth and development of all body systems including the brain. Many of the benefits seem to be enhanced with increased duration of breastfeeding [14, 15]. It provides the brain and immune system with unique living factors that cannot be supplied by other foods. It lays the foundation for lifelong health and reduces the risk of chronic diseases as well as reduces the incidence and duration of common childhood illnesses [16]. As the current American Academy of Pediatrics recommendations for extended breastfeeding beyond 1 year become popular, breastfed toddlers will become more commonplace. Parents may decide to add cow's milk to the toddler's daily menu and continue to nurse at home before naps and bedtime.

Table 4.7   DRIs and contribution of breast milk in toddlers 12 to 23 months

Nutrient	DRI for 1–3 years	% From Breast Milk	% Needed From Complementary Foods
Energy (kcal/day)	1046	33	66
Protein (g/d)	13	36	64
Vitamin B_{12} (mg/d)	0.9	52	48
Vitamin C (mg/d)	15	120	0
Vitamin D (mg/d)	5.0	4.0	96
Calcium (mg/d)	500	25	75
Iron (mg/d)	7.0	1.4	99

Source: Data compiled from "Nutrition, Growth, and Complementary Feeding of the Breastfed Infant," by K. G. Dewey, (2001), *Pediatric Clinics of North America, 48*(1), 87–104. Institute of Medicine. (2002). *Dietary Reference Intakes for Energy, Carbohydrate, Fiber, Fat, Fatty Acids, Cholesterol, Protein, and Amino Acids.* Washington, DC: National Academy Press. Institute of Medicine. (1997). *Dietary Reference Intakes for Calcium, Phosphorus, Magnesium, Vitamin D, and Fluoride.* Washington, DC: National Academy Press. Institute of Medicine. (1998). *Dietary Reference Intakes for Thiamin, Riboflavin, Niacin, Vitamin B_6, Folate, Vitamin B_{12}, Pantothenic Acid, Biotin, and Choline.* Washington, DC: National Academy Press. Institute of Medicine. (2000). *Dietary Reference Intakes for Vitamin C, Vitamin E, Selenium, and Carotenoids.* Washington, DC: National Academy Press. Institute of Medicine. (2001). *Dietary Reference Intakes for Vitamin A, Vitamin K, Arsenic, Boron, Chromium, Copper, Iodine, Iron, Manganese, Molybdenum, Nickel, Silicon, Vanadium, and Zinc.* Washington, DC: National Academy Press. These reports may be accessed via http://www.nap.edu

Breast milk provides 50% or more of the nutrient needs for vitamin A, folate, B_{12}, and vitamin C [8]. Table 4.7 describes the nutrient contribution from breast milk and the need for complementary foods.

PROMOTING HEALTHFUL EATING BEHAVIORS

Beginning in infancy and continuing through the toddler stage, the development of good food habits is crucial. If given only a few selected food items, children will have a limited range of food experiences as well as a limited number of foods from which to receive the necessary nutrients.

Food jags may develop at any age, but are common with 2-year-olds. Food jags in children with autism or sensory issues need expert advice from occupational therapists and registered dietitians.

By age 2, children may show strong preferences for particular foods (food jags). Favorite foods are demanded while most or some foods may be refused. Normal toddlers may be exerting their independence, may be too busy exploring the environment, or may simply be tired and need to rest. To be successful, approach this stage with a good understanding of the "division of responsibility" introduced in Chapter 3.

The parent and care provider play a supportive role by providing nutritious food in a positive environment. As toddlers grow, the following abilities and characteristics will emerge. Toddlers will:

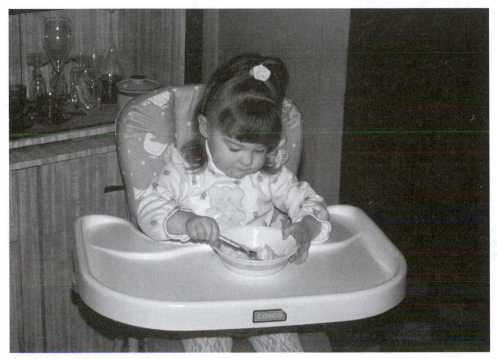

The toddler learns to eat a variety of foods

- feed themselves;
- ask for particular foods;
- show an interest in helping with food preparation and selection;
- learn to like new foods with repeated exposures (5–10 times);
- consume the right amount of food most of the time;
- develop a food preference from one positive exposure to a food;
- be influenced by family food habits and food choices;
- be happy and confident in their ability to self-feed.

Expanding Food Preferences

The effectiveness of various methods of encouraging the child to eat or try new foods has been reviewed by Birch [17] and others [18–27]. The frequency of exposure has been shown to be important at least during the toddler stage. The more a child is exposed to a food, the more likely it is that the child will try the food. However, quality of exposure can also affect food preferences. Rewards for eating or commands to eat more do not expand food preferences. Rather, foods that are presented in a positive situation or along with a rewarding situation (for example, a birthday or holiday) tend to be preferred. Once the care provider has offered the foods and presented a positive and encouraging environment, the child should be allowed to enjoy the mealtime along with the care providers.

Food predispositions are flexible and will change over time with positive influences and repeated opportunities to taste different flavors. When a child observes parents, siblings, peers, or older children enjoying unfamiliar foods in a relaxed atmosphere they are more likely to try it. Parents and caregivers who limit their own food choices should be counseled to increase their own intake and offer unbiased introductions to a variety of foods [17]. The following child feeding practices will help increase the acceptance and variety of foods:

- Offer the child food from the menu, and let the child decide which of the offered foods she will eat and how much.
- Generate curiosity about new foods, talk about its color, size, shape, aroma, and texture while refraining from talking about how it tastes.
- Consider the child's intake over time rather than at each meal.
- Continue serving new foods at least 10 to 15 times before expecting acceptance.
- Let the child participate in food preparation when possible.
- Do not use food as a reward, bribe, or punishment.
- Support the child's efforts to taste a tiny portion of new foods, and let him ask for more.
- Serve favorite foods along with new foods since she may try a new food if it is alongside her favorites.
- Serve new foods and or less favorite foods for snack times; children may be more willing to try the foods if they are hungry and have few competing choices.
- Make trying new foods appealing by involving the child in shopping or preparing food.
- The care provider should not offer a food with plans to restrict its use.

Parental Influence

Researchers have found that toddlers who were breastfed tend to have higher food intakes [19]. It seems that mothers who breastfeed learn early on to relinquish control and allow the baby to lead the feedings. Thus they have trained themselves and the baby to respond to internal cues of hunger and satiety. In fact, the lean and tall toddlers at 18 months of age ate the most food. This can be related to a decrease in maternal control when it comes to feeding. Parental influence on the feeding relationship begins with the first feeding.

Parent–Child Feeding Practices. Some parents want to become more involved in feeding and enter feeding battlegrounds by deciding for their child how much of a food must be eaten or by making treats available but controlling amounts and restricting access. Their children will lose their ability to respond to internal cues of hunger. Figure 4.4 shows the extremes based on the amount of control exerted by the parent.

Parent controls all aspects of feeding *and* determines how much to be eaten.
Parent believes child's eating must be managed.
Parent uses food as rewards, bribes, and treats.
Parent restricts access to favored foods or unhealthy foods.
Parent prompts child to eat

Child controls menu and when to eat.
Child eats only favorite foods.
Child chooses foods and feeding times.
Parent offers no guidance regarding acceptable food choices and amounts.
Child views food as rewards, bribes, and treats.

Figure 4.4   Two extremes of parent–child feeding practices, neither of which are desirable.

Other parents will labor over their child's eating by elaborate coaxing, bribing, or limiting food choices to only favorites for fear of upsetting their child. Mealtime becomes an unpleasant chore for all involved when children are put in charge of the menu. Children in this position miss opportunities to learn about new foods. When eating is not their job they depend on their parents to make sure all foods in all places are favorites. Thus the ability to eat a variety of foods in unfamiliar settings is severely limited and becomes a burden. The parent has lost control of the menu, focusing on getting the child to eat, while the child has dictated that the menu must consist of only favorites. The feeding relationship is out of balance, and both parties have crossed the dividing line of responsibility in feeding. Parents should focus on controlling food choices, not amounts, and allow children to self-regulate food intake. This is an important feeding principle to accept, and in the end it continues to benefit children by allowing them to meet individual needs by choosing to eat or not [20].

Parents' Food Choices.   Parents' food choices for their children can reach extremes, as Figure 4.5 illustrates. Either end can be harmful, causing nutrient deficiencies, undesirable eating behaviors, and/or growth abnormalities. It is a paradox that our food system in the United States is the greatest/safest in the world but the plenty has overwhelmed families with endless choices, including calorie-dense vaguely nutritious foods (e.g., fruit chews with vitamins A, C, and E; heavily sweetened yogurt treats; low-fat pudding snacks which are low in calcium too; and fat-free, cholesterol-free cookies made with hydrogenated coconut oils). These choices are increasingly convenient to eat and direct our eating away from national health goals. On the other extreme, the marketing of health foods has frightened some parents into believing adult health foods are appropriate and better choices for their infants and children.

A review of research on child feeding practices reveals how parents and home environment impact children's eating behaviors, and in fact may be promoting

| Junk food is "regular food": high fat, high sugar, refined food products, and soda are consumed daily. | | All foods must be organic or health foods. May use inappropriate health foods not intended for young children. |

Figure 4.5   Parents' food choices

obesity [21, 22]. Highly controlling styles, characterized by a parent determining how much of certain foods should be eaten, tend to backfire leaving children unable to control their intake of those foods [23, 24]. Similarly, when a parent insists that a child eat more of a healthy food, the food becomes a less favored food and less is eaten. It's not a matter of reverse psychology. Kids need to manage the how much and whether of their eating [20, 24, 25].

This stage is a beginning of letting go for some parents; they need to realize that it is not their job to get their child to eat. Healthy toddlers will eat when hungry, stop when satisfied, and be willing to try a variety of foods. With proper encouragement, toddlers emerge from this fussy stage happy and confident with their ability to eat and satisfy hunger.

Recommend that parents consider their influence as role models for healthful eating practices. As positive role models for healthy eating and activity they can influence their children [26]. Make time for family physical activity so parents and toddlers both get their 1 hour of physical activity each day. Provide structured family meals in a calm and comforting atmosphere, ignoring unpleasant mealtime behaviors. Define acceptable mealtime behaviors. Support children's attempts to self-regulate intake. Increase variety and limit the purchase of unhealthy choices, fast foods, and soft drinks.

Care Provider's Role

The care provider's role is supportive. You do not feed the toddler; the toddler eats! Messy as it may be, this is the time to allow toddlers to become independent. Food is put on the spoon with fingers, or fingers are used in place of a spoon, even for such foods as applesauce and scalloped potatoes. Sometimes foods are just squashed or crumbled to see how they feel. Care providers can cover the floor with newspapers, an old shower curtain, or a vinyl tablecloth, which can be discarded or cleaned.

Mealtime.   As a care provider you will have many opportunities to interact with toddlers and model healthy food behaviors. Be sure to praise good behavior, good manners, and tasting new foods while avoiding praise for its health benefits. Keep personal dislikes to yourself and be positive about trying unfamiliar foods. Mealtime should not be rushed in order to "put the toddler down for a nap." If facilities and resources permit, it is ideal for the care provider to eat with the toddler while carrying on a conversation about the food and eating situation. Encouraging a toddler to try broccoli is much easier if the care provider is eating broccoli.

Imitation is still one of the best means by which children learn. Children like to imitate adults as well as other siblings. Placing the picky eater at the table next to a child who has learned to enjoy all foods often helps encourage the child to try a variety of foods. Offering the new food first, while the child is hungry, also encourages the child to become acquainted with a new food.

Schedules.   If schedules and policies permit, allow the toddlers an opportunity to help prepare food or watch you or the food service personnel prepare foods. Children will want to explore by tasting each ingredient (for example, vegetables for the soup). Involving the food service staff in educational activities often improves the acceptance of food by children and teacher and may improve the quality of food service.

Food should be given at five to six intervals throughout the day with at least 2 to 2 1/2 hours between eating periods. The number of feeding periods may vary, depending on the appetite of the child and length of stay in the center; however, calorie and nutrient consumption tends to increase when the frequency of eating increases. Food and energy intake are positively affected by allowing the toddler to eat more than three times per day.

Self-Regulation

Although children have the ability to regulate their intake of calories they do not have the ability to self-select a nutritious diet from the traditional American diet. Children will choose foods because they are desirable and associated with positive experiences, regardless of nutritional value [27]. Parents and care providers need to remain in control of the menu and provide nutrient-dense choices while encouraging children to eat as little or as much as they desire without coercion or limitations of menu items [23, 6].

Food Refusal.   What if a child does not eat? The first word of caution is to avoid punishment for refusing foods. Then review center schedules (timing of snacks/meals and playtime) so that children come to the table ready to eat. Day care presents an opportunity to provide structure, an unbiased environment, and positive role models for introducing the toddler to new and unfamiliar foods. Meals can be offered at predictable intervals, and foods can be repeatedly offered 5 to 10 times before deciding to remove them from the menu for a while.

When a child does not eat at mealtime, especially the very young child, many care providers become anxious and supplement with snacks between meals. There is nothing wrong with snacks when they are simple nutrient-dense choices from the Food Guide Pyramid. But many times the snacks do not match up nutritionally to the meal because the foods may be high fat or high sugar and they may displace more nutritious foods served at mealtime. Change your view of snacks and treat them as mini meals or a time to try new fruits and vegetables, or a time to add fiber to the diet. Avoid reliance on quick convenience snacks such as cookies, crackers, fruit (jelly) snacks, popsicles, chips, or candy.

Another technique often used when a child refuses to eat is ignoring the behavior by walking away from the "whiny" child, especially if the child is using food to get attention. A frustrated and fatigued child should be allowed to rest before eating; you then avoid a tug-of-war over food.

When the care provider is faced with a child who will not eat, there may be little the center can do but discuss the child's behavior with the family or, if available, a social service professional. The parent–child relationship at home may affect the food intake and preferences. The following list of concerns may help the care provider understand why the child won't eat. Is the child

- developmentally ready for the foods and equipment presented?
- hungry?
- exerting some independence?
- too busy, "on the go," exploring the environment?
- tired and in need of sleep more than food?
- expected to eat foods not eaten by other family members or care providers?
- using utensils, chair, and table of right size?
- served portions that are an appropriate size?
- eating enough?
- becoming ill or recovering from an illness?
- emotionally distressed from interactions at home?

Feeding Disorders.   When does a picky eater become a child with a feeding disorder? When a child's refusal to eat severely impacts his or her growth and development—the child is unable to eat sufficient calories and nutrients to maintain health and sustain appropriate growth for age. These children may appear to be falling off their growth charts or they may linger below the 5th percentile for height and/or weight for age. Feeding disorders will require physician intervention and behavioral management. For more information on feeding disorders go to the Kennedy Kreiger Institute Web site at http://www.kennedykreiger.org/ or call 1-800-554-2080.

Serving Food to the Toddler

Foods should be served in small portions, and less desired foods can be used as snacks or may be offered first while other foods cool or are being prepared; 1 tablespoon per year of age is the general rule for the serving size for cooked foods. This means 1 to 3 measuring tablespoons (15 mg), not "serving" tablespoons (Figure 4.6). Food should be 1/2 inch diameter or less to prevent choking because toddlers will occasionally swallow without chewing [6]. Additional tips are in the following list and in Chapter 7.

- Supervise children while they are eating.
- Have children sit while they are eating. Eating while running or walking may cause them to choke.

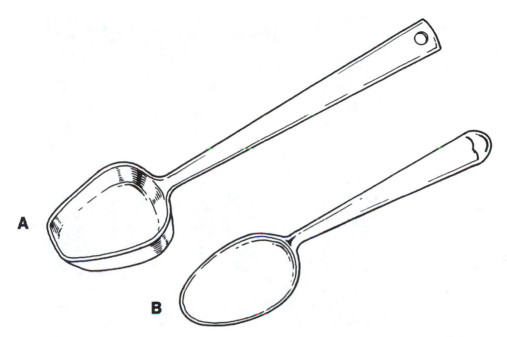

Figure 4.6   General guide for measuring serving size: 1 measuring tablespoon (A), not serving spoon (B), per year of age

- Keep things calm at meal and snack times. If the child becomes overexcited he may choke on food.
- Choking can result when children try to put too much food in their mouth at once.

Serving small quantities permits the child to ask for additional servings [6]. Milk should be given in a small cup (4 to 6 ounces) filled one-quarter to one-half full (2 to 3 ounces), limiting the amount available for spills. Keep the servings small.

Serving family style at an early age helps develop children's capacity to make choices. However, for very young toddlers the plate may need to be prepared in the kitchen because their ability to wait for other children to serve themselves is too limited. On the other hand, the young toddler may come to the serving area after food has been served onto the plate and then be allowed to serve second helpings. By 18 to 24 months children can definitely begin participating in the meal service at least by watching older children serve themselves.

Time and schedules usually run child-care centers, especially centers in which children spend only part of the day. However, the meal service should be expected to take at least 30 minutes if the care provider is using the environment as an educational tool. Discussing the eating process and the foods children are eating is important. Adults should join the table to encourage the children to engage in pleasant conversation and deter risky behavior such as fighting and feeding

Small servings of food work best for the toddler

from each others' plates, as well as activities that lead to choking. This time is also needed to practice the use of a fork and spoon. Care providers are also responsible for introducing the concept of safety while eating, by avoiding running, standing, or walking with food in the mouth, and stressing the need to sit at the table [6]. All activities surrounding food can be used to stimulate language development (Chapter 8).

Commercial Toddler Foods

Although commercially prepared toddler foods are available and convenient, these are not practical from an economic viewpoint, especially in a group-care setting. Although many are now prepared without additional salt and are nutritionally acceptable when plain vegetables and meats are used, toddlers are ready for table foods and the social aspects of eating with a group. When jarred foods are chosen over table foods, the opportunity to learn is missed. If individual baby food jars are used, food must be portioned into a separate clean dish and not spooned directly from the container to avoid contamination [6].

High-fat choices should gradually be replaced with lower fat and higher fiber choices; for a 2-year-old, switch from whole to 2% milk; for a 3-year-old, consider the following strategies:

- Offer five or more fresh fruits and vegetables daily.
- Include beans, legumes, and whole grains as a regular part of the diet.

- Replace potato chips with whole-wheat crackers, roasted potato or sweet potato slices, or whole-wheat pretzels.
- Choose lean meats such as lean cuts of pork and beef, poultry without the skin, and trim fat from meats before cooking.
- Reduce reliance on fried and processed meats; try baked or poached or grilled.
- Choose lower fat choices at fast-food restaurants such as hamburger without cheese and grilled chicken sandwiches, skip the fries or kids meals, and choose low fat milk as a drink.
- Gradually increase fiber from 8 to 19 grams a day.
- Try salsa, chutney, grated Parmesan cheese, or sweet vinagarette as an alternative to high-fat sauces, butter, and margarine.

Equipment. Choosing the right size equipment can enhance the dining atmosphere and ease the transition to independent feeding [6]. High chairs are useful for the very young, but children can quickly graduate to small tables and chairs reaching mid-chest and waist height, allowing the child's feet to touch the floor [6]. Papers may be spread on the floor to simplify cleanup.

Toddlers are ready for small flatware—spoons, (dull) knives, and forks. Choosing plates or bowls with a curved edge enables the child to push the food against the edge in filling the spoon. In case you think this is unnecessary, we suggest you try eating peas from a flat plate, left-handed (if you are right-handed). Glasses or cups with weighted bottoms help to prevent spills. Clear glasses (plastic) allow the care provider and the child to judge how much milk has been poured. Care providers should encourage toddlers to drink from a cup, use a spoon, and use their fingers to self-feed, as much as possible [6]. Young toddlers who still use a bottle for milk should be served milk from the original container poured into a clean disinfected bottle or a disposable liner [6].

NUTRITION-RELATED HEALTH CONCERNS

Obesity

The major health problems that are nutrition related and may be affected by diet during ages 1 to 3 are anemia, dental caries, food allergies, and lactose intolerance. Although obesity is a growing concern with children, the trend toward increased obesity prevalence is more common after 4 years of age, except for Mexican American girls who at ages 2 to 3 show an overweight prevalence of 10.5% [28]. Toddlers who show an early expression of obesity before the age of 2 should be referred to an pediatric obesity treatment center for further evaluation. Guidelines for individual treatment of obesity were discussed in Chapter 2.

During the toddler years prevention is the best medicine. Following the positive child feeding practices discussed earlier in this chapter will increase acceptance of a variety of foods, neutralize the feeding battleground, and empower the child to respond to internal cues of hunger and satiety. In addition, promoting daily physical activity in lieu of television or computer games and allowing a gradual transition to a lower-fat diet are the strategies we currently recommend. The following chapter will address obesity in more detail. Guidance for promoting age-appropriate physical activity is discussed at the end of Chapters 3–6. Obesity prevention strategies important for toddlers include the following:

- Breastfeed for 1 year or longer [15, 29, 30].
- Expand the variety of fruits, vegetables, and whole grains offered at home and school.
- Limit the purchase and personal use of sugar-sweetened beverages, sodas, fast foods, and fatty foods.
- Discourage the use of television for children under 2 and use wisely with 3-year-olds, limiting to 1 hour or less of educational programming per day [31, 32].
- Encourage family style meals in a pleasant atmosphere.
- Model healthful eating behaviors and use positive child feeding practices.
- Model daily physical activity and promote daily physical activity for the toddler.

Anemia

Recent national surveys estimate 13% of 1-year-olds and 5% of 2-year-olds are iron deficient [33]. Iron deficiency anemia affected 3% of 1-year-olds. Researchers have reported a decline of anemia among certain low-income infants and children [34]. The USDA's special supplemental Nutrition Program for Women, Infants and Children (WIC; see Appendix VI) through nutritious food supplements and nutrition education is widely recognized for leading this impressive trend. The consequences of iron deficiency anemia and prevention through diet are discussed in Chapter 2.

Although the incidence of anemia appears to be declining in certain groups it is still commonly seen. Some toddlers have a higher risk of anemia if they have these characteristics [33]:

- Early introduction of cow's milk before 1 year
- Those consuming a diet with few good iron sources and drinking more than 24 ounces of milk daily

Food Allergies

Food allergies were discussed in Chapter 3; however, the toddler may develop food allergies that were not present in infancy. Still, most children will outgrow their allergies to cow's milk protein, wheat, egg, and soy within 1 to 4 years of diagnosis [35]. Toddlers with food allergies face risks for malnutrition and growth failure when overly restrictive diets limit the variety of nutrients and total calories available. These children need an annual nutrition assessment and nutrition education regarding appropriate food avoidance and selection of nutritionally equivalent food substitutes [36]. Resources for families dealing with food allergies were identified in Chapter 3 and are essential for parents of children with severe allergies.

The Food Guide Pyramid can still serve as the basis for a healthy allergen-free diet. Each food to be avoided should be classified into a food group. Within each food group, eliminate the allergenic food and seek out acceptable replacements within the same food group and avoid potential cross-contamination. For instance, if there is a severe allergy to milk, the child still needs the major nutrients from milk, so protein, calcium, and phosphorus sources should be used to replace the dairy group [37].

Lactose Intolerance

Lactose, the disaccharide or carbohydrate found in milk and milk products, is broadly consumed in its natural form and in a variety of manufactured and processed products. The adequacy of lactose digestion and absorption has important implications for care providers in centers that have a predominantly nonwhite population. Throughout the world, lactose intolerance—a lack of sufficient quantities of the digestive enzyme lactase—is far more common than tolerance. Tolerance of lactose and large quantities of milk is peculiar to Northern European and white American ethnic groups; most adults in the world are lactose nondigesters. Although infants and children produce lactase and are able to digest lactose, as they reach school age, most children in the world become lactose nondigesters.

The inability to digest lactose should not be considered abnormal or a sign of illness [38]. It is equally important to recognize that lactose intolerance is not an all-or-none phenomenon. Rather, it is influenced by (1) the availability of the enzyme lactase, which can slowly decline, (2) how fast the food moves through the intestinal tract, (3) the lactose content in the food (cheese, milk, yogurt) consumed, and (4) intake of additional foods. A child may not be able to tolerate a glass of milk by itself, but after or when eating other foods, may tolerate milk well. Likewise, cheese may be tolerated when cow's milk causes gastric distress.

Lactose tolerance can be enhanced by adding lactase to predigest the milk sugar or purchasing products with added lactase. Because milk is an important food source for many vitamins, minerals, and protein, the diet must make up for these nutrients. In addition, try cured cheese and yogurt, in which much of the lactose is broken down in the fermentation process. Finally, one can substitute other foods for the calcium in milk by referring to Table 4.4 for alternate calcium sources. Supplementation with calcium may be necessary in some cases.

Early Childhood Caries

Conditions that affect the incidence of dental caries begin during the toddler years. While many common foods can produce cavities, some foods, such as aged cheddar cheese, can help decrease acid conditions and prevent caries formation. Other foods with protective actions include chocolate, licorice, and nuts [39].

Child-care centers located in areas where water is unfluoridated should alert parents whose children remain in the center all day regarding the need for supplementing the child's intake of fluoride.

The American Academy of Pediatric Dentistry Guidelines for Child Care Settings, introduced in Chapter 3, still apply. An additional recommendation for toddlers is to comfort children who want a bottle between regular feedings or during naps, with a bottle filled with cool water [40].

The center can introduce a toothbrush by 12 to 15 months when the teeth have erupted; however, individual attention to each child's teeth is difficult. As mentioned in Chapter 3, a hands-on demonstration on tooth brushing/oral hygiene can be very helpful to parents and help establish good habits in the home.

Cardiovascular Disease

The debate over the relationship of diet—including the effect of sodium, saturated fat, and cholesterol—to heart disease continues. Excessive amounts of saturated fat, cholesterol, and/or sodium may or may not affect the health of the child later in life [41]. The AAP recommends a lower-fat diet for all healthy children as a means of preventing heart disease [42]. However, the newly introduced Acceptable Macronutrient Distribution Ranges (AMDRs) advocate a safe range of fat intake for toddlers as 30 to 40% of calories. In addition, the Institute of Medicine acknowledged that a diet very high in carbohydrates combined with a very low-fat diet is not beneficial [43]. It is not appropriate for the center to restrict the very young child's intake of red meats, dairy products, and eggs. These foods provide high-quality protein, iron, calcium, and other nutrients necessary for the growth of children. A complete discussion of diet and cardiovascular disease for children after 2 years of age is included in Chapter 6.

EXERCISE AND PHYSICAL FITNESS

Concerned parents often begin pressuring care providers to provide more energy expenditure through exercise for children in this age span. This is the result of a constant barrage of fitness survey reports that are reported over and over on television and in magazines and newspapers. National studies of youth fitness over the past two decades have highlighted the importance of preventing obesity and illness in children aged 6 to 17 years. None have addressed the physical development of younger children and its importance to their overall well-being.

On February 26, 2002, The National Association for Sport and Physical Education (NASPE) released a report titled "Active Start: A Statement of Physical Activity Guidelines for Children Birth to Five Years." The guidelines recommend that toddlers should have safe places to roam indoors and outdoors and get a minimum of 30 minutes daily of well-planned, structured activities [44]. In a reaction to the report, Barbara Willer, the deputy director of the National Association for the Ed-

A toddler enjoys playing with balls

ucation of Young Children stated that "Although the guidelines emphasize the need for planned activities they don't necessarily mean that there should be a checklist of jumping jacks and other things. This should be done in the context of play and routine activities" [44].

Many parents of infants and toddlers are beginning to react by seeking out early childhood programs that offer fitness as part of their curriculums.

Over the past 27 years, a number of franchise fitness programs targeted specifically for children aged newborn through 8 years have begun. The hallmarks of the majority of the franchise programs are songs and games and stretching and climbing exercises in which children participate with one or both parents. Activities are designed to help children develop balance and coordination, and to provide other sensory stimuli while having fun in a play environment. Franchise programs usually require a nonrefundable enrollment fee and offer a variety of play programs ranging in price from $143 to $280 for 12 to 15 forty-five-minute weekly sessions.

The concerns of these parents are valid; however, again we refer you to the cautions regarding exercise programs that were given in Chapter 3.

The early childhood environment should be well stocked with climbers, large cardboard boxes, slides, barrels, large blocks, large balls, puzzles, four-wheeled toys, and push-and-pull play materials [45].

Exercise will occur naturally as the toddlers climb, crawl, pull, walk, bend, and jump. These movements will provide an abundance of exercise for all muscles. Since toddlers are excited and happy about these new movement skills, they will spend much time practicing them over and over, both indoors and out of doors.

Parents should be encouraged to participate in regular play with their children to enhance the development of their child's physical skills. Family activities allow children to see their parents as models for an active lifestyle and let children learn activities they can enjoy through life.

POLICIES THAT PROMOTE NUTRITION AND PHYSICAL FITNESS

The center caring for toddlers accepts the challenge of meeting the diverse needs of toddlers—not quite babies and not fully able to express themselves. At this stage toddlers are learning food preferences based on their experiences with eating. Center policies should promote the best child-feeding practices and incorporate daily physical activity. Consider the following policy components for centers serving toddlers:

- Provide daily opportunities for physical activity in a safe environment.
- Assure that care providers understand the importance of age-appropriate daily physical activity.
- The center's feeding policy should protect children from force-feeding, promote self-regulation of food intake, and prohibit the use of food as rewards or punishment.
- Assure that care providers understand their responsibility for modeling healthy food behaviors and participating in daily physical activity with children.
- Avoid the use of television for children under 2. Instead, promote interactive play, reading stories, singing, and talking. For children older than 2, limit total media to 1 to 2 hours or less of quality media programming [31].

PUBLIC HEALTH RESOURCES

Toddlers are eligible for government food programs that are designed to improve health and nutritional status. For a listing of programs, see Chapter 7.

SUMMARY

- The toddler, age 12 to 36 months, is growing proportionately more slowly than the infant; however, continued attention to the child's height and weight, developmental skills, and dietary intake is important.
- The toddler with a history of breastfeeding may appear leaner and taller and may exhibit a higher food intake with a keen ability to regulate his own food intake when compared to nonbreastfed counterparts.
- The care provider's task is to interest the child in food and eating when the child is hungry and to acquaint the child with a wide variety of food experiences.
- The toddler needs fat in the diet. The AMDR for fat is 30% to 40% of calories. Fat should not be restricted; rather, a gradual transition to a lower-fat diet can begin after 2 years of age. Some toddlers may still need the extra fat and calories from whole milk.
- Foods from the Food Guide Pyramid for Children should be carefully chosen to promote variety, and encourage the child to self-feed small 1/2-inch bits, using fingers and small-sized flatware. A variety of new and interesting combinations of foods along with familiar foods should be offered.
- Some nutrition-related problems develop during the toddler stage. Iron-deficiency anemia may become acute if the infant was not breastfed exclusively or given iron supplements or a diet high in iron-containing foods during the 6- to 12-month period.
- Obesity prevention should be incorporated into the toddler years. Key components include daily physical activity, encouraging children to respond to their feelings of hunger and satiety, and beginning a gradual transition to a lower-fat diet 30% to 40% of calories.
- Dental caries may develop as a result of frequent consumption of foods that contain large quantities of sticky carbohydrates, nursing bottle syndrome, or consumption of an unfluoridated water supply without the addition of fluoride supplements.
- A few toddlers who could tolerate milk during infancy may produce less lactase as they grow older and become lactose nondigesters or lactose intolerant. This is a normal trait for a significant percent of the population.
- Exercise for children during the toddler years can occur naturally as they play with care providers or parents.

DISCUSSION QUESTIONS

1. List preparation methods that could be used with specific foods to stimulate a toddler to use fingers, spoon, and fork.
2. What are some of the reasons a child will not eat? What are some examples of ways to promote healthy eating?

3. A child is anemic. How would you help the mother choose foods that would increase the iron supply in the child's diet? Suppose the child's mother requested that the child consume a vegetarian diet.

4. Many parents are concerned about the growing rate of childhood obesity. How can your center help prevent childhood obesity?

5. How can the care provider create a positive atmosphere for feeding and the development of healthful food behaviors? (What influence do parents have on feeding behaviors exhibited in their children?)

6. When choosing foods from the Food Guide Pyramid for Young Children what considerations should be made when selecting foods from the bread group or dairy group?

7. How do the energy, fat, and nutrient needs of the toddler compare with those of the infant?

8. What type of exercises occurs naturally during the toddler period?

9. What are the dangers presented by structured exercise programs for toddlers?

10. What role can care providers play in providing toddlers with an environment that fosters natural movement and growth experiences?

REFERENCES

1. Lucas, B. (1999). Normal nutrition from infancy through adolescence. In P. Samour, K. Helm, & C. Lang (Eds.), *Handbook of pediatric nutrition* (pp. 99–120). Gaithersburg, MD: Aspen.

2. Joiner, T. A., Foster, C., & Shope, T. (2000). The many faces of vitamin D deficiency rickets. *Pediatrics in Review, 21*(9), 296–302.

3. Erikson, E. H. (1963). *Childhood and society* (2nd ed.). New York: Norton.

4. National Academies' Institute of Medicine. (2002). *Dietary Reference Intakes for energy, carbohydrate, fiber, fat, fatty acids, cholesterol, protein, and amino acids (macronutrients), a Report of the Panel on Macronutrients*. Washington, DC: National Academy Press, Subcommittees on Upper Reference Levels of Nutrients and Interpretation and Uses of Dietary Reference Intakes, and the Standing Committee on the Scientific Evaluation of Dietary Reference Intakes.

5. Yu, J. N., Cunningham, J. A., Thouin, S. R., Gurvich, T., & Liu, D. (2000). Hyperlipidemia. *Primary Care, 27*(3), 541–587.

6. American Academy of Pediatrics, American Public Health Association, and Maternal and Child Health Bureau. (2002, January). *Caring for our children: National health and safety performance standards guidelines for out-of-home child care programs*. Retrieved March 8, 2002 from http://nrc.uchsc.edu/cfoc/index.html

7. Institute of Medicine. (1997). *Dietary Reference Intakes for calcium, phosphorus, magnesium, vitamin D, and fluoride.* Washington, DC: National Academy Press.

8. Dewey, K. G. (2001). Nutrition, growth, and complementary feeding of the breastfed infant. *Pediatric Clinics of North America, 48*(1), 87–104.

9. Institute of Medicine. (2001). *Dietary Reference Intakes for vitamin A, vitamin K, arsenic, boron, chromium, copper, iodine, iron, manganese, molybdenum, nickel, silicon, vanadium, and zinc.* Washington, DC: National Academy Press.

10. National Research Council, Subcommittee on the 10th Edition of the RDAs,

Food and Nutrition Board. (1989). *Recommended Dietary Allowances.* Washington, DC: National Academy Press.

11. Institute of Medicine. (1998). *Dietary Reference Intakes for thiamin, riboflavin, niacin, vitamin B_6, folate, vitamin B_{12}, pantothenic acid, biotin, and choline.* Washington, DC: National Academy Press.

12. Institute of Medicine. (2000). *Dietary Reference Intakes for vitamin C, vitamin E, selenium, and carotenoids.* Washington, DC: National Academy Press.

13. Piovanetti, Y. (2001). Breastfeeding beyond 12 months. An historical perspective. *Pediatric Clinics of North America, 48*(1), 199–206.

14. Butte. (2001). The role of breastfeeding in obesity. *Pediatric Clinics of North America, 48*(1), 189–198.

15. Raisler, J., Alexander, C., & O'Campo, P. (1999). Breast-feeding and infant illness: A dose-response relationship? *American Journal of Public Health, 89*(1), 25–30.

16. Davis, M. K. (2001). Breastfeeding and chronic disease in childhood and adolescence. *Pediatric Clinics of North America, 48*(1), 125–141, ix.

17. Birch, L. L. (1999). Development of food preferences. *Annual Review of Nutrition, 19,* 41–62.

18. Johnson, S. L. (2000). Improving preschoolers' self-regulation of energy intake. *Pediatrics, 106*(6), 1429–1435.

19. Fisher, J. O., Birch, L. L., Smiciklas-Wright, H., & Picciano, M. F. (2000). Breast-feeding through the first year predicts maternal control in feeding and subsequent toddler energy intakes. *Journal of the American Dietetic Association, 100*(6), 641–646.

20. Satter, E. (1990). The feeding relationship: Problems and interventions. *Journal of Pediatrics, 117*(2 Pt 2), S181–189.

21. Birch, L. L., & Fisher, J. O. (1998). Development of eating behaviors among children and adolescents. *Pediatrics, 101*(3), 539–549.

22. Spruijt-Metz, D., Lindquist, C. H., Birch, L. L., Fisher, J. O., & Goran, M. I. (2002). Relation between mothers' child-feeding practices and children's adiposity. *American Journal of Clinical Nutrition, 75*(3), 581–586.

23. Fisher, J. O., & Birch, L. L. (1999). Restricting access to palatable foods affects children's behavioral response, food selection, and intake. *American Journal of Clinical Nutrition, 69*(6), 1264–1272.

24. Evers, C. (1997). Empower children to develop healthful eating habits. *Journal of the American Dietetic Association, 97*(10, Suppl 2), S116.

25. Birch, L. L. (1998). Development of food acceptance patterns in the first years of life. *Proceedings of the Nutrition Society, 57*(4), 617–624.

26. Tibbs, T., Haire-Joshu, D., Schechtman, K. B., Brownson, R. C., Nanney, M. S., Houston, C., et al. (2001). The relationship between parental modeling, eating patterns, and dietary intake among African-American parents. *Journal of the American Dietetic Association, 101*(5), 535–541.

27. Birch, L. L. (1998). Psychological influences on the childhood diet. *Journal of Nutrition, 128*(2 Suppl), 407S–410S.

28. Ogden, C. L., Troiano, R. P., Briefel, R. R., Kuczmarski, R. J., Flegal, K. M., & Johnson, C. L. (1997). Prevalence of overweight among preschool children in the United States, 1971 through 1994. *Pediatrics, 99*(4), E1.

29. Armstrong, J., & Reilly, J. J. (2002). Breastfeeding and lowering the risk of childhood obesity. *Lancet, 359*(9322), 2003–2004.

30. Hediger, M. L., Overpeck, M. D., Kuczmarski, R. J., & Ruan, W. J. (2001). Association between infant breastfeeding and overweight in young children. *Jama, 285*(19), 2453–2460.

31. American Academy of Pediatrics Committee on Public Education. (2001). Children, adolescents, and television. *Pediatrics, 107*(2), 423–426.

32. Robinson, T. N. (2001). Television viewing and childhood obesity. *Pediatric Clinics of North America, 48*(4), 1017–1025.

33. Wu, A. C., Lesperance, L., & Bernstein, H. (2002). Screening for iron deficiency. *Pediatrics in Review, 23*(5), 171–178.

34. Sherry, B., Mei, Z., & Yip, R. (2001). Continuation of the decline in prevalence of anemia in low-income infants and children in five states. *Pediatrics, 107*(4), 677–682.

35. Wood, R. (2002). *Food allergy: From recognition to prevention.* Paper presented at the John's Hopkins' Advances in Pediatrics, Baltimore, MD.

36. Christie, L., Hine, R. J., Parker, J. G., & Burks, W. (2002). Food allergies in children affect nutrient intake and growth. *Journal of the American Dietetic Association, 102*(11), 1648–1651.

37. Koerner C. B., Hays, T. L. (1999). Food allergy: Current knowledge and future directions nutrition basics in food allergy. *Immunology and Allergy Clinics of North America, 19*(3).

38. Koldovsky, O. (1997). Digestive-absorptive functions in fetuses, infants, and children. In W. A. Walker & J. B. Watkins (Eds.), *Nutrition in Pediatrics* (2nd ed., pp. 234–235). Hamilton: B.C. Decker.

39. Schafer, T. E., & Adair, S. M. (2000). Prevention of dental disease. The role of the pediatrician. *Pediatric Clinics of North America, 47*(5), 1021–1042, v–vi.

40. American Academy of Pediatric Dentistry. (January 1997). *The American Academy of Pediatric Dentistry guidelines for child care settings.* Retrieved December 2, 2002, from http://www.cd.civ/ncidod/hip/abc/facts02.htm

41. Kleinman, R. E. (2000). Complementary feeding and later health. *Pediatrics, 106*(5), 1287.

42. American Academy of Pediatrics Committee on Nutrition. (1998). Cholesterol in childhood. *Pediatrics, 101*(1 Pt 1), 141–147.

43. National Academies' Institute of Medicine. (Sept. 5, 2002). *Report offers new eating and physical activity targets to reduce chronic disease risk.* Retrieved January 14, 2003, from http://www4.nationalacademies.org/news.nsf/isbn/0309085373?OpenDocument

44. Manzo, K. K. (2002). Experts map physical activity guidelines for young set. *Education Week, 21*, 22.

45. Ward, A. (1986). Born to jog: Exercise programs for preschoolers. *The Physician and Sports Medicine, 14*, 163.

5

The Preschooler (3 to 5 Years)

LEARNING OBJECTIVES

Students will be able to:

- State the physiological characteristics of the preschooler that may affect eating habits.
- Describe how BMI can be used to monitor healthy weight in preschoolers.
- State the nutrient and energy needs of the preschool child.
- Describe how you can use the Food Guide Pyramid to evaluate the diet.
- Recall what child-feeding practices the teacher or parent can employ to promote healthful eating behaviors in preschoolers.
- List acceptable snack foods from each group in the Food Pyramid Guide.
- Discuss how family and home environment influence the development of childhood obesity.
- Discuss how teachers and the school can adopt practices that help prevent obesity in children.
- Describe the vegetarian diet and its use in the preschool center.
- Describe appropriate exercise for this age group.

Parents often wonder if their energetic preschooler is "hyperactive." However, the bundled up energy is usually directed at chasing friends and physically exploring their world. The child between 3 and 5 years of age is usually a physical child. While the toddler moved around excessively, the preschooler often surpasses the toddler in activity. As new skills develop, those learned during the toddler stage become refined, and the preschooler gains sophistication in motion control. Long gone are the days when the child practiced gaining head control, upright posture, and basic abilities.

The beauty of this preschool age is that the child no longer struggles with the basics of eating and is ready to socialize. If the parents or care providers have regularly eaten with the child and the child has practiced using utensils, only the use of a knife for cutting and spreading may need refinement. Thus, this is the first real opportunity for the care provider and child to actively participate together in the food and nutrition program.

Up to now the challenges for the teacher have been to acquaint the child with a wide variety of foods modified for easy and safe consumption, and to teach the basic use of utensils. A healthy child will respond by trying many foods and counting healthy foods choices as favorites. If this is achieved before 3 years of age, any food can be used as an educational experience. However, if the child has been exposed to only a small number of foods and many foods of poor nutritional quality, the task of expanding food preferences in the child's diet will be added to the responsibilities of the nutrition program at the child-care center.

Physically, these children will want to participate in most activities in the child-care center and enjoy all types of active play. They have better balance and perception of

Care giver and preschoolers participate in use of food as a learning experience

their body, but they can't always judge the amount of effort or intensity that goes into an action [1]. Preschool children thoroughly enjoy gross motor activities, but they may throw too hard, kick and miss a ball, or fall down. As fine motor skills improve, the children can be included in preparing food, setting the table, serving the food, and cleaning up. Occasionally, going to the market can become a regular part of the children's activities. Preschool children at this point can use scissors to cut out and color pictures. These skills can be used to make placemats for the tables and can be incorporated into other activities that will make meals a special learning time. Psychosocially, these children develop initiative and eagerly explore surroundings. For preschoolers, size, form, color, shape, time, and space take on a new meaning and can be related to foods and mealtime.

WEIGHT AND STATURE

Preschool children's relative state of health influences their growth. Ordinary illnesses such as upper respiratory tract infections or the childhood diseases usually are not severe or prolonged enough to interfere with growth. Chronic, repeated, or severe illness, however, may cause preschoolers' bodies to conserve resources, and the rate of growth may slow.

Stature and weight of the preschool child should be taken on a monthly basis and recorded on charts for boys and girls ages 2 to 20 years: stature for age, weight

Table 5.1 Median weights and heights* of children ages 3 to 5

Age	Boys' Length (inches)	Girls' Length (inches)	Boys' Weight (lbs)	Girls' Weight (lbs)
3 years	37 1/2	37	32	30 1/4
4 years	40 1/4	39 1/2	36	35
5 years	43	42 1/4	40	40

*Measurement of height is taken standing.
Source: National Center for Health Statistics in collaboration with the National Center for Chronic Disease Prevention and Health Promotion (CDC). (2000). Growth charts available at http://www.cdc.gov/growthcharts/.

for age, and weight for stature are shown in Appendix IV. The physical growth of the preschooler can be monitored through the use of a scale and measuring stick as described in Chapter 4. Monitoring growth in stature and weight is important, and any prolonged slowdown in growth should be noted.

The preschooler's height and weight do not increase as rapidly as they did during the first 12 months. The 4-year-old probably will weigh five times as much as at birth. Therefore, the 7.5-pound (3.8 kg) baby now weighs about 37 pounds (16.7 kg). This is a general rule and individual weights will vary. Between 3 and 5 years of age, these children will probably gain about 4.5 to 6.5 lbs per year. Gains in height will continue at about 2.5 to 3.5 inches per year (see Table 5.1).

BMI Growth Charts

Body mass index or BMI, described in Chapter 2 (and see Box 5.1, p. 173), can now be applied to the young child. For children, BMI is considered a fairly reliable indicator of the complications associated with childhood obesity, such as high cholesterol levels, high blood pressure, and the eventual development of heart disease [2]. The standards for a healthy BMI for children vary depending on age and gender, so the calculation must be plotted on the appropriate CDC/NCHS growth chart to determine BMI for age. Figure 5.1 shows the BMI-for-age percentiles for girls from 2 to 20 (See Appendix V for BMI Charts). The BMI charts require the following calculation before plotting the measurement.

To Calculate BMI:

Weight in pounds ÷ Height in inches ÷ Height in inches × 703
Weight in kilograms ÷ Height in centimeters ÷ Height in centimeters × 10, 000
Or go to an online Web BMI calculator such as
http://www.keepkidshealthy.com/welcome/bmicalculator.html

To Plot BMI:

Select the BMI growth chart for the appropriate gender.
Locate age along the horizontal scale across the bottom of the chart and draw a line up from the age. Use a straight edge such as an index card to locate the child's BMI and draw a line horizontally. The point where the two lines intersect is the child's growth percentile.

2 to 20 years: Girls
Body mass index-for-age percentiles

NAME _____

RECORD # _____

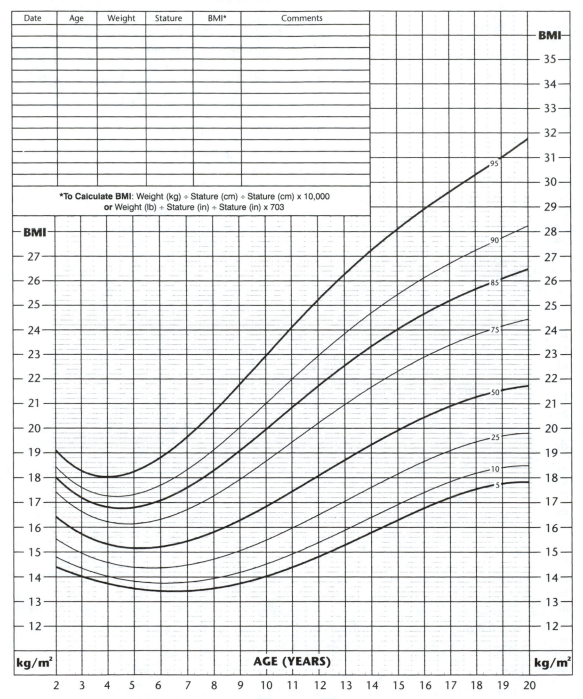

*To Calculate BMI: Weight (kg) ÷ Stature (cm) ÷ Stature (cm) x 10,000
or Weight (lb) ÷ Stature (in) ÷ Stature (in) x 703

Figure 5.1   Body mass index-for-age percentiles

Source: Developed by the National Center for Health Statistics in Collaboration with the National Center for Chronic Disease Prevention and Health Promotion. (2000). Available at http://www.cdc.gov/growthcharts.

Table 5.2 Median BMI based on gender and age

Age	Boys' BMI	Girls' BMI
2	16.6	16.4
3	16	15.8
4	15.6	15.4
5	15.5	15.18
6	15.4	15.2
7	15.45	15.4
8	15.6	15.8

Source: National Center for Health Statistics in collaboration with the National Center for Chronic Disease Prevention and Health Promotion, Body Mass Index. (2000). Available at http://www.cdc.gov/growthcharts/.

To Interpret:

Under weight = ≤ 5th percentile
At risk for overweight = ≥ 85th percentile
Overweight = ≥ 95th percentile

During the preschool years children grow lean. Body fat, adiposity, falls to the lowest level before beginning an upward trend after age 6. This stage is often referred to as the "adiposity rebound." The downward trend in body fat is evident at ages 4 and 5, when you look at Table 5.2 which lists the median BMI for children. If children gain fat before the age of about 5.5 or begin an early adiposity rebound, they have a greater chance of persistent obesity in adulthood [2, 3]. Children who are at risk for obesity can be identified by monitoring BMI and determining which children are approaching the 85th percentile or greater. Obesity in even one parent doubles or triples a child's risk of persistent obesity [2].

The prevalence of obesity in children has doubled in the last 20 years. It is now estimated that 10% to 15% of children and adolescents are overweight, making today's children the fattest generation of children. Determining BMI percentile is an essential tool for monitoring the health of toddlers and preventing their drift toward obesity.

Children with a high BMI share common traits: overweight parents, small families, poor, high-fat diets, many hours in front of the television [4]. Individual counseling or anticipatory guidance to prevent obesity should be directed at the parents of these high-BMI children. Still, the center should address obesity prevention for all children, discussed later in this chapter.

If preschool children gain a pound or two in less than a month, look for the reasons. Weight gain or loss may be a result of chronic illness, overeating, error in measurement,

BMI does not determine body fat percentage. Body fat must be compared to lean muscle mass. Body fat can vary widely for children due to age, muscularity, and onset of puberty and frame size. However, children should not be judged on appearance alone because the general population of children is getting heavier and our view of normal weight is being skewed. Instead, use routine plotting of growth charts including BMI charts to identify children growing outside the norm. To improve your skills at using the BMI charts, refer to the tutorial available at http://www.cdc.gov/nccdphp/dnpa/growthcharts/training/modules/index.htm.

faulty equipment, or stress in the home environment. Such losses or gains of weight for a 2- or 3-month period, without a change in height, should cause concern. After ensuring proper use of measuring equipment, take time to talk with parents about any changes in their children's physical or eating behavior. Then, if necessary, refer children to their physician or the center's consulting dietitian for a review of individual growth, body fat, diet history, health history, and family lifestyle.

Skin Fat-Fold Measurements

An additional anthropometrical measurement taken by health professionals is skin-fat-fold thickness, which estimates body fat under the skin (subcutaneous). This measurement has been most widely used in hospitals to determine the subcutaneous fat and nutritional status of surgery and controlled-research patients. However, it is difficult to accurately measure infants, children, and obese individuals, thereby limiting the technique's usefulness [5].

CHILD DEVELOPMENT SKILLS

Preschool children are now ready for verbal exchanges during meals. Children are eager to help the care provider and parents with food preparation, service, and cleanup. Still, keep in mind that children's quickness in movement and occasional inattentiveness may result in spills or broken dishes. Mishaps are inevitable, but generally these are not intentional. Children simply misjudge situations, and these miscalculations, combined with the haste of preschoolers, cause accidents. Table 5.3 provides a list summarizing the stages of development. During the preschool period the rate of growth stabilizes and appetite is regular and children will still need both meals and several snacks.

Children like to be included in food-related activities and are generally welcomed helpers. Mealtimes will be influenced by the new skills developing in the preschool child. By age 3 to 4 years, preschoolers will be able to do the following:

- enjoy imitating the cook
- hold a cup by its handle
- pour liquids from a small pitcher
- use a fork
- chew most foods
- show an increased appetite
- request favorite foods
- show interest in foods of various shapes and colors
- stop eating most foods when satisfied

As preschoolers approach age 5, peer influence takes on greater significance. In addition, expect 5-year-olds to be capable of the following:

- use a knife and fork
- use a cup well

Table 5.3   Stages of development for preschooler and elementary years*

Stage	Physical	Nutritional	Intellectual
Preschool: 3 to 4 years	Slowed steady height-weight gain; lordosis and prominent abdomen disappear; face grows faster than cranial cavity; jaw widens	Assertion of independence increases; appetite declines with picky food habits	Concept of "conservation" begins (i.e., some features of objects remain the same despite changes in other features)
Elementary I: 5 to 6 years	Steady average weight gain 3 to 3.5 kg/yr and height gain of 6 cm/yr; growth of head slows	Rate of growth stabilizes, accompanied by more regular appetite; likes to be included in food-related activities	Child can begin to take others' viewpoints; school begins

Stage	Gross Motor	Fine Motor	Speech and Language
Preschool: 3 to 4 years	Stands and hops on one foot; jumps heights and distances	Minute degrees of flexion and extension of interphalangeal joints in three-jaw-chuck position	Sentence length and complexity increase; uses language for a variety of purposes (to satisfy needs, pretend, argue; etc.); other consonants emerge
Elementary I: 5 to 6 years	Rides a bicycle, begins organized play activities and perfects game skills	Refinement of individual finger coordination (i.e., piano playing); ability to use one upper extremity for one task, one for a different task	Receptive and expressive language develops in relation to cognitive growth

Stage	Social/Behavioral
Preschool: 3 to 4 years	Moves from parallel to cooperative play; able to conform
Elementary I: 5 to 6 years	Acceptable table manners; peers becoming more important

*This chart provides the health of professional with a standard tool for assessing feeding levels.
Source: Modified from Harvey-Smith, M., et al. (1982). *Feeding Management of a Child with a Handicap: A Guide for Professionals.* Memphis: University of Tennessee Center for the Health Sciences.

- show an increased ability to feed themselves
- show more interest in talking than in eating
- persist with food jags
- enjoy helping to prepare foods
- enjoy set-up or clean-up of mealtime
- show an interest in where food comes from

Table 5.4   Dietary Reference Intakes for children ages 1 to 3 and 4 to 8

Daily Nutrient Needs	1 to 3 years	4 to 8 years
Estimated Energy Requirement (EER)	992*	1642*
Fat % of total calories	30–40	25–35
Protein (g/d)	**13†**	**19**
Fiber (g/d)	19	25
Vitamin A (μg/d)	300	400
Vitamin D (μg/d)	5	5
Vitamin E (mg/d-TE)	6	7
Vitamin C (mg/d)	15	25
Folate (μg/d)	150	200
Vitamin B_6 (mg/d)	**0.5**	**0.6**
Vitamin B_{12} (μg/d)	**0.9**	**1.2**
Calcium (mg/d)	500	800
Phosphorus (mg/d)	460	500
Iron (mg/d)	**7**	**10**
Magnesium (mg/d)	80	130
Zinc (mg/d)	**3**	**5**

*EER based on active females ages 1–2 and 3–8; boys will need 1046 cal/d and 1742 cal/d respectively. All other DRIs based on ages 1–3 and 4–8.

†Amounts in bold are based on RDAs.

Source: Data compiled from *Recommended Dietary Allowances.* (1989). Washington, DC: National Academy Press. Institute of Medicine. (2002). *Dietary Reference Intakes for Energy, Carbohydrate, Fiber, Fat, Fatty Acids, Cholesterol, Protein, and Amino Acids.* Washington, DC: National Academy Press. Institute of Medicine. (1998). *Dietary Reference Intakes for Thiamin, Riboflavin, Niacin, Vitamin B_6, Folate, Vitamin B_{12}, Pantothenic Acid, Biotin, and Choline.* Washington, DC: National Academy Press. Institute of Medicine. (2000). *Dietary Reference Intakes for Vitamin C, Vitamin E, Selenium, and Carotenoids.* Washington, DC: National Academy Press. Institute of Medicine. (2001). *Dietary Reference Intakes for Vitamin A, Vitamin K, Arsenic, Boron, Chromium, Copper, Iodine, Iron, Manganese, Molybdenum, Nickel, Silicon, Vanadium, and Zinc.* Washington, DC: National Academy Press. These reports may be accessed via http://www.nap.edu.

RECOMMENDED ENERGY AND NUTRIENT NEEDS

The recommended energy and daily nutrient needs for 3 to 5 years are discussed in this section and the DRIs are listed in Table 5.4. For a more complete nutrient requirements for age see Appendix III.

Energy

The energy needs of children of the same age, sex, and size can vary as a result of differences in physical activity or the efficiency with which children utilize energy. The DRI is only a guide for energy needs for preschoolers. Table 5.4 shows that the estimated energy requirements of active 4- to 8-year-olds are 1742 cal/day for males 1642 cal/day for females. The energy needs vary with gender and activity level, so very active boys will require the most energy, whereas sedentary girls will require less in order to maintain a healthy weight for height.

Given an energy allowance of approximately 1600–1800 kcal (for 4- to 8-year-olds) and a need for a wide variety of nutrients, the diet should contain foods of high nutrient density. Foods that supply few nutrients at a high calorie level should not be a routine part of the diet. If so, children will expect and prefer these poor choices: candy, soft drinks, juice-type drinks, fruit-flavored chews, cookies, cupcakes, non-whole-grain crackers, and snack chips. These foods supply most of the calories with little fiber or necessary nutrients or additional saturated fat. Moving children to a diet with whole foods will be a greater challenge if these foods compromise the majority of the diet.

Fat

The AMDR for fat from ages 1 to 3 is 30% to 40% of calories; by ages 3 to 5 the child should be transitioning to a lower-fat diet [6]. This may be accomplished easily by choosing reduced-fat dairy products; however from ages 4 and older the diet can be further reduced in fat to range from 25% to 35% of fat. Achieving this range will be difficult if fast-food consumption is routine. A report summarizing U.S. food consumption patterns confirms that fast food consumption by children accounts for more fat intake than foods eaten at home [7]. Increasing meals at home is a good place for parents to start. The center can increase use of whole-grain products, and fruits and vegetables in meals and snacks. Children who are under desirable weight will probably need more fat in the diet as a concentrated form of energy. Children who are vegetarian will need the higher range of fat to make their bulky diet more palatable and increase nutrient density. Box 5.1 describes the method for calculating fat grams based on the AMDR.

For active 4-year-olds, the desired 25% to 35% of calories from fat would be 45 to 65 g of fat per day. One fast-food kids meal with a cheeseburger and fries would supply 27 g of fat. Also, consider that 3 cups of whole milk would provide 24 g of fat compared to 7 g if 1% milk were used.

Protein

The AMDR for protein from ages 1 to 3 is 5% to 20% of calories, as children grow, the AMDR increases to 10% to 30% of calories for children 4 to 8 years [6]. The DRI for protein goes from 13 g/day for ages 1 to 3, to 19 g/day for ages 4 to 8 [6]. An

---

BOX 5.1   Method to calculate fat grams

To calculate and individual fat gram recommendation, take 25% of the estimated energy requirement (EER based on age, gender, and activity level) and divide by 9 cal/g for minimum grams of fat per day. Calculate the maximum range by substituting 35% in the same equation.

   $.25 \times 1642$ cal (EER active female)/9 cal/g = 45 grams of fat per day, minimum
   $.35 \times 1642$ cal (EER active female)/9 cal/g = 63 g/d, maximum

> **BOX 5.2   Method to calculate protein grams**
>
> To calculate an individual protein recommendation, multiply .95 g by kg body weight. Therefore for a 40-pound (17 kg), 4-year-old child, 16 g of protein would be recommended. You may also use the general DRI of 19 g/day for 4 to 8 years of age.

individual calculation can be determined by assigning .95 g protein/kg/day. Box 5.2 describes the method for calculating protein needs based on the AMDR.

The protein recommendation is easily met for children who drink milk and/or eat meat products. To meet the protein recommendation, children should drink between 2 and 3 cups (16 to 24 ounces) of milk (16 to 24 g of protein). This quantity not only supplies protein, but also helps to meet calcium, riboflavin, and other vitamin and mineral needs. Two cups of milk supply 16 g of protein. Two ounces of meat (7 g of protein per ounce of meat) will supply 14 g of protein, making a total of 30 g of protein, more than the recommended. This amount excludes the protein in vegetables and grain products, which would increase the total protein intake. Most children will have no difficulty meeting their protein needs.

Recipes using high-protein foods such as nuts, legumes, and beans as ingredients also provide much-needed magnesium, zinc, folacin, and vitamin B_6. These nutrients are easier to obtain when a wide variety of high-protein sources are included in the diet.

Calcium

In some preschoolers' diets, calcium is one of the nutrients found in less-than-recommended amounts. Less than half of preschool children meet the calcium DRI (see Table 5.4) of 500 mg for 3 years of age and 800 mg for 4 to 5 years [8], which is probably related to the steep increase in carbonated beverage consumption among children [8]. Three cups of milk readily provide the 800 mg of calcium (1 cup supplies approximately 280 mg calcium). If the child likes milk, calcium will probably be taken in sufficient quantities for building bones and teeth as long as juices or sweetened beverages are not also offered. In short, obtaining enough calcium without consuming dairy products is difficult (Chapter 4 includes a list of calcium-rich foods). Dried beans and green vegetables are sources of calcium, but the quantity of these foods necessary to meet the child's calcium needs is large and not a practical option during the growing years. If the child cannot drink fresh, fluid milk, then canned (processed) milk, dry milk, yogurt, or cheese (excluding cream cheese) could be eaten. These products contain comparable quantities of calcium and may be more easily tolerated. Once again, fast food comes up short as it provides less calcium than foods eaten at home.

Iron

The DRI for iron is 7 mg at 3 years and increases to 10 mg for 4 to 5 years (see Table 5.4) [9]. Milk is a poor source of iron, yet consuming it in large quantities (more than 3 to 4 cups) may replace foods with higher iron content. Discontinuing forti-fied infant cereals and iron-rich formula also contributes to iron deficiency ane-mia in the toddler years. In some cases, the toddler may still be eating cooked iron-fortified cereal or iron-fortified infant cereal. But by the preschool years, the cooked cereals (for example, Cream of Wheat®, Malt-O-Meal®) have given way to more dry cereals. Check the labels and keep iron-fortified cereals available for quick snacks.

Preschool children are able to chew most meat products, typically good sources of iron. Grains, legumes, fruits, and vegetables can provide some iron. However, some of that iron may not be readily available because of the phytate and fiber in plants, which, reportedly, bind some iron into an unusable complex. Nevertheless, as more food products on the market are iron-fortified, a meatless diet can supply adequate iron [10].

It is difficult to consume enough food with iron if the energy intake is "wasted" on food with low nutrient density. Good sources of iron with a high nutrient den-sity are meat, greens, and enriched or iron-fortified whole-grain cereal products (see Chapter 4). Similarly dense in nutrients but less popular are these food items: egg yolk, beans, molasses, and dried fruits.

Liver is often cited as one of the best sources of iron, and indeed it is; but liver's high cholesterol value has discouraged its use. One ounce of beef liver supplies al-most 2 mg of iron, whereas 1 ounce of ground beef supplies only 1 mg. Likewise, 2 tablespoons of wheat germ, 3/4 cup of oatmeal or rolled oats, two rye wafers, or 3 tablespoons of cooked spinach supply 1 mg of iron. See Chapter 7 for ways to in-clude iron in menus.

Zinc

Zinc, like iron, is needed in small amounts. The DRI is 5 mg for the preschooler [9]. Table 5.4 shows the DRI for the 1- to 3-year-old compared to the 4- to 8-year-old.

Zinc is an essential nutrient found in many food sources, including organ meats, oysters, egg yolk, beans, and nuts. Milk, meats, legumes, beans, whole-grain cere-als, and wheat germ supply more than 1 mg per serving. Many of these foods are also good protein sources. If the Food Guide Pyramid recommendation of six serv-ings of grains is met with an increased use of legumes and beans, the zinc DRI can easily be met.

Vitamin C

A balance of all nutrients is as important for the 3- to 5-year-old as it is for the younger child. The DRI for vitamin C is 15 mg/day for 3-year-olds and reaches 25 mg/day by age 4 (see Table 5.4) [9]. A daily source of vitamin C is important, since there is evidence that it enhances iron absorption.

Many other nutrients must be included in the diet. See Chapter 1, Tables 1.9 and 1.10 for a review of vitamin and mineral contributions. For this age group we have singled out those nutrients that are often consumed in less-than-recommended amounts or are often presented on child-care centers' menus in less-than-recommended quantities. These nutrients are difficult to supply without careful planning of menus.

Supplementation

Center staff often ask whether they should supplement children's diets with nutritional supplements such as vitamin or mineral pills. Supplementation is a real concern, and if a registered dietitian is available, a group meeting to discuss this issue is often helpful for parents. If a vitamin or mineral—including fluoride—must be added to the diet, it should be prescribed by the physician or public health clinic. This is especially true in the case of iron. Anemia is not always caused by iron deficiency; it may also be caused by lack of folate or may be secondary to other disease states and should be further investigated by a health professional.

The strict vegetarian diet will need supplementation with vitamin B_{12} if animal products (milk, eggs, and fish) are not included in the diet or the child is not consuming a vitamin B_{12} fortified soy product. (Further discussion of the diet is included in the section, Special Concerns Related to Dietary Intake.)

Too many vitamins, especially the fat-soluble vitamins A and D, can be harmful. Because scientists do not completely understand the interaction between certain vitamins and minerals and the effect of megadoses, a word of caution is advised in providing vitamin and mineral supplementation.

Poor growth records are not a signal to start supplementation; instead, they should signal the care provider to advise parents to seek a more thorough examination from a physician or other health professional. The supplement could mask a more serious medical condition.

FOOD NEEDS

The preschooler needs to eat frequently throughout the day. Assessing the child's nutritional needs includes determining a child's acceptance of food. You can use a dietary history along with physical measurements of growth and development. You may use the 24-hour dietary recall method described in Chapter 2 or the Dietary Questionnaire for Children included in Appendix V. Because many preschoolers are frequently on the go/on their own and are now more self-sufficient than during the toddler stage, they open refrigerator doors, climb onto kitchen cabinets, and open jars to find their favorite foods. For example, children may well have stuffed cookies into little pockets when they enter the center at 7:00 A.M. In short, realize that parents might be misinformed regarding their children's diet.

A good dietary history taken by the care provider may reveal that the child is consuming less-than-recommended amounts of food or reveal food behaviors that impact nutrient intake. Such analysis may reveal conflicts that could be avoided by allowing the child to decide how much to eat or not to eat at all. By neutralizing

Table 5.5   Recommended food intake based on the Food Guide Pyramid for Children and suggested serving sizes (ages 3–5)*

Food Group	Servings Per Day§	Suggested Serving Size (3 through 5 years)
Vegetable Group	3	1/2 c
Green vegetables	(1)	
Other vegetables	(2)	
Fruit Group	2	1/2 c
Vitamin C source	(1)	
Grain Group	6	1/2 slice
Bread		
Ready-to-eat cereals, enriched, whole grain		
Cooked cereals: macaroni, pasta, rice		1/4 c, 1/3 oz
Milk Group	2	3/4 c
Milk†: 2%, 1%, 1/2%		
Cheese (1.5 oz = 1 c milk)		
Meat Group	2	1–1 1/2 oz
Lean meat, fish, poultry, eggs		
Nut butters (peanut, soynut), nuts‡	(2–3/week)	3 Tbsp
Cooked dried beans/peas	(1–2)	3/8 c
Fats and Sweets	Use sparingly	1 tsp, small amounts
Butter, margarine, oils, mayonnaise		
Soft drinks		
Candy, desserts, jelly, sugar		

*Serving sizes based on CACFP meal pattern in Table 7.2.
†Whole milk may be used for some underweight children, Food Guide Pyramid milk serving is 1 c.
‡Avoid for allergic children.
§Allow a minimum serving of 1 Tbsp/year of age for cooked fruits, vegetables, cereals, and pasta until children reach 1/2 c portion size. Additional servings of food may be needed to meet energy requirements of some children.

meal and snack times, children may improve their own diets. Additionally, in a supportive environment, overweight and underweight preschoolers can be taught to self-regulate food intake instead of responding to external cues such as time of day and amount of food on plate [11].

If only a limited diet is served, the child learns to enjoy only a few foods. Parents and care providers should expose children to a variety of foods without rewards or punishments [12]. Children will dislike foods presented in a negative context.

Table 5.5 lists the amount of food for each of the Food Guide Pyramid food groups and is a useful tool for evaluating nutrient intake, estimating serving size, and planning menus. Preschoolers would need to consume only 1/2 to 3/4 of a slice of whole-grain bread; however, one slice has been allowed in the example. The general rule for minimum serving size is 1 tablespoon (measuring) per year of age. The guide emphasizes use of beans as a substitute for part of the protein, whole-grain cereals and breads, fruits, milk and milk products, and vegetables, specifically the dark green varieties and those with a high vitamin C content.

Grain Group

The Food Guide Pyramid for Young Children recommends a minimum of six servings of grain products. Items from the bread (serving = 1/2 slice) and cereal group (serving = 1/4 c) are probably the easiest for the preschooler to ingest. Cookies or crackers are easy for the preschooler who wants to "eat and run." They satisfy the child's hunger and may not be as messy as fresh vegetables and fruit, milk, or some meat products, but they can also be high in fat and sugar or salt while providing few nutrients.

Ready-to-eat cereals can be a nutritious snack substitute and may enhance the nutritional value of the menu without compromising variety [13]. Either whole-grain or iron-fortified "breakfast cereals" can be served in the center. Because the nutrient density of whole-grain cereals is higher than that of some fortified cereals, whole-grain cereals should be encouraged. However, check the labels! Look for 6 to 10 grams of sugar or less and 2 or more grams of fiber. Some cereals advertised as whole grain may also include a high sugar and saturated fat content along with fortification with iron and other nutrients. In addition, a spoonful of wheat germ is a good way to add iron and other nutrients to cereal products. One teaspoon of toasted wheat germ can replace a teaspoon of cereal before it is cooked, for example, in oatmeal. Preschoolers accept wheat germ when it is substituted for part of the cooked cereal or sprinkled on top of a familiar favorite.

The center can serve pastas and rice flavored with herbs and spices. Cooked grains with steamed vegetables or fruits, served hot or cold, can increase servings of grains. Birthdays without birthday cake are sometimes difficult to justify to parents. However, many parents welcome the idea of substituting with crafts and games or finding more nourishing treats, such as a basket of seasonal fruit from a local farm. Watermelon or cantaloupe, hollowed out and filled with fruit, with candles around the edge, can substitute for birthday cake. Infrequently providing foods that have a low nutrient density (such as birthday cakes) will not harm the child; however, a center with 15 to 30 children will likely have many birthday celebrations. In this case, plan a once-a-month celebration to limit the impact. Plan, too, to meet the new challenge of candy-filled gift bags. If parents insist on gift bags, suggest alternative treats.

Fruit Group and Vegetable Group

Many preschoolers will not consume unfamiliar vegetables and fruits. Fruits and vegetables introduced in the child-care center may be strange to the child. This situation can easily be remedied if the menus are part of the educational curriculum (Chapters 7 and 8). A planned menu or lesson plan can increase familiarity with fruits and vegetables. Obviously, you will have to pay particular attention to introducing vegetables and fruits with high nutritional content, especially the dark green and yellow vegetables and those with high iron content (Table 5.6).

To familiarize children with a wider variety of fruits and vegetables, engage their participation in preparing and serving those items. During meal service, place small pieces of broccoli and cauliflower in the serving bowls or a "lazy Su-

Table 5.6   Fruits and vegetables high in iron

1.5–2 mg iron per serving

    Spinach
    Lima beans
    Swiss chard

.5–1 mg iron per serving

    Brussels sprouts
    Sweet potatoes
    Kale
    Acorn squash
    Asparagus
    Green beans
    Broccoli
    Tomatoes
    Cantaloupe
    Raisins
    Raspberries, red
    Turnip greens
    Prunes

Source: Foods composition determined using the USDA National Nutrient Database for Standard Reference, Release 15 (August 2002).

san" revolving tray so a child takes only one flower of broccoli, one asparagus spear, or one Brussels sprout. Unfortunately, cooked cabbage is often served to the preschooler in large chunks and spinach greens are frequently served with a large spoon instead of tongs; therefore, the child cannot take a small serving. Also problematic to serving are overcooked, mushy greens. Note that properly chopped, cooked greens or spinach may be easier to serve and may better allow for teaspoon servings, giving children opportunity to experiment and to taste food without being responsible for large portions.

The Food Guide Pyramid for Young Children recommended daily servings for vegetables is three servings and for fruit is two servings. Fruit juices should not become a routine substitution for fruit; and if juices are used, the amount should not exceed 4 to 6 ounces per day. Overconsumption of fruit juices can result in a decreased intake of more nutrient-dense foods [14]. Thirst between meals and snacks should be quenched with cool water [15].

Milk Group

During the toddler years, extended use of bottles may have caused an overconsumption of milk. And, while preschool children may be free of the bottle, many still drink more than 3 cups (24 oz) of milk a day, an excessive amount if it replaces other foods and nutrients in the diet. The recommended amount is two servings per day. Serving size is 3/4 cup to 1 cup.

Imitation milks, or "health food milks," discussed in Chapter 4, are nondairy products usually fortified with vitamins and calcium. The USDA Child Care Food Program does not approve their use where reimbursement is allowed for milk and for meals served to children (Chapter 7). Whole milk, skim milk, or 2% milk can be served in the preschool center, either plain or chocolate-flavored.

The caloric contribution of skim milk is one-half that of whole milk. Most whole milk contains 3.2% to 3.5% butterfat, whereas skim milk has less than 1% butterfat. Two-percent milk contains 2% butterfat. The difference in energy between a half cup of 2% and a half cup of whole milk equals about 15 to 16 kcal, making 2% milk an acceptable product for children.

Ice cream, puddings, and sweetened yogurt may be used on the menu of the child-care center, but the contribution of added sugars should be taken into consideration. Yogurt provides calcium and protein, a small serving of vanilla yogurt served with fruit, such as partially frozen raspberries, is a delicious treat, and may increase the fruit intake. Plain yogurt (unsweetened) or yogurt sweetened with fresh fruit can substitute for fluid milk according to the Food Guide, but current regulations by USDA (Chapter 7) require use of yogurt. Cream cheese, butter, and margarine cannot be used as milk substitutes.

Meat Group

Most preschoolers readily accept popular fast food meat products, such as hamburgers and chicken nuggets. Two daily servings of meats (serving = 1–1 1/2 oz) and meat alternates (serving = 3/8 c) are recommended, because they are the best source of iron. Moreover, frequently include iron-rich meat alternates or protein foods, including lentils and legumes (such as peas, beans, and nuts), which further benefit with folate, magnesium, vitamin E, vitamin B_6, and zinc. A combination of meat alternates and meats raises a diet's nutrient density.

Prepare and cook meats and meat alternates until tender so children can easily serve themselves from serving dishes onto their plates. This means that one half of a hamburger, two baked chicken nuggets, or a small piece of roast beef will be on the serving plate. Meat does not have to be chopped fine or legumes cooked until they appear as puree, but they should be soft and moist enough to cut with table knives or to eat as finger foods. Meats can be paired with a mild fruit or vegetable salsa or ranch dipping sauce to increase palatability. To familiarize children with legumes use a "lazy susan" revolving tray filled with a variety of soft beans of different colors and shapes to taste.

Should you serve luncheon meats, hot dogs, and sausages which are salty and high in fat, but are generally well-liked by children and care providers? Take into account the nutritional content of the foods as well as their potential for providing educational experiences. For example, when a wiener roast is planned as part of the curriculum, hot dogs can be an appropriate part of the child-care menu. Luncheon meats can be on a "make your own sandwich" menu, and these luncheon meats may also be low fat. The final decision regarding food choices may rest with the center food service supervisor who plans the menus. For additional guidance on selecting meat and meat alternates for the menu, see Chapter 7.

PROMOTING HEALTHFUL EATING BEHAVIORS

By their preschool years, children should be capable of putting some foods on their plates. Children progressing normally will be capable of serving independently by 3 1/2 years of age. After a month or two of practice, they will be a better judge of how much food to serve [16]. There are exceptions, as some children overestimate portion sizes and must be monitored by the care provider.

This activity may seem like a small accomplishment to the care provider or parents; however, children have a different perspective. They see an important decision: *How much food will I eat?* This opportunity to participate in determining an appropriate amount of food is lost when teachers serve the food.

Children should try at least a small portion of each menu item. Eating at least one green bean, one flower of broccoli, or one-half spear of asparagus is appropriate when becoming familiar with a new food. More importantly, keep the atmosphere positive and noncoercive; if the child is uncooperative, the exercise's

Preschoolers decide how much to eat when they serve themselves

value is lost and should be temporarily shelved. Regardless, the care provider, honoring the division of responsibility, can remain firm about the menu and what foods are available for meals. Eventually, hunger will push children to try unfamiliar foods.

Family Influence

Family behaviors influence a preschooler's reaction to food and eating behavior. For instance, eating in front of the TV may become an expectation. Foods promoted as healthy and good may end up being disliked or avoided if parents don't eat the foods too. Offering rewards for eating certain food can make that food less desirable. Restricting intake of junk food favorites can generate interest in eating that food and decrease the child's ability to respond to satiety and stop eating [17, 18]. A better solution is to simply avoid purchasing the food on a regular basis.

As children age, controlling the home menu becomes more difficult, especially when children plunder accessible cupboards. Foods like fruit snacks, fruit bars, fruit drinks, puddings, and sweetened yogurts packed in individual serving sizes seem like an appropriate choice to young children. They assume these are "okay" snack foods meant for their intake and will passionately respond to parental restrictions. To win this battle parents must limit their purchases; however, when putting these foods "on the menu," parents should not restrict amounts.

Encourage parents to remain firm about what foods are "on the menu" for snacks or meals. Parents should predetermine menu choices; children may choose

A child who learns to spread butter as a preschooler can now make sandwiches at 6 years of age

Preschooler learns to pour from small pitcher

to eat, or not. But these menu wars might have their cease-fires: in the absence of a precluding medical condition, parents should include at least one food finicky children will eat.

Serving Food to Preschoolers

As discussed in Chapter 7, utensils and cups should be used at mealtime. For preschoolers, include small right-sized equipment such as a spoon, a fork, and a (dull) knife. Children may use the latter to spread soft margarine on bread. They may then use the knife to cut the bread as well as tender vegetables and meat. As discussed in Chapter 4, choose drinking glasses wisely and fill sparingly. For preschoolers, add a small pitcher filled a half to a quarter full for them to refill drinks at the table. Allow children to fully participate in these activities that stimulate fine motor coordination. Use mealtime as a learning experience.

Tables and seating arrangements for young children are important. Select tables with rounded corners and comfortable chairs. Chairs should accommodate small children and allow the child's feet to be placed squarely on the floor. Buy sturdy chairs, because adults should sit on the children's chairs rather than having the children sit on adult chairs.

Seat active or excitable children between quiet and calm children; place children who enjoy eating beside picky eaters. Six and possibly eight children may sit at one table with a care provider. It is important to allow enough room for children to pass the bowls of food from one child to another. Small groups of children allow for a small quantity of food to be placed in each bowl. If there are three or four items served at each meal, at least half of the children can begin serving themselves when food service starts. For example, one child can be pouring milk, one serving broccoli, one serving mashed potatoes, one serving meat, one serving the fruit dish, and one taking a slice of bread. Allowing children to serve food at the center takes 4 to 5 minutes after 4 to 6 weeks of practice. Do not attempt to encourage a child to serve all the foods during the first week at the child-care center. Begin with carrot and celery sticks, and let the child serve these foods onto the plate. If your center has not begun this experience, start with only one serving bowl per table and progress slowly until children are serving all foods onto their plates.

SPECIAL CONCERNS RELATED TO DIETARY INTAKE

It is not the intention of this book to cover all the diet-related concerns of the preschool period. Diet-related health concerns discussed in Chapters 3 and 4 include obesity, lactose, intolerance, and food allergies. Chapter 6 includes cardiovascular disease and dental caries, which also affect the preschooler. There may also be children in the center who require diabetic diets, or who have other conditions that require special dietary treatment. The administrator should have specific written instructions from the physician or nutritionist explaining how the diet can be implemented in the center.

Snack Foods

Snack foods with low nutrient density become more popular as the child gets older. But how do you reduce the child's intake of these convenient snack foods? Avoiding these foods may be easier at the center than at home, if menus are used to promote a healthy diet and limits are placed on the use of these foods.

Very few commercially available snack foods start with wholesome ingredients. If they are high in nutrients, often they have taken a short cut by fortifying with a few missing nutrients. Consider serving whole foods such as fruits and vegetables with yogurt or sour cream dips, or look for whole grain snacks that provide some fiber along with the fat or sugar common in snack foods. Avoid hydrogenated fats (transfats) when possible. Judging whether a food should be served as a snack depends on whether the food:

1. Can be classified as part of the Food Guide Pyramid (see Table 5.5).
2. Contains sufficient nutrients to justify the caloric value (i.e. nutrient dense). Usually whole grain (if grain group), low in added sugar, low in saturated hydrogenated fat, and closer to the unprocessed whole food.

3. Will enhance the educational objectives of the food program at the center, for example, seasonal fruits to coincide with lesson plans.
4. Meets the USDA Child and Adult Care Food Program guidelines (Chapter 7) for which foods are permissible in the food program. These guides offer an excellent source for determining whether a food is an acceptable part of the program. If all the required foods are consumed in addition to high-calorie snacks, and the child is not overweight, the child may simply need the extra energy for growth and physical activity.

A guide to reading food labels in the grain and milk grain group is presented in Figure 5.2. Recommended acceptable ranges for energy, fiber, fat, and select vitamins and minerals are included. Foods from the grain group provide the foundation for the diet. They present the easiest opportunity for selecting foods that are high in nutrients needed in the child's diet. However, using grain products with added sugar raises the energy value, thereby reducing the nutrient density. Convenience foods from the milk group are becoming more popular. Again, be wary of milk products that add excessive amounts of sugar and thereby reduce the amount of calcium available per calorie. Also, when fruits are added to yogurt, expect about 10 more grams of sugar per 4-ounce serving; however, some products, such as yogurt tubes, may exceed this amount because they are only 2 ounces per serving. The guide included (see Figure 5.2) can help target better convenience food choices in the grain and milk group.

Table 5.7 provides a general list of snack foods primarily from the fruit and vegetable group. The list includes opportunities for pouring (and drinking), for using fingers, and for practicing spreading with a knife. Care providers can use snack time as well as mealtime to practice fine motor skills.

Fast Food

The question of whether to eat at fast-food establishments is often asked of nutritionists, especially when the preschool center wishes to take the children "down the street" for a hamburger and french fries. Most fast food establishments will provide complete listings of the nutrient composition of their foods. There are a few low-fat options now available, however "super-sizing" kids' meals or choosing adult-size meal packages can easily lead to overconsumption. Parents can keep serving sizes in a reasonable range by purchasing off the "ala carte" menu. Certainly an occasional meal from a fast-food establishment is not objectionable, but a diet composed primarily of these foods would be nutritionally limited.

Sweeteners

A question that you will be asked is, "Should I serve artificial sweeteners or sugar to preschoolers?" Nutritionists are often tempted to answer with a question, "Is either really necessary?" The relationship of sugar to dental caries is well documented.

	Grain Group	Milk Group
Nutrition Facts **Servings Size:**	1/2 c, 30–50 g	1/2 c–1 c
Amount per Serving Calories Cal. from Fat	60–150 Not more than 50% of calories coming from fat. Avoid hydrogenated (trans) fats.	80–150 Not more than 50% of calories from fat.
% Daily Value **Total Fat** **Saturated Fat** **Total Carbohydrate** **Dietary Fiber*** Sugars† Protein	0–4 g 0–2 g 1–5+ < 10 g 1–4	0–5 g 0–1+ < 18 g/4 oz < 35 g/8 oz 6
Vitamins and Minerals **Vitamin A** **Iron** **Calcium** **Folate** **Vitamin D** **Zinc** **Vitamin B$_6$ and others**	Look for at least two vitamins or minerals greater than 0% or one greater than 25%	Calcium 25% or more and Vitamin D 20% or more Vitamin A 5% or more.

Figure 5.2   Guide to reading food labels to identify nutrient-dense foods from grain and milk groups
*When food choices have added fruit or dried fruit to the product allow 5–10 more grams of sugar.
†Some processed grain products may be fortified to appear more nutritious but they usually do not have more than 1 g fiber per serving. Use these foods less often and in smaller amounts.
Source: Nutrient-dense foods were identified using the USDA National Nutrient Database for Standard Reference, Release 15 (August 2002), and defined by the author.

Otherwise, it is difficult to find extensive scientific literature indicating that consumption of table sugar per se is detrimental to health for the preschooler. Humans are born with a preference for sweet tastes, and sweet tastes are a source of pleasure for many. However, reduction of simple sugars may be advisable for treatment of diabetes, treatment and prevention of obesity, and prevention of dental caries. The Dietary Guidelines for Americans suggest sugar should be used in moderation. For a review of sweeteners see Chapter 1.

Natural and Organic Foods

Natural and organic foods are discussed frequently, and more and more centers are asked if they provide only "natural" foods. Words such as processed, natural, and

Table 5.7   Snacks that provide educational opportunities for children

Activity	Snack
To pour and drink	100% fruit juices, milk, protein shake (1/2 c milk, 1/2 c orange juice, 1/4 c powdered milk), water
For fingers	Fruit*: Orange, grapefruit, tangerine, banana slices, apple, pear, peach slices, pineapple wedges, dried apricots, dates, raisins, grapes, plums, berries
	Ice pop made from fruit juice or pureed fruit, fruit puree, pudding (made with fluid milk), plain yogurt†
	Vegetables: Cherry tomato halves, and other vegetables, raw or cooked crunchy—cucumber, zucchini, turnip, green beans, cauliflower, green pepper strips or wedges, asparagus, broccoli, brussels sprouts, peas (for older children), lima beans, jicima, sugar snap peas
To spread on	Peanut butter, yogurt dips, flavored margarine (make your own)
To use spoon, fork	Yogurt†, cottage cheese, cold meat cubes, pudding, whole-grain or fortified cereals with milk

*Most fresh or canned fruit (e.g., bananas cut in disks or pieces, oranges, grapefruit, pineapple) can be frozen on a tray, brought out 10 minutes before snack time, and enjoyed as a crunchy snack.
†Plain yogurt may be sweetened by adding fresh fruit.

refined provide little solid nutrition information, unless they are defined in a quantitative framework. Unfortunately, "natural" is not a defined term for labeling and it may mean absence of artificial colors, flavors, and additives in one food product and the absence of processing or refinement in another. However, new labeling regulations define the use of the term "organic."

Organic food refers to those products grown without use of chemical fertilizers and pesticides. The USDA organic seal is an easy way to identify various levels of organic foods. The categories range from 100 Percent Organic, to use of some organic ingredients and to those that contain less than 70% organic ingredients [19].

Food Additives

The question of additives is often bothersome for the care provider, and parents may question the use of food with additives. Table 5.8 provides a list of some of the additives and their functions. Because of the use of additives, mainly preservatives, the marketplace is filled with a variety of products that would otherwise not be marketable. Without additives, the shelf life of a loaf of bread, including whole-wheat bread would be a day or two instead of more than a week. The cost of such a product would be at least doubled or tripled, making bread an unobtainable product to the lower-income family that depends on it for many nutrients.

Table 5.8   Role of some common additives in food

Additive	Function
Acetic acid	Commonly used to give tartness to dressing, sauces, relishes. The key ingredient in vinegar.
Ascorbic acid (vitamin C, sodium ascorbate)	Keeps fruit slices from darkening, inhibits rancidity in fatty foods. Enhances nutrition value of beverages, beverage mixes.
Carrageenan	Improves consistency and texture of chocolate milk, frozen desserts, puddings, syrups. The most common stabilizer used in ice creams. Derived from seaweed.
Modified food starches	Special starches with desired characteristics (heat-stable, freeze-thaw stable) "built-in." Give body to pie fillings, gravies, and sauces. Derived from cereal grains and potato.
Pectin	Jelling substance extracted from citrus rind; provides consistency of body in all jams, jellies, and preserves.
Potassium sorbate	Controls surface molds on cheese, syrups, margarine, mayonnaise.
Sulfur dioxide	Inhibits browning in fresh and dried fruits. Prevents undesirable color changes when wine is exposed to air.
Vitamin B_6	Needed to help body use protein, carbohydrate, and fat. Added to cereals, other foods.
Vitamin B_{12}	Helps all body cells function normally. Added to cereals, other foods.
Zinc	Mineral added to cereals to promote proper growth. Deficiency can cause dwarfism.

On the other hand, many of the products in which additives are used could be eliminated from the child's diet if the calories are not required for weight gain (for example, gelatin, cake mixes, chips, grain group snacks, or cured meats). For more information go to the Food Additive Web site at http://www.fao.org/es/ESN/jecfa/database/cover.htm.

NUTRITION-RELATED HEALTH CONCERNS

Obesity

The prevalence of childhood obesity has continued to increase with each national nutrition survey over the last 20 years. Overweight prevalence among preschoolers aged 4 to 5 years has increased from 5.8% in the 1971–1974 National Health and Nutrition Examination Survey I (NHANES I) to a prevalence of 10% in the 1988–1994 NHANES III [3, 20]. In the general population, this marks the start of the trend toward obesity in this age group but not in younger children. However, certain subgroups begin to show earlier trends; Mexican American girls aged 2 to 3 have a 10.5% prevalence of overweight compared to a overall prevalence of 5% for 2- to 3-year-olds [3]. When greater than 5% of children are defined as overweight, having a weight for stature or weight for length that plots above the 95th percentile curve of their growth, the population is at risk for persistent obesity.

Threats to Long-Term Health.   The researchers at the CDC have clearly shown that today's children are at an increased risk for becoming overweight adults. Obese children are experiencing increased health risks normally associated with adult obesity. Cardiovascular disease risk factors are noted in 60% of overweight 5- to 10-year-olds. Also there is an increased incidence of type II (adult onset) diabetes among youth [21].

The Influence of Diet.   Traditionally diet and genetics have been blamed for causing obesity. However, preschoolers' food intake data from several national food consumption surveys did not reveal an increased intake of calories or fat in this age group. So caloric intake is an unlikely cause in this age group [3]. Many researchers agree that the trend toward excess weight is largely due to low physical activity level and increased sedentary hours spent with television or computers [2, 3, 21, 22].

Genetics and Obesity.   The role of genetics and obesity was reviewed by Strauss [2]. Twin studies imply that children inherit a susceptibility to gain weight from their parents. Although genetics has a role in the expression of obesity, it can account for only a small percentage of the increase seen in the last 30 years. In addition, researchers have been unable to find metabolic differences causing low metabolism in obese children. Experts agree that prevalence of obesity has reached "epidemic" proportions that can be explained only by changes in our environment and society [2, 20].

Prevention.   What should be done? "Prevention" is the obvious quick and easy response given to parents concerned that their child may be becoming obese. But the goal of preventing obesity in preschool children must become integrated into values at home and in the center. The American Academy of Pediatrics issued a new policy statement regarding the prevention of pediatric obesity [22]. Although research has not yet identified the best strategies, the need for proactive steps in preventing obesity is stressed. Routine calculation and plotting of BMI on growth charts will aid in identifying children at risk (those in the 85th to 95th percentile).

The strategies for preventing obesity must include the family and the school environment. Both should be targeted because of their combined effect on dietary intake and physical activity. Tables 5.9 and 5.10 identify factors that impact obesity in the home and in the school environment.

In the home, families contribute to obesity by sliding into poor eating behaviors, discouraging physical activity by favoring "push-button entertainment," and selecting the least physically challenging mode of transportation within the community. See Table 5.10 for a detailed list.

The school environment can contribute to obesity, as well, by accepting sedentary lifestyles and junk foods as the cultural norm and allowing the degradation of physical education components within its curriculum.

The authors believe that promotion of healthful eating behaviors and increased physical activity is grounded in a few essential themes promoted throughout this text and described in the following list with regard to obesity prevention.

Table 5.9   Home and family influence on obesity

Factors contributing to intake	Factors contributing to inactivity
• Food preparation techniques that add fat • Food selections brought into the home: low nutrient density, high fat • Infrequent family meals • Child not allowed to decide whether or not to eat • Parent–child feeding relationship • Parent food behaviors and dieting • Use of sweetened beverages, sodas/soft drinks • Number of hours watching TV/day • Parent's inability to set limits • Portion size • Parent's obesity	• TV/computer in bedrooms • Number of hours watching TV/day • Hours spent at video games or computer • Inability to walk to/from school • Poor neighborhood safety • Number hours inactive during daily routines • Access to playmates for TV/video/computer free-play time • Access to exercise facilities, playgrounds sidewalks, YMCA

Table 5.10   The influence of teachers and school on obesity

Factors affecting caloric intake	Factors affecting physical activity level
• Access to vending machines • School lunch/breakfast menu food choices • Snacks provided in school and after school programs • Sack lunches sent from home • School fund-raising sales • Time allowed for meal consumption • Child food acceptance/preferences	• Physical education (PE) offered and how often • PE content • Recess time • Support of walking to/from school • Activity incorporated in after-school programs

1. Keep mealtimes pleasant by following the division of responsibility in feeding and avoiding coercive techniques or bribes to eat. This approach enables the child to enjoy eating, feel and respond to satiety, and resist external hunger cues.
2. Expand food acceptance patterns by continuing to offer a variety of healthy nutrient-dense foods. Improving the acceptability of a diet lower in fat and simple carbohydrates is necessary for maintaining a healthy weight.
3. Breastfeed exclusively for 6 months and thereafter use breast milk and complementary foods. Breastfeeding impacts obesity because breastfed children show an increased ability to self-regulate food intake [23]. Breastfeeding mothers use less controlling and less restrictive child feeding practices [24] and some studies show that adults who were breastfed have lower rates of obesity [25].
4. Setting limits on the use of TV, videos, and computers in favor of creative and interactive play is one of the most effective means of preventing obesity [26]. When employing this strategy, parents must accept a certain amount of

boredom as a necessary part of creativity. Limiting TV time reduces exposure to mass marketing of junk foods and reduces time spent inactive, both of which seem to have an effect on obesity [26].

5. Offer daily opportunities for physical activity (group and individual). The physically active child will spend enough energy to balance caloric intake. In addition, research shows that the physically active child feels more attractive and enjoys body satisfaction in contrast to the sedentary child who may feel lonely, shy, and a sense of hopelessness [2].

Vegetarian Diet

With an apparently increasing interest in the vegetarian diet and requests by some child-care centers to serve vegetarian meals, a discussion of the types and nutrient composition of each seems appropriate. Although the following classifications exist, individual diets differ in the extent to which they avoid animal products so an individual assessment is needed.

- Vegans or total vegetarians avoid meat, fish, fowl, eggs, dairy, and other animal products.
- Lacto-ovo vegetarians avoid meat, fish, and fowl.

According to the American Dietetic Association [27], when planning a diet one should choose a wide variety of foods from the food groups in the Food Guide Pyramid. The foods may include fresh fruits, vegetables, whole-grain breads and cereals, nuts and seeds, legumes, low-fat dairy products or fortified soy substitutes, and a limited number of eggs, if desired. Vegetarians are advised to limit their intake of foods with low nutrient density. Consuming a food source rich in vitamin C with meals will further enhance absorption of available iron. Grains, vegetables, legumes, seeds, and nuts eaten over the course of the day complement one another in their amino acid profiles to form complete proteins, and precise planning and complementation of proteins within each meal, as urged by the recently popular "combined proteins theory," is unnecessary.

With the help of a registered dietitian or public health nutritionist, care providers can discuss the adequacy of vegetarian diets of children with parents. The CDC growth charts should be used to record and monitor height, weight, and BMI in the center for children on modified diets as well as for all children.

Children on vegetarian diets will need a regular source of vitamin B_{12} and, if sunlight exposure is in question, supply vitamin D. Foods rich in iron, calcium, and zinc should be emphasized. Consider including frequent meals and calorie-dense snacks to meet energy needs. Also consider offering fortified soy milk (calcium, vitamins A & D) through the preschool years. Another good protein alternate is tofu, the curd produced from clotting soy milk (soybean product). A good protein and calcium source, this custard-like product can be used in a variety of ways, and it appeals to many children.

The U.S. Department of Agriculture allows reimbursement for meals served to vegetarian children if a suitable protein substitute is included in the meal (for

Baked beans and brown bread
Lentil soup with rice
Hopping John (beans and rice)
Split pea soup with bread
Cereal, hot or cold, with milk
Cereal cooked with milk
Pizza, cheese, with whole-wheat crust
Cheese sandwich
Peanut butter sandwich
Tamale pie with beans and cheese
Toast and eggs
Granola with cereal, nuts, and seeds

Figure 5.3   Food combinations that supply complete protein (See Chapter 7 for combinations and quantities of foods that qualify for Child Care Food Program reimbursement)

example, eggs, cheese, legumes, soy protein) in the amounts required. Combination dishes with complementary proteins or which include milk and eggs are included in Figure 5.3.

Is the Vegetarian Diet Safe for Children?   Many care providers are concerned whether the diet will retard growth and development of children. Use of a vegetarian diet that allows ample energy and adequate supplies of dairy products and eggs is safe for children as long as fat is not restricted in children under 2. Researchers have found that preschool children raised in families using lacto-ovo-vegetarian diets compare favorably for most nutrients [28].

On the other hand, multiple nutritional deficiencies have been found in infants raised in a strict vegetarian community without the use of fortified soy milk products [29]. Some vegetarian groups who describe their diets as "macrobiotic" do not include any egg and dairy products in their diets. The growth curves, especially for height, for one group of macrobiotic vegetarian children were more depressed than those of other vegetarian children. Growth patterns among vegetarians vary; when diets were more restricted as to animal foods, children's growth was consistently more affected. Obtaining enough energy in the diet appears difficult for some vegetarian children. Although protein intake may fall within the normal range, energy levels for some vegetarian children may be below recommended levels.

Nutrients that are most difficult to acquire on a vegan or strict vegetarian diet are listed in Table 5.11 along with the animal and plant sources for the nutrients. The nutrients include protein, vitamin A, riboflavin, vitamin B_{12}, vitamin D, calcium, and iron. Most experts agree with the American Dietetic Association, which states that vegan and lacto-ovo vegetarian diets can meet nutrient needs throughout the lifecycle if "appropriately planned." The ADA offers a food guide pyramid for vegetarian meal planning [27] as a way to assure nutrient needs are met, and it is available on their Web site http://www.eatright.org.

Table 5.11　Nutrients often limited in vegan or strict vegetarian diets

Nutrient	Food Sources	
	Animal	Plant
Protein-amino acids	Meat, poultry Fish Eggs Milk, cheese Yogurt	Legumes Nuts, seeds Soy milk Meat analogs
Vitamin A value	Liver Butter Whole milk Cheese Fortified low-fat milk	Orange vegetables and fruits Greens Fortified margarine
Riboflavin (B^2)	Liver Milk products Red meat	Fortified cereals Fortified soy milk
Vitamin B^{12}	Liver, meat Poultry, fish Milk products Eggs	Fortified soy milk, cereals, and 　meat analogs
Vitamin D	Fortified milk Fish oils	Fortified soy milk
Calcium	Milk, cheese Yogurt Sardines and salmon with 　bones	Calcium-fortified soy milk Greens Almonds, filberts
Iron	Liver Red meat	Fortified grain products Dried beans and lentils Whole-wheat bulgar

Source: Modified from National Dairy Council. (1979). *Vegetarian Nutrition.* Rosemont, IL.

Diet and Hyperactivity

In the 1970s the Feingold diet [30] became popular for the treatment of hyperactivity. The diet is based on the idea that much of the hyperactivity associated with learning disabilities that occurs in school-age children can be attributed to ingestion of food additives and salicylates (an ingredient commonly found in aspirin). Feingold asserted that hyperactivity could be treated effectively through dietary changes in up to two-thirds of the children. Claims of the diet's success have had an impact on care providers and parents who have children with hyperkinesis (severe hyperactivity) in their care.

Since that time, the scientific community, the National Institutes of Health, the Food and Drug Administration, and the National Education Association have studied the issues and diet. A recent review of research by Wolraich [31] finds no credible evidence for the success of this diet. Parents who attempt to use this strict diet should be cautioned that they are imposing a strict diet with no scientific evidence proving its efficacy. Wolraich proposes the following possible consequences: (a) teaching children to blame their behavior on what they eat, (b) making children perceive themselves as fragile and unhealthy, (c) promoting eating behaviors that may seem peculiar to other children, and (d) depriving children of an appropriate medical or psychological evaluation of their behavior [32].

Does Sugar Cause Hyperactivity?   Studies have failed to prove this myth to be true [31, 33]. Sucrose does not adversely affect behavior of children. Parents of hyperactive children often attempt to control sugar intake but are unsuccessful. Attempting to impose restrictions may exacerbate already strained parent–child interactions. However, a change in family lifestyle to adopt a healthier diet, increase physical activity, and increase attention to the life of the child may indeed have beneficial effects on nutritional status as well as behavior.

EXERCISE AND PHYSICAL FITNESS

Fine motor control steadily improves while 3- to 5-year-olds also develop their large muscles in their legs, arms, and torso. They love to run, jump, throw, and catch, and need little encouragement for active movement. However, the caregiver needs to be acutely aware of the necessity to include gross motor fitness into the total curriculum.

The 2002 National Association for Sport and Physical Education (NASPE) guidelines recommend at least 60 minutes of physical activity daily for preschoolers. They emphasize that during the preschool years, children should be encouraged to practice movement skills in a variety of settings [34].

Preschoolers exercise naturally

Javernick reports that "although most preschool programs purport to encourage gross motor development, we teachers often neglect this area of development and emphasize instead fine motor, cognitive, and social development" [35]. Javernick also cites Broadhead and Church [36], who wrote, "Without enriching experiences, children are often thought to be at risk educationally. Typically, intervention programs aimed at compensating for existing or expected problems are cognitively and socially oriented. There is little emphasis upon motor development."

In their position statement on Good Teaching Practices for 4- and 5-year-olds, the National Association for the Education of Young Children recommends "children have daily opportunities to use large muscles, including running, jumping, and balancing. Outdoor activity is planned daily so children can develop large muscle skills, learn about outdoor environments, and express themselves freely. Children have daily opportunities to develop small muscle skills through play activities such as pegboards, puzzles, painting, cutting, and other similar activities" [37].

Gallahue and Ozumun categorize fundamental movement abilities developed through play as locomotor, manipulative, and stability abilities [38]. He feels that teachers should integrate into their daily program opportunities for movement activities that reflect preschoolers' needs, interests, and levels of ability.

Vannier and Gallahue [39] classify the fundamental abilities into three groups: locomotor, manipulative, and nonlocomotor. They define locomotor movement abilities (LMA) as those by which the body is transported in a horizontal or vertical direction from one point in space to another. Activities that are considered to be fundamental LMA are running, jumping (vertical or horizontal), leaping, galloping, skipping, hopping, sliding, and climbing.

Manipulative movement abilities (MMA) are those that involve giving force to objects or receiving force from objects. Activities are overhand throwing, catching, kicking, striking, dribbling, ball rolling, trapping, and volleying.

Nonlocomotor movement abilities (NLMA) are those where the body remains in place but moves around on its horizontal or vertical axis. Nonlocomotor movements place a premium on gaining and maintaining equilibrium in relation to the force of gravity. Axial movements such as reaching, twisting, turning, bending, stretching, lifting, carrying, pushing, and pulling are fundamental nonlocomotor abilities.

The following suggestions will help you offer a better balanced fitness program:

1. Be aware that preschoolers are involved in developing and refining fundamental movement patterns in the three categories of movement. These movements are developed and refined through exploration and discovery. Plan your environment to facilitate such activity.
2. Follow the NAEYC's "Good Teaching Practices for 4- to 5-Year-Olds" [37] to provide a program that daily encompasses all areas of child development, including physical development.
3. Get into the act. The teacher/caregiver needs to participate enthusiastically but not to dominate or control motor activities. It will help you to become physically fit also.

Preschoolers make the most of a movement opportunity

4. Be aware that preschoolers need at least 60 minutes of daily physical activity. Under "normal" conditions (that is, in a balanced program), preschoolers will acquire movement skills through everyday activity.*

5. Beware of unusual-sounding movement activity programs that make extravagant but untested claims. (See Appendix VII for a listing of appropriate play materials for 3-, 4- and 5-year-olds.)†

*In special situations with special needs children, more structured motor experiences may be necessary. See Cook, Ruth E., Tessier, Annette, and Klein, D. (2000). *Adapting Early Childhood Curricula for Children in Inclusive Settings.* Upper Saddle River, NJ: Merrill/Prentice Hall.

†For additional resources, consult these recent publications on play: Isenberg, J. P., and Jalongo, M. R. (2001). *Creative Expression and Play in Early Childhood.* Upper Saddle River, NJ: Merrill/Prentice Hall. Frost, J. L., Wortham, S., and Reifel, S. (2001). *Play and Child Development.* Upper Saddle River, NJ: Merrill/Prentice Hall. Pica, R. (1995). *Experiences in Movement.* Albany, NY: Delmar Publishing.

POLICIES OF THE CENTER

The center caring for the preschooler has many opportunities to promote their health and well-being. Center policies should be consistent with good nutrition, promote positive child-feeding practices, limit inactive leisure time, and promote daily physical activity. Consider the following components for center policies:

- Limit media time to no more than 1 to 2 hours a day, including time at home.
- Provide a total of at least 1 hour for physical activity.
- Allow children to participate in nutrition education activities on a regular basis.
- Offer a variety of healthy food choices in a positive atmosphere.
- Encourage children to identify and respond to their hunger and satiety sensations.

PUBLIC HEALTH RESOURCES

School-age children are eligible for a variety of school-based feeding and nutrition programs. See Chapter 7 for program specifics.

SUMMARY

- Preschool children should interact with each other and the teacher regarding food, food preparation, food service, and cleanup.
- Mealtime should be related to other educational activities in the center (for example, those fostering language development skills).
- Energy needs per pound of body weight are decreasing during the preschool years, although the total amount of energy required has been increasing over the previous 3 years.
- Dietary intakes of the preschooler may be less-than-recommended for iron, calcium, vitamin C, and vitamin A.
- The care provider, along with the dietitian or nutritionist, can assess growth patterns and dietary intake patterns to ensure that growth is progressing within normal limits and that the dietary intake contains enough of the energy and nutrients known to be essential for the preschooler.
- Snacks should be offered from the Food Guide Pyramid groups. They should contribute nutrients without supplying excessive energy to the diet.
- Children can be well nourished if their diets contain all the essential amino acids.
- When considering the use of sweeteners, care providers and food service personnel must take responsibility for preparing foods with a high nutrient density and without excessive calories from fat and sugar.
- Studies of the Feingold diet for hyperactivity show no evidence to support the additive-free diet as the cure. Yet the only effects from this diet may be limited to psycho-social consequences from severe dietary restrictions and a lack of proper medical evaluation.
- The early childhood environment provides numerous opportunities for both fine and gross motor development, yet teachers often neglect the gross motor, which results in an unbalanced program.
- Preschoolers should have at least 60 minutes of daily physical activity.

DISCUSSION QUESTIONS

1. List the reasons you may record a gain of 2 pounds or more per month for a 4-year-old.
2. How do the nutrient and energy needs of the preschooler compare with those of the toddler?
3. State how the food needs of the preschooler differ from and are similar to your own.
4. What special considerations should be given to the arrangements of the eating situation?
5. Describe guidelines for choosing snacks to use in the preschool center.
6. Should foods containing additives be eliminated from the preschool diet to control hyperactivity?
7. Should low-fat foods with a sugar substitute ever be used in the center?
8. How can obesity development be monitored within the center or school?
9. What is the role of the teacher and family in creating an environment that prevents obesity?
10. What do you feel can be done to ensure a balanced program that will include opportunities for total motor fitness?

REFERENCES

1. Patel, D. R., Pratt, H. D., & Greydanus, D. E. (2002). Pediatric neurodevelopment and sports participation. When are children ready to play sports? *Pediatric Clinics of North America, 49*(3), 505–531, v–vi.
2. Strauss, R. S. (2002). Childhood obesity. *Pediatric Clinics of North America, 49*(1), 175–201.
3. Ogden, C. L., Troiano, R. P., Briefel, R. R., Kuczmarski, R. J., Flegal, K. M., & Johnson, C. L. (1997). Prevalence of overweight among preschool children in the United States, 1971 through 1994. *Pediatrics, 99*(4), E1.
4. United States Department of Agriculture. (May 1999). *Profile of overweight children.* Retrieved January 26, 2003, from http://www.usda.gov/cnpp/insight/ins13a.pdf
5. Bessler, S. (1999). Nutritional assessment. In P. Q. Samour, K. K. Helm, & C. E. Lang (Ed.), *Handbook of pediatric nutrition* (p. 21). Gaithersburg, MD: Aspen.
6. Institute of Medicine (2002). *Dietary Reference Intakes for energy, carbohydrate, fiber, fat, fatty acids, cholesterol, protein, and amino acids.* Washington, DC: National Academy Press.
7. Lin, B. H., G. J., Frazao E. (May-August 2001). Examining the well-being of children: American children's diets not making the grade. *Food Review, 24,* 8–17.
8. Institute of Medicine. (1997). *Dietary Reference Intakes for calcium, phosphorus, magnesium, vitamin D, and fluoride.* Washington, DC: National Academy Press.
9. National Research Council, Subcommittee on the 10th Edition of the RDAs, Food and Nutrition Board. (1989). *Recommended Dietary Allowances.* Washington, DC: National Academy Press.

10. Hunt, J. (2002). Moving toward a plant-based diet: Are iron and zinc at risk? *Nutrition Reviews, 60* (5), 127–130.

11. Johnson, S. L. (2000). Improving preschoolers' self-regulation of energy intake. *Pediatrics, 106* (6), 1429–1435.

12. Birch, L. L. (1998). Development of food acceptance patterns in the first years of life. *Proceedings of the Nutrition Society, 57*(4), 617–624.

13. Briley, M. E., Jastrow, S., Vickers, J., & Roberts-Gray, C. (1999). Can ready-to-eat cereal solve common nutritional problems in child-care menus? *Journal of the American Dietetic Association, 99*(3), 341–343.

14. Committee on Nutrition. (2001). The use and misuse of fruit juice in pediatrics. *Pediatrics, 107*(5), 1210–1153.

15. American Academy of Pediatrics, American Public Health Assocation, & Maternal and Child Health Bureau. (January 2002). *Caring for our children: National health and safety performance standards guidelines for out-of-home child care programs.* Retrieved March 8, 2002, from http://nrc.uchsc.edu/cfoc/index.html

16. McConahy, K. L., Smiciklas-Wright, H., Birch, L. L., Mitchell, D. C., & Picciano, M. F. (2002). Food portions are positively related to energy intake and body weight in early childhood. *Journal of Pediatrics, 140*(3), 340–347.

17. Birch, L. L. (1998). Psychological influences on the childhood diet. *Journal of Nutrition, 128*(2 Suppl), 407S–410S.

18. Fisher, J. O., & Birch, L. L. (1999). Restricting access to palatable foods affects children's behavioral response, food selection, and intake. *American Journal of Clinical Nutrition, 69*(6), 1264–1272.

19. U.S. Department of Agriculture. (January 9, 2003). *The National Organic Program: Labeling packaged products.* Retrieved January 14, 2003, from http://www.ams.usda.gov/nop/ProdHandlers/LabelTable.htm

20. Dietz, W. H., & Gortmaker, S. L. (2001). Preventing obesity in children and adolescents. *Annual Review of Public Health, 22,* 337–353.

21. Dietz, W. (1999). How to tackle the problem early: The role of education in the prevention of obesity. *International Journal of Obesity Related Metabolic Disorders 23 Suppl 4,* S7–9.

22. American Academy of Pediatrics. (2003). Prevention of pediatric overweight and obesity. *Pediatrics, 112*(2), 424–430.

23. Dewey, K. G., Heinig, M. J., Nommsen, L. A., Peerson, J. M., & Lonnerdal, B. (1993). Breast-fed infants are leaner than formula-fed infants at 1 year of age: The DARLING Study. *American Journal of Clinical Nutrition, 57*(2), 140–145.

24. Fisher, J. O., Birch, L. L., Smiciklas-Wright, H., & Picciano, M. F. (2000). Breast-feeding through the first year predicts maternal control in feeding and subsequent toddler energy intakes. *Journal of the American Dietetic Association, 100*(6), 641–646.

25. Butte, N. F. (2001). The role of breast-feeding in obesity. *Pediatric Clinics of North America, 48*(1), 189–198.

26. Robinson, T. N. (2001). Television viewing and childhood obesity. *Pediatric Clinics of North America, 48*(4), 1017–1025.

27. American Dietetic Association. (1997). Vegetarian diets—Position of the ADA. *Journal of the American Dietetic Association, 97,* 1317–1321.

28. Tayter, M., & Kaye, L. S. (1989). Anthropometric and dietary assessment of omnivore and lacto-ovo-vegetarian children. *Journal of the American Dietetic Association, 89*(11), 1661–1663.

29. Zmora, E., Gorodischer, R., & Bar-Ziv, J. (1979). Multiple nutritional deficiencies in infants from a strict vegetarian community. *American Journal of Diseases of Children, 133,* 141.

30. Feingold, B. F. (1975). *Why your child is hyperactive.* New York: Random House.

31. Wolraich, M. (1998). Attention deficit hyperactivity disorder. *Professional Care of Mother and Child, 8*(2), 35–37.

32. Barrett, S. (March 11,2002). *The Feingold Diet: Dubious benefits, subtle risks.* Retrieved January 14, 2003, from http://www.quackwatch.org/01QuackeryRelatedTopics/feingold.html

33. Young, S. N. (2002). Clinical nutrition: 3. The fuzzy boundary between nutrition and psychopharmacology. *Canadian Medical Association Journal, 166*(2), 205–209.

34. *NASPE releases first ever Physical Activity Guidelines for Infants and Toddlers.* (February 6, 2002). Retrieved January 23, 2003, from http://apherd.org/naspe/template.cfm?template=toddlers.html

35. Javernick, E. (1988). Johnny's not jumping: Can we help obese children? *Young Children 42*(5):59, 1987, 43(21).

36. Broadhead, G., & Church, G. (1985). Motor characteristics of preschool children. *Research Quarterly for Exercise and Sport, 56,* 208–214.

37. National Association for Education of Young Children. (1986). *Good teaching practices for 4 and 5 year olds—A position for the National Association for Education of Young Children.* Washington DC: National Association for Education of Young Children.

38. Gallahue, D. L., & Ozumun, J. C. (2002). *Understanding motor development* (5th ed.). Columbus, OH: McGraw-Hill.

39. Vannier, M. H., & Gallahue, D. (1978). *Teaching physical education in elementary schools.* Philadelphia, PA: Saunders.

6

The 6- to 8-Year-Old

LEARNING OBJECTIVES

Students will be able to:
- Describe growth patterns of school-aged boys and girls.
- State food needs related to nutrient and energy recommendations.
- Describe acceptable foods for after-school snacks.
- List appropriate strategies to prevent cardiovascular disease in children.
- State the concern for dental caries at this age.
- Describe physical activities that can facilitate energy balance.

Middle childhood is generally defined as beginning at 6 years of age and ending at the onset of puberty. This chapter describes growth and nutrition needs from age 6 to 8; additional resources describe middle childhood and adolescence in more detail [1, 2]. Growth patterns that have been similar during the preschool years now begin to differentiate by gender. Whereas the young girl at 7 to 8 years may already have accelerated growth, rapid growth rate will not be seen in the young boy until 9 or 10 years at the earliest. For both girls and boys, the period from 6 to 8 years is a relatively stable growth period and may even be called latent compared to the preschool years or what is still to come during adolescence.

The influence of school and extracurricular activities becomes more important during middle childhood. The significance of body image, especially for young girls, may be seen in what clothing is worn and what foods are eaten. School and community activities allow children to use their increased physical ability. Attendance at school for a full day provides regularity for activities, including food service. Foods are generally accepted and appetites improve as the children participate in activities that increase energy expenditure. The routines and activities of full-day school encourage adaption of regular times for snacks and meals.

WEIGHT AND STATURE

Before 6 years of age, boys may be a little taller and heavier than most girls, but by 8 to 9 years the girls are catching up and many weigh almost as much as the average boy in the same class. The 7- to 8-year-old girls begin to admire their older peers, and "dieting" can occur at this early age.

From infancy to 6 years of age, the percentage of body fat for both boys and girls decreases, while lean body mass increases. However, at about 6 years girls begin to have a higher proportion of their weight as fat, a trend that will continue into adolescence and adult years. The 6- to 8-year-old gains approximately 2 to 3 inches in height and 4.5 to 6.5 pounds per year. Table 6.1 shows the average height and weight of boys and girls at this age.

Table 6.1   Median weights and heights for 6- to 8-year-olds.

Age	Boys Height (inches)	Girls Height (inches)	Boys Weight (pounds)	Girls Weight (pounds)
6 years	44	45	46	45
7 years	50	48	50	48
8 years	56	50.1	56	50.25

Source: National Center for Health Statistics in collaboration with the National Center for Chronic Disease Prevention and Health Promotion (CDC). (2000). Growth charts available at http://www.cdc.gov/ growthcharts/.

Ongoing measures of weight and stature continue to be important indicators of health status. Continue plotting these measures and BMI on the NCHS/CDC growth charts discussed in Chapters 4 and 5 and Appendix IV. In particular, look for trends toward obesity or weight loss represented by a BMI at or above the 85th percentile or below the 5th percentile. Such changes will alert the care provider to any abnormalities that need further evaluation from a physician.

ENERGY AND NUTRIENT NEEDS

A review of children's nutrition reveals that most 6- to 11-year-olds are not eating five fruits and vegetables a day. If french fries and fruit juices would not be counted as servings, the numbers would be worse. Children are drinking more sodas and consuming less milk, thereby sinking calcium and vitamin D intake below recommended levels and threatening the children's ability to achieve optimum bone health. Overall there are trends toward eating more calories and abstaining from physical activity. Parents who have been concerned about their preschooler's appetites often find their 6- to 8-year-old child willing to eat more foods now. Teachers will find they have limited influence during meals, as children now sit together.

Energy

Dietary recommendations for 6- to 8-year-olds are listed in DRIs for ages 4 to 8 (Table 6.2). Energy requirements may increase or decrease based on physical activity; increases in caloric needs are due not only to aging and growth. Energy needs during middle childhood may vary widely; therefore, plotting monthly heights and weights on growth charts should indicate needs for more or less energy.

Active 6- to 8-year-olds' energy needs, according to the DRI, remains 1742 calories for boys and 1642 calories for girls [3]. Energy needs vary with activity level, so very active children require additional energy whereas sedentary children, perhaps those who watch more than 2 hours of TV daily and play computer games, will require less energy to maintain a healthy weight. To achieve optimal growth, ensure that children balance energy intake with physical activity. As described earlier in the chapter, track height and weight on BMI-for-age growth charts.

Table 6.2   Dietary Reference Intakes (DRIs) for children ages 4 to 8

Daily Nutrient Needs	4 to 8 years
Requirement (EER)	
Estimated Energy	1642*
Fat % of total calories†	25–35
Protein (g/d)	19‡
Fiber (g/d)	25
Vitamin A (μg/d)	400
Vitamin D (μg/d)	5
Vitamin E (mg/d-TE)	7
Vitamin C (mg/d)	25
Folate (μg/d)	200
Vitamin B_6 (mg/d)	0.6
Vitamin B_{12} (μg/d)	1.2
Calcium (mg/d)	800
Phosphorus (mg/d)	500
Iron (mg/d)	10
Magnesium (mg/d)	130
Zinc (mg/d)	5

*EER based on active females ages 1–2 and 3–8; boys will need 1046 cal/d and 1742 cal/d respectively. All other DRIs based on ages 1–3 and 4–8.
†Fat % is Acceptable Macronutrient Distribution (AMDR).
‡Numbers in bold are RDAs, otherwise numbers are adequate intakes or AIs.
Source: Data compiled from *Recommended Dietary Allowances.* (1989). Washington, DC: National Academy Press. Intitute of Medicine. (2002). *Dietary Reference Intakes for Energy, Carbohydrate, Fiber, Fat, Fatty Acids, Cholesterol, Protein, and Amino Acids.* Washington, DC: National Academy Press. Intitute of Medicine. (1997). *Dietary Reference intakes for Calcium, Phosphorus, Magnesium, Vitamin D, and Fluoride.* Washington, DC: National Academy Press. Intitute of Medicine. (1998). *Dietary Reference Intakes for Thiamin, Riboflavin, Niacin, Vitamin B₆, Folate, Vitamin B₁₂, Pantothenic Acid, Biotin, and Choline.* Washington, DC: National Academy Press. Intitute of Medicine. (2000). *Dietary Reference Intakes for Vitamin C, Vitamin E, Selenium, and Carotenoids.* Washington, DC: National Academy Press. Intitute of Medicine. (2001). *Dietary Reference Intakes for Vitamin A, Vitamin K, Arsenic, Boron, Chromium, Copper, Iodine, Iron, Manganese, Molybdenum, Nickel, Silicon, Vanadium, and Zinc.* Washington, DC: National Academy Press. These reports may be accessed via http://www.nap.edu.

Fat

By 6 years of age, children should have made the transition to lower-fat milk, dairy, and to leaner cuts of meat. Limiting use of fried foods on the menu can also contribute to lowering the total fat in the diet to the AMDR of 25% to 35% of calories [3, 4], or about 25 g per day (see Table 6.2).

Calculating the Low-Fat Diet.   Care providers may wish to determine how to plan a diet with 25% to 35% of calories from fat. Rather than excluding fatty foods, include a greater amount and variety of fruits, vegetables, legumes and nuts, and enriched whole grains. The result will be a reduction in fat. See Chapter 5 for steps to calculate percent of fat in the diet.

Fat restriction or elimination is harmful to children because fat is an essential diet component and carries many nutrients. Too little fat in the diet can result in excessive intake of sugar, stunted growth, growth failure, and vitamin or protein deficiencies [5].

Calcium

Calcium intake of U.S. children is below the recommended level of 800 mg/d [6]. This trend is particularly true for girls ages 6 through 11 who meet only 59% of the requirement. As caloric intake has increased over the last 10 years, calcium consumption has fallen short. Usually drinking milk at mealtime is the best way to ensure adequate calcium intake [7], yet many school lunch programs offer orange drink as a substitute beverage. Also worth concern is milk's declining consumption in relation to soft drinks' increases. Heightened obesity is not coincidental [8]. Thus, ensure that fat reduction strategies are not misinterpreted as messages to "drink less milk" [7].

> Kosher practices restrict the use of milk with meat. For children eating kosher, find acceptable methods to increase milk intake. Chapter 1 discusses the influence of religion and culture on food practices.

Keep in mind, the DRI for calcium can easily be met with three servings of low-fat or skim milk served daily [6].

Dietary Supplementation

According to the American Academy of Pediatrics (AAP), national dietary and health surveys have shown little evidence of vitamin or mineral inadequacies, with the exception of iron, for this age group [1]. There is little basis for routine vitamin and mineral supplementation in healthy children, especially as the growth rate decreases after infancy. However, the AAP has identified the need for supplements for some children, including those

- from deprived families, especially children who suffer from parental neglect or abuse;
- with anorexia, poor and capricious appetites, or poor eating habits;
- on dietary regimens to manage obesity; and
- consuming vegetarian diets without adequate dairy products (vitamin B_{12} is absent from vegetable foods).

FOOD NEEDS

Meeting the food needs of middle childhood requires consumption of food in slightly greater quantities than at earlier years. Children will gradually increase serving sizes to meet the serving size recommendations from the Food Guide Pyramid for Young Children to the general Food Guide Pyramid serving sizes. The number of servings will be similar to, and in some cases larger than, the adult serving size. Table 6.3 shows a recommended food pattern that meets nutrient needs

Table 6.3   Recommended food intake according to food group and average serving sizes (ages 6 to 10 years)

Food Group	Servings/Day*	Average Serving (ages 6 to 10)
Vegetables	3–5	
Emphasize green or yellow vegetables		1/2 c*
Fruits	2–4	
Vitamin C source (citrus fruits, berries, melons)		1/2 c
Breads and Cereals (Whole Grain)	6–11	
Bread		1 slice
Ready-to-eat cereals, whole grain, iron-fortified		1 oz
Cooked cereal including macaroni, spaghetti, rice, etc. (whole grain, enriched)		1/2 c
Milk and Milk Products	3–4	
Whole or 2% milk (1.5 oz cheese = 1 c milk) (c = 8 oz or 240 g)		1 c
Meat and Alternates	3–4 including:	
Lean meat, fish, poultry, eggs†	2	3 oz
Nut butters (peanut, soynut)	1–2§	4 Tbsp‡
Cooked dried beans or peas		1/2 c
Nuts	1 oz	
Fats and Oils	3	
Butter, margarine, mayonnaise, oils		1 tsp

*Allow a minimum service of 1 Tbsp/year of age for cooked fruits, vegetables, cereals, and pasta until the child reaches 1/2 c portion size or 8 years.

†To enhance overall nutrient content of diet, include eggs (two to three times a week) and liver occasionally.

‡Serving size recommended by Illinois State Board of Education, Department of Child Nutrition: Child Care Food Program—required meal patterns, Springfield, IL, June 1986, The Board.

§Include nut butters, dried (cooked) beans, or peas as often as possible to meet nutrient recommendations and use additional servings of meats when legumes, beans, and nuts are omitted.

for children 6 to 8 years of age. The food pattern is a guide from which to choose foods for a nutritionally adequate, low-fat diet. Table 6.4 gives additional suggestions for planning low-fat meals and snacks. Also, Figure 6.1 answers frequently asked questions regarding feeding school-age children.

Snacks

From ages 6 through 8, many children still consider snacks as treats; they may expect chips, cookies, toaster pastries, cupcakes, doughnuts, french fries, or soda for snacks. Reserve these foods for occasional treats and don't purchase these "goodies" every week. Additionally, if treats are offered on the menu, do not restrict intake even for overweight children. Table 6.5 lists snack food and nutrient composition. Snacks still supply needed calories and nutrients, but school-age children need only two snacks

How can I get my child to eat more fruits and vegetables?

- Be a positive role model—eat more fruits and vegetables yourself.
- Keep a variety of fresh fruits and vegetables in the home.
- Keep juice in the refrigerator.
- Put a bowl of fruit on the kitchen table or counter.
- Eat fruits with meals or for dessert.
- Pack fruits or vegetables to eat at school.
- Wash and cut up fruits and vegetables and keep them in a clear container (so they can be seen easily) in the refrigerator, along with low-fat dip or salsa.
- Serve two or more vegetables with dinner (including at least one your child likes).
- Serve a salad with a choice of dressing.
- Use plenty of vegetables in soups, sauces, and casseroles.
- Plant a garden with your child.
- Offer a variety of fruits and vegetables, but don't force your child to eat.

How can I help my child, who does not drink milk, get enough calcium?

- Serve low-fat flavored milk.
- Use low-fat dairy foods in recipes (for example, in puddings, milkshakes, soups, casseroles, and cooked cereals).
- Serve low-fat dairy foods for snacks (for example, cheese, yogurt, and frozen yogurt).
- Offer unusual dairy foods (for example, yogurt juice drinks and new flavors of low-fat yogurt).
- Serve other calcium-rich foods (for example, tofu [if processed with calcium sulfate], broccoli, and turnip greens).
- If your child is lactose intolerant, try serving small portions of milk and other dairy foods frequently; milk with a meal or snack; yogurt or lactose-reduced milk; aged hard cheeses (for example, cheddar, colby, Swiss, and Parmesan) that are low in lactose; or lactase tablets or drops in the milk.
- Serve calcium-fortified foods (for example, orange juice or cereal).
- If these strategies don't work, talk to a health professional about giving your child a calcium supplement.

How can I teach my child to make healthy food choices away from home?

- Encourage your child to make healthy food choices when purchasing food at school, stores, and restaurants, and from vending machines.
- Review school and restaurant menus with your child and discuss healthy food choices.
- Identify on these menus foods that are low in fat and calories.
- Encourage your child to eat salads, low-calorie dressings, and broiled or baked meats.
- Encourage your child to avoid eating fried foods or to reduce the serving size (for example, by splitting an order of French fries with a friend).
- Teach your child to be assertive and to request food modifications (for example, asking the server to "hold the mayonnaise").

My child snacks on high-fat and high sugar foods. What should I do?

- Limit the availability of high-fat and high-sugar foods (for example, chips, candy, and soft drinks) at home.
- Keep a variety of easy-to-prepare and healthy foods on hand and teach your child to prepare them.
- Stock up on healthy snack foods (for example, pretzels, baked potato chips, popcorn, juice, fruit, vegetables, low-fat granola bars, and yogurt).
- Help your child to determine healthy food choices at school, stores, and restaurants, and from vending machines.

My child has become a vegetarian. Should I be concerned?

- With careful planning, a vegetarian lifestyle can be healthy and meet the needs of a growing child.
- A vegetarian diet that includes dairy foods and eggs usually provides adequate nutrients; however, your child may need to take an iron supplement.
- A vegan diet restricts the use of all animal products, and may be low in certain nutrients if not carefully planned; be sure to seek out resources such as The American Dietetic Association's Food Guide Pyramid for Vegetarians at http://www.eatright.org.

Figure 6.1   Frequently asked questions about feeding school-age children
Source: Story, M., Holt, K., & Sofka, D. (2000). *Bright Futures in Practice: Nutrition.* Arlington, VA: National Center for Education in Maternal and Child Health, Georgetown University.

Table 6.4   Specific recommendations to lower fat intake

Use	Include Less Often
Skim milk, 1% milk	Whole milk
Yogurt, skim cottage cheese, low-fat sour cream and dips*	Dairy dips with sour cream
Fruit ices, sorbets, and low fat ice cream	Ice cream, prepared pudding
Low-fat meats	High-fat meats
Margarine (sparingly), low-fat margarine (free of hydrogenated fat)	Butter, palm and coconut oil
Low-fat cheese*	High-fat cheese
Low-fat dressings	Regular oil- or fat-based dressings
Legumes, beans, and peas	High-fat meats, fried meats
Fruits and vegetables, fresh, or frozen, steamed	Deep-fried vegetables and fruit breads
Crackers or low-fat snack chips, pretzels, crusty bread low in saturated fat	Snack chips, crackers made with hydrogenated fats

*Check labels for fat content.

School friends talk and eat during a lunch break

at about 200 calories each [4]. Regularly select nutrient-packed fruits and vegetables or whole grains, lean meats, or low-fat dairy, nuts, and nut butters. Good timing will keep meals and snacks from running together. Watch the clock, and be sure to offer snacks more than 1 1/2 hours from a planned meal. Also, brush teeth after snacks to prevent cavities or choose less sticky foods. (For a list of less sticky foods see the Dental Health section later in this chapter.)

Table 6.5   Energy, fat, and fiber content for snack foods

Food (serving size)	Total Kcal	Fat Kcal	Fat % Kcal	Fiber
Favorite snacks				
Snickers (1bar)	280	153	55	1
Reese's Peanut Butter Cups (2)	270	149	55	1.5
Chocolate chip cookie (1)	52	21	40	0
Poptart, S'mores, frosted (1)	200	54	27	1
Oreo (1)	53	18	34	0.3
Ice cream, 10% fat (1c)	273	131	48	0
Soda (12 oz)	144	0	0	0
Potato chips (1 oz)	161	102	63	1
Cheetos	160	90	56	1.5
Doritos	140	63	45	1
Recommended Snacks				
Apple (1 medium)	81	4	5	4
Soynuts (1/3 c)	140	54	39	4
Banana (1 medium)	105	5	5	3
Grapes (1c)	107	5	5	2
Orange (1)	64	3	5	3
Saltine crackers (6)	78	19	24	0.6
Graham cracker (4 squares)	118	25	22	0.8
Wheat multigrain cracker (4 small)	58	23	31	0.4
Yogurt, plain, low fat (1 c)	155	34	22	0
Triscuits, low fat (4)	130	27	21	4
Whole-wheat bagel with 2 tsp jelly	188	9	5	2

Source: Information as interpreted from manufacturer's labels by the NDDA Laboratory, Southern Illinois University at Carbondale, 2002, and the USDA National Nutrient Database for Standard Reference, Release 15 (August 2002).

PROMOTING HEALTHFUL EATING BEHAVIORS

As school children mature, peers, mass media, and school environment exert a greater influence upon eating behaviors. In response, teachers and parents should continue positive dietary practices:

- Help children recognize internal hunger cues, as distinguished from external influences such as TV commercials.
- Aid children in recognizing satiety and slowing down to avoid overeating.
- Invite children to participate in selecting and preparing foods.
- Encourage school programs to include fruits, vegetables, string cheese, peanut butter, yogurt, and breadsticks as staple choices and to reduce chips and treats.
- Support school policies requiring a variety of fruits and vegetables.
- Limit access to vending machines.
- Model healthful eating and activity.

A child should be able to read before using a microwave

- Promote friendly conversations and social experiences at meals.
- Encourage tasting of new foods.

What Influences Eating Patterns?

Television and Media.   Hours viewing television/videotapes and computer games by school-age children have increased, reaching an average of 2.5 hours per day for 6- to 7-year-olds and 4.5 hours per day for 8 years and older [9]. Recent research by Robinson has identified a most direct causal relationship between TV viewing and obesity [9]. In addition, television shows directed toward children notoriously advertise calorie-dense, low-nutrient foods, and carbonated beverages. Television or movie characters entice children to request these items, especially with packaging displaying favorite characters.

Family.   Some studies show that preteens are influenced more by peer pressure than by parental actions [10]. However, family income and economic status do influence the types and amounts of food purchased and where foods will be eaten (restaurants or in the home). Family structure and parental work schedules reduce the time available for preparing healthy meals at home. Busy families typically select convenience foods, fast foods, and restaurants.

Children at 6 to 8 years old can prepare some of their own meals, especially breakfast, from what is available in the kitchen. They can be responsible for choosing from 15% to 20% of their foods every day. With microwaves and prepackaged frozen microwave items, children have a wider variety of foods from which to choose and can learn at an earlier age to prepare nutritious meals for themselves.

Resources like the USDA's Team Nutrition at http://www.fns.usda.gov/tn/ may help parents maintain healthy habits during this stage and make better choices for quick, nutritious food preparation at home.

School.   As children spend more time at school they make more of their own food decisions; parents have less control over what their children eat. Responsibility rests with the school system to provide at least one-third of recommended nutrients for children participating in school lunches, and at least one-half if breakfast is eaten at school. An after-school care provider may provide another 150 to 300 calories (for example, with crackers or cookies and milk), 10% to 15% of energy and nutrients. Parents, therefore, may be responsible for less than 40% of total energy needs, serving children only one meal per day.

After-school providers are challenged to select children's menus from available and accepted foods. Menus should provide nutrients that help children maintain a desirable body weight and contribute to growth and development. Teachers, coaches, and after-school providers influence children's food choices through their words of advice and their behaviors. Getting involved in the food programs at school and demonstrating a positive attitude toward nutritious foods served at school will encourage children to adopt healthful eating behaviors. Likewise, complaining about food service influences children negatively. Teachers should support the food service, or if changes are needed, they should help make changes.

Schools can access a variety of resources to improve health such as the USDA's Team Nutrition at http://www.fns.usda.gov/tn/.

Carbonated Beverages.   Carbonated beverages have become commonplace in children's diets. Calories from sodas account for a higer proportion of caloric intake in obese children [7].

The influence of media, schools, and the use of snack foods and carbonated beverages will affect children's eating patterns. Evaluate each area for its contribution to weight abnormalities. Individual or school-wide goals can be developed to reduce the impact on children.

NUTRITION-RELATED HEALTH CONCERNS

Lactose intolerance, dental caries, cardiovascular disease, and persistent weight problems are directly related to nutrition. Lactose intolerance, discussed in detail in Chapter 4, may be seen in as many as 30% of school-age children. Many children will have learned that they prefer milk with meals, not alone for the afternoon milk break. Some children tolerate flavored milk better than regular, whole, or skim milk and should be allowed to make this food choice. The importance of continuing a supply of calcium to this age group is essential. Bone density is established during the early years of life; it is crucial to aid the prevention of osteoporosis during early years by establishing a pattern of eating dairy products high in calcium.

Dental Health

For children, the most common chronic infectious disease is dental caries—tooth decay. Among 6-year-olds, at least 40% experience dental caries in their primary teeth. By adolescence, 85% of 17-year-olds will have dental caries. Prevention hinges on keeping the oral cavity free of cariogenic microbes and reducing exposure to sticky carbohydrate foods and carbonated beverages [7]. Not surprisingly, children who consume a diet high in simple carbohydrates and who are late to initiate oral hygiene practices or who are not monitored in caring for their teeth are at a greater risk for tooth decay. The prevalence of dental caries is greatest among special population groups that include the following: children from families who have a low socioeconomic status, homes where parents do not have a high school education, and certain ethnic groups—African Americans, Hispanics, and Native Americans. In modern society, dental caries is becoming a disease of the poor [11].

Low-Caries Diet.   The "stickiness" of snack foods and the length of time taken for the saliva to remove the snack from the teeth should be considered when providing nutritious snacks. Of the following foods studied by dental researchers [5], some barely stick to the teeth while others are rated "stickiest."

Barely sticky: apples, bananas, hot fudge sundaes, milk chocolate bar
Moderately sticky: chocolate caramel bars, white bread, caramels, creme-filled sponge cake
Stickier: dried figs, jelly beans, plain doughnuts, chocolate-caramel-peanut bars, raisins
Stickiest: granola bars, oatmeal cookies, sugared cereal flakes, potato chips, corn chips, pretzels, salted crackers, puffed oat cereal, creme sandwich cookies, peanut butter crackers, french fries

Sticky snacks leave particles on the teeth for longer periods of time, which makes the teeth susceptible to attacks from the enamel-eroding acids produced by bacteria. Typical snack foods—cereals, crackers, and cookies (even plain, low-fat/sugar)—are stickiest. According to research, some foods like cheese, nuts, milk, and chocolate appear to have an anticariogenic effect [11].

In addition, carbonated beverages are highly cariogenic. In fact, drinking soda is of increasing concern. Drinking sodas prolongs the exposure of teeth to carbohydrates, producing a new attack on the teeth with every sip. The sugar in the soda combines with bacteria in the mouth to form acid that degrades the tooth enamel. Even diet sodas have acid that tears down the tooth enamel. Each acid attack may last up to 20 minutes. The Missouri Dental Association has developed a new media campaign aimed at reducing soda consumption by children. For educational materials go to their Web page: http://www.modental.org/Stop_The_Pop.html.

Snack Foods.   Emphasizing snacks that are less sticky may help reduce dental problems seen in this group. However, any snack can be eaten if the teeth are cleaned after eating.

Oral Health Care.   Children should have a regular routine established for care of teeth and gums at home and brush after meals at school. They should be familiar with the dentist, participating in regular visits at least once a year. Many dentists apply sealants as new permanent teeth emerge to deter the development of caries. This can be an effective treatment for children with high risk of dental caries.

Centers should encourage oral health screening and promote sound dental health by (1) providing nutritious low-caries-risk diet, (2) restricting sweets to mealtimes when salivary flow is greater, (3) promoting follow-up on dental screenings, and (4) promoting oral health practices such as teeth-brushing and flossing.

Cardiovascular Disease

Children 6 to 8 years old are generally healthy and at low risk for nutrition-related problems. Still, there is general agreement that coronary heart disease may begin in youth and undergo progression through young adulthood, even though symptoms usually do not appear until middle age or later [12–14]. Perhaps due to increased media coverage of cardiovascular disease, care providers and parents are concerned that children's diets protect the heart.

Whether to recommend diet restrictions for young children and at what age has been hotly debated over the last decade. Two long-term studies involving dietary fat modification in childhood found success in lowering cholesterol levels without adversely affecting growth development [15, 16]. Nonetheless, there is evidence that higher-fat diets cannot guarantee nutritional adequacy compared to moderate-fat diets [17]. Researchers found that nutrient inadequacies for calcium, zinc, and vitamin E persist at all fat-intake levels.

The 2002 National Academy of Science's DRI recommendations propose one hour of daily physical activity for children and diets that meet the new Acceptable Macronutrient Distribution Ranges, AMDR, as the best method for modifying diet to improve long-term cardiovascular health in children [3]. For children 4 to 8, the AMDR for fat levels are 25% to 35% of total calories while carbohydrates should not exceed 45% to 65% of calories because eating very low levels of fat combined with very high levels of carbohydrates does not reduce risks for cardiovascular disease. In regards to type of fat, the DRIs recommend the lowest possible level of cholesterol, trans fatty acids (hydrogenated fat often used in margarine) and saturated fatty acids achievable in a nutritionally adequate diet [3].

National health surveys reveal an alarming trend toward persistent obesity threatening the cardiovascular health and quality of life of our nation's children. Although a decrease in physical activity plays a significant role in the obesity epidemic, the general population (except for preschoolers) seems to have switched to eating less fat but still overeating [18, 19]. Thus an overemphasis on reducing fat intake as a preventive measure against heart disease may be unsuccessful if obesity is ignored in favor of simply reducing fat.

To reduce risks for cardiovascular disease, obesity prevention is the most promising strategy. Early studies of childhood coronary risk factors identified elevated BMI as the most predictive risk factor of cardiovascular disease [20]. Each risk condition for cardiovascular disease is exacerbated by obesity. Childhood obesity is associated with increased prevalence of elevated cholesterol levels, hypertension, and Type II Diabetes in adulthood. In fact, studies of overweight children have found double the rate of cardiovascular disease and hypertension and triple the rates of Type II Diabetes [21], an alarming tread.

Measures to reduce fat in the diet and improve nutrient density of the diet have been included earlier in this chapter and each preceding chapter. Obesity prevention strategies have been discussed in Chapter 5. Obesity interventions are discussed in this chapter, and recommendations for increasing physical activity are discussed in Chapters 3–6.

Children with increased risk for heart disease should be identified and screened by their physicians by age 7. Those with hypertension, elevated plasma cholesterol, and/or with high-risk parents (parents who have cardiovascular disease or have one or more of the known risk factors such as elevated cholesterol, diabetes, or obesity) may need additional dietary measures at school. For these children, modifying the fat in diets below the AMDR but not less than the National Cholesterol Education Program's lower limit of 20% of calories seems appropriate, as long as sufficient calories and nutrients are available for adequate growth [13].

Obesity

We hope that you adopt our view that proper eating behaviors produce healthful habits and optimal health. For each age group, we describe positive child feeding practices, ones enabling children to self-regulate food intake, to increasingly choose nutritious foods, and to enjoy a lower-fat, fiber-rich, nutrient-dense diet. At the same time, parents and schools can make a conscious effort to engage in daily physical activity and discourage inactive leisure pastimes. In spite of adopting all these practices you will still find childhood obesity at your school. Prior to this age, prevention is the accepted approach for most children. Chapter 5 discussed many aspects of a preventive approach. At age 6 and older the obese child can achieve success in long-term weight maintenance; therefore we will explore aspects of obesity intervention in children.

Strauss [21]defines childhood obesity as a cultural problem, not a medical problem, because until adulthood most children will resist the medical complications of obesity—high blood pressure, heart disease, and some forms of cancer [21, 22]. The most immediate consequence for these children is emotional pain from lowered social status and self-esteem [21, 22]. Therefore, teachers, caregivers, and parents should promote a positive body image in children. Some actions to promote positive body image are discussed in Figure 6.2.

Ikeda and Mitchell [23] reviewed guidelines for the treatment and prevention of obesity, as issued by recognized national health authorities: American Academy of Pediatrics, American Dietetic Association, and the American Heart Association. All groups recognize the need for a multidimensional family-based intervention that focuses on improving eating and activity behaviors, while promoting self-esteem and avoiding extremes such as eating disorders.

- Demonstrate healthy eating behaviors, and avoid extreme eating behaviors.
- Focus on non–appearance-related traits when discussing yourself and others.
- Praise children for academic and other successes.
- Demonstrate interest and affection to children regardless of weight.
- If children are overweight, don't criticize their appearance—offer support instead.
- Share with a health professional any concerns you have about eating behaviors or body image.
- Read children's magazines or watch shows to identify and eliminate ones focusing on appearance, dieting, and thinness as the ideal.
- Promote physical activities in which children of all sizes and skill levels can be successful.
- Discuss the normal variation in body sizes and shapes among children.
- Consider ways school practices may negatively affect body image and seek to change.
- Refer children and parents with weight control issues to a pediatric obesity treatment center.

Figure 6.2   Teacher actions to foster positive body image among children
Source: Story, M., Holt, K., & Sofka, D. (2000). *Bright Futures in Practice: Nutrition.* Arlington, VA: National Center for Education in Maternal and Child Health, Georgetown University.

A review of successful obesity treatment programs for children revealed commonalities [24]. Parents and children were treated separately, in programs that emphasized reduction in inactivity, reduction in TV time, and increased physical activity.

Goals should be achievable and allow for the existence of a healthy and active, yet overweight child who would not benefit from weight loss. The treatment goal, generally, is the slowing of the rate of weight gain in proportion to linear growth, not an actual loss in weight. Dietary restrictions are not effective for most children. A prominent children's study found that parents who exerted a high degree of control over their children's eating may be too severe [25]. The result was a loss of lean tissue, inhibited growth, and depleted energy reserves needed for periods of stress.

Parent Involvement.   Parent involvement is an important determinant of children's success at achieving a healthy weight [26], but parents can go overboard. Research shows that parents advocating the eating of healthy foods may, in fact, be teaching their children to dislike these foods. Children yearn for high-fat, energy-dense foods when they are denied access to those "goodies" while peers and other family members are allowed to indulge [27]. In addition, parental adiposity relates to their children's adiposity; however, this correlation is probably a product of the home environment and family lifestyle rather than genetics.

Screen Time.   Amount of time spent viewing television is one of the most powerful predictors of obesity for 6- to 11-year-olds even when controlling for other known variables associated with childhood obesity [9]. Therefore, parents and care providers should work together to limit the total number of hours their children spend with media at home and school to no more than 1 to 2 hours or less per day [28, 29].

Dietary Approaches.   Ikeda and Mitchell reviewed dietary approaches to childhood obesity and concluded that using dieting to treat obese children can create problems and has not proven to be an effective technique [23]. Child feeding practices should remain positive and nonpunitive. Strict control of intake will not improve children's ability to regulate their own intake. Instead, they advocate improving the quality of the diet.

Strategies for Maintaining Healthy Weight.   Once the BMI standards ($\geq$ 95%) identify overweight or obese children (Chapters 2 and 5), parents should discuss the problem with their children's pediatrician and teacher. When all parties recognize the need to address the weight problem, ask the consulting dietitian or nutritionist to assist in developing an action plan leading to behavior change in the school and in the home. Planning and implementation of school activities should include the following:

- Increase activity. Plan more gross motor activities during the day and select activities that the overweight child can enjoy and accomplish. Find ways to make it fun for everyone.
- Reduce inactivity or sedentary behaviors. Screen time, TV, computer games, and the Internet, should be discouraged in favor of social interaction, reading, and conventional games. Aim for $\leq$ 1 hour per day total screen time.
- Promote self-esteem by offering "constructive blame-free alternatives" [30]. Figure 6.2 lists important practices that foster self-esteem and a positive body image.
- Reduce or eliminate soft drink consumption, an excessive source of calories [7]. Between meals use water to satisfy thirst. Also, limit juices to 6 to 8 oz/day or less. Serve skim milk with meals.
- Decrease fat, saturated fat, and cholesterol by increasing fruits and vegetables to five or more servings per day and switching to whole-grain breads and cereals.
- Decrease frequency of high-fat menu items such as french fries, macaroni and cheese, or pizza. Offer smaller portion sizes of these foods, or seek reduced fat options.

Monitor Progress.   Behavior goals should describe actions that can be accomplished at the school and home. Provide this information to the family's pediatrician to verify that modifications in exercise and diet will not interfere with any other medical treatment; you might track, and thereby monitor for progress, these actions/behaviors in a journal.

In addition, weigh obese or overweight children each month and record these weight and height measurements on appropriate growth charts, including BMI charts. Provide this information, along with the children's educational progress, to the parents. However, the value of this practice (weighing children) is lost if the procedure becomes negative and singles out overweight or obese children. It is important to track progress, but centers may want to leave this type of tracking to health care professionals. Instead, the centers might focus on tracking behaviors that increase physical activity, reduce inactivity, and improve diet quality.

Teachers can help parents understand and practice sound eating and child feeding practices in the home by reviewing Chapters 3–6. Parents can encourage their children to adopt healthful eating practices by eating nutritious foods with their children, setting up a positive structured eating environment in the home, allowing children to self-regulate their food intake, and helping their children find age-appropriate ways to participate in family meals.

Obesity Resources
- Shape Up America!
  6707 Democracy Boulevard, Suite 306
  Bethesda, MD 20817
  Tel: (301) 493-5368
  Fax: (301) 493-9504
  Web site: http://www.shapeup.org/

- Weight-Control Information Network
  1 WIN Way
  Bethesda, MD 20892-3665
  Tel: (301) 984-7378, (800) WIN-8098
  Fax: (301) 984-7196
  Web site: http://www.niddk.nih.gov/health/nutrit/win.htm

- American Dietetics Association
  Web site: http://www.Eatright.org

Eating Disorders

As our culture has increasingly promoted dieting and thinness, eating disorders have become more common. Children's concern with dieting, thinness, and achieving the ideal body—which puts them at risk for eating disorders—is now reported in those as young as 5 years of age. Thus, teachers should be familiar with symptoms of eating disorders (Figure 6.3) and the resources for coping with the condition.

Eating Disorders Resources
- American Anorexia Bulimia Association
  165 West 46th Street, Suite 1108
  New York, NY 10036
  Tel: (212) 575-6200
  Fax: (212) 501-0342
  Web site: http://www.aabainc.org/home.html

Common symptoms of anorexia nervosa are as follows:
- Excessive weight loss in a short period of time
- Continuation of dieting although thin
- Dissatisfaction with appearance, belief that body is fat, even though severely thin
- Loss of menstrual period
- Unusual interest in certain foods and development of unusual eating rituals
- Eating in secret
- Obsession with exercise, and depression

Common symptoms of bulimia nervosa are as follows:
- Loss of menstrual period
- Unusual interest in certain foods and development of unusual eating rituals
- Eating in secret
- Obsession with exercise
- Depression
- Binge-eating
- Binge-eating with no noticeable weight gain
- Vomiting or laxative use
- Disappearance into bathroom for long time periods, possibly to induce vomiting
- Alcohol or drug abuse

Figure 6.3   Recognizing a child with eating disorders
Source: Story, M., Holt, K., & Sofka, D. (2000). *Bright Futures in Practice: Nutrition.* Arlington, VA: National Center for Education in Maternal and Child Health, Georgetown University.

- Anorexia Nervosa and Related Eating Disorders
  P.O. Box 5102
  Eugene, OR 97405
  Tel: (541) 344-1144, (800) 931-2237
  Web site: http://www.anred.com

- National Association of Anorexia Nervosa and Associated Disorders
  P.O. Box 7
  Highland Park, IL 60035
  Tel: (847) 831-3438
  Fax: (847) 433-4632
  Web site: http://www.anad.org

EXERCISE AND PHYSICAL FITNESS

Children 6 to 8 years old have gained better control of fine motor and can coordinate the small muscles of the hand and eye to an increasing degree. This is a time when children become immersed in games and physical activities. To continually develop and refine locomotor and nonlocomotor skills, they must have many opportunities to test and retest their abilities [31]. This age group benefits from having increased structure in their physical fitness activities both at home and at school.

Components of Fitness

The American Academy of Pediatrics Committee on Sports Medicine and School Health defines the components of fitness to include muscle strength and endurance, flexibility, body fat composition, and cardiorespiratory endurance [32].

Frequency of Physical Education Classes

In its position statement regarding integrated components of appropriate and inappropriate practice in the primary grades, the National Association for the Education of Young Children recommends that physical education be integrated into the curriculum each day [33]. The American Academy of Pediatrics stresses that physical education classes be held at least three times weekly in the primary grades and that such classes are critical to developing and maintaining physical fitness in young children [34].

Parents often feel that their children get plenty of exercise in their school's gym classes and at recess. The fact is that many students get as little as one hour of physical education a week. In addition, schools have traditionally emphasized sports that promote agility and specialized skills (baseball, basketball, football) rather than cardiovascular fitness (bicycling, swimming, running, fast walking, aerobic exercise, tennis). Most physical activity in school-age children occurs outside of physical education classes [35].

In light of these facts, in 1987 the American Academy of Pediatrics issued a policy statement urging parents and pediatricians to appeal to their local school boards to maintain, if not increase, physical education programs [34].

As indicated in Chapter 2, numerous fitness surveys have indicated that children in the United States are underexercised. Society's current emphasis on academics has resulted in an unbalanced curriculum that lacks opportunities for children to develop and refine motor skills. Nevertheless, the United States has more physical educators, more gyms, more swimming pools, and more recreational opportunities than any country in the world. Some would say we also have the best medical science system in the world, yet we lead the world in degenerative diseases [1, 35]. Regularly scheduled physical education classes and incorporating lifelong cardiovascular fitness skills, rather than those that promote game skills that are often not carried into adulthood, must be provided. Without such programs, the risk of latent disorders such as obesity, elevated blood pressure, and high cholesterol level (all of which can lead to coronary heart disease) will continue to threaten children.

The President's Council on Fitness and Sports recommends that the cardiovascular system be stressed for at least 30 minutes a day through vigorous activity. Without this activity, children can progressively decondition with the final result

Physical activity of the 6- to 8-year-old takes many forms

being alarmingly poor cardiac condition [35]. In contrast, the 2002 National Academies' Institute of Medicine report recommends that to maintain cardiovascular health at a maximal level regardless of weight, adults and children should spend a total of at least 1 hour each day in moderately intense physical activity [3]. This amount of activity is double the daily minimum goal that was set by the 1996 Surgeon General's report [36].

Parents' Role

As with all societal problems, the schools can't do it all. Parents can do much to instill awareness of fitness in the primary-age child. We caution, however, that parents must remember that if it is not fun, children won't do it. The American Academy of Pediatrics suggests that parents do the following:

1. Incorporate fitness activities into the family lifestyle.
2. Introduce children to a variety of athletic activities, they are easily bored.
3. Become involved with your children's activities by either playing a sport with them or coaching a team.
4. If safe, encourage your child to walk to school or take a shorter bus ride and walk part way.

5. Encourage after-school activities and limit TV viewing during this time.
6. Set a good example.

The 6- to 8-year-old has everything to gain by being physically fit. Exercise boosts self-image and improves physical strength and stamina as well as scholastic performance.

SUMMARY

- Young children's eating habits during the 6- to 8-year period are influenced by the school setting, coaches, and teachers.
- Girls will continue into adolescence having a higher proportion of their weight as fat.
- Supplementation with vitamins and minerals is needed only in children at high risk for poor dietary intake.
- To limit fat to 25% to 35% of calories, substitutions should be found for high-fat snacks.
- Dental caries are a common problem in school age children. Many parents do not realize the dental health risk of carbonated beverages.
- Poor body image and low self-esteem are the most immediate consequences of childhood obesity.
- Children of parents who are at high risk for coronary heart disease should be screened by their physicians for elevated cholesterol by 7 years of age, and if a true risk exists, a diet intake of 20% to 35% of calories from fat can begin.
- Successful obesity treatment strategies involve parents, increased physical activity, improved diet quality, and reduction in television and computer time.
- Parents as well as schools play a critical role in providing opportunities for 6- to 8-year-olds to participate in both structured and unstructured physical fitness activities.

DISCUSSION QUESTIONS

1. How does the 7-year-old differ from the 4-year-old in eating habits?
2. Compared to the younger child, would you expect to see more or less anemia?
3. How do the nutrient and energy needs of the school-age child compare to those of the preschooler?
4. Calculate the energy you need each day and list foods usually eaten. How can your diet be modified to include only 30% calories from fat?
5. Can snack foods with more than 30% fat be included in the diet?
6. Which foods are most cariogenic?
7. Why is a low-caries diet recommended at this age?
8. Discuss the need to both modify and increase physical education activities.

REFERENCES

1. Story, M., Holt, K., & Sofka, D. (2000). *Bright futures in practice: Nutrition.* Arlington, VA: National Center for Education in Maternal and Child Health, Georgetown University.

2. Nissenberg, S., & Pearl, B. (2002). *Eating right from 8 to 18: Nutrition solutions for parents.* New York: Wiley.

3. National Academies' Institute of Medicine. (2002). *Dietary Reference Intakes for energy, carbohydrate, fiber, fat, fatty acids, cholesterol, protein, and amino acids (macronutrients), A Report of the Panel on Macronutrients.* Washington, DC: National Academy Press, Subcommittees on Upper Reference Levels of Nutrients and Interpretation and Uses of Dietary Reference Intakes, and the Standing Committee on the Scientific Evaluation of Dietary Reference Intakes.

4. Kuzemchak, S. (February 1, 2003). *Smart parent's guide to healthy snacking.* Retrieved January 27, 2003, from http://www.parents.com/articles/health/5218.jsp

5. Symposium: Dietary Guidelines for Children. (1996). *Journal of Nutrition, 126,* 1031–1041.

6. Institute of Medicine (1997). *Dietary Reference Intakes for calcium, phosphorus, magnesium, vitamin D, and fluoride.* Washington, DC: National Academy Press.

7. Johnson, S. L. (2000). Improving preschoolers' self-regulation of energy intake. *Pediatrics, 106*(6), 1429–1435.

8. Jacobson, M. (October 21, 1998). *Liquid candy: How soft drinks are harming Americans' health.* Retrieved January 14 2003, from http://www.cspinet.org/sodapop/liquid_candy.htm

9. Robinson, T. N. (2001). Television viewing and childhood obesity. *Pediatric Clinics of North America, 48*(4), 1017–1025.

10. Baskett, L. M. (1984). Ordinal position differences in child's family interactions. *Developmental Psychology, 20,* 1026–1031.

11. Schafer, T. E., & Adair, S. M. (2000). Prevention of dental disease. The role of the pediatrician. *Pediatric Clinics of North America, 47*(5), 1021–1042, v–vi.

12. American Academy of Pediatrics Committee on Nutrition. (1998). Cholesterol in childhood. *Pediatrics, 101*(1 Pt 1), 141–147.

13. U.S. Department of Health and Human Services (1991). *National Cholesterol Education Program: Report of the Expert Panel on Blood Cholesterol Levels in Children and Adolescents.* (No. NIH Publication No. 91-2732) Washington, DC: U.S. Government Printing Office.

14. Strong, J. P., Malcom, G. T., McMahan, C. A., Tracy, R. E., Newman, W. P., 3rd, Herderick, E. E., et al. (1999). Prevalence and extent of atherosclerosis in adolescents and young adults: Implications for prevention from the Pathobiological Determinants of Atherosclerosis in Youth Study. *Journal of the American Medical Association, 281*(8), 727–735.

15. Obarzanek, E., Kimm, S., Barton, B., Van Horn, L., & Kwiterovich, P., Simons-Morton, D.G., et al. (2000). Long-term safety and efficacy of a cholesterol-lowering diet in children with elevated low-density lipoprotein cholesterol: Seven-year results of the Dietary Intervention Study in Children (DISC). *Pediatrics, 107*(2), 256–264.

16. Simell, O., Niinikoski, H., Ronnemaa, T., Lapinleimu, H., Routi, T., Lagstrom, H., et al. (2000). Special Turku Coronary Risk Factor Intervention Project for Babies (STRIP). *American Journal of Clinical Nutrition, 72*(5 Suppl), 1316S–1331S.

17. Ballew, C., Kuester, S., Serdula, M., Bowman, B., & Dietz, W. (2000). Nutrient intakes and dietary patterns of young children by dietary fat intakes. *Journal of Pediatrics, 136*(2), 181–187.

18. U.S. Department of Agriculture. (May 1999). *Profile of overweight children.* Retrieved January 26, 2003, from http://www.usda.gov/cnpp/insight/ins13a.pdf

19. Ogden, C. L., Troiano, R. P., Briefel, R. R., Kuczmarski, R. J., Flegal, K. M., & Johnson, C. L. (1997). Prevalence of overweight among preschool children in the United States, 1971 through 1994. *Pediatrics, 99*(4), E1.

20. Valente, A., Newburger, J., & Lauer, R. (2001). Results of expert meetings: Conducting pediatric cardiovascular trials: Hyperlipedemia in children and adolescents. *American Heart Journal, 142*(3), 433–439.

21. Strauss, R. S. (2002). Childhood obesity. *Pediatric Clinics of North America, 49*(1), 175–201.

22. United States Surgeon General. (2002). *Overweight and obesity fact sheet: Overweight in children and adolescents.* Retrieved November 11, 2002, from http://www.surgeongeneral.gov/topics/obesity/calltoaction/fact_adolescents.htm

23. Ikeda, J. P., & Mitchell, R. A. (2001). Dietary approaches to the treatment of the overweight pediatric patient. *Pediatric Clinics of North America, 48*(4), 955–968, ix.

24. Dietz, W. H., & Gortmaker, S. L. (2001). Preventing obesity in children and adolescents. *Annual Review of Public Health, 22,* 337–353.

25. Oliveria, S. A., Ellison, R. C., Moore, L. L., Gillman, M. W., Garrahie, E. J., & Singer, M. R. (1992). Parent-child relationships in nutrient intake: The Framingham Children's Study. *American Journal of Clinical Nutrition, 56*(3), 593–598.

26. Birch, L. L., & Davison, K. K. (2001). Family environmental factors influencing the developing behavioral controls of food intake and childhood overweight. *Pediatric Clinics of North America, 48*(4), 893–907.

27. Birch, L. L., & Fisher, J. O. (1998). Development of eating behaviors among children and adolescents. *Pediatrics, 101*(3), 539–549.

28. American Academy of Pediatrics Policy Statement. (2001). Children, adolescents, and television. *Pediatrics, 107*(2), 423–426.

29. American Academy of Pediatrics Committee on Public Education. (2001). Children, adolescents, and television. *Pediatrics, 107*(2), 423–426.

30. Davison, K. K., & Birch, L. L. (2001). Weight status, parent reaction, and self-concept in five-year-old girls. *Pediatrics, 107*(1), 46–53.

31. Arnheim, D. D., & Sinclair, W. A. (1979). *The clumsy child: A program of motor therapy.* St. Louis, MO: Mosby.

32. American Academy of Pediatrics Fact Sheet (1987). *Fitness: The myths and the facts.* Elk Grove Village, IL: American Academy of Pediatrics.

33. National Association for the Education of Young Children. (January 1988) Position statement on developmentally appropriate practice in the primary grades, serving 5- through 8-year-olds. *Young Children, 43,* 64–68.

34. American Academy of Pediatrics policy statement. (1987). Physical fitness and the schools. *Pediatrics, 80*(3), 449–450.

35. The President's Council on Physical Fitness and Sports (1986). *National School Population Fitness Survey.* (No. Research Project 282-84-0086). HHS—Office of the Assistant Secretary of Health and University of Michigan Press.

36. *Physical activity and health: A report of the Surgeon General.* (1996). Atlanta, GA: U.S. Department of Health and Human Services, Centers for Disease Control and Prevention, National Center for Chronic Disease Prevention and Health Promotion.

7

Center Food Service

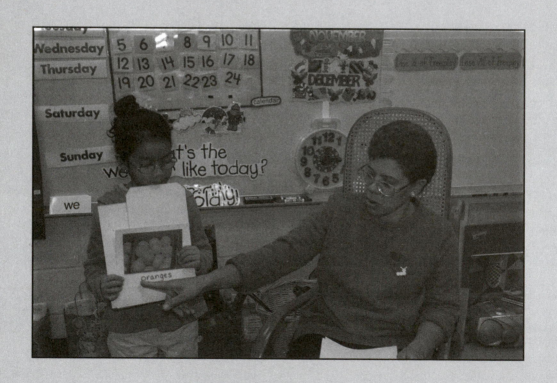

LEARNING OBJECTIVES

Students will be able to:

- List and describe standards and guidelines for food served to young children in child-care programs and use the food guides to plan and evaluate menus for infants, toddlers, and preschoolers.
- Describe programs that address child health and nutrition issues.
- Describe how food service personnel, the dietitian, and teachers may participate in making the menu a focal point of the curriculum.
- Consider the various styles of meal service and describe the setting where you might use each.
- State the Seven Steps to Successful Ethnic Meals.
- Using food safety Web sites and the text, identify food safety risks in food preparation and service in child-care centers.

Food service for the child cared for away from home can occur in a variety of settings. Some of the settings, especially those receiving public funds, must follow regulations outlined by the U.S. Department of Agriculture and the Department of Health and Human Services, as well as state and local agencies. In addition to providing nourishment, the foods served can be used to teach nutritional practices that will lead to a healthy lifestyle. To provide nourishment and nutrition education in the classroom, the principles of food service must first be understood and practiced. The menu and lesson plan (Chapters 8–9) can be the tools used to help coordinate the nutrition and food needs of children with learning activities in the classroom and home.

When teachers and food service personnel work together to select foods and plan the style in which they are served, both professional groups feel committed to making food and nutrition work in the classroom. The teacher and food service personnel plan the food service activities described in this textbook jointly. An outcome of this joint planning may be seen when teachers do not have to "beg the food service personnel" for a fresh pineapple or have to purchase one themselves for the classroom. Instead, the teacher and food service personnel plan "menus for learning" from which educational experiences naturally evolve. Although you, as the teacher, may not take direct responsibility for writing the menus or preparing foods, you are an important component of the process if the menu, food preparation, foods, and food service are to be used in the curriculum. Without center food service there can be no nourishment. Likewise, without curriculum planning involving food service activities there can be few educational activities around food and mealtime. This chapter is intended to help the teacher understand the regulations and processes used by the dietitian and food service personnel in providing food for children. The teacher is then in a better position to use the food service activities when teaching children.

FOOD SERVICE GUIDELINES IN CHILD-CARE CENTERS

Before one begins to plan menus or to discuss the planning of the curriculum around the menu, it is necessary to review the food standards that apply to feeding children. The Dietary Guidelines (see Chapter 2; http://www.health.gov/dietaryguidelines/dga2000/document/summary/default.htm) are important in planning healthy diets and activity.

The Food Guide Pyramid (http://www.nal.usda.gov:8001/py/pmap.htm) modified for young children ages 2 to 6 years was introduced in Chapter 2 and used to plan a full day's menu for a preschooler. The Food Guide Pyramid is an outline of what to eat each day based on the Dietary Guidelines. It's not a rigid prescription but a general guide that lets you choose a healthful diet. The Pyramid calls for eating a variety of foods to get the nutrients needed and at the same time the energy or calories needed to maintain healthy weight.

Most centers will not be providing all the meals and snacks but only portions of the daily food intake and will be following not only the Dietary Guidelines but also guidelines for one or more of the Child Nutrition Programs (see Box 7.1).

Child and Adult Care Food Program

USDA's Child and Adult Care Food Program (CACFP) plays a vital role in improving the quality of child care and making it more affordable for many low-income families. Each day, 2.6 million children receive nutritious meals and snacks through CACFP. CACFP serves nutritious meals and snacks to eligible children and adults who are enrolled for care at participating child-care centers, day-care

---

BOX 7.1   Child nutrition programs

Child Nutrition Programs (http://www.fns.usda.gov/cnd/Default.htm) include:

Child and Adult Care Food Program (http://www.fns.usda.gov/cnd/care/cacfp/cacfphome.htm) gives information about providing nutritious meals and snacks to infants, young children, and impaired adults who receive day care. This program also offers after-school snacks in sites that meet eligibility requirements.

National School Lunch Program (http://www.fns.usda.gov/cnd/Lunch/default.htm) provides information about nutritious lunches and the opportunity to practice skills learned in classroom nutrition education. This program also offers after-school snacks in sites that meet eligibility requirements.

School Breakfast Program (http://www.fns.usda.gov/cnd/Breakfast/Default.htm) provides information about nutritious breakfasts to promote learning readiness and healthy eating behaviors.

Special Milk Program (http://www.fns.usda.gov/cnd/Milk/Default.htm) provides information about offering milk to children who do not have access to other meal programs.

Summer Food Service Program (http://www.fns.usda.gov/cnd/Summer/Default.htm) provides information about serving healthy meals and snacks to low-income children during long school vacations.

homes, and adult day-care centers. CACFP also provides meals to children residing in homeless shelters, and snacks to youths participating in after-school care programs. This section primarily describes services to child-care centers.

History and Administration. In 1977, Public Law 95-627 made the then-titled Child Care Food Program (CCFP) permanent and it was authorized under the National School Lunch Act (42 U.S.C. 1766). The U.S. Department of Agriculture (USDA), Food and Nutrition Service (FNS), which administers CACFP through grants to states, issues program regulations. The program is usually administered within most states by the state educational agency. In a few states it is administered by an alternate agency, such as the state health or social services department; and in Virginia, the FNS Mid-Atlantic Regional Office directly administers CACFP. Independent centers and sponsoring organizations enter into agreements with their administering state agencies to assume administrative and financial responsibility for CACFP operations. Eligible public or private nonprofit child-care centers, outside-school-hours care centers, Head Start programs, and other institutions that are licensed or approved to provide day-care services may participate in CACFP, independently or as sponsored centers.

Meal Reimbursement. Independent centers and sponsoring organizations receive cash reimbursement for serving meals to enrolled children that meet federal nutritional guidelines. The CACFP meal pattern varies according to age and types of meal served. Child-care centers and day-care homes may be approved to claim up to two reimbursable meals (breakfast, lunch, or supper) and one snack, or two snacks and one meal, to each eligible participant, each day. Shel-

> **Sponsors for family day-care homes**
>
> Individual family day-care homes must be sponsored by an organization that has been approved by CACFP. CACFP provides reimbursement for meals and snacks served to small groups of children receiving nonresidential day care in licensed or approved private homes. A family or group day-care home must sign an agreement with a sponsoring organization to participate in CACFP. The sponsoring organization organizes training, conducts monitoring, and helps with planning menus and filling out reimbursement forms. Day-care homes must be licensed or approved to provide day-care services.

ters may serve each child up to three reimbursable meals (breakfast, lunch, and supper) each day. After-school care programs may claim reimbursement for serving each child one snack each day. In addition to cash reimbursement, USDA makes donated agricultural commodities or cash-in-lieu-of commodities available to institutions participating in CACFP.

Centers participating in CACFP may charge a single fee (nonpricing program) to cover tuition, meals, and all other child-care services, or they may charge separate fees for meals (pricing program). All day-care homes and the vast majority of centers participate in CACFP as nonpricing programs, because the fees they charge cover all areas of their child-care services.

Cash assistance for meals served to eligible children in centers is based upon the participant's eligibility under specific income eligibility guidelines for free, reduced-price, or paid meals. Participants from households with incomes at or below 130% of poverty are eligible for free meals. Participants in centers with household incomes

BOX 7.2   Reimbursement for CACFP*

Meal Type	Free	Reduced-Price	Paid
Breakfast	$1.17	$0.87	$0.22
Lunch or Supper	2.14	1.74	0.29
Snack	0.58	0.28	0.05

*2002 data

between 130% and 185% of poverty are eligible for meals at a reduced price. Institutions must determine each enrolled participant's eligibility for free and reduced-price meals served in centers. (At the time of this writing 130% of the poverty level was $22,945 for a family of four; 185% was $32,653.) A participant's eligibility for free and reduced-price meals in centers may be established by submission of an income eligibility statement, which provides information about family size and income. The information submitted by each household is compared with USDA's Income Eligibility Guidelines (http://www.fns.usda.gov/cnd/IEGs&NAPs/IEGs.htm). Children whose families receive benefits from the Food Stamp Program, Food Distribution Program on Indian Reservations (FDPIR), or state programs funded through Temporary Assistance for Needy Families (TANF) are categorically eligible for free meals. Children who are income-eligible participants of Head Start or Early Head Start programs are automatically eligible for free meals, without further application or eligibility determination. Centers receive payments based on the type of meal served and the number eligible for free, reduced-price, or paid meals. As of July 1, 2002, centers in most states (payments are higher in Alaska and Hawaii) received an average of 15.5¢ in commodities (or cash in lieu of commodities) for each lunch or supper they serve, in addition to the meal rates (Box 7.2).

Menu Planning.   The CACFP program reimburses for meals that are served to eligible children and that follow the meal pattern for either infants or young children. Child Care Infant Meal Pattern for breakfast, lunch, or supper, and snack is included in Table 7.1 and can be found online at http://www.fns.usda.gov/cnd/care/ProgramBasics/Meals/InfantBreakfast.htm. To encourage breastfeeding, centers may claim reimbursement for meals where infants are breastfed [1]. Meal patterns for breakfast, lunch, or supper, and snack for children after one year are included in Table 7.2 (http://www.fns.usda.gov/cnd/care/ProgramBasics/).

To learn more about CACFP services to other centers and instititutions, contact your state agency at http://www.fns.usda.gov/cnd/Contacts/StateDirectory.htm or telephone at (703) 305-2286, 3101 Park Center Drive, Room 914, Alexandria, Virginia 22302.

The National School Lunch Program (NSLP)

Most child-care centers participate in the CACFP. However, if a child-care center is located in a school setting served by the National School Lunch Program (NSLP),

Table 7.1 Child-care infant meal pattern

Breakfast		
Birth–3 Months	**4–7 Months**	**8–11 Months**
4–6 fluid ounces of formula[1] or breast milk[2,3]	4–8 fluid ounces of formula[1] or breast milk[2,3]; 0–3 tablespoons of infant cereal[1,4]	6–8 fluid ounces of formula[1] or breast milk[2,3]; 2–4 tablespoons of infant cereal[1]; 1–4 tablespoons of fruit or vegetable or both
Lunch or Supper		
Birth–3 Months	**4–7 Months**	**8–11 Months**
4–6 fluid ounces of formula[1] or breast milk[2,3]	4–8 fluid ounces of formula[1] or breast milk[2,3]; 0–3 tablespoons of infant cereal[1,4]; 0–3 tablespoons of fruit or vegetable or both[4]	2–4 tablespoons of infant cereal[1]; 1–4 tablespoons of meat, fish, poultry, egg yolk, cooked dry beans or peas; 1/2–2 ounces of cheese; or 1–4 ounces (volume) of cottage cheese; or 1–4 ounces (weight) of cheese food or cheese spread; 1–4 tablespoons of fruit or vegetable or both
Snack		
Birth–3 Months	**4–7 Months**	**8–11 Months**
4–6 fluid ounces of fruit juice[5]; formula[1] or breast milk[2,3]	4–6 fluid ounces of formula[1] or breast milk[2,3]	2–4 fluid ounces of formula[1] or breast milk[2,3]; 0–1/2 bread[4,6] or 0–2 crackers[4,6]

[1]Infant formula and dry infant cereal must be iron-fortified.

[2]Breast milk or formula, or portions of both, may be served; however, it is recommended that breast milk be served in place of formula from birth through 11 months.

[3]For some breastfed infants who regularly consume less than the minimum amount of breast milk per feeding, a serving of less than the minimum amount of breast milk may be offered, with additional breast milk offered if the infant is still hungry.

[4]A serving of this component is required when the infant is developmentally ready to accept it.

[5]Fruit juice must be full-strength.

[6]A serving of this component must be made from whole-grain or enriched meal or flour.

Source: Amendments to the Child Nutrition Infant Meal Pattern. (2002). Department of Agriculture, Food and Nutrition Service, 7 CFR Parts 210, 220, and 226. *Federal Register, 67*(102), 36779–36788.

the center may follow the guidelines for reimbursement under the NSLP. The NSLP (http://www.fns.usda.gov/cnd/Lunch/AboutLunch/AboutNLSP.htm) is a federally assisted meal program operating in approximately 98,000 public and nonprofit private schools and residential child-care institutions. The program was established under the National School Lunch Act in 1946. It provides nutritionally balanced, low-cost or free lunches to more than 27 million children each school day. In 1998, Congress expanded the National School Lunch Program to include reimbursement for snacks served to children in after-school educational and enrichment programs

Table 7.2   Child and adult care food program meal pattern

Food Components	Ages 1–2	Ages 3–5	Ages 6–12[1]
Breakfast (select all 3 components)			
• 1 milk, fluid	1/2 c	3/4 c	1 c
• 1 fruit/vegetable juice, fruit and/or vegetable[2]	1/4 c	1/2 c	1/2 c
• 1 grains/bread[3]			
bread or	1/2 slice	1/2 slice	1 slice
cornbread or biscuit or roll or muffin or	1/2 serving	1/2 serving	1 serving
cold dry cereal or	1/4 c	1/3 c	3/4 c
hot cooked cereal or	1/4 c	1/4 c	1/2 c
pasta or noodles or grains	1/4 c	1/4 c	1/2 c
Lunch (select all 4 components)			
• 1 milk, fluid	1/2 c	3/4 c	1 c
• 2 fruits/vegetables juice, fruit and/or vegetable	1/4 c	1/2 c	3/4 c
• 1 grains/bread			
bread or	1/2 slice	1/2 slice	1 slice
cornbread or biscuit or roll or muffin or	1/2 serving	1/2 serving	1 serving
cold dry cereal or	1/4 c	1/3 c	3/4 c
hot cooked cereal or	1/4 c	1/4 c	1/2 c
pasta or noodles or grains	1/4 c	1/4 c	1/2 c
• 1 meat/meat alternate			
meat or poultry or fish[4] or	1 oz	1 1/2 oz	2 oz
alternate protein product or	1 oz	1 1/2 oz	2 oz
cheese or	1 oz	1 1/2 oz	2 oz
egg or	1/2	3/4	1
cooked dry beans or peas or	1/4 c	3/8 c	1/2 c
peanut or other nut or seed butters or	2 Tbsp	3 Tbsp	4 Tbsp
nuts and or seeds or	1/2 oz	3/4 oz	1 oz
yogurt	4 oz	6 oz	8 oz

[1]Children age 12 and up may be served adult-size portions based on the greater food needs of older boys and girls, but shall be served not less than the minimum quantities specified in this section for children age 6 to 12.
[2]Fruit or vegetable juice must be full-strength.
[3]Bread, pasta or noodle precuts, and cereal grains shall be whole grain or enriched; cornbread, biscuits, rolls, muffins, etc. shall be made with whole grain or enriched meal or flour; cereal shall be whole grain or enriched or fortified.
[4]A serving consists of the edible portion of cooked lean meat or poultry or fish.

to include children through 18 years of age. The USDA's Food and Nutrition Service administers the program at the federal level. At the state level, the National School Lunch Program is usually administered by state education agencies, which operate the program through agreements with school food authorities. School districts and independent schools that choose to take part in the lunch program get cash subsidies and donated commodities from the U.S. Department of Agriculture (USDA) for each meal they serve. In return, they must serve lunches that meet federal requirements, and they must offer free or reduced-price lunches to eligible children. School

Table 7.2 *Continued*

Food Components	Ages 1–2	Ages 3–5	Ages 6–12[1]
Snack (select 2 of the 4 components)			
• 1 milk, fluid	1/2 c	1/2 c	1 c
• 1 fruit/vegetable juice, fruit and/or vegetable	1/2 c	1/2 c	3/4 c
• 1 grains/bread			
bread or	1/2 slice	1/2 slice	1 slice
cornbread or biscuit or roll or muffin or	1/2 serving	1/2 serving	1 serving
cold dry cereal or	1/4 c	1/3 c	3/4 c
hot cooked cereal or	1/4 c	1/4 c	1/2 c
pasta or noodles or grains	1/4 c	1/4 c	1/2 c
• 1 meat/meat alternate			
meat or poultry or fish or	1/2 oz	1/2 oz	1 oz.
alternate protein product or	1/2 oz	1/2 oz	1 oz.
cheese or	1/2 oz	1/2 oz	1 oz.
egg or	1/2	1/2	1/2
cooked dry beans or peas or	1/8 c	1/8 c	1/4 c
peanut or other nut or seed butters or	1 Tbsp	1 Tbsp	2 Tbsp
nuts and or seeds[5] or	1/2 oz	1/2 oz	1 oz
yogurt[6]	2 oz	2 oz	4 oz

[5]Nuts and seeds may meet only one-half of the total meat/meat alternate serving and must be combined with another meat/meat alternate to fulfill the lunch requirement.

[6]Yogurt may be plain or flavored, unsweetened or sweetened.

Source: Amendments to the Child Nutrition Infant Meal Pattern. (2002). Department of Agriculture, Food, and Nutrition Service, 7 CFR Parts 210, 220, and 226. *Federal Register, 67*(102), 36779–36788.

food authorities can also be reimbursed for snacks served to children through after-school educational or enrichment programs. Snacks are not part of the regular school lunch program for preschool children.

Any child at a participating school may purchase a meal through the National School Lunch Program. Similar to the CACFP program, children from families with incomes at or below 130% of the poverty level are eligible for free meals. Those with incomes between 130% and 185% of the poverty level are eligible for reduced-price meals, for which students can be charged no more than 40¢. Children from families with incomes over 185% of poverty pay a full price, though their meals are still subsidized to some extent. Local school food authorities set their own prices for full-price (paid) meals, but must operate their meal services as nonprofit programs. Most of the support USDA provides to schools in the National School Lunch Program comes in the form of a cash reimbursement for each meal served. The school will receive cash reimbursement of more than $2.00 for a "free meal" to approximately 20¢ for a "paid" meal. In addition to cash reimbursements, schools are entitled to receive commodity foods or "entitlement" foods, at a value of 15.5¢ for each meal served.

The National School Lunch Act mandates that school meals "safeguard the health and well-being of the Nation's children" [2]. Participating school lunches must meet the Dietary Guidelines for Americans, which recommend that lunches contain no more than 30% of calories from fat, and less than 10% from saturated fat. Regulations also establish a standard for school lunches to provide one-third of the Recommended Dietary Allowances [3] for protein, vitamin A, vitamin C, iron, calcium, and calories.

To provide local food service professionals with flexibility, there are four menu-planning approaches to plan healthful and appealing meals. Schools choose one of the approaches but local schools make the choice of what specific foods are served and how they are prepared and presented.

Menu Planning Approaches.   Under the **Traditional Food-Based Menu Planning Approach,** schools must comply with specific component and quantity requirements by offering five food items from four food components. These components are: meat/meat alternate, vegetables and/or fruits, grains/breads, and milk. Ages and grade groups (see Appendix VIII) establish minimum portion sizes.

The **Enhanced Food-Based Menu Planning Approach** is a variation of the Traditional Menu Planning Approach. It is designed to increase calories from low-fat food sources in order to meet the Dietary Guidelines. The five food components are retained, but the component quantities for the weekly servings of vegetables and fruits and grains/breads are increased (Appendix IX).

Nutrient Standard Menu Planning (sometimes called "NuMenus") is a computer-based menu planning system that uses approved computer software to analyze the specific nutrient content of menu items automatically while menus are being planned. It is designed to assist menu planners in choosing food items that create nutritious meals and meet the nutrient standards.

Assisted Nutrient Standard Menu Planning (sometimes called "Assisted Nu-Menus") is a variation of Nutrient Standard Menu Planning. It is for schools that lack the technical resources to conduct nutrient analysis themselves. Instead, schools have an outside source, such as another school district, state agency, or a consultant, plan and analyze a menu based on local needs and preferences. The outside source also provides schools with recipes and product specifications to support the menus. The menus and analyses are periodically updated to reflect any changes in the menu or student selection patterns. The required minimums for nutrients and calories for these nutrient standard menu-planning approaches are included in Appendix X.

Alternate Menu Planning Approach is a menu-planning approach that allows states and school districts to develop their own innovative approaches to menu planning, subject to the guidelines established in the regulations. These guidelines protect the nutritional and fiscal integrity of the program.

Resources for Child Nutrition Programs

Team Nutrition, Healthy School Meals Resource System (HSMRS), Child-Care Nutrition Resource System, and National Food Service Management Institute (NFSMI) are resources that can be accessed by school personnel to help the food service program become an important part of the overall educational environment.

Team Nutrition (http://www.fns.usda.gov/tn/) is a nationwide integrated program designed to help implement the School Meals Initiative for Healthy Children. It provides schools with technical training and assistance to help school food service staff prepare healthy meals, and with nutrition education to help older children understand the link between diet and health.

> **School meals initiative for healthy children**
>
> USDA's School Meals Initiative for Healthy Children underscores our national health responsibility to provide healthy school meals that are consistent with the Recommended Dietary Allowances, the calorie goals, and the Dietary Guidelines for Americans. This eating plan is illustrated in the Food Guide Pyramid.

Healthy School Meals Resource System (HSMRS), as part of Team Nutrition, provides access to resources and training materials for Child Nutrition Program personnel in a timely manner. It also facilitates dissemination of pertinent information, provides a conduit for industry and professional groups working in the National School Lunch and Breakfast Programs and other Child Nutrition Programs, and aids in the collection and sharing of state and local resources.

The HSMRS Web site includes a database of training materials, several online discussion groups for specific target audiences, full text resources, Web links to pertinent materials and food service professional groups, regulations, and food safety information. Special categories of interest to school food service personnel provide added resources of mutual benefit. These include the Chef's Connection, a cooperative program where chefs and school personnel are working together. Industry partnerships with the USDA provide for cooperative efforts, and food service software vendors help with nutrient analysis of menus and foods.

Child Care Nutrition Resource System (http://www.nal.usda.gov/childcare/) provides recipes, resources, and information on nutritious meals and food safety. Child-care centers that participate in the CACFP will find the practical information useful in daily operations.

National Food Service Management Institute (NFSMI) information service provides information or referrals about any Child Nutrition Program for free. NFSMI answers questions, identifies information, and works in conjunction with the National Agricultural Library (NAL) to lend materials (see Box 7.3). There are school meal specialists, experienced with school meals in buying, preparing, and serving. Materials available from NAL are searchable via NAL's Web Gateway to AGRICOLA (http://www.nal.usda.gov/ag98). Anyone associated with a Child Nutrition Program who has a question related to serving healthy food might use this service.

BOX 7.3   The National Agricultural Library (http://www.nal.usda.gov/)

The National Agricultural Library (NAL), part of the Agricultural Research Service of the U.S. Department of Agriculture, is one of four National Libraries in the United States. NAL is a major international source for agriculture and related information. This Web site provides access to NAL's many resources and a gateway to its associated institutions.

Center Choice: CACFP or NSLP

Child-care centers may enroll in either the CACFP or School Lunch and Breakfast Programs in order to be reimbursed for meals served. Both follow the Dietary Guidelines for Americans (see Chapter 2). If the program is within a school setting serving kindergarten children, the center would probably follow the NSLP guidelines. If the child-care program is within a school district and serving prekindergarten children, it can enroll and claim reimbursement from either CACFP or NSLP. In many cases the prekindergarten program may want to participate in the CACFP because, unlike the NSLP, snacks are provided. Appendix XI includes a description of the School Breakfast Program, Special Milk Program, and Summer Food Service Program. These programs may serve young children under special circumstances.

OTHER FOOD PROGRAMS AFFECTING YOUNG CHILDREN

Teachers may be in a position to recommend other food and nutrition programs that can assist the parents of young children. The following information includes two programs that are directly related to parents with children less than 5 years of age.

Special Supplemental Nutrition Program for Women, Infants, and Children (WIC)

Description of Program (http://www.fns.usda.gov/wic/).   The WIC program mission is to safeguard the health of low-income women, infants, and children up to age 5 who are at nutritional risk by providing nutritious foods to supplement diets, information on healthy eating, and referrals to health care. Food, nutrition counseling, and access to health services are provided to low-income women, infants, and children under WIC. Established as a pilot program in 1972 and made permanent in 1974, WIC is administered at the federal level by the Food and Nutrition Service of the U.S. Department of Agriculture. Formerly known as the Special Supplemental Food Program for Women, Infants, and Children, WIC's name was changed under the Healthy Meals for Healthy Americans Act of 1994, in order to emphasize its role as a nutrition program.

Most state WIC programs provide vouchers that participants use at authorized food stores. A wide variety of state and local organizations cooperate in providing the food and health care benefits, and 46,000 merchants nationwide accept WIC vouchers.

WIC is effective in improving the health of pregnant women, new mothers, and their infants. A 1990 study showed that women who participated in the program during their pregnancies had lower Medicaid costs for themselves and their babies than did women who did not participate. WIC participation was also linked with longer gestation periods, higher birth weights, and lower infant mortality [4].

Eligibility.   Pregnant or postpartum women, infants, and children up to age 5 are eligible. They must meet income guidelines, a state residency requirement, and be individually determined to be at "nutritional risk" by a health professional. To be eligible on the basis of income, applicants' gross income (i.e., before taxes are withheld) must fall at or below 185% of the U.S. poverty income guidelines.

Head Start

Description of Program (http://www2.acf.dhhs.gov/programs/hsb/). Head Start and Early Head Start are comprehensive child development programs, which serve children from birth to age 5 years and their families. They are child-focused programs and have the overall goal of increasing the school readiness of young children in low-income families.

The Head Start Bureau in the Administration on Children, Youth, and Families (ACYF), Administration for Children and Families (ACF), Department of Health and Human Services (DHHS) administers the Head Start program. The ACF Regional Offices and the Head Start Bureau's American Indian and Migrant Program Branches award grants directly to local public agencies, private organizations, Indian tribes, and school systems for the purpose of operating Head Start programs at the community level.

The Head Start program has a long tradition of delivering comprehensive and high-quality services designed to foster healthy development in low-income children. Head Start grantee and delegate agencies provide a range of individualized services in the areas of education and early childhood development; medical, dental, and mental health; nutrition; and parent involvement. In addition, the entire range of Head Start services are responsive and appropriate to the family's developmental, ethnic, cultural, and linguistic heritage and experience.

Eligibility. Children from birth to age 5 years from families that meet the federal poverty guidelines are eligible for Head Start services. Programs throughout the country establish priorities for enrolling children based on community needs and available funds. In order to enroll a child in a local Head Start program, a family's income must be below the poverty line or be a family that is receiving public assistance; that is, SSI or TANF benefits. Children that exceed the low-income guidelines may fill 10% of the enrollment opportunities in each program. There is also a requirement that 10% of enrollments should be offered to children with disabilities.

The 1994 Head Start Reauthorization Act established the Early Head Start program, which serves low-income pregnant women and families with infants and toddlers from birth to age 3. Early Head Start programs are operated under grants awarded by the federal government.

Food Patterns. Although the Head Start program is administered by DHHS, reimbursement through CACFP for meals is allowed within the Head Start Program. Head Start follows the CACFP guidelines for the meal patterns. The Recommended Dietary Allowances (RDAs) [3] are used to establish the nutritional needs of children in order to insure that one-third of the nutritional needs of children in part-day programs, and one-half to two-thirds of the nutritional needs of children in full-day programs are met.

Head Start Guidelines [5] go beyond the CACFP regulations. Cycle menus of three weeks or longer are generally used in the Head Start Center, and help in formulating balanced and varied menus, as well as in planning purchase orders and work schedules. Posting menus in the food preparation and dining areas and sending menus home to parents helps facilitate the integration of nutrition activities, especially if such menus are designed to cover an entire food cycle. To keep staff, parents, and children informed of changes, substitutions are indicated on all menus. The Head Start program emphasizes the cooperation between food service staff and teachers in planning and implementing an educationally focused program.

FOODS FOR INFANTS AND YOUNG CHILDREN

The importance of nutrition for infants and children has been covered in Chapters 3 through 6. Even though the food service staff is following the guidelines presented previously, some decision about what foods to provide children is left to the center staff, food service, and teachers.

Purchasing commercially prepared foods may be advisable for infants at child-care centers with fewer than four to six children. FDA requires labeling on "infant" food for babies under a year of age to be more complete than that of other foods intended for adults. It is not easy today to select the right baby food because manufacturers have a variety of foods available for the child from birth through the toddler years, and babies may not fit the narrow developmental patterns attributed to each level. One company has infant, 2nd, 3rd, and "graduate" foods (http://www.gerber.com) while another has a four-step nutrition plan (http://www.heinzbaby.com) and another three stages (http://www.babycenter.com). To obtain the best nutrition for the least cost, use the following guide:

Recommended	*Not Recommended*
Strained vegetables	Creamed vegetables
Strained meats	Vegetable and meat dinners
Fruit juice	More than 4–6 oz per day
Single-grain infant cereal	Custards (check labels)
Yogurt (plain or check label for excessive sugar)	Fruit puddings and desserts with added starch
	Honey
Fruits without added sugar	Fruits with sugar and starch added
Cheese	Cream cheese, cheese spread, soft cheese*

*Feta, Brie, and Camembert cheeses, blue-veined cheeses, and Mexican-style cheeses such as "queso blanco fresco" may contain listeria (http://www.foodsafety.gov/). Do not use!

Center-Prepared Infant Foods

The center may prepare foods for infants if fresh or frozen foods are available that have been properly prepared in the kitchen for the infants. Foods can be pureed or ground from fresh or frozen vegetables (no salt added) and fruits. Leftovers that

---

BOX 7.4   Choking and foods to avoid

Insist that children eat at the table or at least sitting. Watch young children while they eat. Encourage them to eat slowly and chew food well. Cut up foods that are firm and round and can get stuck in the child's airway.

Foods to Avoid

- Chunks of meat
- Chips
- Hot dogs (not recommended for young children)
- Whole grapes (if used, cut into quarters)
- Cherries with pits
- Large pieces of fruit with skin
- Raw vegetables (cut them into small strips or pieces that are not round)
- Single foods such as:
  - Mini marshmallows
  - Nuts and seeds (don't give peanuts to children under age 7)
  - Popcorn
  - Pretzels
  - Round or hard candy
  - Spoonfuls of peanut butter (use small amounts spread thinly)
  - Raisins and other dry fruit
  - Firm peas
- Peanut butter (not recommended for infant)

---

have been prepared for older children and allowed to stand in cooking water or on the table are not acceptable. Extra portions of freshly cooked food can be prepared (ground or pureed), placed in ice cube trays, and immediately frozen. One or two cubes per feeding will be sufficient for the young infant. Frozen cubes kept in a covered container can be thawed in the refrigerator overnight or cooked in the microwave oven before serving (see "Use of Microwave Ovens" in the Food Safety section of this chapter). Always stir foods taken from the microwave and test food in several places to ensure the food is not too hot.

By 6 to 7 months, the infant will be ready to accept center-prepared foods with a texture other than pureed. The infants are developmentally ready to chew and will do so with their gums, even though teeth have not erupted. Any cooked, chopped, or mashed bite-sized pieces of table foods are acceptable, excluding those that promote choking (see Box 7.4). These foods should not contain seasonings or additional sugar and salt.

The issue of sodium and fat has become important. Some infants given home-prepared strained foods or table foods receive more sodium than would be found in commercial baby foods [6]. Teachers who prepare food for infants should not add salt or seasoning with sodium. Studies have failed to demonstrate a relationship between salt intake in infancy and early childhood and the development of salty taste preference. Also, evidence is lacking to establish the time of onset of "diet sensitivities" in those hypertensive individuals who are "diet-sensitive" or sodium sensitive [7]. Since 1978 no excessive sodium or preservatives have been added to commercial infant foods. Sugar is usually added only to custards, puddings, and desserts. No added modified food starch, salt, artificial flavors, colors, or preservatives are used in most of the products.

Foods for Toddlers and Preschoolers

Food service for the toddler and the preschooler is different from the infant feeding routine. Toddler or Graduates® foods may be used for the toddler shortly after one year of age. Foods that are hard and can become lodged in the throat (such as raw celery, nuts, hot dogs, and popcorn) should be avoided. Foods such as biscuits, cookies, toast, and crackers should be eaten in an upright position to reduce the possibility of choking on crumbs [8]. Most centers find that when the toddler can use a spoon and self-feed, crackers, cookies, and table foods can be introduced. Interaction among children is limited at the early toddler stage; however, this does not preclude the use of conversation about foods and eating. The amount of food is generally smaller for the toddler and served more frequently when compared with the preschooler. Young children, 12 to 20 months, may still be fed individually, but shortly after age 2 years, they like and can learn from eating with other children in the center.

By 30 months, they can be using tablespoons to take food from serving bowls. Chapters 4 and 5 include the recommended food patterns to meet children's daily nutritional needs. Frequent use of legumes, beans, fruits, and green or yellow vegetables contributes significantly to specific nutrients often difficult to acquire in the diet. Whole-grain cereals have been included, while "dessert" (something sweet at the end of the meal) is fruit or a component of the meal. Children are allowed to take a serving of all the menu items at the start of the meal. No food is withheld at the beginning of a meal. The Child Nutrition Program establishes the food pattern requirements (Table 7.1 and Table 7.2).

Coordinating Center and Home Food Intake

Is the child getting enough food? Meals following the CACFP pattern are required to provide only one-third of the child's RDA for lunch plus a snack. If the lunch provides only one-third of the recommended amount of the nutrients, the parents at home must supply an additional two-thirds of the recommended allowances through the other meals. In many cases the child must leave home early, possibly without a morning meal, and return late in the evening. Staff of centers may need to evaluate what foods are eaten at home compared to those eaten in the center in order to help parents provide all the nutrition necessary for growth and development.

FOOD SERVICE AS A TEAM EFFORT

Menus are often planned to include foods that children like and will eat. This process seems logical because it reduces food waste and appears to be most cost-effective. However, this approach is based on the fact that food service personnel are in charge of planning as well as serving foods, and the teacher has little, if any, responsibility for these activities. We believe the meal service and foods served should be both educational and nutritional. It is important to include not only the dietitian and food service supervisor but also the teacher and parent.

Children eat the foods they know, but new or less familiar foods may be viewed with suspicion or rejected. The menu-planning system that involves teachers and food service personnel can accomplish the goal of good nutrition while introducing the child to a wide variety of foods.

Menus are usually viewed as the foundation of food service operation. The process of using an educational approach to develop a center's menu requires the food service personnel and the teacher to coordinate activities. The menus still must contain the basic foods and consider the constraints of the food service facility, but, in addition, the menu will be used as a tool for learning (Figure 7.1). The day's menu should be a written translation of the CACFP patterns, the Food Guide, and the teacher's learning objective.

The proper menu has foods with the appropriate combinations of taste, texture, and color. Producing a menu that (1) meets the child's requirements and (2) meets the constraints of the food service facility and is part of the educational curriculum takes careful planning.

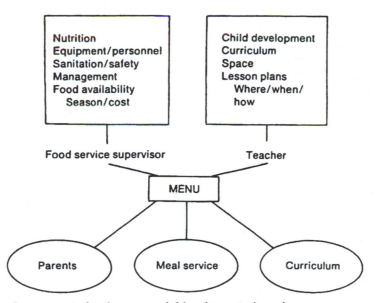

Figure 7.1 Components for the successful implementation of a menu

Food Service Supervisor's Contribution

As indicated in Figure 7.1, the registered dietitian and food service personnel come to the menu-planning session with a set of food and nutritional guidelines for children. They have knowledge of the guides, standards, and food production. Dietitians and food service staff can provide teachers with educational materials for children. They are often in communication with Child Nutrition Program consultants who provide teaching materials for the classrooms.

The equipment and personnel may limit the number and kinds of food items. Teachers can better understand the role of the food service personnel by understanding a few situations that arise in daily food service operations. For example, baked potatoes and meat loaf may not be served together, if the oven is not large enough to prepare both at the same time. The number of products to be prepared in the preschool kitchen may be limited by personnel. Some foods may need to be prepared from mixes, or frozen entrees served. Preparing mashed potatoes for 30 to 50 children requires special equipment, and instant potatoes may be the only solution. Baked ham, baked sweet potatoes, and hot rolls require large oven space. Fruited gelatin (gelatin prepared with fruit juice), tossed salad, and cold meat and cheese platters may require too much refrigerator space. Fruited gelatin is impractical to serve on Monday in a Monday-to-Friday center, because it must be prepared on Friday and allowed to stand over the 2-day weekend. Some programs serve food prepared in one site and transported to another; therefore, some foods cannot maintain high quality. Equipment and personnel may also limit the use of various types of meal services. Large numbers of bag lunches may be difficult to prepare. Food service personnel understand the process of food purchasing, preparation, and service.

Foods and Educational Activities. The food service supervisor knows the availability of foods and can alert the teachers to foods that are locally grown and could be used in teaching young children. The foods in season are usually available in your locality and fit within the budgetary constraints. However, in some areas many fresh foods, especially fruits and vegetables, are available all year.

The food service supervisor is the link between the foods served and the curriculum prepared by the teacher. Those in food service can help children that are developmentally ready to assist with certain kinds of food preparation. Activities such as making cream into butter provide a multitude of language experiences and develop thinking skills as teachers encourage children to guess, observe, and draw conclusions about what they experience. A fresh pineapple provided by the food service personnel can be incorporated into the educational activities when pineapple is on the menu. See Chapter 8 for further details in using food in the educational program.

Dietitian's Contribution

Both child-care workers and food service personnel find it helpful to consult with a registered dietitian (RD) or public health nutritionist.

The center director should expect that the dietitian will

1. use the tools of nutrition assessment, planning, and evaluation to help teachers, food service workers, and parents solve children's food- and nutrition-related problems.
2. manage chronic conditions such as overweight, underweight, diabetes, heart disease, allergies, bottle mouth caries, or anemia.
3. negotiate with food service supervisors and teachers in planning menus.
4. have the ability to verify and interpret the nutrient content of the menus ensuring compliance with established state and federal guidelines.
5. negotiate with regulatory agencies during their visits with the program.
6. train food service personnel in sanitary requirements and use of safe practices when handling food.

The public health nutritionist has had courses in public health and community nutrition from an accredited college or university and an approved dietetic internship or equivalent training and experience in a health care program that meets requirements for the RD. A dietitian is experienced in working with food and nutrition programs for mothers and children in a variety of settings such as day care, supplemental feeding programs, and institutions. Dietary consultation can be located through the state agency that administers the funding for the food programs. In addition, local university food and nutrition programs, state or local dietetic associations (www.eatright.org), public health departments, and Cooperative State Research, Education, and Extension Service (CSREES) offices may be contacted to help your center locate professionals with experience in the areas of child feeding.

Some training for the food service personnel is required. In no other facility where food is prepared do we expect the extent of involvement of the teacher and food service personnel. The dietitian, the public health department, and the state agency that monitors the Child Nutrition Programs (NSLP and CACFP) can help in training food service personnel.

Teacher's Contribution

The teacher brings to the menu-planning session knowledge of the educational needs of children. Available space, equipment, and location will limit some activities; for example, inner-city schools find it difficult to pick apples from nearby orchards, whereas rural preschoolers cannot walk to the grocery or nearby parks.

The food service personnel can suggest various options for involving children in food preparation, service, and cleanup, but the teacher is the director of the learning activities. Without the teacher's cooperation the food service will not be used effectively to help children learn about food.

The teacher may use the menu as a tool to learning through a specific food service style; for example, family (formal, informal), buffet, cafeteria, bag lunch, and picnic. A particular food item may also be used in conjunction with a learning resource center in the classroom. A new food or preparation method with which the child is becoming familiar may be used along with a science activity (see Chapter 8).

Teachers rely on food service staff to prepare nutritious meals and follow food safety guidelines

When food service personnel are planning menus, a checklist of foods and preparation methods (Appendix XII) can be made available to the teacher. The teachers can circle or indicate which food items or preparation methods are new for the child and could be a part of the child's learning experiences. This list also includes many vegetables and fruits high in fiber and in vitamins A and C.

Parent's Contribution

Most centers assume the large task of educating parents as well as children about nutrition. Menus and basic nutrition education programs are shared with parents. Because food idiosyncrasies and poor eating habits may be a result of foods served in the home or eaten out with parents, parents must be included in the program so that sound nutrition principles are followed at the center and home. Parents can be participants in the food programs by helping plan menus and by participating in food preparation, service, and eating with the children. Chapter 9 is devoted to parent involvement, including their contribution to the menu. Many preschool centers require parents to serve on advisory or policy boards, which approve cycle menus before they are used; however, too often, parents "rubber stamp" a menu or set of menus without being provided with proper information on which to judge the quality of the menus. If possible, a parent should participate in the total planning process. At minimum, the parents should receive a copy of the menus, which should explain how foods would be used in the center to help the child learn about new foods and accept a wide variety of foods. In some states the licensing regulations require that menus be posted at least 2 weeks in advance and must be kept on file for up to 6 months. Many centers arrange group sessions conducted by a dietitian on the food and nutrition needs of children. These sessions include the nutritional needs of children as related to the specific menus of the center. The dietitian, along with the food service personnel and teacher, must be accountable to parents for the food served, how foods are used in the child-care center, and for the education of the child's parents so that the efforts begun in the center will be continued at home.

STYLES OF FOOD SERVICE

Children love variety. Therefore, weather permitting, teachers may plan some meals outside, picnic style. Inside, a variety of settings are available (for instance, a Christmas buffet for older preschoolers). Food service styles include family, buffet, cafeteria, picnic, and bag lunch.

In **family style** food service, all children sit at a table, which has been prepared with individual plates and flatware. Food is placed on the table in serving bowls and is passed. Children help themselves from serving bowls with the assistance of the teacher or other staff.

> **Head start performance standards for family style meal service**
>
> All toddlers, preschool children, and assigned classroom staff, including volunteers, eat together family style and share the same menu to the extent possible. 45 CFR Part 1304 (2001). *Federal Register* 4(5), 181–183.

A **modified family style** may be used with a group of children new to the center. Only one or two items are placed in serving bowls and the teacher places other foods on the plates. This method is used only until the children are not familiar with this style of meal service.

Food, flatware, and plates are placed on the serving table in a **buffet style** presentation. The child takes a plate, flatware, and food from the table with or without assistance from adults, but foods are not "dished up" for the child. This style may be used with an experienced group of preschoolers to add variety. The younger children's flatware may be placed at the table, and the child takes only a plate on which food is placed from the buffet table.

In **cafeteria style** service, food, flatware, and plates are placed on a serving tray. An adult places foods on the child's plate or tray. The child may select one or more items. The server usually sets portion sizes. However, children may be asked how much they can eat. This service is not recommended for preschoolers.

No formal definition exists for **picnic style** meal service, except that the meal is usually eaten at a picnic table or on the ground out-of-doors. This style has been used indoors where playgrounds or parks have not been available or where the weather has not cooperated. Children love picnics! Foods should be easy to prepare and carry. One or more of the foods may be prepared outside over an open fire; however, outdoor cooking is not necessary for a successful picnic. Paper plates, cups, and plastic utensils may be used. Remember, infants as well as preschoolers like to eat outside.

For the **bag lunch,** easy-to-prepare foods are packed in a bag. A spoon may be added for eating some foods, but most foods should be finger foods. Bag lunches can be used for field trips. All the nutrients in a regular lunch can be supplied through the bag lunch—candy bars, potato chips, and sweet cakes do not have to be included. A menu may include peanut butter or cheese sandwich on whole-wheat bread, raw vegetables and fruit, and milk. Remember, providing liquids for children in hot weather is important.

PLANNING CYCLE MENUS

Planning menus well in advance is a key to good management. Cycle menus are a series of carefully planned menus, used for a definite period of time, and then repeated. They can be planned for an odd number of days not divisible by five, such as 11, 13, 21, or 29 days, to ensure that a menu is not repeated on the same day in consecutive weeks.

Using cycle menus reduces the time required for menu planning. After the initial cycle has been completed, the menu can be changed to account for special occasions such as holidays and vacations. To make a cycle menu successful, at least three to four new menu items should be added in the subsequent cycle. This ensures that meals do not become monotonous or boring. In addition, with a cycle menu, food preparation procedures can be standardized and costs can be identified and controlled.

Teacher activities can be easily varied from the first 3- or 4-week cycle to the second time the cycle is used. A menu can be thought of as a road map, always allowing opportunities to change direction. The menu should be flexible for side trips, but the food service supervisor and teacher should be conscientious enough not to get seriously sidetracked into a poor nutritional program.

Several forms will assist the food service manager and the teacher in the preparation of menus to meet CACFP guidelines. Figure 7.2 was taken from materials supplied to home day-care teachers who may have children at their homes for breakfast, lunch, dinner, and snacks.

Although no rule dictates how the menu should be planned, food service planners usually start with the meat, meat alternate, or protein foods and add other components in order to get a wide variety. You could begin with any food component. Appendix XII gives a variety of foods and preparation methods to assist in planning. At least one fruit and vegetable for lunch and dinner (main meals) should be chosen. Vegetables, fruits, and grains are now the foundation of the diet and provide many vitamins and minerals as well as fiber. A minimum of *11 servings* a day should be included in the menus, two from fruits, three from vegetables, and six from the grain products.

Ten menus are included as examples in this chapter (Table 7.3). These menus have been planned for one meal and a snack, meeting approximately one-third of the Recommended Dietary Allowances (RDA) for the 4-year-old in the center for one-half day. With additional servings from the foods listed on the menus, more energy can be added to the diets and these menus will easily meet 50% of the RDA.

USE WHEN PREPARING YOUR MENU—WRITE IN EVERYTHING SERVED		
BREAKFAST: (Time)	**LUNCH: (Time)**	**SUPPER: (Time)**

1. Juice or fruit or vegetable
   AND
2. Cereal or bread or pasta or rice (enriched or whole grain)
   AND
3. Fluid milk
	1. Meat or meat alternative (cheese, eggs, legumes, peanut butter, other nuts or seed butters, fish, or poultry) (nuts, seeds—no more than 50%)
	AND 2. Bread or cooked grains, pasta (enriched or whole grain) or rice.
	3. (a) and (b) Vegetables and/or fruits:
	AND 2 fruits or 2 vegetables or 1 fruit and 1 vegetable
	4. Fluid milk	

1. Ju/Fr/Veg	1. Protein	1. Protein
	2. Grain	2. Grain
2. Grain	3a. Fr/Veg	3a. Fr/Veg
	b. Fr/Veg	b. Fr/Veg
3. Milk	4. Milk	4. Milk

Figure 7.2   Menu planning worksheet
Source: A portion of worksheet record illustrating use of the Child Care Food Program requirements prepared by Association for Child Development, Lansing, Michigan, a home day-care sponsor in Illinois and Michigan.

The daily energy allotment has been set at 1,500 kcal for the 4- to 5-year-old. Guidelines for CACFP and NSLP still use the RDAs; however, newer data and Dietary Reference Intakes (Appendix III) may change the recommended nutrient values for children's meals [9].

Some states require that if children are in the center 8 hours or more they should receive one-third and preferably one-half of the RDA. However, in at least one study children were given breakfast, lunch, and two snacks but still could not meet 75% of the standard for energy, iron, zinc, magnesium, vitamin A, and folic acid [10]. Looking at both the home and the day-care food intake, children did not eat foods with nutrients meeting the RDA for folic acid and iron [11].

Child Nutrition Labeling

To assist in purchasing foods that meet meal pattern requirements, some foods are identified with a Child Nutrition (CN) label. Child Nutrition labeling is a voluntary federal labeling program that provides a warranty for CN-labeled products. The program requires an evaluation of a product by the Food and Nutrition Service (FNS) of the USDA to determine the contribution of the product toward the

Table 7.3   Sample menus and nutrient analysis

Menus for preschooler, lunch and snack

Day 1	Day 2	Day 3	Day 4	Day 5
Beef/vegetable stew	Stir-fry chicken with celery, carrots, and bok choy	Lean roast pork	Baked chicken	White beans and ham
Molded salad with orange sections	Orange slices	Sweet potato	Broccoli	Cooked greens
Whole-wheat bread	Spinach salad with fat-free dressing	Baby lima beans	Cooked tomatoes and pasta	Fresh broccoli with fat-free ranch dressing
Margarine	Whole-wheat bread	Carrot sticks	Whole-wheat bread	Apple slices
2% milk	2% milk	Whole-wheat bread	Margarine	Cornbread
		Margarine	2% milk	Margarine
		2% milk		2% milk
Snack:	Snack:	Snack:	Snack:	Snack:
Hard-cooked egg	Pineapple chunks	Grapefruit sections	Dried fruits— peach slice, apricot slice, dates	Grapes (green)
Blueberries	2% milk	2% milk	2% milk	2% milk
2% milk				

Day 6	Day 7	Day 8	Day 9	Day 10
Soy-enhanced chicken patty	Chili with tomato sauce, beans, and hamburger	Roast turkey	Vegetable burger with tomato, pickle, lettuce	Seafood chop suey with bean sprouts, bamboo shoots, water chestnuts, and green pepper
Baked potato	Spinach salad with fat-free dressing	Sweet potatoes	Oven-baked potatoes	Brown rice
Fresh cantaloupe	Grapefruit	Cranberry salad	Baked beans in tomato sauce	Fresh fruit salad
Brussels sprouts	Whole-wheat crackers	Whole-wheat bread	Apricots	Whole-wheat bread
Whole-wheat bread	2% milk	Margarine	Whole-wheat bun	Margarine
Margarine		2% milk	2% milk	2% milk
2% milk				
Snack:	Snack:	Snack:	Snack:	Snack:
Pineapple	Sliced peaches	Citrus cup	Apple slices	Strawberries
2% milk	2% milk	Toasted wheat germ	Peanut butter	2% milk
		2% milk	2% milk	

meal pattern requirements, and manufacturers are allowed to state the contribution on their labels. This protects the consumer from exaggerated claims about a product; however, it does not provide any assurance of product quality. Neither does it mean the foods are safer to eat, or free of pathogens or allergens.

Products eligible for CN labels include main dish products that contribute significantly to the meat/meat alternate component of the meal pattern requirements and juice and juice drink products that contain at least 50% full-strength juice by volume.

Table 7.3 *Continued*

Week 1 (Day 1–Day 5)

Percent Energy Distribution:

Fat	28%
SFA	11%
Carbohydrate	49%
Protein	25%

Total	Nutrient	% RDA	0%	20%	40%	60%	80%	100%
393.0 kcal	Energy	60%						
24.8 g	Protein	103%						
892.0 RE	Vitamin A	178%						
30.5 mg	Vitamin C	68%						
337.0 mg	Calcium	42%						
3.3 mg	Iron	33%						

Week 2 (Day 6–Day 10)

Percent Energy Distribution:

Fat	24%
SFA	10%
Carbohydrate	54%
Protein	24%

Total	Nutrient	% RDA	0%	20%	40%	60%	80%	100%
353.0 kcal	Energy	68%						
21.51 g	Protein	90%						
284.0 RE	Vitamin A	57%						
26.0 mg	Vitamin C	58%						
288.0 mg	Calcium	36%						
3.28 mg	Iron	33%						

A facsimile of a CN label is presented in Figure 7.3. Note the distinct border of the CN logo, the meal pattern contribution statement, the 6-digit product identification number, the USDA/FNS authorization, and the month and year of approval.

Foods from Many Cultures

Knowledge of cultural food patterns helps the centers establish rapport with the child and family. Serving foods that represent different cultural food patterns can be a nourishing and educational experience for children. What people eat depends on ethnic, social, and economic factors. Children who were born in this country generally like and will eat foods that are readily available.

Table 7.4 illustrates the similarities among traditional foods of six ethnic groups—black, Hispanic American, Japanese, Chinese, Vietnamese, and American

Figure 7.3   Facsimile Child Nutrition (CN) label
(The six-digit CN identification number in the upper right corner is assigned by the FNS, CND headquarters office. This date is written using numbers to reflect the month/year of final approval.)

Indian, while Chapter 1 reviews foods used by different cultural groups. Using these common foods, menu planners will find it relatively easy to accommodate diverse tastes. However, preparation methods vary greatly from one ethnic group to another. Although there are many similarities, the teacher can capitalize on the diverse ethnic cuisines found in this country and make an effort to incorporate as many of the foods as possible into the child-care menu and curriculum.

Seven Steps to Successful Ethnic Meals.   The following guidelines were developed by the authors when working with preschool centers to foster ethnic meal preparation:

1. Obtain information. Acquire materials (e.g., cookbooks and articles) from the library, book stores, USDA Child Nutrition Program, National Food Service Management Institute (http://www.olemiss.edu/depts/nfsmi/), American Dietetic Association (http://www.eatright.org) [12].

Table 7.4   Foods common to most ethnic food patterns

Meat and Alternates	Milk and Milk Products	Grain Products	Vegetables	Fruits	Others
Pork* Beef Chicken Eggs	Milk, fluid Ice cream	Rice White bread Noodles, macaroni spaghetti Dry cereal	Carrots Cabbage Green beans Greens (especially spinach) Sweet potatoes or yams Tomatoes	Apples Bananas Oranges Peaches Pears Tangerines	Fruit juices

*May be restricted because of religious custom.

2. Standardize recipes. Include standardized recipes among the resource materials.
3. Get a commitment. Involve all teachers, food service personnel, dietitians, and those responsible for menus and food preparation in planning
   a. the number of ethnic meals to serve.
   b. the kind of ethnic meals.
   c. the lesson plans and educational use of menus.
   d. a list of parents as resources.
4. Meet with parents. Serve ethnic foods suggested by parents from different ethnic backgrounds. Have them write down their favorite menu or recipes and try to match the foods they like with standardized recipes in ethnic cookbooks. Develop complete ethnic menus and corresponding recipes.
5. Consult with specialists. Consult with a registered dietitian to be sure the CACFP guidelines are met. Low-fat products can make traditional menus lower in fat.
6. Pilot test menus/recipes. Unless the food service supervisor is familiar with the ethnic food, prepare samples of food at least a week in advance and have parents, teachers, and children sample just a little taste of the new food. Build anticipation!
7. Publicize ethnic day. Let all staff, parents, and the community know through newsletters, newspapers, and other media.
8. Evaluate and modify. Make changes as necessary for the next cycle of menus.

MENU CHECKLIST

The following questions help you consider the components in the menu-planning process:

1. Do the lunches meet the minimum requirements for the group served?
2. Is a raw vegetable or fruit included often for preschoolers and finger foods for toddlers?
3. Is a carotene-rich fruit or vegetable included daily or at least twice a week? Is a dark green vegetable included almost every day?
4. Is a vitamin-C-rich fruit or vegetable included each day?
5. Are foods that are good sources of iron included daily?
6. Are sugar and salt used in limited quantities (for example, potato chips not served with ham or lunch meats, limit sweet desserts)?
7. Do the lunches include a good balance of color, texture, shape, flavor, and temperature?
8. Are the foods varied from day to day and week to week from cycle to cycle?
9. Is at least one new food or preparation method introduced each week?
10. Are new foods introduced in combination with popular foods?
11. Are the teacher's objectives integrated into the menus?

12. Can the lunches be prepared successfully within the time available?
13. Can the lunches be prepared with the staff, facilities, and equipment available?
14. Can food be purchased with money budgeted?
15. Do cycle menus reflect both the children's own culture and that of unfamiliar cultures?
16. Do the menus give opportunities for the child to develop motor skills (foods for spoon, knife, and fork for the preschooler; finger foods and foods for the spoon for the toddler)?
17. What role will the parents have in the planning process?

GOOD MANAGEMENT PRINCIPLES

Quantity food service principles and procedures are applied through planning the menu, ordering and purchasing food, controlling supplies, preparing food, and analyzing costs. Planning the menu is the start of good management of the food program in child care. The contributions of the teacher, food service personnel, and dietitian were discussed earlier. During menu planning, continually evaluate menus for adequacy, appearance, acceptance, and workload as well as the contribution the foods will make to the educational curriculum. Other areas to consider are:

1. Plan preferably a month or more in advance.
2. Maintain up-to-the-minute inventories on which menus are based.
3. Use locally abundant foods.
4. Order and use commodities, if available.

Ordering and Purchasing Food

1. Develop purchase orders or grocery lists in advance.
2. Order by the case or in quantities that are least expensive. (Small centers may purchase with other nearby child-care centers, senior citizen programs, or schools.)
3. Obtain competitive quotations each time purchases are authorized.
4. Check deliveries for quantity, quality, weight, and conformity to all specifications.

Controlling Supplies

1. Record correctly all merchandise issued from storage.
2. Refrigerate food that needs to be kept cold, and keep frozen foods in a freezer.
3. Prevent loss from the kitchen and warehouse by keeping records and making regular checks. (Keep freezers locked.)
4. Allow no leftover food to be taken from the kitchen.

Preparing Food

1. Follow tested recipes. This assures a uniform product, prevents waste, and makes it easier to provide portions of the correct size. Recipes for child-care services are available from the USDA [13].
2. Avoid providing too much or too little food by keeping accurate records of participation. If all the food is used, the extra handling and storage of left-over food is avoided. If there is too little food, nutrition and educational programs will suffer.
3. In estimating the number to be served, consider the weather, center activities, and other factors.
4. Simplify preparation and serving.
5. Maintain food production records.

Analyzing and Comparing Costs

1. Keep accurate daily cost records.
2. Do not repeat expensive menu items unless they can be balanced by inexpensive items or unless funds are available.
3. Control inventory so that food is used wisely.

Food service personnel should be encouraged to attend School Food Service Certification Workshops as well as to receive the Certification for Food Service Managers in states where available. Contact the regional or state agency that administers the Child Nutrition Programs for more information and the specific requirements of each state.

We strongly encourage the directors of early childhood education programs as well as directors of food service facilities to obtain good food service textbooks [14,15] as well as *Food for Fifty* [16], a frequently used reference for quantity recipes if your center has 25 or more children.

FOOD SAFETY

The topic of food safety deserves special attention, especially in preparation of foods for vulnerable, "high-risk" groups such as infants and young children. Some states now require a food handler's certificate. The largest number of food-borne illnesses in centers are enteric (small intestine) infections, which usually show themselves as diarrhea and other disturbances in the gastrointestinal tract. Enteric illnesses are commonly associated with "food poisoning." But in the nation's day-care centers, tainted food is often not the culprit. Rather, the illnesses most often result from fecal contamination because staff and children fail to follow the dictates of ordinary common sense about things like hand washing and cleanliness.

The major contributors to the spread of enteric diseases—person-to-person contact, water, and food—are interrelated and part of a persistent cycle. Attacking one part of the problem will have little effect. What's needed is a concerted effort directed at all sources of transmission of enteric pathogens.

Studies show that children less than 3 years old who are cared for in child-care centers are more subject to diarrhea than other youngsters. Likewise, child-care center workers and families of these young children seem to suffer more bouts of diarrhea [17].

The human gut, including that of small children, normally contains many of the pathogenic bacteria and viruses that can cause diarrhea, but the body's natural defenses usually keep them well under control. More important, these potentially dangerous organisms don't ordinarily get spread around. But fecal contamination can be a prime source of disease in centers that care for children less than 3 years old who are being toilet trained. Hands, toys, diaper-changing areas, and just about everything else can be contaminated with fecal matter. Children and adults who touch these contaminated objects and then put their fingers to their mouths are prime candidates for disease.

Child-care centers can minimize the danger of infection caused by fecal contamination by hand washing. As simple as it may seem, hand washing is probably the single most preventive measure in the child-care center. Child-care staff members should wash their hands when they start work, before preparing or serving food, after diapering a child or wiping the nose or cleaning up messes, and after a trip to the bathroom, according to the Food Safety Code (Box 7.5).

For children, the routine is much the same. CDC advises that children's hands are washed when they arrive, before they eat or drink, and after they use the toilet or have their diapers changed. It's also important that the diaper-changing area is located well away from food-serving areas and that a separate sink is used for preparing food and washing dishes. CDC recommends that only washable, preferably hard-surfaced toys be used around children still in diapers. Toys should be washed daily. Stuffed toys should be washed at least once a week if children in diapers use them.

All facilities and supplies at child-care centers should be washed with soap and water and then disinfected on a regular, frequent schedule. For disinfectants, CDC recommends a commercial product that kills bacteria, viruses, and parasites, such as a bleach solution. To make the bleach solution, mix one-fourth cup of bleach with a gallon of water (or one tablespoon per quart). The solution should be made daily but can be stored in a spray bottle. Disinfectants must be kept out of the reach of children [18].

Food-Borne Organisms

Child-to-child contact spreads organisms causing most infections in the child-care centers. However, microorganisms that cause food-borne illnesses are found everywhere, on everything, in the air we breathe, on the things we touch—we even carry them on our skin, hair, and clothing. Food, moisture, and moderate temperatures promote life and growth of these organisms. When all these conditions are present, they grow and multiply at a rapid rate. About every 20 minutes the organism may split, grow, and divide again and again. In 24 hours, one may grow and divide into 281 trillion organisms.

BOX 7.5   FDA Food Safety Code

Embodied in the FDA Food Safety Code, this statement is intended to apply to child-care centers. There are several provisions in the Code which can help prevent the spread of food-borne diseases:

- Child-care center operators must maintain oversight of their employees who prepare food to ensure that those who are ill or exhibit certain symptoms associated with food-borne illness do not prepare food or engage in other activities that could contaminate the food.
- Employees who prepare food are required to report certain symptoms, illnesses, and high-risk conditions related to food-borne illness with which they may have been associated.
- The Code specifies an acceptable method for food employee *hand washing* during the preparation of food and special hand-washing products (washing twice and using a nail brush) that are necessary in certain situations, for example, after using the toilet.
- Touching ready-to-eat food with bare hands is prohibited. Proper utensils or single-service gloves may be used to satisfy this requirement.
- In order to destroy disease-causing organisms, potentially hazardous foods (this means those that can support the growth of disease-causing organisms and includes many foods like cut melons, boiled potatoes, fried rice, and others that you might not think could be dangerous) must be:
  - Cooked to certain temperatures for 15 seconds, depending on the type of food;
  - Held cold at 41° F or less* or hot at 140° F; and
  - Reheated rapidly to at least 165° F.

Consult the FDA Food Code for specific temperature requirements and for special provisions related to microwave cooking and reheating.

Young children attending child-care centers are particularly susceptible to food-borne illness and special precautions apply. For example: individual packages of food, like crackers, must not be reserved if they are not eaten, even if they remain unopened; and pasteurized eggs should be used instead of shell eggs.

*With home thermometers, use about 40° F (5° C) or less.
Source: Adapted from http://www.cfsan.fda.gov/~dms/wh-dcare.html.

The U.S. Public Health Service has identified the following microorganisms as being the biggest culprits of food-borne illness, either because of the severity of the sickness or the number of cases of illness they cause (http://www.fightbac.org/).

Campylobacter Jejuni is the most common cause of diarrhea. Sources include raw and undercooked meat and poultry, raw milk, and untreated water. It is underreported as a cause of food-borne illnesses because symptoms may not be severe in some cases.

Clostridium botulinum organism produces a toxin, which causes botulism, a disease characterized by muscle paralysis. Sources are home-prepared foods and herbal oils.

E. coli O157:H7 is a bacterium that can produce a deadly toxin. Sources include meat, especially undercooked or raw hamburger, produce, and raw milk.

Listeria monocytogenes causes listeriosis, a serious disease for pregnant women, newborns, and adults with a weakened immune system. Sources include soil and water. It has been found in dairy products, including soft cheeses, as well as in raw and undercooked meat, in poultry and seafood, and in produce (Box 7.6). Refrigeration does not stop its growth.

Salmonella is the second most common cause of food-borne illness. It is responsible for millions of cases of food-borne illness a year. Sources include raw and undercooked eggs, undercooked poultry and meat, dairy products, seafood, fruits, and vegetables.

Staphylococcus aureus is a bacterium that produces a toxin causing vomiting shortly after ingesting. Sources are cooked foods high in protein (e.g., cooked ham, salads, bakery products, and dairy products).

Shigella causes an estimated 300,000 cases of diarrhea illnesses. Poor hygiene causes Shigella to be easily passed from person to person. Sources include salads, milk and dairy products, and unclean water.

Toxoplasma gondii is a parasite that causes toxoplasmosis, a very severe disease that can produce central nervous system disorders, particularly mental retardation and visual impairment in children. Sources include meat, primarily pork.

Vibrio vulnificus causes gastroenteritis or a syndrome known as primary septicemia. People with liver diseases are especially at high risk. Sources are raw or undercooked seafood.

Yersinia enterocolitica causes yersiniosis, a disease characterized by diarrhea and/or vomiting. Sources include pork, dairy products, and produce.

Methyl-Mercury

Although not a living organism, foods with high concentrations of methyl-mercury should be avoided. Although the foods associated with methyl-mercury may not be commonly eaten in all areas, there is an FDA advisory that concerns centers caring for young children. Fish such as shark, swordfish, king mackerel, and tilefish contain high levels of a form of mercury called methyl-mercury that may harm a young child's or unborn baby's developing nervous system. These long-lived, larger fish that feed on smaller fish accumulate the highest levels of methyl-mercury and therefore pose the greatest risk to the unborn child. Mercury can occur naturally in the environment, and it can be released into the air through industrial pollution and can get into both fresh and salt water. The FDA advises pregnant women and women of childbearing age who may become pregnant not to eat shark, swordfish, king mackerel, and tilefish. The FDA is also recommending that nursing mothers and young children not eat these fish as well [19]. The FDA advisory acknowledges that seafood can be an important part of a balanced diet. Eat other kinds of fish, including shellfish, canned fish, smaller ocean fish, or farm-raised fish. The Environmental Protection Agency has also issued advice on possible mercury contamination to pregnant

---

BOX 7.6 Reducing the risk of *Listeria monocytogenes*

USDA 's Food Safety and Inspection Service (FSIS) and the U.S. Food and Drug Administration (FDA) provides the following foods that have a likelihood of containing *Listeria monocytogenes* and should be avoided by at-risk individuals such as pregnant women, infants, or immune-compromised individuals, for example, those with HIV.

- Do not eat hot dogs and luncheon meats, unless they are reheated until steaming hot.
- Do not eat soft cheese such as Feta, Brie, and Camembert cheeses, blue-veined cheeses, and Mexican-style cheeses such as "queso blanco fresco."
- Cheeses that may be eaten include hard cheese; semi-soft cheeses such as mozzarella; pasteurized processed cheeses such as slices and spreads; cream cheese and cottage cheese.
- Do not eat refrigerated pates or meat spreads. Canned or shelf-stable pates and meat spreads may be eaten.
- Do not eat refrigerated smoked seafood, unless it is contained in a cooked dish, such as a casserole. Refrigerated smoked seafood, such as salmon, trout, whitefish, cod, tuna, or mackerel, is most often labeled as "nova-style," "lox," "kippered," "smoked," or "jerky." The fish is found in the refrigerator section or sold at deli counters of grocery stores and delicatessens. Canned or shelf-stable smoked seafood may be eaten.
- Do not drink raw (unpasteurized) milk or eat foods that contain unpasteurized milk.

---

women, nursing mothers, and young children eating fish caught by family and friends (noncommercial fish).

Keeping Food Safe

The most common sources of contamination of food served are

- employees' handling foods
- the food or ingredient used
- ice used as a coolant
- equipment, utensils, not sanitized
- children eating or handling food

Food service personnel may bring in disease-causing organisms and, because of careless personal hygiene, pass these on to food. Therefore, it is important that those in food service maintain a high degree of personal hygiene. Disease-ridden insects and rodents will carry organisms in with them. It is the responsibility of the kitchen employee to be on the lookout for signs of pest infestation, such as droppings and food damage, and report any findings to the supervisor so that proper steps for extermination may be taken. The organisms may be carried into the child-care center already on the food. Remember that living organisms need food, moisture, and moderate temperature to grow.

Mercury risk

To protect against the risks of mercury in fish caught in freshwaters, the EPA is recommending that high-risk groups limit fish consumption to one meal per week for adults (6 ounces of cooked fish, 8 ounces uncooked fish). Young children should limit fish consumption to one meal per week (2 ounces cooked fish or 3 ounces uncooked fish). The EPA particularly recommends that consumers check with their state or local health department for any additional advice on the safety of fish from nearby waters. Additional information is available on the EPA's Web site at: www.epa.gov/ost/fish.

Food service supervisors should make sure the child-care center is on guard against contamination that can make people needlessly sick. The risk is not just a bout of diarrhea. The risk can be serious health problems that can—and should—be prevented. Frequently asked questions about food safety are listed in Figure 7.4.

Personnel Sanitation

Personal hygiene means more than just a clean face and hands. It means a clean body, clean clothes, and clean habits. Everyone's skin harbors organisms. Food service personnel should wear clean uniforms or aprons each day. An apron should be changed when it gets soiled. It is necessary that a kitchen cap, chef's cap, or hair net be worn, because organisms are on hair. Also, caps or nets prevent hair from falling onto the food. The hands of a food service worker should be kept clean, with short, clean nails and no jewelry other than a watch or wedding ring. Hands frequently harbor organisms that can be transferred to food. Because of this, it is essential that hands be washed before working, each time they become dirty, after smoking (organisms from your mouth get onto cigarettes and then onto fingers), and after using the toilet. Use soap and hot water to effectively wash hands and follow the Food Safety Code (Box 7.5).

Take time to do a thorough job. Do not lean against the basin; organisms outside the basin will get on your uniform and then onto the work counter and work area. Rinse and dry hands thoroughly with a fresh paper towel. Do not use your clean hands to turn off water. Use a paper towel. This will keep the clean hands from touching the unsanitary water faucet. Food service personnel should not handle the food if they have boils, running sores, skin eruptions, or infected cuts, because these conditions may be sources of infection. It is possible to work in a non-food-handling part of the kitchen until the skin condition has disappeared.

Food should not be handled by anyone with an illness. Turn away from food to sneeze or cough, and cover mouth and nose with a disposable tissue. (A sneeze alone will explode millions of organisms into the air and contaminate not only food but also work areas, equipment, and coworkers.) Because organisms from a sneeze or cough can penetrate the tissue used and get onto the hands, dispose of the tissue after use and wash hands.

The warmth of a kitchen often causes one to perspire. When wiping perspiration from the face, use a paper towel, not a kitchen towel. After using, dispose of the paper towel and wash hands. Always comb hair in the lavatory, not in the kitchen. Try not to touch hair or skin while working, for the hand could then serve as a carrier of organisms to the food.

Food Handling

After preparation, keep foods in a cold refrigerator, 40° F, and store and keep hot foods at least 140° F when holding. Do not leave food out for more than 2 hours, and less if the temperature is higher. Use thermometers on a regular basis to check foods for correct temperatures when cooking and holding food. There are various

1. **Are fruits and vegetables safe to eat?**
   Yes. In fact, health authorities such as the National Cancer Institute, the National Academy of Sciences and The American Dietetic Association recommend that we eat more fruits and vegetables—at least five servings a day—to reduce the risk of cancer and other chronic diseases and for better health.

2. **How can I be sure that foods grown using pesticides are safe to eat?**
   Pesticides, like pharmaceuticals, are extensively tested and regulated. The U.S. Environmental Protection Agency and state regulatory agencies review the test data and grant a registration, or license to sell, only if the product meets its standards. A single pesticide is subjected to more than 120 tests. It takes 8 to 10 years and $35 to $50 million to develop and register a pesticide product. On average, only one in 20,000 chemicals makes it from the laboratory to the farmer's field.

3. **Who ensures that the food is safe?**
   Our government sets strict standards and monitors food safety very closely. The U.S. Food and Drug Administration, U.S. Environmental Protection Agency, U.S. Department of Agriculture, and individual states all play important roles in protecting the safety of our food supply. In addition, agricultural chemical companies work closely with these government regulatory agencies and continuously assess the safety and efficacy of their products to be sure they meet today's high standards and satisfy the needs of both growers and consumers.

4. **How much pesticide residue remains on food? How can I tell if residues are there? Can I taste residues?**
   Very little, if any, pesticide residue remains on the foods we buy. According to the U.S. Food and Drug Administration's Residue Monitoring Program, the majority of foods on the market have no detectable residues. If residues do exist, they are at levels so small that special laboratory equipment is necessary to detect them. These small amounts are described as parts per million (ppm). One ppm is equivalent to one cent in $10,000. You cannot taste or smell them.

5. **Should I wash produce before serving?**
   Washing produce is always recommended for sanitary reasons. However, do not wash foods in soapy water because the soap can leave residues of its own.

6. **Who should I look to about the safety of our food?**
   The scientific and regulatory communities, including the Food and Drug Administration, the U.S. Public Health Service, and the Environmental Protection Agency, agree that any risk to humans of all ages from pesticide residue is negligible—so small that there should not be cause for concern. Health experts, including the former U.S. Surgeon General C. Everett Koop, believe that dietary exposure to pesticides is not a source of danger to children or adults.

7. **Are there pesticide residues in processed foods?**
   Processed foods must meet the same rigorous standards for safety as fresh foods. Any residue remaining in processed foods must not exceed the amount established to be safe by the Environmental Protection Agency.

8. **Should I be concerned about the waxy coating on some fruits and vegetables?**
   The thin, waxy coat on some produce (such as apples and cucumbers) is not a cause for concern. This practice helps maintain the quality of the produce by retaining the moisture, protecting the food from bruising, and preventing spoilage. Waxed produce should also be washed (in water only).

Figure 7.4   General food safety questions
Source: Taken from The Children's Food Safety Kit, developed by the National Center for Nutrition and Dietetics of the American Dietetic Association and made possible by an educational grant from the Du Pont Company.

thermometers for selective uses but whatever thermometer, follow minimum temperatures and holding times (Figure 7.5).

Centers, parents, and children should follow safe food handling tips for parents and children shown in Figure 7.6 when handling food. A system for monitoring the food service process to reduce the risk of food-borne illness is called HACCP. Food service workers can be trained to identify critical control points in food service operations (Box 7.7).

Resources for Food Safety

Food service textbooks can provide additional information [14–16]. Professional and consumer information is available from the American Dietetic Association [20–21] on safe cooking, eating, storage, and food-borne illness in the home and center.

You can also find helpful information about food-borne illness by going online at the following sites.

Centers for Disease Control and Prevention

Health Topic: Food-Borne Illness

http://www.cdc.gov/health/foodill.htm

This site provides links describing a vast number of food-borne illnesses, and is useful and informative for teachers and food specialist. Additionally, information is available about food-borne disease regulation, identification, prevention, and elimination.

Food-Safe Schools

http://www.foodsafeschools.org

The National Coalition for Food-Safe Schools (NCFSS)— a collaboration of over 50 organizations, trade associations, federal agencies, education agencies, and health agencies that work together to improve food safety—has launched a portal site featuring links to resources and information for parents, students, teachers, school nurses, school administrators, school food service professionals, health departments, cooperative extensions, and other members of the school community.

Resources and links are organized by audience and topic area. Topic areas include kitchen tips, harmful food-borne organisms, school food service safety, hand washing, food recalls and alerts, and food allergies. Searches also can be performed with key words.

Food-borne Illness: Prevention Strategies

http://hgic.clemson.edu/factsheets/HGIC3620.htm

The information contained within this site is fundamental and essential for any food handler. The challenging aspects of food organization, common diseases

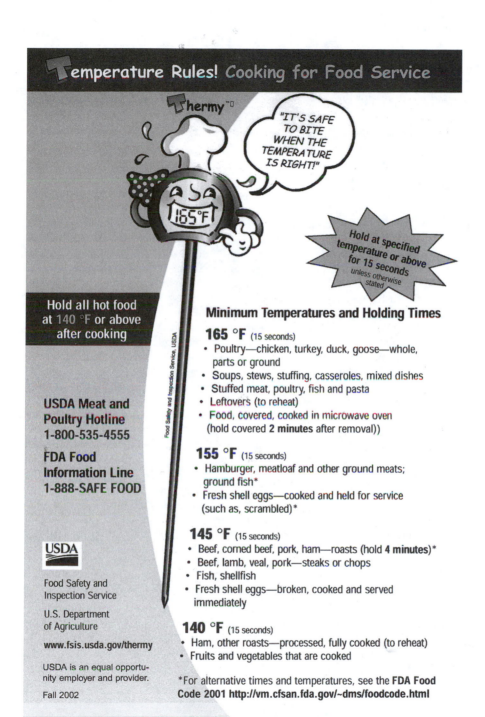

Temperature Rules! Cooking for Food Service

Thermy™

"IT'S SAFE TO BITE WHEN THE TEMPERATURE IS RIGHT!"

165°F

Hold at specified temperature or above for 15 seconds
unless otherwise stated

Food Safety and Inspection Service, USDA

Hold all hot food at 140 °F or above after cooking

USDA Meat and Poultry Hotline
1-800-535-4555

FDA Food Information Line
1-888-SAFE FOOD

USDA

Food Safety and Inspection Service

U.S. Department of Agriculture

www.fsis.usda.gov/thermy

USDA is an equal opportunity employer and provider.

Fall 2002

Minimum Temperatures and Holding Times

165 °F (15 seconds)
- Poultry—chicken, turkey, duck, goose—whole, parts or ground
- Soups, stews, stuffing, casseroles, mixed dishes
- Stuffed meat, poultry, fish and pasta
- Leftovers (to reheat)
- Food, covered, cooked in microwave oven (hold covered **2 minutes** after removal))

155 °F (15 seconds)
- Hamburger, meatloaf and other ground meats; ground fish*
- Fresh shell eggs—cooked and held for service (such as, scrambled)*

145 °F (15 seconds)
- Beef, corned beef, pork, ham—roasts (hold **4 minutes**)*
- Beef, lamb, veal, pork—steaks or chops
- Fish, shellfish
- Fresh shell eggs—broken, cooked and served immediately

140 °F (15 seconds)
- Ham, other roasts—processed, fully cooked (to reheat)
- Fruits and vegetables that are cooked

*For alternative times and temperatures, see the **FDA Food Code 2001** http://vm.cfsan.fda.gov/~dms/foodcode.html

Figure 7.5 Temperature rules

Food-borne illness (food poisoning) can strike anyone, but kids are especially susceptible. Here are 10 basic food-handling tips that you should know:

1. Wash your hands thoroughly with soap before and after handling food.
2. Wash all work surfaces, cutting boards, utensils, and your hands immediately after they have come into contact with any raw meat, raw fish, raw poultry, or raw eggs. Never let any raw juices from these foods touch any other food.
3. Use acrylic, not wooden, cutting boards. Wooden surfaces harbor bacteria. Acrylic boards can be scrubbed with hot soapy water or cleaned in the dishwasher.
4. Don't serve raw fish (i.e., sushi, oysters, clams) or dishes made with raw eggs that could contain harmful bacteria, viruses, or parasites. If cookie, bread, or cake dough contains raw eggs, don't lick the bowl or spoon. Homemade ice cream is often made with raw egg yolks. Instead, use an egg substitute which has been pasteurized or follow a recipe that calls for cooking the ice cream mixture before freezing.
5. Freeze foods at 0° F or below. Refrigerate foods at 40° F or below. Buy a freezer/refrigerator thermometer at the supermarket and check temperatures regularly.
6. Thaw meats and poultry in your refrigerator overnight or in a microwave oven. If thawed in the microwave, cook immediately. Never thaw meats on the counter at room temperature.
7. Refrigeration and freezing slows bacterial growth, but does not kill the bacteria. Once frozen foods thaw to room temperature, bacteria continue to thrive. Only heating foods to a high enough internal temperature can kill bacteria, so cook foods thoroughly. Use a meat thermometer to check the internal temperature of food.

Beef	Internal temperature of at least 160° F
Pork	Internal temperature of at least 170° F
Lamb and poultry	Internal temperature of at least 180° F

Foods cooked in the microwave may heat unevenly, resulting in some parts of the food not being heated to safe temperatures. Be sure to follow microwave directions, rotating dishes and allowing standing time if required. Check internal food temperature in a variety of areas.

8. Keep hot foods above 140° F and cold foods below 40° F. Don't allow foods to sit at room temperature for more than two hours. The "danger zone," when bacteria multiply the fastest, is between 40° F and 140° F.
9. If canned food is not completely consumed when opened, either cover the can securely or transfer food to another container. Store leftovers in the refrigerator.
10. Cool leftovers quickly in a refrigerator or freezer. Large batches should be divided into small portions in shallow containers so food can cool more quickly. Do not stack items during cooling or freezing in order to allow air to circulate. Reheat leftovers to at least 165° F.
11. Do not save raw or cooked food too long. A complete chart of holding times is available (ask your dietitian). However, a simple rule of thumb applies: *"When in doubt, throw it out!"* Food harboring harmful bacteria does not necessarily have a foul odor or spoiled appearance.
12. Be sure to separate diapering from food handling and preparation activities. Always wash hands well after diapering.

Figure 7.6   Safe food handling tips for parents and children
Source: Taken from The Children's Food Safety Kit, developed by the National Center for Nutrition and Dietetics of the American Dietetic Association and made possible by an educational grant from the Du Pont Company.

BOX 7.7   HACCP

Hazard Analysis of Critical Control Points (HACCP) is a system for monitoring the food service process to reduce the risk of food-borne illness. It involves looking at the food-handling practices as food flows through the food service operations, from purchasing through serving.

A critical control point is any step, place, or procedure in a food's production where food safety hazards can be controlled or prevented. Critical control points may include issues with purchasing, receiving, storing, preparing, cooking and holding, cooling and reheating. Failure to take appropriate action at these critical control points could result in food-borne illness. Critical control points and steps food service workers can take to ensure food safety are included in food service courses and available online at: http://www.nal.usda.gov/fnic/foodborne/index.html.

---

originating from improper food management, and preventative measures for avoiding food-borne illness are topics covered by this site.

Partnership for Food Safety Education—Fight Bac!

http://www.fightbac.org/main.cfm

This site is fundamental education for any food handler. Its educational structure is primarily targeted to young audiences, but the educational material is meant for anyone. It emphasizes four primary elements of food safety (clean, separate, cook, chill), which should be core understandings of any food handler.

Shigella—An Infectious Food-Borne Illness

http://ohioline.osu.edu/hyg-fact/5000/5563.html

This site discusses known information about the food-borne illness Shigella. It answers factual questions concerning its symptoms, transmission, and regulation.

U.S. Food and Drug Administration Center for Food Safety and Applied Nutrition

Food-Borne Illness

http://vm.cfsan.fda.gov/

This site is an incredible resource containing several highly informative Web links that discuss topics ranging from specifying individual food-borne pathogens to procedural requirements for maintaining food safety. It is an invaluable educational resource for any food service professional.

Food-Borne Illness and Seafood

http://vm.cfsan.fda.gov/

This site contains highly descriptive information about various pathogens associated with certain kinds of seafood. Information is provided on the nature and diagnosis of certain pathogens, as well as population and outbreak analysis.

U.S. Department of Agriculture Food Safety and Inspection Service

Food-Borne Illness Peaks In Summer? Why?

http://www.fsis.usda.gov/

This site explains why the potential for contracting food-borne illness rises in the summertime. It attributes the cause of the increased incidence to two primary sources: better circumstances for bacterial growth and less environmental regulation of bacterial growth.

U.S. Department of Agriculture/U.S. Food and Drug Administration

Food-Borne Illness Education Information Center

http://www.nal.usda.gov/foodborne/index.html

This site should be helpful to anyone interested in food safety education. It contains links to food safety training materials, informational resources, HACCP training materials, and other vital assets needed by the food safety professional.

Use of Microwave Ovens

Microwave ovens have become popular for child-care centers that have foods prepared in locations other than the centers or if special diets are required for which the food has been frozen. Microwaves are very-high-frequency radio waves that swing back and forth at a frequency of about 2 billion cycles per second. During this process, they make certain molecules move, and once they're moving, they're hot. Microwaves enter food from the outside, and penetrate instantly into a chunk of food, heating and cooking as they go. Microwaves heat fats, sugars, and liquids more quickly than carbohydrates and proteins.

Some basic rules apply when using the microwave.

- Always use containers or plastic wrap designed for microwave.
- Cover food with plastic wrap or a glass covering and add a little liquid to food. This creates steam, which readily kills pathogens.
- To ensure uniform heating, if the microwave oven does not come with a turntable, turn the dish several times during cooking. Stir soups and stews periodically during reheating to ensure even heating.
- When done cooking, make sure the food is hot and steaming. Use a food thermometer and test the food in 2 or 3 different areas to verify that it has reached a safe internal temperature. Foods tend to have hot and cold spots and bacteria can survive in the cold spots.

- Do not put closed plastic bottles in the microwave—they may explode from the heat and steam.
- Never warm a baby bottle in the microwave.
- Children who are too young to read are too young to use microwaves.
- Always check temperature of food after it is stirred.
- When defrosting food in the microwave, cook the food immediately. Some areas of the food may become warm and begin to cook during the defrosting process. The internal temperature of the food probably hasn't reached the temperature needed to destroy bacteria and, indeed, may have reached optimal temperatures for bacteria to grow. So don't let foods sit in the danger zone!
- Heat to a temperature of at least 165° F (74° C) in all parts of the food and allow to stand covered for 2 minutes after cooking to obtain temperature equilibrium.
- Fruits and vegetables that are cooked for hot holding shall be cooked to a temperature of 140° F (60° C).

Teachers and Aides Preparing Food

In many cases it is necessary and even advantageous for teachers and aides to assist the food service personnel. In some centers unions may forbid this activity. However, where permitted, they should participate in food safety training and follow the same procedures to ensure maintenance of sanitary conditions in the food service facility. Personal hygiene principles should be followed. (Hands should be washed before personnel come into the kitchen area.) Likewise, providing a clean apron and wearing a hair net or cap are essential during food preparation and cleanup.

Eating and drinking of food by staff should be permitted only outside the kitchen or food preparation area. It is disruptive for teachers to take "tastes" from the containers of food while food service personnel are preparing and serving it.

SUMMARY

- Federal Child Nutrition Programs facilitate child-care centers in serving nutritious foods and provide reimbursement for meals served.
- Two programs that are designed to enhance the health and well being of the young child include Women, Infants, and Children (WIC) and Head Start.
- If the menu is to become a tool for the educational curriculum, the food service personnel and teachers must participate together in the food service activities.
- Cycle menus, which are flexible enough to be changed frequently, not only help meet the nutritional needs of the individual child but also assist the food service personnel and teacher in planning food service and the curriculum.

- Without the use of good management principles, foods will not provide the quality necessary to encourage children to actively participate in the educational process.
- Following food safety guidelines can help keep children from suffering food-borne illness.

DISCUSSION QUESTIONS

1. How are the food patterns for the various age groups different?
2. How might the teacher, food service personnel, dietitian, and parents participate in planning?
3. Are there foods or combinations of foods that meet the Child and Adult Food Program requirements but might be questioned for the child given the principles outlined in Chapters 4, 5, and 6?
4. Describe how you have observed the good management principles outlined in this chapter in preschool or child-care facilities.
5. List possible constraints from the food service management viewpoint of preparing the following menu: meat loaf, baked potato, cooked broccoli, tossed salad, freshly baked whole-wheat rolls, baked apple, and milk.
6. Identify and describe the most frequent food-borne illnesses in the nation and in your state, using the Internet.
7. From your experience, describe a situation in a child-care center where food may have become contaminated.
8. Evaluate the menu of ham salad sandwich, gelatin with orange and apple pieces, carrot sticks, chocolate pudding, and graham crackers and milk. Would this menu meet the CACFP guidelines?

REFERENCES:

1. U.S. Department of Agriculture, Food and Nutrition Service, 7 C.F.R. pts. 210, 220, and 226. Amendments to the Child Nutrition Infant Meal Pattern. Fed. Reg. 36,779 (2002); 67(102).
2. U.S. Department of Agriculture, Food and Nutrition Service. National School Lunch Act 42 U.S.C. 1751.
3. National Research Council, Subcommittee on the 10th Edition of the RDA's Food and Nutrition Board, Commission on Life Sciences. (1989). *Recommended dietary allowances.* Washington, DC: National Academy Press.
4. Koaleski-Jones L., & Duncan, G. J. (May 2002). Effects of participation in the WIC program on birthweight: Evidence from the National Longitudinal Survey of Youth. *American Public Health Association*, 92(5), 799–804.
5. U.S. Department of Health and Human Services, Food and Drug Administration, 45 C.F.R. Pt. 1304. Program Performance Standards for the Operation of Head Start Programs by Grantee and Delegate Agencies. Fed. Reg. (2001); 4: 181–183.
6. Endres, J., Poon, S. W., Welch, P. (1987). Dietary sodium intake of infants fed

commercially prepared baby food and table food. *Journal of the American Dietetic Association, 87,* 750–753.

7. Kleinman, R. E. (Nov. 2000). Complementary feeding and later health. *Pediatrics, Supplement, 106*(5), 1287.

8. Centers for Disease Control and Prevention. Preventing choking among infants and young children. Retrieved September 3, 2002, from http://www.cdc.gov/safeusa/home/choke.htm

9. Food and Nutrition Board, Institutes of Medicine. (2002). *Dietary Reference Intakes for energy, carbohydrates, fiber, fat, protein, and amino acids (macronutrients).* Washington DC: National Academy Press.

10. Drake, M. A. (1992). Menu evaluation, nutrient intake of young children, and nutrition knowledge of menu planners in child-care centers in Missouri. *Journal of Nutrition Education, 24*(3), 145–147.

11. Drake, M. A. (1991). Anthropometry, biochemical iron indexes, and energy and nutrient intake of preschool children: Comparison of intake at day-care center and at home. *Journal of the American Dietetic Association, 91,* 1587–1588.

12. Ethnic and regional food practices: A series. (1995–1998). Chicago, IL: American Dietetic Association and American Diabetes Association.

13. U.S. Department of Agriculture. *Healthy school meals resources system: Recipes and menus.* Retrieved September 3, 2002, from http://www.nal.usda.gov:8001/Recipes

14. Knight, J. B., & Kotschevar, L. H. (2000). *Quantity food production, planning, and management* (3rd ed). New York: Wiley.

15. Payne-Palacio, J., & Theis, M. (2001). *West and Wood's introduction to foodservice* (9th ed.). Upper Saddle River, NJ: Prentice Hall.

16. Molt, M. (2001). *Food for fifty* (11th ed.). Upper Saddle River, NJ: Prentice Hall.

17. Bartlett, A. V., Moore, M., Gary, G. W., Starko, K. M., Erben, J. J., & Meredith, B. A. (1985). Diarrheal illness among infants and toddlers in day care centers. II. Comparison with day care homes and households. *Journal of Pediatrics 107,* 503–509.

18. Young, F. E. (August 1989). *In day-care centers, cleanliness is a must.* Updated June 2002. FDA Consumer Retrieved August 5, 2002, from http://www.cfsan.fda.gov/~dms/wh-dcare.html

19. Center for Food Safety and Applied Nutrition, U.S. Food and Drug Administration. (March 2001). *An important message for pregnant women and women of childbearing age who may become pregnant about the risks of mercury in fish.* Consumer Advisory. Retrieved September 4, 2002, from http://vm.cfsan.fda.gov/~dms/admehg.html

20. Cody, M. M., & Kunkel, M. E. (2002). *Food safety for professionals* (2nd ed.). Chicago: American Dietetic Association.

21. Cody, M. M. (1996). *Safe food for you and your family* (American Dietetic Association *Nutrition Now* Series). New York: Wiley.

8

Integrating Food and Nutrition Concepts into the Early Childhood Curriculum

LEARNING OBJECTIVES

Students will be able to:

- List and describe the four major curriculum approaches used in early childhood education programs.
- List the characteristics of the cognitive–interactionist approach.
- List six programmatic insights to be gained in using any approach to learning.
- State the goals and objectives for teaching nutrition directly to young children (3 to 5 years).
- Using one food from each of the food groups, describe how the food can be used according to Blank's model [1].
- Write nutrition education objectives and list activities to teach the young child (birth to 3 years) good nutrition principles.
- Discuss the use of the menu as a key resource for nutrition education in early childhood programs.
- Write a lesson plan for at least one curriculum area, incorporating food or nutrition in the activities.
- List the four developmental areas used to integrate food and nutrition activities in the learning environment.
- Develop written lesson plans using nutrition activities related to the four developmental skills.
- List some precautions to be observed when cooking in the classroom.

In compiling information for this chapter, we considered the following questions: How do children develop intellectually? Which concepts do they acquire? At which age do they begin to develop these concepts? How can we as teachers of young children teach concepts using foods as one of the primary teaching tools? Can food and nutrition concepts be integrated into the curriculum? Is cooking in the classroom feasible? Are there classroom recipes that young children can prepare? How can recipes be followed by nonreaders? We have attempted to answer these questions through the use of one approach or model, while presenting additional common teaching approaches that are practical in early childhood settings. All these approaches can be adapted to the nutrition curriculum.

PROGRAMMATIC APPROACHES TO LEARNING

As we examine the development of thought and the many implications it has for teaching, it becomes evident that the environment and the kind of stimulation and interaction with adults to which a child is exposed in the early years will have a significant impact on the child's capabilities.

269

The child learns through interaction and encounters with objects and persons in the environment. Food, the eating situation, and those persons who provide the food and food service are components of the environment. Thus, the child learns through observing and interacting with foods and the eating situation, manipulating foods, and modeling or imitating those significant adults who participate with the child in the eating situation. The child's perception of the world becomes stabilized, and concepts about the world develop into usable entities. How much and how well this is learned and the kinds of things learned depend on the child's exposure to examples of foods and the eating experiences. The nutrition education curriculum in early childhood settings should provide the appropriate kinds of experiences, materials, and opportunities to explore and interact for each child's complete development.

It is generally agreed that the early years in a child's life are critical to development and that appropriate early childhood programs can have a positive influence [2]. There is less agreement on which kind of educational program is appropriate, and this, too, has a significant relationship to nutrition education for the young child. The Head Start planned variation studies [3] and numerous educational laboratories and universities have been and are involved in trying to answer that question.

There are at least four major types of approaches to early childhood education: the cognitive-interactionist, traditional nursery school, perceptual motor, and the academic skills [4, 5]. We have chosen the cognitive-interactionist approach to express ways of teaching nutrition education concepts to children. This does not mean that the other approaches are not appropriate for helping children select the proper foods. Any of the methods can be used with success.

Cognitive–Interactionist Approach

Cognition refers to mental growth and activity. It defines most of the processes of thinking and knowing that children employ daily—planning what to do in the morning, learning the rules of a game, or making up an excuse for not going to bed early. Cognition includes thinking, remembering, problem solving, understanding, planning, imagining, judging, and deciding. These processes develop in a predictable way according to Piaget [6]. Cognitive ability, which makes understanding possible, develops in three major stages: sensorimotor (birth to 24 months), preoperational (24 months to 6 years), and concrete operational (7 years to 11 years).

Sensorimotor Stage.   This stage covers the period of growth from birth through 24 months. During this period the child depends on inborn sensorimotor reflexes for interaction with the environment. The environment does not just turn on and off those tools provided by heredity. The infant profits from experience and actively modifies the reflex schemes. For example, the child learns to recognize the nipple and to search for it [6]. The smell or sight of food can cause the older infant to crawl to the kitchen in pursuit of it.

Preoperational Stage.   This stage of development extends from 2 to 6 years of age. During this period, the child starts to play symbolically and to explore the world in a more able way than the random exploration of an infant. The child has gained more control over the body and thus has freer movement within the environment. Socializing and interacting with others has started. The child's powers of thought are still at a primitive stage, and the sense organs, which have further developed from the sensorimotor period, are still the primary tools for learning. The child needs to look, feel, taste, smell, and even listen to food before, during, and after preparation and to experience this involvement over and over until different experiences (that is, eating a variety of foods) make sense and are internalized.

Concrete Operations Stage.   During this stage of development, which extends from age 7 to 11 years, the child continues to develop in ability to handle concepts both in terms of forming them and in manipulating them in a thought process. Actually, concrete operations are an internalized set of actions that allow the child to do in the head what was previously done with the hands. The child still isn't able to think abstractly but can solve problems with concrete content. As a result, overt trial and error is reduced. At this stage, the child can deal with more than one concrete aspect at once, yet can only consider one abstraction at a time. The child is now able to substitute thought for actual performance. Development of mental process can be encouraged and facilitated during this stage through the use of concrete or real objects as opposed to hypothetical situations and places. The child needs to be involved in a learning setting that promotes experiences with real objects, things, and people; for example, cooking in the classroom, using real utensils, recipes, and ingredients [6].

Concepts.   Concepts play an important role in cognitive development. Understanding is based on concepts, which in turn determine what one knows and believes and, to a large extent, what one does. Flavell [7] states that "once a concept develops, it serves as an experimental filter through which impinging events are screened, gauged, and evaluated, a process that determines in large part what responses can and will occur."

As you work with children, you will find that they frequently possess a number of misconceptions. These misconceptions are often caused by incorrect information, limited experience, gullibility, faulty reasoning, vivid imagination, unrealistic thinking, and misunderstanding of words. For example, a child might say, "Milk comes from the grocery store, not from cows." Once a misconception is formed, it is difficult to change. This is where the care provider plays an important role, since it is the care provider's responsibility to present experiences that teach children about food, thus minimizing the development of nutritional misconceptions.

The cognitive development approach, also referred to as verbal cognitive or interactionist, includes a variety of diverse types of programs. These approaches share a common emphasis on the development of cognitive skills and abilities such as understanding and using language; concept formation, association, and discrimination; problem solving; and memory. The amount of structure and teaching vis-à-vis child-directed activity varies among programs.

The Perry Preschool High/Scope Curriculum exemplifies the cognitive-interactionist approach [8]. This program follows the Piagetian sequence of content areas with respect to motor and verbal levels of operation. The daily routine is one in which teachers carry out their goals and objectives. When teaching nutrition to children, the care provider takes on a directing role. The routine involving food, food service, and nutrition principles is made as tangible and concrete for the child as possible. The approach is similar to the traditional nursery school, or child development model (discussed later), in the number and kinds of materials used and in the prearranged activity areas.

Morrison identified four recurring themes that are present in programs that implement curricula based on Piaget's ideas:

1. Children's thinking is substantially different from that of adults, and adults must not try to impose their way of thinking on children. The educational environment should enable children to think of their own ideas and construct their own models of the world.
2. Children must be actively involved in learning.
3. Learning should involve concrete objects and experiences with both children and adults, particularly at the sensorimotor and preoperational stages.
4. Children learn best by being continually exposed to quality learning experiences. Their comprehension of any event is greatly dependent upon the proximity of the event to concepts involved. If the children have nothing to associate an experience to, it will be meaningless assimilation (fitting or adding new knowledge into already existing knowledge), and accommodation (changing one's ideas of reality to fit the new knowledge one is trying to assimilate) cannot function unless experiences closely parallel each other [9].

Other Approaches

Three additional approaches to early childhood education described by Mayer [4] are the academic skills, traditional nursery school, and perceptual-motor approaches. The academic skills approach teaches the preschool child the academic skills usually learned in the first years of elementary school through a program of planned, sequenced, highly structured activities. The best known example is the Bereiter-Englemann academically oriented preschool program. Children receive direct instruction in language, arithmetic, and reading, with some time for music and semistructured play. Each teacher takes responsibility for one of the subject areas, and the children in small ability groups rotate from one subject area and teacher to the next. The method of instruction is intense oral drill. Sentence patterns are taught as didactic repetitive formulas, and they increase in complexity as children master them. Concepts such as number and volume, for example, are presented as rules and learned by rote memorization. Children may be expected to memorize examples of the concepts "fruit" or "vegetable."

Another common approach is often termed the traditional nursery school. This type stresses the social and emotional development of the child through free play and organized group activities, such as making placemats for mealtime table settings, reading stories about food, and singing songs about food. Also referred to as the child development model [4], this curricular approach has been the pattern for most preschools serving middle-class populations. It is based on the physiological belief that effective development fosters cognitive development. This approach ranks highest in child–child interaction, providing opportunities for children to participate together without teaching intervention. The care providers' role is subtle. By planning and arranging the eating environment, children learn about foods. Observations of each child's readiness to profit from a food experience determine the use of that experience.

Bandura's social cognitive theory fits well with this approach [5]. This theory emphasizes the importance of imitation and observational learning for social and personality development. Children learn many things by watching and imitating others. Modeling is the core of social cognitive theory. It can be live and direct from a peer, care provider/teacher or parent, symbolic from a book, a video or television, or synthesized in a combination of the acts of different models.

The perceptual–motor approach, or sensory–cognitive model, is best illustrated in the Montessori preschool program. This type of program emphasizes self-corrective sensorimotor activities with specially designed materials. The approach ranks high in child-material interaction but lowest of the four approaches in teacher–child interaction [4]. Learning occurs through "doing," with emphasis on concrete nonverbal experiences. The child is free to choose the activity and to move from task to task, and the teaching materials are planned in a carefully prescribed sequence. The importance of the child's having contact with the natural environment is stressed. Specific experiences with food are planned and encouraged.

Programmatic Insights

Much is yet to be learned from educational philosophies and practices inherent in various early child development curriculum approaches. Each has been carefully and meticulously thought through, tested over a considerable period, and critically evaluated in terms of later school achievement and the personal adequacies of the children involved. From the many models and approaches we can glean important information about children and their learning. Important programmatic insights can be summarized as follows [10]:

1. There is no absolute or preferred approach to learning for all children.
2. Educational goals are determined by an emphasis on child growth or child learning. Where growth objectives dominate, curricular items are introduced when the child can integrate them. Where learning is emphasized, a systematic planned sequence of events is in order.
3. The recognition of individual differences is vital in effective preschool training.
4. A child should experience a continuity in education with curriculum introduced at the developmentally appropriate time and reinforced until the behavior indicates the desired achievement.
5. The teacher's commitment to imparting new social and intellectual skills is necessary for a positive educational experience.
6. Stimulating child-centered environments that provide numerous opportunities for exploration and experimentation are crucial for normal personality and intellectual development.

Early childhood programs cannot be homogeneous in a pluralistic society [11]. There is no single "best" approach or system. Each program should reflect the particular orientation, background, and aspirations of the children's community in the educational setting. This provides us the opportunity to maximize the development of each group rather than attempting to equalize the development of all groups in our society.

GOALS AND OBJECTIVES FOR NUTRITION EDUCATION

The goal of the nutrition education program, whether using a direct or indirect method, may be stated as follows:

> Children will eat a well-balanced diet daily to establish and protect their nutritional health for life.

Ideally, after a sound and effective nutrition education program, it should be expected of preschool children that the following would occur:

> Given a choice of foods, the child will select those foods with a high nutrient density (quality) as frequently or more frequently than those with a low nutrient density.

The implication of this objective can be far-reaching. If the nutrition education program is successful, children when confronted with candy or soda should be willing to choose vegetables, fruit, fruit juices, or foods high in nutrient density. Because it is perhaps not practical to expect to change the total environment of the child and the eating habits of all persons coming in contact with the child at home, in the community, and at the marketplace, an alternate overall objective would be the following:

> Given a variety of foods through a well-planned, prepared, and served menu, the child will accept (taste) all foods provided.

This objective is based on the belief that young children with a sufficient number of positive experiences with many high-quality foods will learn to eat a wide variety of foods.

At the close of their preschool experiences children should be able to:

1. state names of all foods served.
2. identify foods by taste, odor, or touch.
3. classify foods into food groups, such as vegetables, fruits, meats/meat alternates (nuts, legumes, lentils), cereals/grains, milk and milk products, fats (butter, margarine, oil), and other foods (low nutrient density foods or "empty calories").
4. match foods served at mealtime with the basic food groups.
5. match foods served at home with the basic food groups.
6. state number of times each day a child should eat foods from each food group (optional).
7. name major nutrients in each food group (optional).

Although it is our belief that the last two objectives are too advanced for the preschooler, some centers find that their children can progress to this stage. Objectives 1 through 5 should be accomplished before progressing to objectives 6 and 7.

TEACHING CHILDREN TO EAT NOURISHING FOOD

The food groups provide the basis for teaching children to eat a wide variety of nourishing foods. The menu provides the substance for the nutrition education activities that ultimately lead to the child's acceptance of these foods.

Food Group Reference

A visual aid provides a concrete reference point to help young children (3 to 8 years) understand the food groups. One such aid can be constructed with six or more boxes (see Figure 8.1). The boxes can be large enough to hold empty food containers brought from home, or they can be used as a receptacle for food models and pictures of foods. Children can help prepare each box as you progress through the food groups, teaching them the concepts of grains and cereals, vegetables, fruits, milk and milk products, meat and meat alternates, and fats, oils, and sweets.

You may choose to combine the food groups into only six categories:

Group 1: bread, cereal, rice, and pasta
Group 2: vegetables
Group 3: fruits
Group 4: milk, yogurt, and cheese
Group 5: meat, poultry, fish, dry beans, eggs, and nuts
Group 6: fats, oils, and sweets

The preparation can include gathering boxes of various sizes. Because the bread, cereal, rice, and pasta and vegetable and fruit groups should contain the

| Bread, cereal, rice, and pasta | Vegetables | Fruits | Milk, yogurt, and cheese | Meat and meat alternates | Fats, oils, and sweets |

Figure 8.1   Boxes representing food groups

Figure 8.2   Divided box emphasizing both meats and meat alternatives

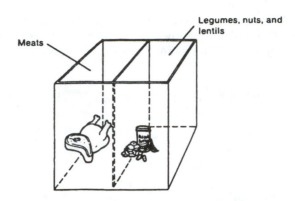

most variety, these boxes may be largest, followed by those for the milk and milk products and the meat and the meat alternates. The fat, oils, and sweets group would be the smallest. The boxes can be sprayed white or color coded, and children can cut out pictures of food from magazines to paste onto the boxes. The meat and meat alternates box may need to be divided to emphasize the importance of including nuts, legumes, and lentils in the diet (see Figure 8.2).

Each food box should be prepared separately, and the foods should be matched with foods served on the menu (objective 4).

The tasting of food items before, during, and after preparation is exciting and educational for children. For example, select a day when white beans appear on the menu. Although children cannot chew a hard, dry bean, they can identify it by touch (objective 2).

Materials for this activity include:

Menu with beans	Pictures of beans in food boxes
Food boxes	Pictures or models of other meats and meat alternates
Uncooked beans	Covered can
Partially cooked beans	

Let the child feel beans placed in a covered can. Pictures of beans can then be placed in the meat and meat alternates food group box (objective 3), and children can note other pictures in the meat alternates box that look similar and that look different. Pinto beans and red beans are similar to white beans, but hamburger and eggs are much different from beans, although they all fall into the meat and meat alternate group.

When planning this event with the cook or food service personnel, you will ask for some partially cooked beans, still crunchy, to taste (objective 2), to feel, to smell, and to note how they have become soft. (In addition, beans may be soaked overnight to allow the children an opportunity to see how they have expanded and become softer.) It is best to teach nutrition education concepts before a meal or snack, since the interest in food and food-related activities will be stronger. At mealtime children can compare the fully cooked beans with the uncooked and partially cooked product as well as with the basic food group "meat and meat alternates" (objective 4).

We have presented the nutrition concept of beans informally. However, if lesson plans were to be written and one needed a model to follow, the following is another illustration using a six-stage model.

Teaching a Nutrition Concept

Objectives 1 through 5 can be taught directly to the child, and each involves teaching a concept. The food and nutrition concepts may be taught through a modified hierarchical sequence of six steps. This is especially true for the 2- through 4-year-old. The six stages as described by Blank [1] are (1) a clear instance, (2) a clear definition of the function or attribute of the instance, (3) extension of the concept to similar instances, (4) extension of the concept to less obvious positive instances, (5) consideration of negative instances, and (6) extension of category.

In giving a preschooler a clear instance, we are in fact giving an example. We associate a word with an object. The following presents a modified version of the hierarchical sequence and examples of the use of this scheme. Whenever possible, let the child taste the example presented—regardless of how small the portion is.

Materials for this activity include:

Food group boxes
Menu with apples
Red and yellow apples, preferably
    with stems
Fresh samples or pictures of dissimilar
    fruits

Other red fruits and vegetables (e.g., onion,
    red grape)
Pictures or models of apples and apple pie
Covered can (Figure 8.3)

Steps	*Example—The Red Apple*
1. Give an example.	"This is an apple; watch the apple roll; this is a big apple."
2. Give a clear definition of the function or attribute of the instance characteristic of the concept. Actions must accompany the verbal dialogue to make the concept clear to the child.	"This apple is round; it has a stem; its skin is smooth. Apples are from the fruit group." Actions: Have the child feel, taste, smell, and listen to the crunchy sound of the apple. Use covered can (Figure 8.3).
3. To extend the concept to similar instances, use contrast. Choose items that are definitely dissimilar.	Use nonfood items or dissimilar food items. An apple may be compared with all the food groups other than fruit. Once again, review the characteristics of the apple.
4. To extend the concept to less obvious instances, present foods with confusing characteristics. These most often will be within food groups but may also be across groups.	Given bananas, grapes, pineapples, lemons, and a yellow apple, ask the child to find another apple. Let the child taste as many fruits as possible.

**Figure 8.3
Identifying item in
covered can by
touch**

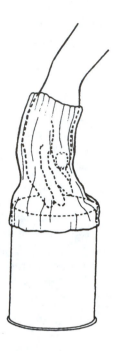

5. Consider subtle negative instances, meaning that the characteristics of the food are primarily present, yet the food is different.

6. Extend the category to relate to activities using the apple either at mealtime or during a special activity.

"Let's find something that is red and round and not an apple." Display red grapes, a red plum, red onion, or a red-orange nectarine. Let child taste even the onion.

When baked or fried apples are served, the children can be asked, "How can we prepare (cook) apples?" Note that the question "What can we make with apples?" will be answered undoubtedly with "apple pie." When this happens, be prepared. Pictures of low-density foods are readily available. Have children place the picture of apple pie in the "other food group" box, thus emphasizing the low nutrient quality.

Because we have provided an example of a meat alternate (beans) and a fruit (apple), vegetables cannot be forgotten. Choose a vegetable high in nutrient quality to provide the child not only with a learning experience but also with a chance to become more familiar with a food that has a high nutrient density. Beans were chosen over other meat products because they have many nutrients that the American diet appears to need in greater quantity. In addition, dietary intake studies show that consumption of meat protein generally is adequate to high. Most homes provide children with meat products. (See preceding chapters for discussion of nutrition and foods.)

Because greens and broccoli have a high vitamin C (ascorbic acid), vitamin A, and iron content, they should be included in the educational curriculum of the preschool center. Because greens are usually less expensive than broccoli, this food has been chosen for illustration.

Materials for this activity include:

Food group boxes	Fresh (if possible) or frozen greens (fresh
Menu with greens	broccoli, lettuce, cabbage, and celery
Facilities to stir-fry greens in center*	leaves, or pictures of these foods).

Steps	*Example—Greens*
1. Give a clear example.	Each child is given a fresh leaf of spinach, turnip, beet, or mustard. "This food is called greens— beet greens, mustard greens, turnip greens, spinach greens."
2. Give a clear definition of the function or attribute.	"Greens are colored green; they are crisp to taste; greens are from the vegetable food group." Actions: Have the children feel, taste, smell, and listen to the crispy sound of the green when they taste it raw.
3. Extend the concept to similar instances.	Use food items from other food groups (e.g., breads, milk, or meat). Compare the greens to at least one item from each of the other food group boxes. Children may select the picture from the boxes of meat, cereals, milk, and fruit. Using the vegetable box with pictures of greens and other vegetables, find a picture of greens.
4. Extend the concept to less obvious positive instances.	In a group of items having the same color or texture (e.g., lettuce, celery leaves), have the child notice the difference between beet greens, spinach greens, and turnip greens.
5. Consider negative instances.	Using broccoli, lettuce, and cabbage leaves (or models or pictures), discuss the differences in appearance and texture between these green vegetables.
6. Extend the category.	"Let's eat these greens, raw, cooked with salad dressing, cream sauce, or margarine." Be sure greens are on the menu. Do not be concerned if the cooked (remember, crunchy cooked) greens are not hot; children prefer foods that are not hot and will eat many cooked vegetables cold.

*The stir-fry method can be used with a frying pan in the classroom. Just use 1/2 tablespoon of margarine for a pound of greens, and stir in frying pan to the "crunchy cooked" stage (takes less than 5 minutes).

Teaching About Nutrients

Those care providers who wish to stress nutrient content of specific foods (such as protein in meats, iron in meats, vitamins A and C in fruits and vegetables) can follow the same format. Appendix I provides the nutrient composition of most foods.

A discussion of protein, fat, and carbohydrate can be found in Chapter 1 and in basic nutrition textbooks.

The Very Young Child.   With a child of 4 to 6 months (when food is first introduced) or one of 12 to 16 months (when language becomes useful), the preceding objectives are inappropriate. The child is not expected to indicate wants by pointing until approximately 15 to 18 months. Many children can, however, indicate desire for food before this time and can identify the foods they are eating by repeating or imitating care providers and the names given to the food. Therefore, with the 1-year-old child, begin with objective 1, "State names of all foods served." The child at 12 months can look at pictures of foods and hear the sound of their names, can begin to imitate words, and can and generally will follow simple instructions such as "Please eat the carrots."

Children may first need to become familiar with the food and like it before they actually eat it. With foods high in nutritive value we may have to allow the child to practice getting acquainted with the texture and flavors by frequently serving and having the child taste the food item. Infants will refuse some new foods, but given continual exposure they will accept them. This is perhaps best illustrated in breast-fed infants. When breastfed infants are suddenly switched to infant formula, they often do not like the formula and refuse to drink it. Likewise, infants who are milk intolerant dislike being switched to soy formulas, but parents and care providers persist, since the health and well-being of the child are at stake. Eventually they "learn" to like the new formula, as older infants and toddlers learn to like a variety of foods.

Specific activities for the very young child from birth to 12 months include the following:

1. Hold the very young infant while bottle-feeding. When several infants are being cared for at the center, their feeding schedules may need to be adjusted, with parents' cooperation, so that each child can be held, just as infants who are breastfed are held.

2. Talk to the infant and young toddler about the food in a pleasant voice while looking at the child, although the child cannot respond with verbal communication.

3. State the names of all foods and eating utensils you are using or that you let the child use; for example: "Would you like a drink of milk? Here is your blue cup. Can you take the handle of the cup? See the milk in the cup. You're drinking the milk by yourself. Good! I only put a small amount of milk into the cup, but I will give you more milk. Would you like more milk? I'll give you just a little more milk from this carton to see if you would like more milk. See, I'm pouring the milk from the carton into the blue cup. Now, I'll give you the blue cup. Can you take the blue cup? [Baby does not take the cup.] Okay, I think you've had enough milk and you don't seem to want any more milk. Perhaps later you'd like some more milk." The child needs to hear your voice and the names of food and eating utensils. Note that after the child has taken at least a taste of the food, any signal from the nonverbal child that additional food or drink is not desired should cause you to stop feeding at once.

When the toddler or older infant is accepting table foods and is fed individually, the care provider must provide a model for the child to imitate by eating the same foods.

1. Make the eating experience pleasant by allowing the child to eat the quantity desired of a variety of foods. Praise the child for trying new, less favorite foods, but expect the child to taste all foods. Refusing a food one day should signal that this food must be reintroduced in small quantities on another day.
2. Give the child finger foods as soon as the child can manipulate the foods in the hand. It is important for the child to experience the touch of the food as well as the taste. This also encourages hand-to-mouth coordination and strengthens finger manipulation. Ideas for finger-feeding have been given in previous chapters. Be sure food is appropriate (for example, cubes of cheese, crunchy cooked vegetables, dry whole-grain toast).
3. Encourage the child to share finger foods with you.
4. Be sure infant seats are fastened to table when feeding small infants, or strap the infant into the high chair securely.
5. Use dishes with sides that facilitate filling by spoon. Use spoons and forks sized for the young child.
6. Tolerate spills and learn to plan for them. Have equipment for spilled milk ready for the cleanup job. As soon as children are capable, have them participate in the cleanup activity.

The Young Toddler (12 to 24 Months)
1. Initiate objective 1. Name all foods served.
2. Let the child begin to put cup, plate, spoon, and fork on table setting.
3. Allow the child to develop self-help skills at mealtime.
4. Allow the child to help you prepare food. Children this age can mix several ingredients with spoons, and they like to taste as they explore.
5. Introduce all foods by this stage, except those that may become lodged in the throat (popcorn, nuts).

The Older Toddler (24 to 36 Months)
1. Continue with objective 1. Name all foods served.
2. Begin with objectives 2 and 3. Classify and match foods eaten with the food groups.
3. The child should be able to set the table with minimal assistance.
4. The child should be able to use spoon and fork and begin using knife for spreading.
5. Provide a low cabinet drawer or shelf for unbreakable cooking utensils to use in play to imitate food preparation activities.
6. Provide a table and table-setting equipment—cups, plates, flatware—to practice table setting.
7. The child should be able to serve self from serving bowls.
8. Provide opportunity to prepare food and practice objectives 1 to 3. Prepare fresh green beans, make tossed salad, mix ingredients for fruit breads, and so on.

Strategies for Incorporating Nutrition Education

Although feeding or eating times are excellent settings for nutrition education, the staff must be cautious not to make them the only setting, since nutrition education can be incorporated in the total early childhood curriculum. Careful consideration should be given to a method of curriculum construction, and a plan should be developed for implementation.

It is not unusual to see children as young as 2 years old serving themselves at mealtime in early childhood centers across the nation. They set the table and pass dishes filled with fresh vegetables and meat. They butter bread that they have baked themselves. They pour their own milk. They are joined at the table by their teachers and other staff members who engage in conversation. The children eat, giggle, and talk about their favorite foods, often discussing important nutrition concepts in the process.

Through this process, positive attitudes toward food can be developed in early childhood settings. However, only through planning based on assessment of needs of individual children and calculations of future status can you be sure that you are helping the child.

THE MENU

The menu can be considered the major raw material in planning and implementing nutrition learning activities in early childhood education. Chapter 7 discussed use of the menu as a process for planning with the food service personnel. In this

A preschooler pours milk

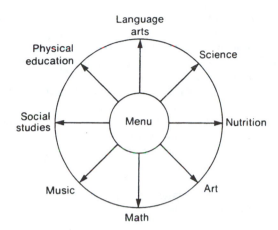

Figure 8.4   The menu as a source for activities in all curriculum areas

chapter, we have indicated that menu items can be used to teach basic nutrition concepts. Figure 8.4 shows the menu at the hub of many of the curriculum areas, including nutrition education.

Care providers may integrate the menu into the early childhood curriculum in a variety of ways; two approaches are presented in this chapter. In the first approach, the care provider uses a single food (in our example, a raisin) to develop instruction in various curriculum areas—language, science, art, math, social studies, music, and physical education (motor development). Next, the behavioral–objective approach is used to teach skills related to personal–social, sensorimotor, language, and perceptual–cognitive areas.

Use of Food from the Menu

When you are selecting a food for use in the curriculum, the first consideration should be its nutritional quality. To encourage the intake of nourishing foods, exposure to these foods is important. Raisins are used as the first example [12].

Class Introduction to Raisin (Prekindergarten)

Nutrition

 1/2 cup of raisins (approximate measure)
 230 kcal energy (15% of energy allowance, based on 1500 kcal)
 2 g protein
 Trace fat
 60 g carbohydrate
 45 g calcium
 3 mg iron (30% of iron allowance)

General Introduction.   Raisins can be introduced in the following way:
ACTIVITY: Let's solve a mystery.
MATERIALS: Menu with raisins, opaque container with holes, raisins, clear glass or plastic container with water, and clear glass or plastic container (empty).

PROCEDURE: Have each member of the class smell raisins that have been placed in an opaque container with holes in the lid. Ask them not to guess what is in the container until everyone has smelled the raisins. Then ask those who think they know to raise their hands but not to name the mystery item. (About half of some 4-year-old groups will have no idea what they have smelled.) Then have the class members close their eyes. Hand each child a few raisins and have them describe the mystery item. Such observations may be "small," "squishy," "soft," "round," and even "square": one child squished the raisin into a perfect cube after hearing classmates agree that raisins were round. After much discussion, ask the children to open their eyes to check their identification.

Discuss such additional questions as: "What color is a raisin? How big is it? Is it smooth? What do you do with it?" Finally, ask, "What does it taste like?" Following the discussion, the children again can close their eyes and count as several raisins are dropped into water ("plop") and then into an empty cup, noting the difference in sound. Talk about how the raisins look in the water; they do not float, but they fall more slowly than when dropped into an empty cup.

At the end of the day, compare the raisins in the two cups. What happened? Are they the same color? Are they the same size? Do they float? How do they taste? Note that the raisins in water have absorbed liquid, diluting the concentration of natural sugar and making them taste less sweet than the dried product. At mealtime be sure to review and ask the children to identify raisins in other foods such as salads (menu) or raisin bread or cereal. Discuss how to prepare grapes to make raisins. Grapes may be covered with cheesecloth and set to dry in the sun. Let the children observe the changes in the grapes and try to guess what will happen next. A warm oven turned off, door ajar, may be used for drying overnight (see Science Activity).

Language Arts.   Let children discuss a variety of sensory experiences with raisins. How do they smell? (Put in opaque container with holes in lid.) How do they feel? Squishy, small, round, soft. How do they look? Black, little, bumpy, sort of shaped like an egg. How do they sound? Drop raisins in water, empty cups, on paper, and so on. How do they taste? Do different kinds have different tastes?

ACTIVITY: Mr. Raisin pictures

PROCEDURE: Have each child draw a picture of Mr. Raisin and tell you what he is doing. Write dialogue on the picture: "He's going to punch a hole through the raisin box so he can get out!" Have them make other pictures and combine these into their own Mr. Raisin book. A class may talk about iron helping to keep them strong and healthy. Mr. Raisin may be endowed with bionic powers. Ask each child to draw a series of pictures showing how a grape turns into a raisin. Let them cut these out, back them with flannel (or Velcro), and use them for their own flannel board story. How does Mr. Grape feel? What does Mr. Raisin think about when he's sitting out in the sun? For the older preschooler, you may use the letters in the word *raisin*. Find the same letters in the children's names on the name chart or in signs around the room. See how many words, silly or real, you can rhyme with raisin. Then write a poem or song using those words. Find words that start with the same sound and other foods, animals, and things in school that start with the same sound.

Science.   What is a raisin? A raisin is a dehydrated grape. What does dehydrated mean? It means "dried." How do you remove the water? Most commercially processed raisins are dried in the vineyard in bunches on wooden or paper trays.

ACTIVITY: Making raisins

MATERIALS: Fresh, ripe, firm seedless Thompson grapes; scales; large pan or bowl of water; plastic-coated trays or paper plates; pieces of clean cheesecloth, mosquito netting or wire screen, large enough to cover the trays; and glass container with tight-fitting lid.

PROCEDURE: Weigh the grapes and record the weight. (Measuring weight of grapes will be meaningful only for older preschooler.) Handle carefully, as grapes bruise easily. Save a few for comparison later or be prepared to purchase grapes 4 to 5 days later for children to compare to dried grapes. Place grapes in a container of water, and wash them thoroughly. Lift the grapes from the water, and blot with a towel. Remove the grapes from the stem, and spread one layer of grapes evenly on the tray. Cover the tray with the cloth or screen to keep insects and dust from getting on the grapes. Fasten the cloth so it will not blow off. Place the tray in direct sunlight to dry, away from dirt and dust and where air can circulate freely over and under the tray. Temperatures under 80° F are not recommended. Rotate the grapes daily to help in the drying process. After 4 days test the grapes for dryness by squeezing them in your hand. If there is no moisture left in your hand and the grape springs apart when the hand is opened, they are dry enough. They should be pliable and leathery to touch. If they are not dry enough, test them again the next day. When the grapes are dry, remove them from the tray and weigh. Record the weight and compare with the first weight. Compare raisins' qualities to those of the grapes you set aside (or a fresh bunch of grapes).

	Comparisons
Color	Green to brown
Form	Sphere to flat
Texture	Smooth to wrinkled
Taste	Sweet and mild to sweeter and rich

Put several raisins in a cup of water. Do they sink or float? What happens after they soak for an hour or two? Are they the same color? Size? Texture?

How long will raisins keep? In tight containers in a cool, dry place they will keep for 6 months. How long will grapes keep? In the refrigerator they will keep for 3 to 5 days.

Experiment! Try observing the effect of different locations on raisins: What happens to them in the sun, the dark, the refrigerator, the oven, and so on?

If you have pets in the classroom, find out which ones can eat raisins. One teacher reported, "For several days we had a young guinea pig in the class. The children fed him raisins and other bits of fresh fruit and vegetables. Then one day the baby went home, and papa was brought in for a day. The children were very excited and decided the raisins, with all that iron, had made him grow fast."

Art.   Raisins can be used for art projects.

ACTIVITY: Edible artwork

MATERIALS: Give the children graham crackers or large cookies, softened peanut butter or cream cheese as paste, and light and dark raisins, and let them make their own pictures—for example, funny faces. You might add nuts, cereal, coconut, or other small edibles for interest.

PROCEDURE: Use raisins for features on gingerbread men or as faces on peanut butter sandwiches. Put them on a table with a bunch of toothpicks, and let the children make raisin critters. Children can make a grapevine by drawing green scribbles and pasting on leaves and raisins (for the grapes). Or they can draw pictures of Mr. Raisin in various moods. (See suggestions in Language Arts Section.)

Math.   Let the children pass out and divide the completed food. Passing out the food is an excellent one-to-one math activity for very young children, and older children can work out how to share a loaf of raisin bread or 31 raisin cookies with 11 children.

Some of the best math work done with foods is in actual cooking. To follow a recipe, you must practice numeral recognition, one-to-one counting, adding and subtracting, measuring, fractions, weights and volume, and time intervals. As the children are cooking, ask them questions that will help them work out how to follow the recipe accurately. How many cups of flour have we used? How many more do we need? Of course, the answers will depend on age level.

Give the children a small cup filled with raisins and nuts. Let them sort and count. How many nuts? How many raisins? Which do you have more of? How can you make them the same? What can you do so you will have more raisins? Children enjoy eating their way through these math problems.

Give each child several raisins. Have the child find and eat the smallest and the largest. Sort the rest by size, and eat the middle one. You may have to use grapes and raisins for comparison, since often young children cannot determine small differences in size.

Have the child close his eyes and count as you drop raisins into a cup of water.

Social Studies.   The following are questions from which to develop your plans:

1. Which kinds of grapes are used to make raisins? Thompson seedless, Muscat, and Black Corinth are used. (Unless you are an expert on grape varieties, buy several kinds, if available, or cut out pictures of grapes.)
2. What growing conditions do they require? Hot, dry summer climate at harvest time is needed. Could we grow them here?
3. How are grapes grown? Who grows them?
4. Are machines used to pick grapes?
5. How are grapes prepared to be dried? How are they dried? How long does it take?
6. Who packages them? Do they use a machine?
7. How are they stored?
8. What can they be used for?
9. What are the advantages of drying fruit? Where might we use dried fruits?

Music.   After a number of experiences with raisins, a care provider asked her preschool children to make up a song about raisins, as follows:

Kelly: Five little raisins sitting on a bench. Along came a witch and ate them.

Sarah: (Started setting it to music to the tune of "Five Little Ducks Went Out to Play.")

Three little raisins sitting on a bench,
Sitting there as quiet as could be.
Along came a witch and ate one.
Two little raisins sitting on a bench.
Along came a witch and ate one.
One little raisin sitting on a bench.
He jumped off so the witch couldn't get him.
Zero little raisins sitting on a bench.

If you are a 4-year-old, and you make it up yourself, that's a great song! You may write the music for the song using raisins as the musical notes.

Physical Education.

Fine Motor Development.   Any of the math or art activities requiring the picking up of individual raisins aids in fine motor development. Stabbing raisins with toothpicks for construction materials or stick people requires a good deal of coordination.

Gross Motor Development (Raisin Treasure Hunt).   Make a treasure map leading to a treasure of individual boxes or containers of raisins. Children can be required to crawl under tables, hop around chairs, and climb over gross motor equipment or appropriate furniture to find the treasure. You can substitute raisins for the "candy" associated with Easter, along with hard-cooked eggs.

Developmental Areas

The cognitive–interactionist approach and most other approaches to learning feature commonly emphasized areas or skills around which the objectives for a curriculum can be constructed. These areas are personal and social, sensorimotor, language, and perceptual–cognitive.

It is crucial to remember that some children are able to demonstrate all or most of the following behaviors as measured by teacher observation or objective-referenced instruments. Some children attain even higher levels of achievement, whereas others continue to progress toward mastery of some of these objectives during their primary school experience.

Personal and Social Development.   Personal and social development involves becoming aware of the environment. Children identify themselves in relation to peers and others in their surroundings. Young children depend on adults to meet their needs, and this dependence motivates children to obey parents' rules and demands. Between the ages of about 2 and 3 years, children go through a transitional period where they are seeking independence and resisting adults. This is a time when the young child attempts to make independent decisions. Personal growth is evidenced by the child's ability to be independent.

In the next stage of development, from ages 3 to 5 years, the child tries to win the approval and acceptance of peers and is becoming more sensitive to the opinions of adults. Children in this age group are friendly and cooperative. They begin to express emotions and seek solutions to problems. By seeking solutions, children learn to control their behavior.

Children need to be loved, enjoyed, and needed. Preparing food helps children to feel both useful and needed and allows direct interaction with adults. Being able to complete a task and having others enjoy the finished product contributes to the child's self-worth and provides convenient avenues for meeting basic ego needs.

Sensorimotor Skill Development.   Everything a child learns is dependent on sensorimotor skills. Sensorimotor refers to a combination of the input of sensations and the output of motor activity. It reflects the development of the central nervous system. To discover the functions of the body and its parts, the child will try all the possible muscular reactions, large muscle groups, and small muscle groups. Beginning at the head, muscle control moves to the foot in a systematic fashion. In addition, development takes place from the axis of the body outward to the periphery, the outer surfaces of the body.

The body can be used in a variety of ways during food preparation, thereby fostering the development of sensorimotor skills. Stirring, beating, slicing, rolling, breaking eggs, peeling, scrubbing, holding, spreading, and shaking are but a few of the movements that, with repetition, evidence gradual mastery and increased coordination.

Language Development—Receptive and Expressive.   Language development depends on past sensorimotor experiences and exposure to a variety of people, places, and things. Language is learned through imitation and reinforcement. Receptive

Sensory motor skills are developed in food preparation

language is language that is spoken or written by others and received by the individual. The receptive language skills are listening and reading. Expressive language is language that is used in communicating with other individuals. Speaking and writing are expressive language skills.

Between the ages of 3 and 4, children acquire the ability to comprehend most of the language they will use in conversation throughout their lives. At 3 years of age most children use 900 words; by 4 years they use about 1,550.

Expressing emotions and ideas is also vital to language development. Provide stimulating situations in which the child has ample time to give opinions and to express creatively without being interrupted. Language skills will affect all endeavors in learning. Having acquired these abilities, the child will be ready to attempt other learning skills.

Expressive and receptive language development is facilitated while children prepare snacks

Food preparation and serving are heavily supported by communication. Communication begins between parent and child during feeding. Mealtime can be a prime time for language stimulation as children become older. As children become involved in such situations as planning and preparing snacks and meals, receptive and expressive language are facilitated.

Perceptual–Cognitive Skill Development.   Cognitive learning prospers when a child is socially competent, emotionally stable, and physically healthy. Cognitive objectives represent an intertwining of creative arts, mathematics, and science skills. A young child is a natural explorer, with a built-in curiosity mechanism that wants to find out how and why. Using real situations, an adult will be able to teach mathematical and scientific concepts. The child will learn to reason and analyze, developing processes for ordering, sorting, spatial relationships, sequencing, and becoming aware of the physical environment.

Providing meaningful experiences in the three areas of creative arts—music, art, and drama—develops a child's creativeness and improves self-concept. The creative arts can also be used to develop and improve personal and social, sensorimotor, and language skills. A social skill that could be taught is distinguishing between happy and sad music; a sensorimotor skill would be clapping and marching to the beat of a song or kneading or patting bread to the sound of music. Music education should encourage all types of movements and sounds. Art allows children to exhibit their view of the world. Because children love to role-play at this stage, drama activities should be an integral part of the curriculum. Children should be allowed to express themselves by acting out a nursery rhyme or a fairy

Food preparation offers numerous perceptual discrimination opportunities

tale or putting on dress-up clothes. Food puppets can help children express feelings about food and what food contributes to their well-being.

Taking part in food preparation is a good way to help create an environment rich in perceptual stimulation and to encourage use of all sensory receptors. The smells, tastes, sounds, textures, and sights of food are varied. As children arrange raw vegetables and fruits on a plate, they are exposed to a variety of textures, shapes, colors, and odors, with unlimited opportunities to discriminate perceptually.

OBJECTIVES AND NUTRITION EDUCATION

A curriculum plan serves as a framework through which the staff can implement various approaches to achieving nutrition education goals.

Before writing any curriculum, the teacher must first possess basic knowledge and concepts of the chosen field. In this case, before attempting to write a nutrition curriculum, the care provider should know basic food and nutrition concepts (Chapters 1 to 6) and should have developed a basic educational approach.

When writing a curriculum, the teacher must take the lead in developing a plan or procedure to reach defined goals. This procedure is similar to the development of plays for a football game. In each instance, someone must do the planning, which includes identifying elements and recognizing the interrelationships that exist so that goals and objectives can be obtained at a specified time. A comprehensive system of steps in which all the elements are interrelated is vital. Steps in the system contribute to a common goal of improved nutrient intake through nutrition education.

Ten Steps

The following steps, essential in any curriculum, provide a systematic approach to instruction:

1. Developing objectives
2. Developing activities
3. Assessing entering skills
4. Choosing a teaching strategy
5. Organizing the group
6. Allocating time
7. Allocating space
8. Choosing teaching resources
9. Evaluating performance
10. Analyzing feedback

Developing Objectives.   The care provider first states in behavioral objectives what the learners should be able to do upon completion of the curriculum. Learning objectives vary according to children's chronological age and developmental level. As was mentioned earlier, learning objectives are crucial to the development of an effective curriculum. The teacher must clearly define objectives for children not only to plan the curriculum but also to assess individual progress and to evaluate program effectiveness.

Early childhood programs must acknowledge developmental variability in children but be cognizant of objectives appropriate to their age level and toward which they should be progressing.

Developing Activities.   The care provider selects and develops activities that will help children attain the stated objectives. Content selection should include a variety of activities that are developmentally suitable for preschoolers.

Assessing Entering Skills.   The child's entering behavior must be evaluated. The teacher can make use of the previously developed behavioral objectives with a checklist to record the child's progress. Another approach is to develop an informal inventory to assess the child's existing knowledge of or skill in a particular area. This screening device might indicate a child's ability to define basic terms related to nutrition and the ability to describe basic concepts. For example, if all 3-year-olds can identify all the food items present, the care provider should progress to the next objective.

The essential question to be asked by the pretest is, "To what extent has the child previously acquired the terms, concepts, and skills that are a part of this curriculum?"

Choosing a Teaching Strategy.   An approach should be chosen that will provide the teacher with a method to most effectively present learning activities. We have chosen the cognitive–interactionist approach previously discussed.

Organizing the Group.   Group organization is determined by the objectives. Which objectives can be reached by the learner individually? Which objectives can be achieved only through interaction among the learners themselves? Which objectives can be achieved through a presentation by the teacher and interaction between the learners and the teacher?

Allocating Time.   The teacher must estimate the time necessary to accomplish defined objectives, teaching strategies, and use of resources, considering the abilities and interests of the children. The teaching plan should take into account the estimated time for each type of activity. Yet no teacher should feel bound by any formula allocating time; rather, analyze the learning objectives and space availability and make the best use of each.

Allocating Space.   Space allocation involves the decision to use or have available large spaces, small spaces, and independent learning spaces. Space should be allocated on the basis of meeting the objectives taught by the lesson.

Choosing Teaching Resources.   While the teacher is the most important resource for the child, a variety of instructional materials also enable the learner to obtain knowledge.
    Gerlach and Ely [13] classify resources into five general categories:

1. Real materials and people (care providers, cooks, parents, food, real things)
2. Visual materials for projection (videotapes, computer programs, filmstrips, movie projectors, television, opaque projectors)
3. Audio materials (radio, recordings, tapes)
4. Printed materials (books, pictures, duplicating masters)
5. Display materials (food boxes, bulletin boards, flannel boards, chalk boards)

A good curriculum will make use of all these resource categories to provide a rich variety of learning experiences for the child.

Evaluating Performance.   A vital component of the curriculum, performance evaluation, asks the question, "Did the child meet the objective?" When evaluating a preschool curriculum, the teacher observes the child's behavior and actions. Evaluation by child observation is naturally enhanced by properly stated behavioral objectives.

Analyzing Feedback.   The care provider asks, "Is this approach to teaching effective? Are all the elements working together as a unit to do what was originally proposed?" The care provider self-evaluates performance by continually analyzing the interaction of the children with the activities and by noting their performance evaluations. The teacher can observe not only the strong points the curriculum presents but also those areas that call for improvement. The teacher must be flexible enough to change activities or any step if the objectives are not being met.

Lesson Plans for Preschoolers

Now that you are familiar with a format for curriculum construction, you should be ready to begin the development of nutritional experiences that can be incorporated into the total early childhood program. The following plans follow the objective-oriented format. This formula can be adapted easily to any of the educational approaches previously detailed in this chapter. The activities are used with the interactionist approach, where routines are as tangible and concrete for the children as possible. An activity may be listed under one particular skill but could be applied to several.

Personal and Social Skills

Gross Motor Skills.
ACTIVITY: Tacos
OBJECTIVE: Child is able to take turns and share.
MATERIALS: Taco shells, ground beef, taco seasoning and sauce, head of lettuce, cheddar cheese, onions, tomatoes.
PROCEDURE: Divide the children into five small groups. Each is responsible for a particular task in preparing the tacos. Group One—cook ground beef, adding sauce and seasoning. Group Two—heat taco shells for 10 minutes and shred the head of lettuce. Group Three—chop onions. Use a manual chopper, not a sharp knife. Group Four—shred cheese. Group Five—chop tomatoes. All children will then take turns filling the taco shells halfway with ground beef and adding toppings.
EVALUATION: Children are observed meeting the stated objectives.

Sensorimotor Development

Gross Motor Skills.
ACTIVITY: Making butter
OBJECTIVE: Child moves body to rhythm of music while making butter from whipping cream.
MATERIALS: Record (any rhythm music), small jars with lids (baby food jars), whipping cream (at room temperature), salt (optional).
PROCEDURES:

1. Child or care provider pours 3 tablespoons of whipping cream into the small jars.
2. Child places lid on the jar.
3. The jar is shaken to the rhythm of the music until whipping cream turns to butter (5 to 10 minutes).
4. Liquid is poured off butter into container. Butter is put into bowl (stirring will take out additional liquid).
5. A pinch of salt is added to butter for taste.
6. Butter can be spread on crackers or bread for eating, and liquid can be drunk.

EVALUATION: Child can keep beat of music until butter is made.

Fine Motor Skills.
ACTIVITY: No-bake cookies
OBJECTIVE: The child rolls, pounds, squeezes, and pulls dough.

MATERIALS: Bowl, large spoon, measuring cups, drawing-type recipe that children can read, 1/2 cup wheat germ, 1 1/2 cups peanut butter, 1 1/2 cups brown sugar, 3 cups dried milk, 3/4 cup graham cracker crumbs, powdered sugar.

PROCEDURES:

1. Measure ingredients into bowl.
2. Mix ingredients with large spoon.
3. Take small amount of dough in hands and roll into small ball.
4. Roll balls in powdered sugar.

EVALUATION: Child is observed meeting the stated objective.

Kinesthetic Tactile Discrimination.

ACTIVITY: Which food is missing?

OBJECTIVE: Child identifies food by touch.

MATERIALS: Ear of sweet corn, cauliflower, carrot (use items on menu), paper or cloth bag or covered can.

PROCEDURES:

1. Show children three types of food, and let them examine each by sight and touch.
2. Place the three foods in a bag or covered can.
3. Have the children remove the food you call for by touch identification only.
4. Replace the food and pass on to another group member.
5. Repeat the process.

EVALUATION: Child is observed meeting the stated objective.

Taste–Olfactory Discrimination.

ACTIVITY: Taste and touch

OBJECTIVE: Child discriminates between the following taste qualities: sweet, sour, and salty.

MATERIALS: Variety of foods to taste, including three tastes distinguishable by a preschooler (sweet—fruit; salty—apple slice with salt; and sour—pickle or lemon); pictures of food items; blindfold.

PROCEDURES:

1. Blindfold child.
2. Have child taste item.
3. Remove blindfold.
4. Have child describe what was tasted.
5. Have child find picture of what was tasted.

EVALUATION: Child is observed meeting the stated objective.

Auditory Discrimination and Memory.

ACTIVITY: Rotten potato

OBJECTIVE: The child carries out a series of three or more directions.

MATERIALS: One sheet of poster board, lined and cut into 64 equal pieces; 16 foods from each of the food groups on the cards to facilitate pairing.

PROCEDURE: Play "Rotten Potato" using the same pairing format used when playing "Go Fish."

EVALUATION: Children observed meeting the stated objective.

Visual Discrimination and Memory.

ACTIVITY: Tell a story with pictures

OBJECTIVE: The child describes objects or experiences from memory.

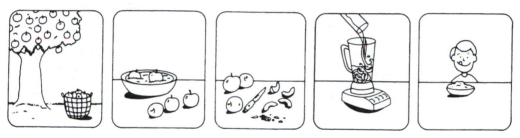

Figure 8.5   Sequence cards depicting the making of applesauce

MATERIALS: Sequence cards depicting nutritional activity.
PROCEDURES:

1. Give the child cards depicting a previous food activity.
2. Have the child arrange the cards in the proper sequence (Figure 8.5).
3. Have the child relate the story to other children.

EVALUATION: Child is observed meeting the stated objective.

Language Development (Receptive and Expressive).

ACTIVITY: Relating an experience
OBJECTIVE: Children dictate ideas in an organized, sequential pattern. This activity is to follow a field trip to an apple orchard.
MATERIALS: Newsprint, Magic Markers.
PROCEDURE: Following a trip to an apple orchard, the children dictate to the care provider their interpretation of the trip from its beginning until its end. The care provider records what the children say. This activity also helps children to listen and appreciate the contributions of others as well as enlarging their vocabulary. If the written material can be reproduced, parents enjoy seeing what the child has contributed.
EVALUATION: Children observed meeting the stated objective.

Cognitive Development

Mathematics and Science Skills.

ACTIVITY: Outline matching
OBJECTIVE: The child matches, recognizes, and identifies a variety of shapes. The child also establishes a one-on-one correspondence through matching.
MATERIALS: Two 12 × 18 inch pieces of poster board, outlines of food items to match shapes outlined on poster board (e.g., apple, lemon, banana, grape, peanut, lettuce), small box.
PROCEDURE: Child takes food items out of box one at a time, names the item, and then attempts to place the object on its outline form. Teacher might say, "Can you find which shape this banana is on the answer board?"
EVALUATION: Child is observed meeting the stated objective.

Sets and Subsets

ACTIVITY: Choose a set
OBJECTIVE: The child identifies and constructs sets and subsets from 1 to 10.

MATERIALS: Pocket chart; numerals 1 through 5 written on top line of chart; index cards; pictures of basic food groups in 10 sets of 1, 10 sets of 2, 10 sets of 3, 10 sets of 4, and 10 sets of 5 glued on index cards.

PROCEDURE: The child counts the set on each card and matches the card with the appropriate numeral (i.e., child picks a card). Count five lemons and then place the card with five lemons on it in the pocket chart under the numeral 5.

EVALUATION: The child is observed using the number concepts.

Numeration and Place Value.

ACTIVITY: Cans

OBJECTIVE: The child recognizes numerals 1 to 10.

MATERIALS: Ten tin cans, numerals 1 through 10 painted on cans, 55 peanuts in the shell.

PROCEDURE: Child puts the appropriate number of peanuts in the cans. Child then can arrange the cans in order 1 through 10.

EVALUATION: The child recognizes numerals.

Addition and Subtraction.

ACTIVITY: Dry fruit mix

OBJECTIVE: The child adds by joining sets.

MATERIALS: Small paper plates for each child, dried fruit (e.g., banana slices, apricots, raisins, and apples).

PROCEDURE: Place small amounts of dried fruit mix on table in front of each child. Direct the child to put two apple slices on his plate. Now ask, "How many pieces of fruit are on your plate?" Next direct the child to add one banana slice. Then ask, "How many pieces of fruit do you have now?" or "How many pieces do you have altogether?" Continue process by adding various sets according to the child's ability. When finished, let the child eat the fruit mix.

EVALUATION: Child is able to add or join sets.

Measurement.

ACTIVITY: Cups

OBJECTIVE: Child identifies concepts of volume: full, half full, and empty.

MATERIALS: Clear plastic cups of various sizes, container for pouring material, pouring material (water, rice, navy beans, or cornmeal).

PROCEDURE: The teacher discusses and demonstrates the concepts of full, half full, and empty. The children are then given time to take a container and then pour the material following the teacher's or child's directions, "Give me a full cup," "Give me an empty cup," or "Give me a half-full cup." This activity can be reinforced at mealtime or snacktime.

EVALUATION: Child is observed meeting the stated objectives.

Fractions

ACTIVITY: Tangerines

OBJECTIVE: Child determines one-half of the whole or small group.

MATERIALS: Tangerines (one per child); graph with children's names, one per column, with a different color for each child's area to aid in their visualization of the graph (Figure 8.6).

PROCEDURES:

1. Have the children peel their tangerines.
2. Break the tangerines into sections.
3. Let the children count their sections and circle the corresponding number on the graph.
4. Teacher-child interaction includes comparisons: "How many in Tim's tangerine?" "How many in Mary's tangerine?" "How many pieces make a whole tangerine?" "How many pieces in half of a tangerine?"

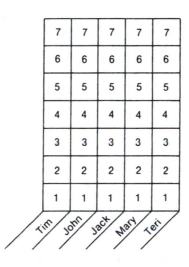

Figure 8.6 Graph for visualizing number concepts

EVALUATION: Child is observed meeting the stated objective.

Geometry.
ACTIVITY: Straight and curved
OBJECTIVE: The child recognizes straight and curved lines.
MATERIALS: An assortment of food-packaging materials (e.g., boxes, jars, cans, and bottles).
PROCEDURES:

1. The child examines the food packages.
2. The child separates the packages into two classifications—those with straight planes and those with curved planes.

EVALUATION: Child is observed meeting the stated objective.

Problem Solving.
ACTIVITY: Use of a recipe
OBJECTIVE: Child uses the five senses to gather information and then communicates observations to others.
MATERIALS: Illustrated recipe, ingredients for recipe.
PROCEDURE: Give the child an illustrated recipe; see whether the child can "cook" from the recipe.
EVALUATION: Child is observed meeting the stated objective.

Creative Arts.
ACTIVITY (ART): Drawing
OBJECTIVE: Child expresses a mental image, design, or happening from actual experience or verbal motivations. This activity follows a field trip to an apple orchard.
MATERIALS: Crayons (primary colors), newsprint.
PROCEDURE: Children are to draw and color their interpretations of the field trip highlights.
ADDITIONAL ACTIVITY: Children can make applesauce, then use the stems, seeds, and peelings to make a collage.
EVALUATION: Children are observed meeting the stated objective.

Sociodramatic Play.
ACTIVITY: Fruit stand

OBJECTIVE: The child interprets realistic roles played by family and community members.
MATERIALS: Variety of fruits, shopping bags, a stand made from a refrigerator packing box or cardboard box of similar size, a scale.
PROCEDURE: Set up a fruit stand. Have some small boxes filled with a variety of fruits and set up a cash register, shopping bags, and a scale. After the children have purchased the fruit, they can use it as a snack.
EVALUATION: Children are observed meeting the stated objective.

As stated earlier, the curriculum serves as a guide for the teacher. Often curriculums are placed in folders, filed away, and used only when programs are evaluated or scrutinized by outside consultants. This should not be allowed to happen. A curriculum should always be open-ended. One should keep it updated with new activities and approaches.

Cross curricular nutrition program guides prekindergarten through grade five are available at a reasonable cost from the National Food Service Management Institute (nfsmi@olemiss.edu). These curricular guides include lessons, teacher handbooks, audio tapes, take-home newsletters, and reproducible worksheets.

The U.S. Department of Health and Human Services Project Head Start has developed a Head Start Nutrition Curriculum for preschoolers. It contains nine units and 147 lessons, which provide background information, specific directions for conducting the lessons, and pertinent resources to reinforce the concepts taught. The entire curriculum guide is available at no cost via Internet access at http://www.bmcc.org/Headstart/NECurriculum/.

> For more information on food and nutrition curriculum resources for grades preschool through six visit: Food and Nutrition Information Center
>
> http://www.nal.usda.gov/fnic/bibs/edu/preschool.html
>
> http://www.nalusda.gov/fnic/pubs/bibs/edu/98-child.htm

RECIPES FOR NONREADERS

The menu, if planned with cooperation between food service personnel and care provider, is perhaps the best tool with which to teach nutrition education; creating a food product in the classroom is also exciting and fun for care provider and student. Often the first task in deciding what to cook is selecting a recipe. There are many cookbooks for children with illustrated recipes for nonreaders. However, any standard cookbook recipe may be used for cooking in the preschool center.

Use of a Recipe for Nonreaders

One of the most important lessons in reading readiness for the preschool student is that words have value. They tell us something. In a recipe, they tell us how to make something that we want to eat. The preschooler discovers that reading is something that can be personally exciting and useful.

By reorganizing, simplifying, and using illustrations, a recipe can be written so that a preschooler can read it nearly independently. A properly organized recipe gives the child such prereading skills as top-to-bottom and left-to-right sequencing. Most recipes as they appear in cookbooks do not do this. Usually the ingredients are listed, followed by a series of instructions. The teacher can rewrite the recipe on a large poster so that cooking can progress from the first to the last step in sequence. (These posters should be saved and used again and again.) After a few cooking experiences, the child will be able to help you to read the next step in sequence and will recognize the words that appear frequently on recipe posters.

The large recipe poster also teaches a variety of math concepts: numeral recognition, counting, measurement, and so on. Following the steps of a recipe gives an added dimension to the actual measuring the child is doing and gives the children who are waiting their turn something to refer to as they help count the ingredients being added. Figure 8.7 is a recipe for nonreaders for "Never-Fail Cookies," which can be made as follows:

Equipment: Cookie sheet; oven (preheat to 350° to 375° F); old newspapers for floor; waxed paper—approximately 12 × 12 inch pieces, one piece per child—or plastic bags; washcloth and water or hand-washing facilities nearby; deep cup and spoon; napkins or paper towels for eating cookies; at least 3 large bowls; 3 serving tablespoons; and 3 serving teaspoons.

Ingredients: Margarine (shortening or fat); sugar (granulated or brown); flour (whole wheat) with 1 teaspoon baking powder per cup of flour; water or milk; decorative items such as raisins, coconut flakes, fruit, and nuts (chopped). Allow approximately 1 1/2 tablespoons of the ingredient per child (e.g., 10 children = 1 cup fat, 1 cup sugar, and 1 1/4 cups flour).

Procedure: The child takes a spoon of each of the ingredients from the bowls and places it on waxed paper. The child then makes one cookie and puts it on the cookie sheet. The teacher observes and adds more liquid or flour as needed. The cookies may be marked with a slip of paper. Have children help put cookies into oven. Bake 15 to 20 minutes. After cookies are cool, children can remove them to a plate. Sit at a table or in a circle to review activities for children, and let children explain what they have accomplished. **Note:** A "never-fail muffin" can be made using the same principles. The child should add eggs (one or two), milk, and raisins, nuts, or fruit to the batter. The batter must be thinner, and the child uses bowl and spoon. Personal experiences with 3-year-olds indicate that they can accomplish this task! (No matter what the product looks like, they eat it!)

Reading, math, and science skills have much more value if the child actually experiences them. Cooking affords this opportunity. A recipe allows you to expose the child to a number of specific academic skills without formal instruction.

In using a recipe with preschoolers, do not belabor each step or insist that they understand each concept. Treat the recipe as a tool. For example, say, "Let's see what we do first." Ask occasional questions about what you are doing, and let the

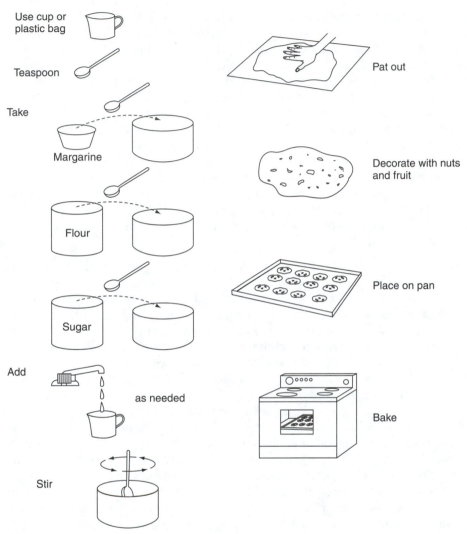

Figure 8.7 **A recipe poster for nonreaders for "Never-Fail Cookies"**

children's comments and questions guide the discussion. Let the equipment and ingredients be the tools to stimulate the discussion.

COOKING IN THE CLASSROOM

Relatively few early childhood programs have child-sized cooking facilities; therefore, electrical appliances are frequently used. When using electrical appliances, be sure that the equipment is in proper working order. It is dangerous to allow chil-

A child learns from experience

dren to stand on stools and chairs to do stovetop cooking in the kitchen. No matter where cooking is done or how, safety precautions must be emphasized, and supervision is imperative. Children can be taught the precautions to use around cooking equipment. Sharp knives should be kept by the teacher. The children can be taught how to use them properly for slicing, cutting, or chopping but only under close supervision. There will undoubtedly be some burns and cuts, but it is hoped that with adequate supervision these will not be serious. If a child should get burned or cut, administer first aid immediately.

Of course, along with food preparation comes cleanup. Children can and should be involved in the various cleanup chores, which vary from wiping countertops and tables to washing, rinsing, and drying dishes. The degree of involvement in cleanup will depend on the facilities and legal requirements.

SUMMARY

- The development of thought and the process of learning are significantly influenced by a child's interactions with objects and persons in the environment. Nutrition may be learned through a curriculum that provides enriching experiences and materials and encourages interaction and exploration for the developing child.
- Four major approaches to early childhood education are cognitive–interactionist, academic skills, traditional nursery school, and perceptual–motor. Any of the methods can be used to successfully teach nutrition education concepts to children.
- The cognitive–interactionist method approaches cognitive ability as a process that develops in a predictable way. This process is separated into three major categories, according to Piaget. The sensorimotor stage ranges from birth to 24 months, the preoperational stage ranges from 2 to 6 years, and the concrete operations stage ranges from 7 to 11 years. Concepts play an important role in cognitive development. The care provider is extremely important in guiding and forming sound concepts.
- The cognitive development approach incorporates a variety of diverse types of programs. Common to all the approaches is the emphasis on the development of cognitive skills and abilities such as understanding and using language, concept formation, association and discrimination, problem solving, and memory.
- There is no one best approach to learning for all children. Six important programmatic insights are presented as applicable to any approach to learning. The child-care worker is encouraged to choose and develop a program that will maximize the development of the group under consideration.
- The basic goal of the nutrition education program is to establish a lifetime pattern of eating a well-balanced daily diet.
- Teaching based on the food groups and the menu can help lead the child to accepting and eventually eating a wide variety of nourishing foods.
- The optimal time for teaching nutrition concepts directly to young children is just before a meal or snack, since the interest in food-related activities will be stronger.
- A hierarchical six-stage sequence for teaching a concept to young children was developed by Blank. The food and nutrition concepts may be taught through a modified version of this hierarchy. The six stages consist of giving a clear instance, giving a clear definition of the function or attribute of the instance, extending the concept to similar instances, extending the concept to less positive instances, considering negative instances, and extending the category.
- The very young child (birth to 18 months) can benefit from verbal stimulation provided by the care provider. Hearing a voice describe foods and eating utensils during mealtime enriches the eating experience of the young child. The older infant or toddler learns through observation of the care

provider, who provides a model of appropriate nutrition and eating practices.

- By integrating food and nutrition concepts into various curriculum areas, the total early childhood curriculum can be used and enhanced.
- The menu can be considered the major raw material in planning and implementing learning activities in early childhood education.
- The major consideration in selecting a food for use in the curriculum should be the nutritional quality of the food.
- Curriculum objectives for preschool programs usually emphasize the following areas of development: personal and social, sensorimotor, language, and perceptual–cognitive.
- To write an effective nutrition curriculum, one must possess a knowledge of food and nutrition concepts.
- A systematic approach to instruction must be operational for a curriculum to be successful. The elements involved must be recognized as interrelated; steps in the system contribute to improved nutrient intake through nutrition education.
- Teaching preschoolers that words have value is very important for reading readiness. A recipe can be rewritten by simplifying, reorganizing, and including symbols or illustrations to facilitate the child's reading and understanding of it.
- An important component of nutrition education is safety during food preparation. Safety precautions should be emphasized, and supervision is imperative.

DISCUSSION QUESTIONS

1. Discuss the similarities and differences of the four programmatic approaches used in early childhood programs.
2. Name the program characteristics of the cognitive–interactionist approach.
3. What role does modeling play in the child's acceptance of new foods?
4. List six programmatic insights to be gained in using any approach to learning.
5. What is the basic goal of the nutrition education program? Name an objective that would be representative of this goal.
6. Describe how the food groups can be used to present nutrition education activities in early childhood centers.
7. Using Blank's hierarchical stages, select and describe a nutrition concept as you would present it to a group of preschoolers.
8. List the activities that would be appropriate to teach good nutrition principles to the very young child (6 months to 2 years).
9. Explain how mealtime experiences can function as settings for nutrition education.
10. Why is the menu considered the major raw material in planning and implementing learning activities in early childhood education?

11. Discuss the importance of selecting foods high in nutrient density for use in the curriculum.
12. Name and explain the four developmental areas used to integrate food and nutrition activities into the learning environment.
13. List and describe the steps involved in a systematic approach to instruction.
14. How are learning objectives crucial to the development of an effective curriculum?
15. Explain how you would convert a recipe from a standard cookbook into one that would stimulate learning in preschoolers.
16. List some precautions to be observed when cooking in the classroom.

REFERENCES

1. Blank, M. (1983). *Teaching learning in the preschool—Dialogue approach.* New York: Merrill/Macmillan.
2. Kostelnik, M. J., Soderman, A. K., & Whiren, A. P. (1999). *Developmentally appropriate curriculum.* Upper Saddle River, NJ: Merrill/Prentice Hall.
3. Goffin, S. G., & Wilson, C. S. (2001). *Curriculum models and early childhood education.* Upper Saddle River, NJ: Merrill/Prentice Hall.
4. Mayer, R. S. (1971). A comparative analysis of preschool curriculum models. In R. H. Anderson, and H. G. Shane (Eds.), *As the twig is bent.* Boston: Houghton Mifflin.
5. Roopnarine, J. L., & Johnson, J. E. (2000). *Approaches to early childhood education* (3rd ed.). Upper Saddle River, NJ: Merrill/Prentice Hall.
6. Ginsberg, H., & Opper, S. (1988). *Piaget's theory of intellectual development* (3rd ed.). Upper Saddle River, NJ: Prentice Hall.
7. Flavell, J. H. (1970). Concept development. In P. H. Mussen (ed.), Carmichael's Manual of Child Psychology, Col. 3, Vol. 1. New York: Wiley.
8. Hohmann, M. (2002). *Study guide to educating young children: Exercises for adult learners* (2nd ed.). Ypsilanti, MI: High Scope Press.
9. Morrison, G. S. (2001). *Early childhood education today.* Upper Saddle River, NJ: Merrill/Prentice Hall.
10. MacFadder, D. N. (Ed.) (1972). *Early childhood development programs and services: Planning for action.* Washington, DC: National Association for the Education of Young Children.
11. Lasser, G. (1971). The need for diversity in day care. In E. Grotberg (Ed.), *Day care: Resources for decisions.* Washington, DC: Office of Planning, Research, and Evaluation.
12. Clemens, B. (1976). *Presentation in Elementary Education 422 health and nutrition class.* Edwardsville, IL: Southern Illinois University.
13. Gerlach, V. S., & Ely, D. P. (1980). *Teaching and media: A systematic approach* (2nd ed.). Upper Saddle River, NJ: Prentice Hall.

SUGGESTED READINGS

Appleton, J., McCrea, N., & Patterson, C. (2001). *Do carrots make you see better? A guide to food and nutrition in early childhood programs.* Beltsville, MD: Gryphon House.

Bredekamp, S., & Copple, C. (Eds.) (1997). *Developmentally appropriate practice in early childhood programs* (Rev. ed.). Washington, DC: National Association for the Education of Young Children.

Cook, R. E., Tessier, A., & Klein, D. (2000). *Adapting early childhood curricula for children in inclusive settings* (3rd ed.). Upper Saddle River, NJ: Merrill/Macmillan.

Elkind, D. (1976). *Child development and education—a Piagetian perspective.* New York: Oxford University Press.

Hendrick, J. (2001). *The whole child* (7th ed.). Upper Saddle River, NJ: Merrill/Prentice Hall.

Hendrick, J. (2003). *Total learning: Developmental curriculum for the young child* (6th ed.). Upper Saddle River, NJ: Merrill/Prentice Hall.

Margerey, A., Worsley, A., & Boulton, J. (1986). Children's thinking about food: 1. Knowledge of nutrients. *Journal of Nutrition* 43(1), 2–8.

Margerey, A., Worsley, A., & Boulton, J. (1986). Children's thinking about food: 2. Concept development and beliefs. *Journal of Nutrition* 43(1), 9–16.

Robertson, C. (1998). *Safety, nutrition, and health in early education.* Albany, NY: Delmar.

Rockwell, R. E., Sherwood, E. A., & Williams, R. A. (1983). *Hug a tree and other things to do outdoors with young children.* Beltsville, MD: Gryphon House.

Rockwell, R. E., Williams, R. A., & Sherwood, E. A. (1992). *Everybody has a body: Science activities from head to toe.* Beltsville, MD: Gryphon House.

Rockwell, R. E., Hoge, D. R., & Searcy, B. (1999). *Linking language: Simple language and literacy activities throughout the curriculum.* Beltsville, MD: Gryphon House.

Rockwell, R. E., & Kniepkamp, J. K. R. (2003). *Partnering with parents: 28 easy programs to involve parents in the early learning process.* Beltsville, MD: Gryphon House.

Sherwood, E. A., Williams, R. A., & Rockwell, R. E. (1990). *More mudpies to magnets—Science activities for young children.* Beltsville, MD: Gryphon House.

Williams, R. A., Rockwell, R. E., & Sherwood, E. A. (1987). *Mudpies to magnets—A preschool science curriculum.* Beltsville, MD: Gryphon House.

Wortham, S. C. (2002). *Early childhood curriculum* (2nd ed.). Upper Saddle River, NJ: Merrill/Prentice Hall.

Wolfgang, C., & Wolfgang, M. E. (1992). *School for young children, developmentally appropriate practices.* Needham Heights, MA: Allyn & Bacon.

9

Parent Involvement in Nutrition Education

LEARNING OBJECTIVES

Students will be able to:

- Describe the value of parent involvement in early childhood nutrition programs.
- List several methods of contacting parents regarding the nutrition education program.
- Identify and describe ways in which parents' contributions of time and talent can be used for nutrition education programs.
- Describe the need for evaluation of parent-involvement programs.
- Identify and describe methods of recognizing parent contributions of time and talent.

The child masters many skills during the first 8 years of life. Learning to eat is one of the most important. What the parent learns about nutrition, food, food preparation, and the importance of mealtime in the home all help to mold the child's food habits and attitudes.

Early childhood programs provide an excellent setting for nutrition education for the entire family. Therefore, it seems only practical that some ideas and approaches for working effectively with parents be discussed.

The increasing interest in parent involvement at both the preschool and elementary school levels has gained momentum over the past four decades. Involving parents in their children's education is hardly a new concept. Since at least the 1960s, the value of parental participation has been recognized in federal law, which mandated that parents be partners in a host of programs funded by the U.S. government. The Individuals With Disabilities Education Act (Public Law 94–142) of 1975 authorized public education to serve 3- to 5-year-olds with disabilities, and in 1986 Public Law 99–457 expanded these services to children from birth through age 2. Under these laws parents were given a pivotal role in planning, implementing, and monitoring their children's education. The federal Head Start initiative put parents in the classroom as well as members of advisory councils. Early childhood programs that focus on parent involvement have also been spearheaded by state governments. In 1990, public schools in 35 states had begun implementing prekindergarten programs. There is no question that federal programs have put and continue to put parent involvement on the agenda of early childhood programs. The major focus of this emphasis has been founded on the theory that if the school and parents work together as partners, the result will be success for the child at school [1].

WHY INVOLVE PARENTS?

Parents are the first and most influential teachers of nutrient intake and healthful food choices for their children. According to the American Dietetic Association, large numbers of parents are sharing that role with teachers and care providers in child-care centers, preschools and family child-care homes. The U.S. Department of Agriculture reports that in 1997, 1.5 billion meals were provided to children in child-care centers and homes that participated in their Child and Adult Food Care Program. This number of meals is nearly half as many as in 1992 and three times as many of the 493 million served in 1982 [2]. They further relate that children typically consume 50% to 100% of their RDAs during their time at the child-care facility. This indicates that many families may be relying on child-care programs to meet most of their children's needs for nutrition and nutrition education. These facts strongly suggest that families and child-care providers need to work together as partners. The child's eating habits are established early in life and are greatly influenced by the interactions and encouragement given not only by the staff at the child-care facility but also by the family at home.

In a position statement on nutrition standards in child-care programs, the American Dietetic Association stresses, "All child-care programs should achieve recommended standards for meeting children's nutrition education needs in a safe, sanitary, supportive environment that promotes healthy growth and development" [3].

Nutrition education involves the entire family

A by-product of parental involvement is that parents themselves benefit. The sense of being needed and useful is evident among those parents who have become involved in various center programs. There is a sense of giving of oneself. At the same time, parents learn how they may best help their youngsters at home, how they can provide a nutritious meal and snacks, or exciting ways in which they can introduce new foods.

Finally, the children's care providers benefit from parental involvement. For example, parent contributions of time and talent often free teachers for instruction and perhaps allow more time for individualization. In addition, parents provide a basis for a more thorough understanding of a child and the child's nutritional habits, thereby assisting the teacher in providing a stimulus to help the child acquire better food habits. The answer to why early childhood programs should seek to involve parents is to enhance the overall development of the children.

First Steps in Getting Parents Involved

If it is agreed that parent involvement is beneficial to children, how can early childhood educators encourage such parent participation in the nutrition program? Where does a teacher begin? Which methods may be worth trying? The following sections give several methods of initiating parent involvement. One or several of the methods may be used to motivate participation in children's learning experiences about food. Modifications and adaptations for specific neighborhoods and their specific needs must be made, of course, but taking advantage of these ideas should result in some forward movement in parent–teacher cooperation.

Informal Contacts. Most of the initial contacts with parents can be made on an informal basis. Some will be incidental, a matter of taking advantage of a given situation. Perhaps when a parent stops by to pick up a child for a doctor appointment, if time permits, a teacher should move toward the door with a smile and at least say a few words about the eating activities of the child. In casual conversations so often parents say, "If there is anything I can do, please let me know." They do not really expect the teacher to say, "As a matter of fact, there is something you can do." But the gate is open, and a teacher or director can step in with a simple way in which that parent can assist the child or the program.

The same procedure of openness and friendly conversation can be used during a center open house, parent–teacher conference periods, and parent meetings. When parents feel at ease and get the idea that their child will benefit, they are more willing to contribute their time and talent.

Registration. Another opportunity for the center to encourage parent participation occurs at registration. If a parent is asked to fill out a registration form, a simple and general statement such as "I will volunteer to help the center in food and nutrition activities (yes _____ no _____)" might be included. Or an open-ended statement such as "I will volunteer to assist my child in the program by _____" could be used. If a secretary or teacher fills out a registration form while interviewing the parents, willingness to help could be ascertained through casual conversation. However, the interviewer must be careful to broach the subject in a matter-of-fact way so that the parent feels no pressure to participate.

Telephone Calls.   Telephone calls offer an opportunity for personal conversation with the parents. Parents are often afraid when they receive calls from the teacher. This is the result of past experiences when only bad news was communicated from the school to the home [4]. This tradition can be changed by setting aside a short period each day to make phone calls to parents. Initial calls can include information about who you are, why you are calling, and a short personal anecdote about the child. Health and nutritional concerns can also be shared. Such phone calls take only a few minutes each, but they let the parents know of a teacher's or director's interest in and knowledge of their child.

Advanced Technology.   Some programs have successfully utilized advanced technology afforded by computers to communicate with families. Weekly menus, home snack recipes, health tips, family nutrition activities, and daily school happenings can be shared. Many school districts are using voice mail to promote better communication between teachers and parents. Each teacher is given an electronic voice mailbox and 1 to 3 minutes of message time. Parents can call a designated number to play a message from a specific teacher. Content of the message can vary from what we had to eat today to suggestions to encourage the family to talk about the colors of the food that they will be eating tonight.

Many families have the ability to communicate with the center or school via electronic mail (e-mail). An e-mail bulletin board system for families can be an efficient and effective strategy of communicating nutritional information from the center to the home. Utilizing World Wide Web access can provide the family with a wealth of nutrition information (see Box 9.1).

BOX 9.1   Nutrition Web sites

---

http://www..fns.usda.gov/tn/parents/index.htm
U.S. Department of Agriculture Web site for family nutrition information.

http://cnn.k12.ar.us/federal.ohtm
Federal Web sites related to child nutrition.

http://www.asfsa.org/about/statenutritionprog
A child nutrition e-source that lists state nutrition program sites and nutrition information links.

http://www.doh.state.fl.us/ccfp/info/links.ht
USDA Child Care Food Program Web site and useful nutrition information links.

Families should be reminded of online safety strategies if their children have access to the World Wide Web. A valuable resource for online safety cautions by age group 2 through 17 years is available at http://www.getnetwise.org/safetyguide/age.

Audio and Videotapes.   Many families have access to both audio and video tape recorders. This technology provides an innovative way of communicating with families, especially those that are unable to attend family meetings or other school functions due to restrictive family situations or conflicting work schedules. Some ideas include:

- Have a volunteer videotape a nutrition information family meeting or speaker so that the families unable to attend can still benefit.
- Videotape everyday classroom routines that show the children engaged in developmentally appropriate nutrition education activities.
- Use a cassette tape to record a volunteer reading a book that has a nutrition theme. Send the book home with the tape so the family can follow along with the reader.
- Videotape the children as they do their daily physical exercise routine with their teacher.

Some resources for nutrition videotapes are: National Dairy Council, American Heart Association, USDA's Nutrition Education and Training Program, State Agricultural Extension Service, Special Supplemental Nutrition Program for Women, Infants and Children, The American Public Health Association, Child and Adult Care Food Program, local branches of the American Dietetic Association, and local public libraries, community colleges, and universities.

Resource Person.   Once the children are in the classroom, the teacher should be alert to any comments they might make about what their parents do. For example, if a child casually mentions that his family has beehives in the backyard, the teacher should determine through reviews of the records or even a phone call to the parents whether the family would be willing to share their special interest. Perhaps the parents have some slides, a beehive, or just some frames with honey on them to show the children. They might enjoy bringing samples of honey for the children to taste, or sitting and talking with the children about bees. The teacher might provide pictures or slides so the learning situation would be a cooperative effort. Many parents have skills or hobbies in which children are interested, and they might be flattered to be asked to share them in the center. It may be necessary for the teacher to reassure them and to preplan together, but parents are often fine resources for specific areas of study and should never be overlooked.

A Special Letter.   A direct way to find out whether parents are willing volunteers is to send a letter telling them that their help is needed. Specific tasks for which they could volunteer should be included in an interest inventory that accompanies the letter. The inventory should provide an open-ended section to enable the parent volunteer to suggest activities that may not have been listed. Frequently parents are most willing to volunteer their talents, but when asked to list them, they respond in a limited manner.

Notes and Happy-Grams.   Notes written by the teacher and carried home by the child are a most effective form of communicating with the home. These notes should never be hastily scratched criticisms of the child or his work. Notes are a useful means of communicating positive, personal observations and anecdotes about the child. Often mealtime conversations abound with items that can be shared with a parent; for example, "Christine tried kiwi fruit today and loved it. She said, "It tastes like strawberries and watermelon mixed together!' "

Orientation.   Just a few days before the beginning of a program year, all parents may be invited to attend an informal "get-acquainted-with-our-room" program orientation. Each parent is invited to the center to meet with the teacher and all the other parents. The teacher presents the routine for activities as well as the food and nutrition program. During this time the teacher extends an invitation for parental assistance and has a prepared list of some kinds of activities for which help is needed. For example, if parent aides are to be used daily for eating activities, a sign-up sheet should be available. Those parents who would like to go on field trips or who could provide transportation could sign another sheet so labeled. The teacher might merely keep a list of those who say they would like to help and then determine later which specific contribution the parent might prefer. However, advanced planning helps parents commit their time.

Standardized Informational Techniques.   Techniques for exchanging information between the parents and the care provider must be standardized and clear, particularly in infant programs. Nutritional information passed between the home and center always involves the accurate recording of daily and nightly occurrences such as times of feeding and types and amounts of food. In addition, naps, diaper changes, amount of sleep, unusual behavior, and home routines are recorded on standardized forms (Appendixes XIII, XIV, XV). Sharing information helps to establish a sense of trust and a partnership between the home and the center as it contributes to an accurate 24-hour record of the child's health and well-being.

Newsletter.   Another method of maintaining home-center contact is the newsletter. A monthly newsletter can include a copy of the menus and the activities that have been used to help children "get to know" the foods on the menu. The newsletter also provides an opportunity to list materials needed from home for classroom activities involving food, to present recipes used, and to solicit recipes parents have used with children. Nutrition information may also be included.

Parent Teacher Conferences.   Parent–teacher conferences provide the time and the opportunity for parents and teachers to consider together all aspects of a child's overall development including health and nutritional concerns. It is an opportunity that establishes or furthers a sense of working together with shared information and common goals. The teacher has the responsibility for setting the tone of a partnership at this meeting by preparing parents for their participatory role, guiding and encouraging them by the use of questions and active listening. Careful planning, evaluation, and follow-up of conferences all work together to make this a productive experience for both the parents and the teachers [4].

Home Visits.　The most time-consuming method of contact with families, yet probably the most successful and beneficial to all, is the home visit. This is by no means a new method of reaching families as it has existed since Elizabethan times in England [5]. There has been an increasing enthusiasm for this strategy of family involvement in recent years, with large initiatives being launched or recommended at both the federal and state levels. For many successful classroom teachers the concept of home visiting may be unfamiliar; however, when making a home visit the teacher is able to gain information that often would not emerge in a parent–teacher conference held at the center. When families are on their "own turf," they may relate unanticipated areas of concern when talking in a comfortable environment. A home visit can build trust, rapport, and a belief that feelings are valued and respected. If conducted effectively, a home visit will generate goals that are the result of a sincere and cooperative effort between the teacher and family. When families believe that what is important to them is being addressed, more cooperation is inevitable.

During such visits, which are preferably arranged at the family's convenience, it is imperative that the visitor convey a sincere understanding and interest in the child and the family. A nutrition-focused visit might be to inform the family of the nutrition learning activities provided by the program during their child's center time. In addition, specific examples and hands-on demonstrations as to what the family can do to extend and expand the program's nutrition learning activities into the home can be provided. The following guidelines can help make the home visit a success [6].

- Be a good listener.
- Set specific goals for each visit.
- Be flexible.
- Be prompt.
- Realize the limitations of your role.
- Help parents become more independent.
- Dress appropriately and comfortably.
- Be confident.
- Remember that small improvements lead to big ones.
- Be yourself.
- Respect cultural and ethnic values.
- Monitor your own behavior—the parent is observing you.
- Include other members of the family in the visit.
- Bring visitors only when you have the parent's permission.
- Don't socialize excessively.
- Don't impose values.
- Don't talk about families in public.
- Don't expect perfection from the parent.
- Don't ask the parent to do something you wouldn't do.

- When you arrive for the home visit do you direct your attention and greeting toward the parent?
- Do you discuss the last home visit and follow up on previous activities that had been suggested?
- Does the parent co-plan the activities for the home visit? Do you make sure that the child is sitting beside the parent?
- Does the parent demonstrate each new activity?
- Do you review each activity with the parent before presenting it?
- Do you hand all materials to the parent?
- Do you identify and reinforce the parent's teaching strengths?
- When the parent has difficulty understanding, do you intervene with the parent rather than the child?
- Do you let the parent be the primary reinforcing agent?
- Do you help the parent problem solve when problems arise instead of jumping in to the rescue?
- Do you work on activities the parent feels are important?
- Do you ask the parent to provide as many materials as possible?
- Do you give the parent the lead when appropriate?
- Do you incorporate the parent's ideas into each activity?
- Do you let the parent present new and exciting experiences?
- Do you individualize parent activities for each parent?
- Do you accept the parent's values?
- Do you involve the parent in evaluation of the home visit?

Figure 9.1   Are your home visits parent-focused?
Source: U.S. Department of Health and Human Services. (1987). A self-evaluation form for home visitors.

- Make parents the focus of your visits. Help develop the parent's role as a teacher.
- Begin working with the parent and child on specific activities immediately. This sets a tone for the home visits, and parents will feel good about their abilities as they see that they can and do teach their children.
- Plan activities around daily routines.
- Make it a habit to discuss the reason for the activity before you or the parent presents it to the child [6].

It is important that home visitors evaluate themselves after each visit. Figure 9.1 suggests questions that can be asked after each visit to determine if the visits are parent-focused [6].

Ways in Which to Use Parent Contributions

Once parent-center contacts have been made—and this may be a continuing process throughout the year—initiation of actual involvement must begin. Parent contributions will be more meaningful if parents are given an opportunity to plan with the care provider those areas that they mutually believe can be of benefit to the program. One goal for the care provider is to be organized but not so static that parents think their suggestions and ideas are not welcomed. In presenting options to the parent, the care provider may wish to organize activities into the following categories. (It should be noted that contributions listed in one area may also be pertinent to another category of parent–caregiver cooperation.)

1. Ways in which parents may assist children during center hours
2. Ways in which parents may work with materials and equipment during center hours
3. Ways in which parents may contribute time and effort to the program after center hours
4. Ways in which parents may participate without leaving their homes

Assisting Children During Center Hours.   The following listing offers some ideas for parental assistance with children in the child-care center. Some parents may want and need on-the-job training. Remember that some states may require a health examination for all persons helping with preparation of food. It is important to capitalize on parents' strengths, hobbies, and interests. For example, someone who has worked as a food service employee in a restaurant would have contributions to make concerning food preparation and occupational information about food. Parents may participate in the following ways:

1. Supervise and contribute to learning centers
   a. Talk with children to develop language skills; that is, discuss food concepts following procedure described in Chapter 8; supervise games; tell and read stories about foods to children; listen to children read aloud.
   b. Demonstrate and supervise a garden plot.
   c. Demonstrate and supervise a cooking center.
   d. Lead and supervise science and mathematics as food-related activities.
2. Share hobbies and demonstrate how they are done (as food related).
3. Share and demonstrate career information (as food related).
4. Prepare snacks and interact with children during eating times.
5. Prepare basic mixes with children (Chapter 7) or for food-service personnel.
6. Supervise bathrooms and hand washing, especially before mealtime and food preparation activities.
7. Share cleanup of kitchen equipment, table, and chairs with the children, or assist food service personnel.

Working With Materials and Equipment During Center Hours.   There are many ways that parents can assist at the center during, before, or after class hours; however, they will need a place to do their work. We suggest a parent resource room. This room is a place within the school where parents can meet, show information, work, and relax. The room can be equipped with comfortable chairs, tables, coffee pot, hot plate, telephone, computer, typewriter, and a bulletin board. Parents and

Parents can assist
and interact with
children

teachers can plan together about how to design, stock, and use the room. Some suggested tasks might be:

1. Typing menus
2. Taking pictures of food and making food displays or scrapbooks
3. Laminating materials, such as food pictures, child-developed recipe books, and recipe cards
4. Making food boxes for the center
5. Arranging for field trips to food-producing sites, manufacturers, and sellers
6. Recruiting, orienting, and training parent volunteers
7. Typing and copying monthly menu and activity calendars

The parent room implies that parents are expected to be a part of the program. This is a place for them to stop and a base from which they can reach out in their involvement.

Contributing Time and Effort at School After Center Hours. One of the most common forms of parent–teacher contact takes place at parent–teacher conferences. However, informal committees, discussion groups, and personal phone calls may provide for parent–teacher cooperation, too. Workshops are especially enjoyable and provide an inviting format for the care provider to offer information regarding basic nutrition, how nutrition objectives are met in the center program, and how the parents can work cooperatively with the staff to achieve objectives [7].

Early in the year, possibly even before the program starts, a teacher should list a number of activities that parents might work on during workshops. The list should be long enough so that an element of choice is offered to the parents at each gathering. Some of the following ideas might be considered and specific tasks planned around them:

1. Invite nutritionists and other health professionals from the local health department, hospitals, and other community agencies to discuss basic nutrition concepts. It is important that these discussions
   a. be organized, with the presentation of basic nutrition concepts first as a home foundation for the use of food and nutrition.
   b. directly involve parents with hands-on nutrition experiences. (Appendix XVI presents a guideline for preplanning, conducting, and evaluating a nutritionally oriented family workshop.)
2. Create work jobs, games, and toys that can be used in nutrition education; for example, prepare pocket charts for categorizing and classifying food items, pictures, and designs for a food bulletin board, or taste jars. (For additional ideas, see Chapter 8.)
3. Meet with care providers and food-service personnel to plan menus that can demonstrate the teaching of specific nutrition concepts.
4. Invite parents to share with professionals the importance of physical activities as related to food consumption.
5. Share nutritious recipes, that is, recipes with high nutrient density.
6. Share activities that parents have used to encourage their children to accept a wide variety of foods.

Parent Advisory Committee (PAC).   Some programs may find parent advisory boards advantageous. This form of parent participation offers parents an opportunity to become involved as joint decision-makers. This committee is in constant touch with all phases of the program. It is critical that parents who serve as members receive continuous training regarding relevant program information to enable them to become knowledgeable as well as effective policy and decision makers. The PAC is a credibility link—a positive step in successful communication and collaboration between parents and staff members. Parents should be free to suggest and recommend anything, but final authority and decision making probably should remain with the professionals, those trained educators who are responsible for all of the children at the center. This is particularly true of decisions about curriculum or specific individual behavior problems. In addition, parents should not be allowed to have access to an individual child's records or to discuss a specific child's problems, especially if names or the data being discussed would identify the child. Those responsibilities must be retained by the care providers and administrators [8].

Participating Without Leaving the Home.   One important way in which parents may participate at home is to help the child with developmental activities. The care provider may list activities or games that provide nutrition experiences and readiness for later learning. For example, a care provider may suggest some of the following for follow-up activities to strengthen nutrition principles learned in the centers.

1. While walking through a store together, talk to your child about the various products and their uses.
2. Look around the house for objects or foods whose first letters sound alike— cup, can, cap; pickle, pear, peach, pineapple.
3. Encourage your child to talk with you about food.
4. While preparing food, allow your child to help.
5. Let your child share in cleanup activities.
6. Test new food activities at home. Provide feedback to teacher on strengths and weaknesses of activities.

Only imagination will limit the number of ways in which parents may help their children at home. The suggestions will vary from year to year and community to community, although some may be duplicated. Ideally, they would vary from child to child, so the suggestions would be geared to individual needs. Several short lists of ideas sent home at different times are more effective than one long list at the beginning of the year. Some of the same activities may be discussed during casual conversations or even at workshops, if parents express an interest. The purpose is to help parents realize they may take advantage of incidental learning opportunities as they arise.

Often parents are willing to help children in the center but cannot take time away from home. Perhaps they work full-time or have younger children at home. Perhaps a handicap prohibits them from coming to the center. Nonetheless, there are ways in which these parents may be encouraged to help provide a better learning environment for their children.

Lending Library.   A lending library provides educational toys, books, and activities for children and parents to take home and use together [9]. A lending library is similar to the public library concept with the exception that materials are selected for inclusion in the lending library to provide a broad range of learning activities related to school readiness, and/or it includes books, toys, cassette tapes, tape players, and manipulatives. Parents and teachers work together to choose items that will be developmentally appropriate and useful to the individual child. If a parent is unable to come into the library, he or she may telephone or send a note and the materials will be sent home with the child. The lending library can also include a parent resource section with books, magazines, and videotapes on various parenting issues. Some lending libraries also have TV/VCR units that can be loaned to parents to view parenting tapes. The lending library is an excellent means of providing nutrition awareness to the entire family.

Calendars.   An activity calendar can be sent home at the beginning of each month. It can include simple daily activities that the parents and the child can do at home. The activities correspond with what is happening in the daily curriculum. The daily menu for a one-month time frame can also be shared.

Snacks and Treats.   Teachers frequently request that parents provide snacks and treats for birthdays and holidays. High-calorie foods with few nutrients are most often sent. This problem can be avoided only by developing a policy that endorses the provision of nutritious foods for party times. Parents, teachers, and children can work together to develop the party snack list, which can be presented to parents in a letter or in a parent handbook at the beginning of the school year.

EVALUATION OF PARENT INVOLVEMENT

A simple method to help evaluate the effectiveness of parental participation is to keep attendance records from workshops, discussion groups, and programs. Of course, such statistics on attendance cannot indicate the quality of participation; they indicate only the number of participants. Although exposure of parents to program purposes and activities may be advantageous, evaluation should not be based exclusively on program turnout [4].

Evaluating the quality of participation is much more difficult than counting noses or calculating percentage of parent participation. Both long-range (perhaps yearly) and short-range (daily) objectives need to be considered. Observations and discussions between parents and care providers, possibly with checklists, are means of informal evaluation. Parent grievances to administrators and care providers may indicate areas toward which improvement efforts need to be directed. All these sources of evaluative information should be used.

Each area of parent–school involvement must be evaluated. For example, after a parent acts as a volunteer, the parent and the caregiver should immediately review both positive and negative points of that particular day's activities. The aim is to improve the quality of interaction on succeeding days. Neither parent nor care provider should be afraid of criticism, which needs to be given and accepted in a positive way.

Evaluations of clerical tasks should be done in two ways, one aimed at the self-fulfillment of the participant and the other at the quality of work. Do the participants feel useful and needed? Excessive typographical errors cannot be tolerated, nor can equipment constantly in need of repair because of mishandling. If the clerical chores involve total class interruptions, then alternate methods of completing the tasks must be created. Wastefulness of materials might be noted, also. As with other areas of evaluation, any benefit must be a result of frank and open discussion between parent participant and caregiver.

After workshops or programs, a short, informal checklist could be passed to each parent in attendance. They should be encouraged, but not required, to fill it out. Questions might include: "Was this gathering worth your time and effort? What did you like about it? What did you dislike about it? Was it too long? Too short? Just right? What would you like to do at a future meeting? How could our gatherings be improved?" (If there were an outside resource person or persons, a question such as, "Would you invite him or her back? Why not?" might be included.) Parents need not sign their names. From these informal instruments some worthwhile suggestions for improvement of a parent-participation program may be forthcoming.

The teacher and care provider might use a checklist to help evaluate their own involvement with parents. Such a list might be scanned several times a year as a reminder of some important points to remember when cooperating with parent volunteers.

1. Am I a good listener?
2. Do I try to make parents feel needed?
3. Have I given personal recognition in the form of compliments and notes to all participants? Have I had the children send thank-you notes? Would a year-end recognition coffee session be useful?
4. Do I try to learn about each parent's interests, hobbies, or work so that each may contribute according to his or her strengths and training?
5. Do I accept all suggestions for activity and discuss programs and problems openly?
6. Do I preplan alone or with the parents?
7. Am I a dictator?
8. Do I keep all meetings and workshops informal and encourage interaction?
9. Do I keep parents informed through meetings, newsletters, notes, or phone calls?
10. Do I provide baby-sitting and transportation services if needed for greater participation?
11. Have I elicited cooperation and understanding of the center administration?
12. Am I careful not to discuss children in front of their parents? Am I sure all records are confidential and unavailable to any parents?
13. Am I aware that some parents may force their views on others?
14. Do I believe there are too many interruptions in the center when parents are involved?
15. Do I expect every parent to be involved? Do I exploit their generosity of time, talent, and effort?

At the end of the year, suggestions for improving the program should be solicited from all parent participants—clerical aides, parent resources, and home participants. A letter could be sent home and returned with each child. Some portions of the programs may be dropped, others added, and some modified according to the combined responses of parents, children, director, and care provider.

RECOGNITION

Every parent volunteer, regardless of the time devoted to the program, should receive frequent praise and encouragement for service. Parents can gain much satisfaction when they believe they have been accepted as colleagues by their coworkers. Another form of satisfaction results when parents believe they have contributed to the progress and growth of an individual child or group of children. Teachers must make a continual effort to express their acceptance of the volunteers and the skills they are contributing.

A special "thank you" is in order for the parents. This can be done at a meeting where the main order of business is the public recognition of parents for their services. Some form of tangible recognition is recommended: a certificate of appreciation, a letter of congratulations, a "good egg award," a happy-gram. It should be something the volunteer can take as a memento of the experience. Newspaper and television coverage of the awards and recognition ceremonies can be helpful in drawing public attention to the program.

Recognition, no matter which form it takes, is essential. A single thank-you as the parent volunteer leaves is a courtesy that will pay dividends. A parent volunteer who enjoys the work is thanked in many ways. The general reception and attitude that the staff expresses toward the volunteer is a form of recognition. In addition, the parent volunteer represents the people of the community. When we recognize the volunteer, we recognize the community.

Parents, care providers, and children may all benefit from effective participation based on clear-cut objectives and goals. It is natural that as the year progresses, more and more responsibility and freedom may be allowed to parent participants, according to their responsiveness and abilities. Effective participation grows like a seed, a little each day. If properly nurtured, it produces fine fruit by the end of a growing season.

SUMMARY

- Children and their well-being are major concerns for parents and early childhood educators. Parent involvement in early childhood nutrition programs provides unity for the parent and child in sound educational experiences about food.
- Benefits of parent participation are realized by parents, early childhood care providers, and the children involved.
- Effectiveness of parent recruitment is maximized when several methods are used. Contacts can be made through informal conversation during various parent–teacher meetings, notes, letters, newsletters, telephone calls, e-mail, lending libraries, home visits, advisory committees, and inclusion of appropriate questions on registration forms.
- To ensure maximum participation, parents should be given options for involvement. Suggested categories for contribution include (1) assisting

children during center hours, (2) working with materials and equipment during center hours, (3) contributing time and effort to the program after center hours, and (4) participating without leaving the home.

- Ideas for parental assistance are vast; parents' strengths, hobbies, and interests should be explored. Parents can also serve as valuable resource persons for early childhood nutrition education.
- Evaluating the effectiveness of a parent involvement program is necessary to maintain and improve the quality of interaction. Suggested evaluation techniques are attendance records at various meetings, questionnaires, parent/caregiver feedback, and self-evaluation by teachers concerning involvement with parents.
- Recognition of parent participation is vital. Frequent praise or other tangible expressions of appreciation provide encouragement and satisfaction for parents.

DISCUSSION QUESTIONS

1. Discuss the value of parent involvement in early childhood nutrition programs.
2. Briefly outline the methods of initiating parent involvement in a nutrition education program.
3. What purpose do home visits serve in nutrition education?
4. Describe four ways parents can contribute to the early childhood nutrition program during center hours.
5. Discuss opportunities for parents to contribute to the school's nutrition program after center hours.
6. List three suggestions for parents to use at home to reinforce nutrition concepts learned at school.
7. Discuss the necessity of evaluating a parent involvement program. Which aspects of the program should be evaluated?
8. Access and list Web sites that offer nutritious snack recipes for young children.
9. Describe methods of recognizing parents for their involvement in early childhood nutrition programs. Why is this important?

REFERENCES

1. Gough, P. B. (1991). Tapping parent power. *Phi Delta Kappan, 72,* 339.
2. Position paper on dietary guidance for healthy children aged 2 to 11 years. (1999). *Journal of the American Dietetic Association, 99,* 93.
3. Position paper on nutrition standards for child care programs. (1999). *Journal of the American Dietetic Association, 99,* 982.
4. Rockwell, R. E. (1993). Parent involvement. In B.J. Howary (Ed.), *Early childhood handbook.* Springfield, IL: Illinois State Board of Education. Illinois Resource Center, Des Plaines, IL.
5. Behrman, R. E. (Ed.). (1993). *Home visiting: The future of children, 3*(3). Los Altos, CA: Center for the Future of Children, The David and Lucille Packard Foundation, 3:3.

6. U.S. Department of Health and Human Services. (1987). Office of Human Services; Administration for Children, Youth and Families; Head Start Bureau. *The Head Start Home Visitor Handbook.* B. Wolfe & J. Herwig (Eds.), for Portage Project, Cooperative Educational Service Agency 5. Washington DC: U.S. Government Printing Office.

7. Rockwell, R. E., & Kniepkamp, J. K. R. (2003). *Partnering with parents: 28 easy programs to involve parents in the early learning process.* Beltsville, MD: Gryphon House.

8. Rockwell, R. E., Hawley, M. K., and Andre, L. C. (1995). *Parents and teachers as partners: Issues and challenges.* Fort Worth, TX: Harcourt Brace College.

9. Owocki, G. (2001) *Make way for literacy.* Portsmouth, NH: Heinemann.

SUGGESTED READINGS

America goes back to school: Partners activity kit, Partnership for Family Involvement in Education. (1997). Washington, DC: U.S. Department of Education.

Bauer, A. M., & Shea, T.M. (2003). *Parents and schools: Creating a successful partnership for students with special needs.* Upper Saddle River, NJ: Merrill/Prentice Hall.

Berger, E. H. (2000). *Parent as partners in education.* Upper Saddle River, NJ: Merrill/Prentice Hall.

Bigner, J. J. (2002). *Parent-child relations: An introduction to parenting.* Upper Saddle River, NJ: Merrill/Prentice Hall.

Klass, C. S. (1998). *Home visiting.* Baltimore, MD: Paul H. Brooks.

Levine, J., Murphy, D., & Wilson, S. (1993). *Getting men involved.* New York: Scholastic.

Swinney, B. (1999). *Healthy food for healthy kids.* New York: Simon and Schuster.

Wright, K., Stegelin, D. A. (2003). *Building school and community partnerships through parent involvement.* Upper Saddle River, NJ: Merrill/Prentice Hall.

List of Book Appendixes

Appendix I
Online Diet Analysis Programs for Consumers

Listed in descending order, from the ones that students felt were the easiest to use to those that were most difficult or did not meet criteria specified.*

Very good site, easy to use, and no advertising.

Site: http://147.208.9.133 (Interactive Healthy Eating Index)
Sponsor: USDA
Description: Compares daily intake to the Food Guide Pyramid, and provides a chart that shows areas for improvement. Gives an extensive breakdown of nutrients in analysis along with a percentage of how the diet compares to Food Guide Pyramid recommendations.
Available Activities: This site keeps a record of all foods entered under a specific log-in; this allows users to compare today's diet with the diet they had last week to see if improvements were made.
Options: Provides a "score" on the overall quality of the entered diet. This score looks at the types and amounts of food eaten compared to the recommendations of the Food Guide Pyramid. Graphs are provided to visualize the diet and how it meets Food Guide Pyramid requirements.
Helpful Hints: Use a log-in that you will remember so that you can compare diets in the future to the one you are currently entering.

Site had an advertisement banner included.

Site: www.dietsite.com
Sponsor: dietsite.com Inc.
Description: This site provides an analysis that compares RDA values and allows comparison of different meals (i.e., comparing today's lunch to yesterday's). This allows you to see progress in your diet.
Available Activities: Can search for specific foods in a large database. Can enter an item not in the database if you have the nutrition label (this food can be stored and used again). Site allows participants to enter height, weight, age range, gender, and activity level.

---

*The sites were contacted during 2001 and may have changed by the time the reader accesses them.

Options: This Web site keeps a record of your previous diet entries and your previously entered weight. It will graph your progress in weight loss or gain. Foods are listed by meal to keep track of foods entered.
Helpful Hints: Be prepared to spend up to 20 minutes entering diet information.

Site: http://www.healthsurvey.org/
Sponsor: The site is a project of Paul T. Williams, Ph.D, Lawrence Berkeley National Laboratory, University of California, National Health Study.
Description: This site covers activities extensively. Compares entered diet to RDA values.
Available Activities: Nutrition comparison is limited; printouts give percentage of diet for calories, saturated fat, monounsaturated fat, polyunsaturated fat, and carbohydrates. It also provides percentage values for cholesterol, calcium, zinc, iron, vitamin A, C, E, B_6, B_{12}, and folic acid. This site does not compute values for protein and fiber. Provides a comparison of your diet to the BMI table and the Food Guide Pyramid.
Options: Participants are given the option of submitting their information for use in the National Health Study. Gives the option of e-mailing results to up to five people.
Helpful Hints: This site may take 35 minutes or more to complete.
Variety of foods limited compared to other databases.

Be prepared to spend a great deal of time with this site. No advertising.

Site: www.nat.uiuc.edu/mainnat.html (Nutrition Analysis Tool version 2.0)
Sponsor: University of Illinois
Description: Provides an analysis for calories, protein, fat, carbohydrates, sodium, vitamin A, vitamin C, saturated fat, and cholesterol.
Available Activities: Can enter age range and gender only. This site has an energy calculator to calculate the daily amount of calories needed using height, weight, and activity level. Has a link for nutrition education resources.
Options: Has an option that suggests foods to include in your diet if you come up deficient in any particular nutrient. Has option to learn more about nutrients that are analyzed by the program.
Helpful Hints: Be patient; the number of foods listed can be overwhelming and it can be hard to find exactly what you want.

Appendix II
Daily Values (DV)

The new label reference value, Daily Value (DV), comprises two new sets of dietary standards: Reference Daily Intakes (RDIs) and Daily Reference Values (DRVs). Only the Daily Value term will appear on the label to make label reading less confusing.

The RDIs replace the term "U.S. RDAs," which was introduced in 1973 as a label reference value for vitamins, minerals, and protein. The name change was sought because of confusion with "RDAs" (Recommended Dietary Allowances). The values for the new RDIs follow.

Daily Reference Values (DRVs) for nutrients are based on the number of calories consumed per day. A daily intake of 2,000 calories has been established as the reference. This level was chosen because it has the greatest public health benefit for the nation.

DRVs for the energy-producing nutrients are calculated as follows:

- Fat based on 30% of calories
- Saturated fat based on 10% of calories
- Carbohydrate based on 60% of calories
- Protein based on 10% of calories
- Fiber based on 11.5 g of fiber per 1,000 calories

Because of current recommendations, DRVs for the following nutrients represent the uppermost limit that is considered desirable. The DRVs for fats and sodium are:

- Total fat: less than 65 g
- Saturated fat: less than 20 g
- Cholesterol: less than 300 mg
- Sodium: less than 2400 mg

Reference Daily Intakes (RDIs)

Nutrient	Unit of Measurement*	Adults and Children 4 or more Years of Age	Children Less than 4 Years of Age†	Infants‡	Pregnant Women	Lactating Women
Vitamin A	Retinol equivalent§	875	400	375	800	1,300
Vitamin C	Milligrams	60	40	33	70	95
Calcium	Milligrams	900	800	500	1,200	1,200
Iron	Milligrams	12	10	8.0	30	15
Vitamin D	Micrograms‖	6.5	10	9.0	10	10
Vitamin E	α-Tocopherol equivalents	9.0	6.0	3.5	10	12
Vitamin K	Micrograms	65	15	7.5	65	65
Thiamin	Milligrams	1.2	0.7	0.4	1.5	1.6
Riboflavin	Milligrams	1.4	0.8	0.5	1.6	1.8
Niacin	Niacin equivalent§	16	9.0	5.5	17	20
Vitamin B$_6$	Milligrams	1.5	1.0	0.5	2.2	2.1
Folate	Micrograms	180	50	30	400	280
Vitamin B$_{12}$	Micrograms	2.0	0.7	0.4	2.2	2.6
Biotin	Micrograms	60	20	13	65	65
Pantothenic acid	Milligrams	5.5	3.0	2.5	5.5	5.5
Phosphorus	Milligrams	900	800	400	1,200	1,200
Magnesium	Milligrams	300	80	50	320	355
Zinc	Milligrams	13	10	5.0	15	19
Iodine	Micrograms	150	70	45	175	200
Selenium	Micrograms	55	20	13	65	75
Copper	Milligrams	2.0	0.9	0.6	2.5	2.5
Manganese	Milligrams	3.5	1.3	0.6	3.5	3.5
Fluoride	Milligrams	2.5	1.0	0.5	3.0	3.0
Chromium	Micrograms	120	50	33	130	130
Molybdenum	Micrograms	150	38	26	160	160
Chloride	Milligrams	3,150	1,000	650	3,400	3,400

*The following abbreviations are allowed: "mg" for "milligram"; "μg" for "micrograms"; "μg RE" for "retinol equivalents"; "mg α-TE" for "α-tocopherol equivalents"; "mg NE" for "niacin equivalents."
†The term "children less than 4 years of age" means persons 13 through 47 months of age.
‡The term "infants" means persons not more than 12 months of age.
§1 retinol equivalent = 1 microgram retinol or 6 micrograms β-carotene; 1 α-tocopherol equivalent = 1 milligram d-α-tocopherol; 1 niacin equivalent = 1 milligram niacin or 60 milligrams of dietary tryptophan.
‖As cholecalciferol.

Appendix III
Dietary Reference Intakes (DRI)

The Food and Nutrition Board of the National Academy of Sciences determines recommended nutrient intake levels that apply to healthy individuals. Beginning in 1997, the Food and Nutrition Board began releasing updated recommendations under a new framework called the Dietary Reference Intakes (DRIs). The DRI values include a set of Tolerable Upper Intake Levels (UL), which are levels of nutrient intake that should not be exceeded due to the potential for adverse effects from excessive consumption.

Dietary Reference Intakes (DRI): Vitamins and Minerals

Life stage group	Vitamin A (µg/RE)	Vitamin C (mg/d)	Vitamin D (µg/d)[3]	Vitamin E (mg/d)[4]	Vitamin K (µg/d)	Thiamin (mg/d)	Riboflavin (mg/d)	Niacin (mg/d)[1]	Vitamin B6 (mg/d)	Folate (µg/d)[2]	Vitamin B12 (µg/d)	Pantothenic Acid (mg/d)	Biotin (µg/d)	Choline (mg/d)	Calcium (mg/d)	Fluoride (mg/d)	Iodine (µg/d)	Iron (mg/d)	Magnesium (mg/d)	Phosphorous (mg/d)	Selenium (µg/d)	Zinc (mg/d)
Infants																						
0–6 mo	400*	40*	5*	4*	2.0*	0.2*	0.3*	2*	0.1*	65*	0.4*	1.7*	5*	125*	210*	0.01*	110*	0.27*	30*	100*	15*	2*
7–12 mo	500*	50*	5*	6*	2.5*	0.3*	0.4*	4*	0.3*	80*	0.5*	1.8*	6*	150*	270*	0.5*	130*	11	75*	275*	20*	3*
Children																						
1–3 y	300	15	5*	6	30*	0.5	0.5	6	0.5	150	0.09	2*	8*	200*	500*	0.7*	90	7	80	460	20	3
4–8 y	400	25	5*	7	55*	0.6	0.6	8	0.6	200	1.2	3*	12*	250*	800*	1*	90	7	130	500	30	5

This table presents Recommended Dietary Allowances (RDA) and Adequate Intakes (AI) indicated by an asterisk (*). RDAs and AIs may both be used as goals for individual intake.

[1]As niacin equivalents (NE).

[2]As dietary folate equivalents (DFE).

[3]As cholecalciferol.

[4]As α-tocopherol.

Sources: Data compiled from *Dietary Reference Intakes for Calcium, Phosphorus, Magnesium, Vitamin D, and Fluoride.* (1997). Washington, DC: National Academy Press. *Dietary Reference Intakes for Thiamin, Riboflavin, Niacin, Vitamin B₆, Folate, Vitamin B₁₂, Pantothenic Acid, Biotin, and Choline.* (1998). Washington, DC: National Academy Press. *Dietary Reference Intakes for Vitamin C, Vitamin E, Selenium, and Carotenoids.* (2000). Washington, DC: National Academy Press. *Dietary Reference Intakes for Vitamin A, Vitamin K, Arsenic, Boron, Chromium, Copper, Iodine, Iron, Manganese, Molybdenum, Nickel, Silicon, Vanadium, and Zinc.* (2001). Washington, DC: National Academy Press. These reports may be accessed via www.nap.edu. Reprinted with permission from (Dietary Reference Intakes: Recommended for Individuals, Food and Nutrition Board © 1997–2003) by the National Academy of Sciences, Courtesy of the National Academies Press, Washington, D.C.

Dietary Reference Intakes (DRI): Energy, Carbohydrate, Fiber, Essential Fatty Acids, and Protein

Age	Energy EER[a] (cal/day)[b]	Carbohydrate (g/day)	Total Fiber (g/day)	Linoleic Acid (g/day)	α–Linoleic Acid (g/day)	Protein (g/kg/day)
Males						
0–6 mo	570	60	—	4.4	0.5	1.52
7–12 mo	743	95	—	4.6	0.5	1.5
1–3[c] y	1,046	130	19	7	0.7	1.1
4–8[c] y	1,742	130	25	10	0.9	0.95
Females						
0–6 mo	520	60	—	4.4	0.5	1.52
7–12 mo	676	95	—	4.6	0.5	1.5
1–3[c] y	992	130	19	7	0.7	1.1
4–8[c] y	1,642	130	25	10	0.9	0.95

Note: For all nutrients, values for infants are AI; AI is not equivalent to RDA. Dashes indicate that values have not been determined.

[a]Estimated Energy Requirement (EER) is the average dietary energy intake predicted to maintain energy balance and is consistent with good health in healthy adults. EER values are determined at four physical activity levels; the values above are for the "active" person.

[b]Kilocalories per day

[c]For energy, the age groups for young children are 1–2 years and 3–8 years.

Source: Dietary Reference Intakes for Energy Carbohydrate, Fiber, Fat, Fatty acids Cholesterol, Protein, and Amino Acids. (2002). Washington, D.C.: National Academy Press. Reprinted with permission from (Dietary Reference Intakes: Recommended for Individuals, Food and Nutrition Board © 1997–2003) by the National Academy of Sciences, Courtesy of the National Academies Press, Washington, D.C.

Dietary Reference Intakes (DRI): Tolerable Upper Intake Levels (UL[a])

Life stage group	Vitamin A (µg/RE)[b]	Vitamin C (mg/d)	Vitamin D (µg/d)[3]	Vitamin E (mg/d)[c,d]	Vitamin K (µg/d)	Thiamin (mg/d)	Riboflavin (mg/d)	Niacin (mg/d)[d]	Vitamin B$_6$ (mg/d)	Folate (µg/d)[d]	Vitamin B$_{12}$ (µg/d)	Pantothenic Acid (mg/d)	Biotin (µg/d)	Choline (mg/d)	Calcium (mg/d)	Fluoride (mg/d)	Iodine (µg/d)	Iron (mg/d)	Magnesium (mg/d)[e]	Phosphorous (mg/d)	Selenium (µg/d)	Zinc (mg/d)
Infants																						
0–6 mo	600	ND[f]	25	ND	ND	ND	ND	ND	ND	ND	ND	ND	ND	ND	ND	0.7	ND	40	ND	ND	45	4
7–12 mo	600	ND	25	ND	ND	ND	ND	ND	ND	ND	ND	ND	ND	ND	ND	0.9	ND	40	ND	ND	60	5
Children																						
1–3 y	600	400	50	200	ND	ND	ND	10	30	300	ND	ND	ND	1.0	2.5	1.3	200	40	65	3	90	7
4–8 y	900	650	50	300	ND	ND	ND	15	40	400	ND	ND	ND	1.0	2.5	2.2	300	40	110	3	150	12

[a]UL = The maximum level of daily nutrient intake that is likely to pose no risk of adverse effects. Unless otherwise specified, the UL represents total intake from food, water, and supplements. Due to lack of suitable data, ULs could not be established for arsenic, chromium, silicon, vitamin K, thiamin, riboflavin, vitamin B$_{12}$, pantothenic acid, biotin, or carotenoids. In the absence of ULs, extra caution may be warranted in consuming levels above recommended intakes.

[b]As pre-formed vitamin A only.

[c]As α-tocopherol; applies to any form of supplemental α-tocopherol.

[d]The ULs for vitamin E, niacin, and folate apply to synthetic forms obtained from supplements, fortified foods, or a combination of the two.

[e]The ULs for magnesium represent intake from a pharmacological agent only and do not include intake from food and water.

[f]ND = Not determinable due to lack of data of adverse effects in this age group and concern with regard to lack of ability to handle excess amounts. Source intake should be from food only to prevent high levels of intake.

Sources: Data compiled from *Dietary Reference Intakes for Calcium, Phosphorus, Magnesium, Vitamin D, and Fluoride.* (1997). Washington, DC: National Academy Press. *Dietary Reference Intakes for Thiamin, Riboflavin, Niacin, Vitamin B$_6$, Folate, Vitamin B$_{12}$, Pantothenic Acid, Biotin, and Choline.* (1998). Washington, DC: National Academy Press. *Dietary Reference Intakes for Vitamin C, Vitamin E, Selenium, and Carotenoids.* (2000). Washington, DC: National Academy Press. (2000). *Dietary Reference Intakes for Vitamin A, Vitamin K, Arsenic, Boron, Chromium, Copper, Iodine, Iron, Manganese, Molybdenum, Nickel, Silicon, Vanadium, and Zinc.* (2001). Washington, DC: National Academy Press. These reports may be accessed via www.nap.edu. Reprinted with permission from (Dietary Reference Intakes: Recommended for Individuals, Food and Nutrition Board © 1997–2003) by the National Academy of Sciences, Courtesy of the National Academies Press, Washington, D.C.

Appendix IV
Growth Charts for Birth to 36 months and Children 2 to 20 years

CDC Growth Charts: United States

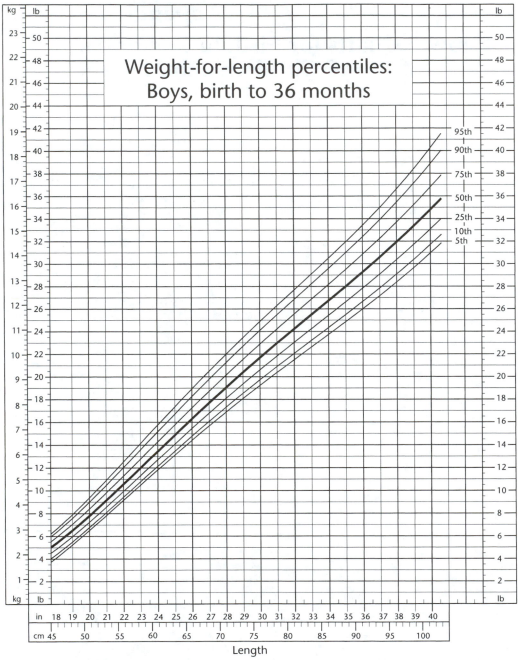

Weight-for-length percentiles:
Boys, birth to 36 months

Revised and corrected June 8, 2000.

SOURCE: Developed by the National Center for Health Statistics in collaboration with the
National Center for Chronic Disease Prevention and Health Promotion (2000).

336

CDC Growth Charts: United States

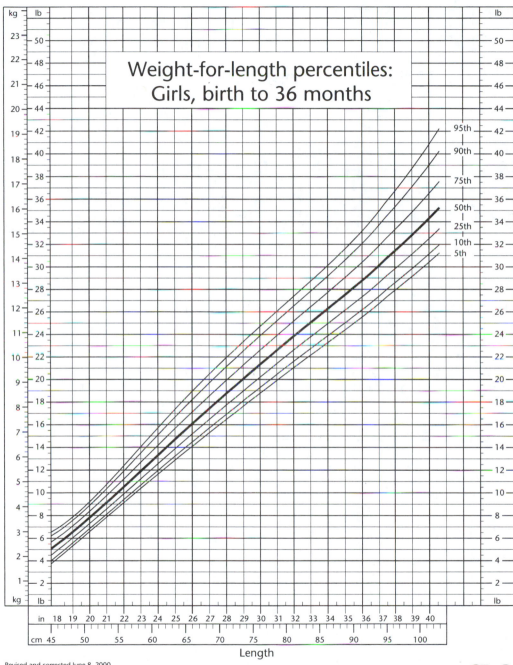

Weight-for-length percentiles:
Girls, birth to 36 months

Length

Revised and corrected June 8, 2000.

SOURCE: Developed by the National Center for Health Statistics in collaboration with the
National Center for Chronic Disease Prevention and Health Promotion (2000).

CDC
CENTERS FOR DISEASE CONTROL
AND PREVENTION

CDC Growth Charts: United States

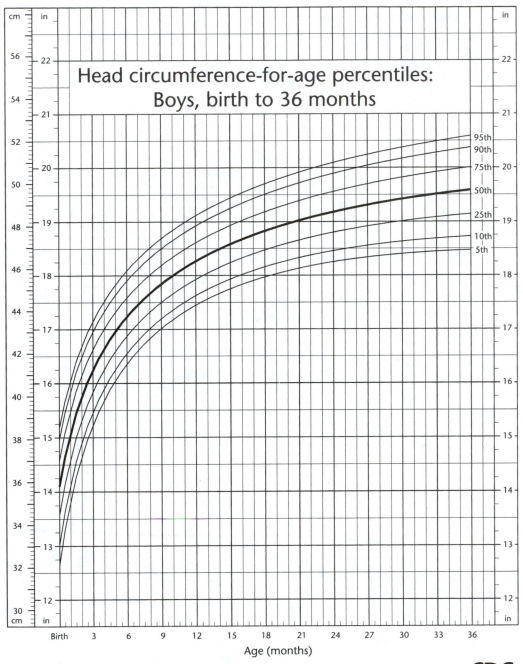

Head circumference-for-age percentiles:
Boys, birth to 36 months

95th
90th
75th
50th
25th
10th
5th

Age (months)

Birth 3 6 9 12 15 18 21 24 27 30 33 36

SOURCE: Developed by the National Center for Health Statistics in collaboration with the
National Center for Chronic Disease Prevention and Health Promotion (2000).

CDC Growth Charts: United States

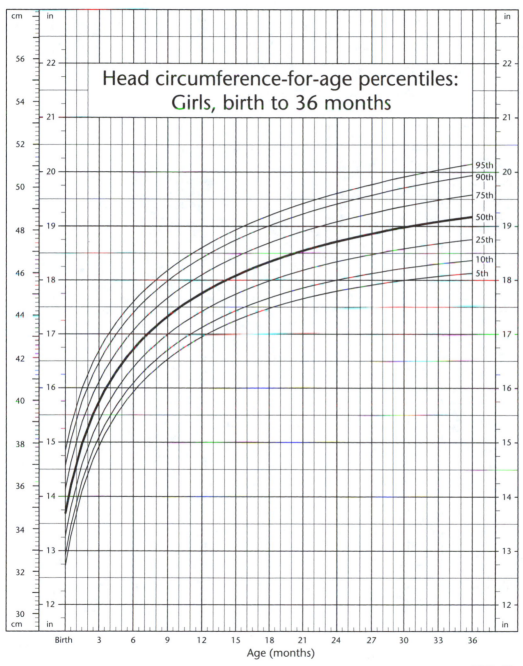

Head circumference-for-age percentiles:
Girls, birth to 36 months

95th
90th
75th
50th
25th
10th
5th

Age (months)

Birth   3   6   9   12   15   18   21   24   27   30   33   36

SOURCE: Developed by the National Center for Health Statistics in collaboration with the
National Center for Chronic Disease Prevention and Health Promotion (2000).

CDC Growth Charts: United States

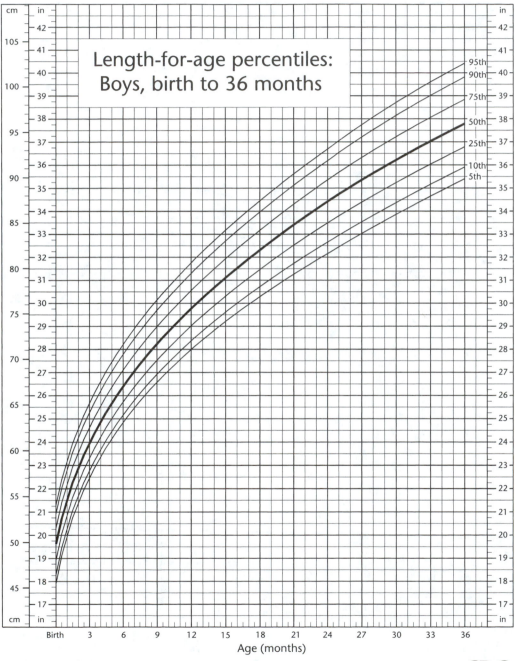

Length-for-age percentiles:
Boys, birth to 36 months

SOURCE: Developed by the National Center for Health Statistics in collaboration with the
National Center for Chronic Disease Prevention and Health Promotion (2000).

CDC Growth Charts: United States

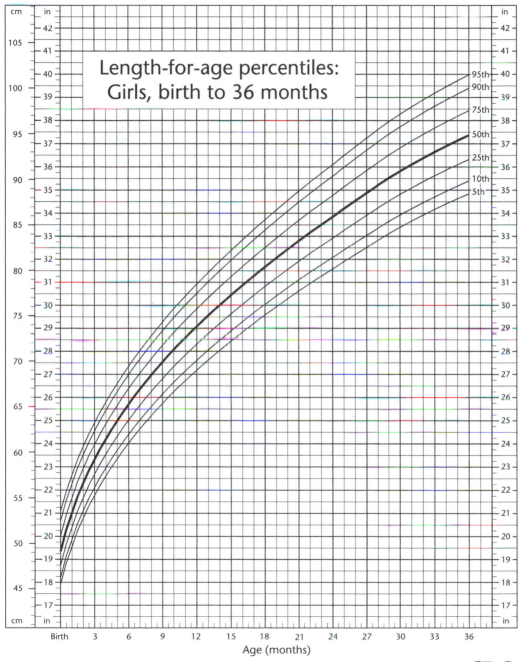

Length-for-age percentiles:
Girls, birth to 36 months

Age (months)

SOURCE: Developed by the National Center for Health Statistics in collaboration with the
National Center for Chronic Disease Prevention and Health Promotion (2000).

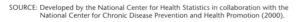

CDC
CENTERS FOR DISEASE CONTROL
AND PREVENTION

CDC Growth Charts: United States

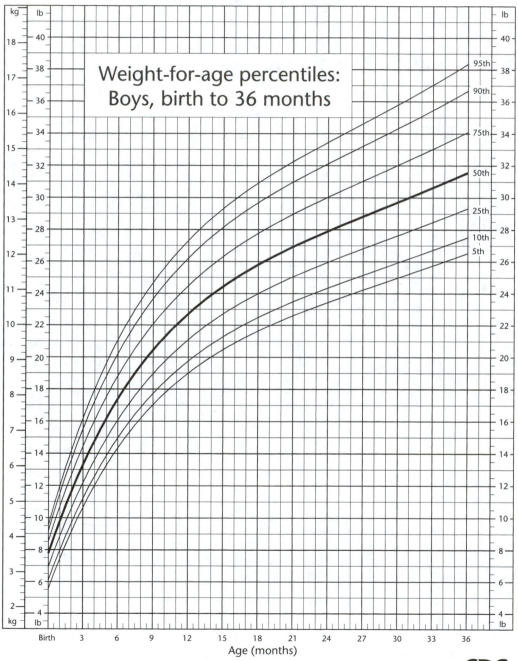

Weight-for-age percentiles:
Boys, birth to 36 months

Age (months)

SOURCE: Developed by the National Center for Health Statistics in collaboration with the
National Center for Chronic Disease Prevention and Health Promotion (2000).

CDC
CENTERS FOR DISEASE CONTROL
AND PREVENTION

CDC Growth Charts: United States

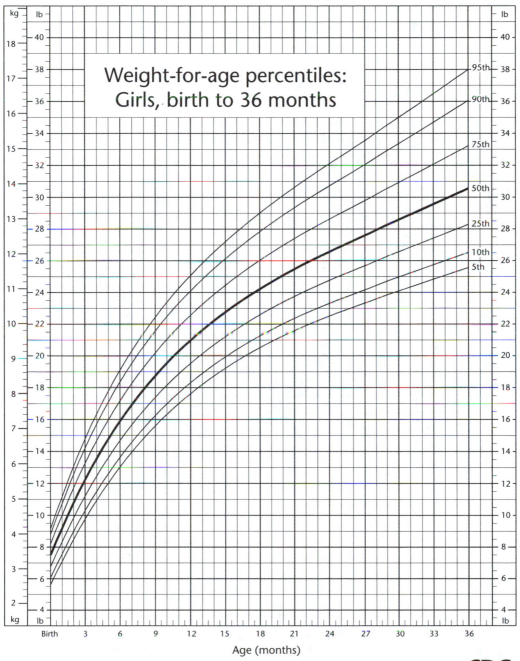

Weight-for-age percentiles:
Girls, birth to 36 months

SOURCE: Developed by the National Center for Health Statistics in collaboration with the
National Center for Chronic Disease Prevention and Health Promotion (2000).

CDC
CENTERS FOR DISEASE CONTROL
AND PREVENTION

CDC Growth Charts: United States

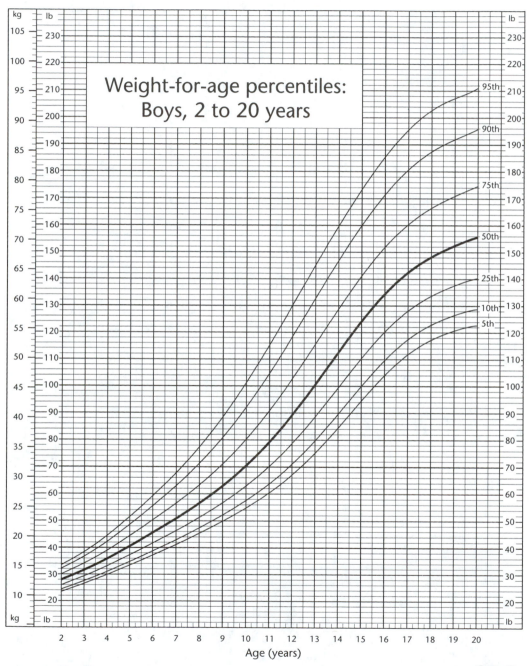

Weight-for-age percentiles:
Boys, 2 to 20 years

95th
90th
75th
50th
25th
10th
5th

Age (years)

SOURCE: Developed by the National Center for Health Statistics in collaboration with the
National Center for Chronic Disease Prevention and Health Promotion (2000).

CENTERS FOR DISEASE CONTROL
AND PREVENTION

CDC Growth Charts: United States

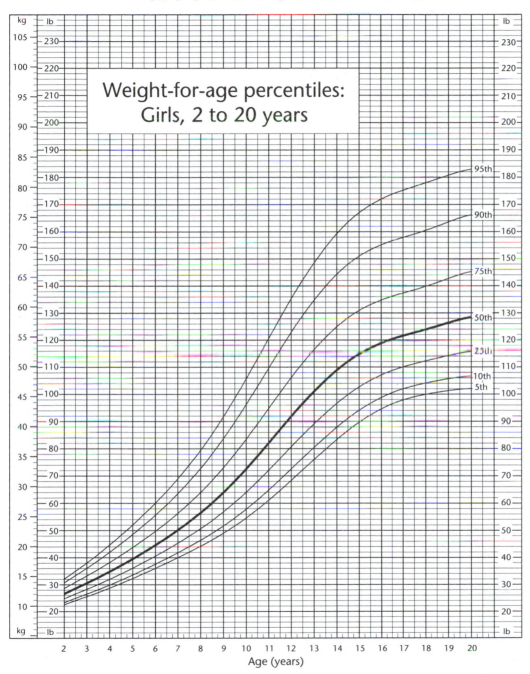

Weight-for-age percentiles:
Girls, 2 to 20 years

95th
90th
75th
50th
25th
10th
5th

Age (years)

SOURCE: Developed by the National Center for Health Statistics in collaboration with the
National Center for Chronic Disease Prevention and Health Promotion (2000).

CDC
CENTERS FOR DISEASE CONTROL
AND PREVENTION

345

CDC Growth Charts: United States

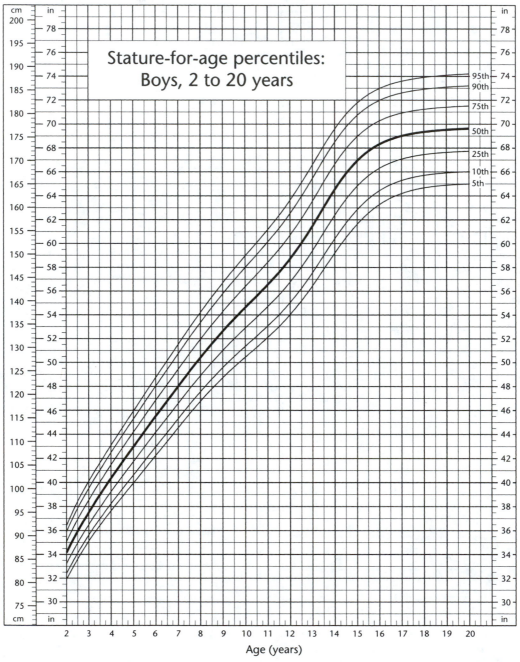

Stature-for-age percentiles:
Boys, 2 to 20 years

SOURCE: Developed by the National Center for Health Statistics in collaboration with the
National Center for Chronic Disease Prevention and Health Promotion (2000).

CDC Growth Charts: United States

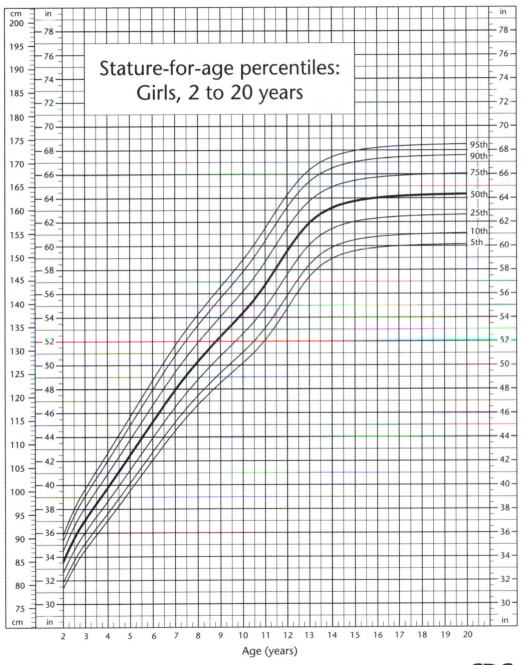

Stature-for-age percentiles:
Girls, 2 to 20 years

SOURCE: Developed by the National Center for Health Statistics in collaboration with the
National Center for Chronic Disease Prevention and Health Promotion (2000).

CDC Growth Charts: United States

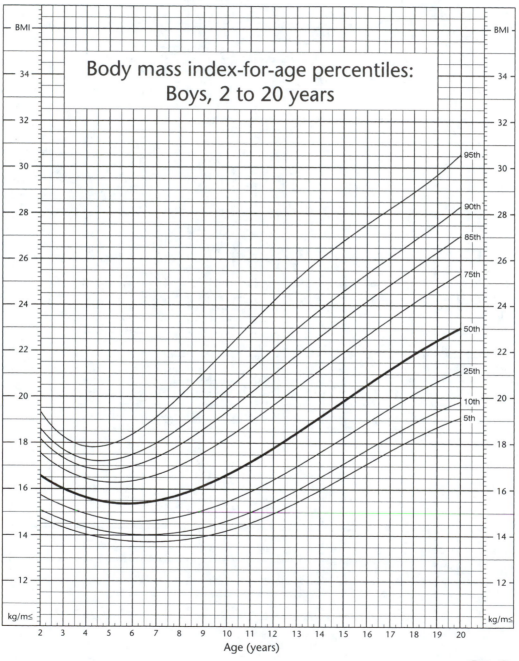

Body mass index-for-age percentiles:
Boys, 2 to 20 years

Age (years)

SOURCE: Developed by the National Center for Health Statistics in collaboration with the
National Center for Chronic Disease Prevention and Health Promotion (2000).

CDC Growth Charts: United States

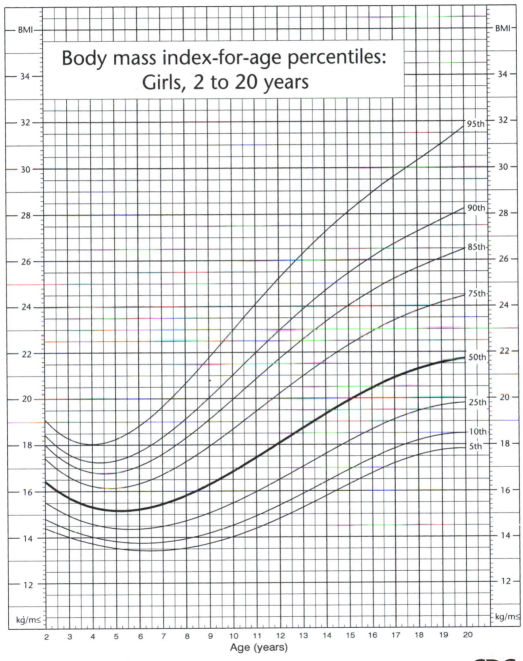

Body mass index-for-age percentiles: Girls, 2 to 20 years

BMI

34

32

30

28

26

24

22

20

18

16

14

12

kg/m²

95th
90th
85th
75th
50th
25th
10th
5th

Age (years)
2 3 4 5 6 7 8 9 10 11 12 13 14 15 16 17 18 19 20

SOURCE: Developed by the National Center for Health Statistics in collaboration with the National Center for Chronic Disease Prevention and Health Promotion (2000).

CDC
CENTERS FOR DISEASE CONTROL AND PREVENTION

Appendix V
Diet Assessment Tools for Infants and Children

Diet History Assessment Form for Infants 7 Through 11 Months

Date: Name: Age:	
List ALL feedings in 24 hours (use the back as needed) Time Feeding/Food Length of Breastfeeding OR Amount of Formula/Food	
Goals Used to Score Diet—if goal is NOT met, check the box.	**7–11 months**
Breastfed for the 1st year with solids beginning at ~6 months	
Offer a variety of nutritious foods	
Use a cup for all liquids (other than breast milk or formula)	
Use a spoon to feed solid foods	
Hours between breast or formula feedings: About every 4–6 hours	
Number of breast or formula feedings/24 hours: About 4–6+ times	
Length of breastfeedings only: About 10+ minutes	
"Extra water" about 4–8 ounces/24 hours **after** protein rich solid foods have been introduced	
Mix formula according to directions	
Baby fed amount listed below for age: *Age* *Ounces of formula* 7–8 mos. 27–32 ounces 9–12 mos. 24–32 ounces	
Total Checks: 3 or more, inadequate diet	
Optional Selections: # of wet diapers in 24-hour period? # of stools in 24-hour period? How do you hold or position your baby at feedings? How much juice does the infant consume in 24 hours? Are food safety precautions followed (i.e., wash hands and containers, use refrigeration for breast milk or formula)?	

Diet History Assessment Form for Infants Birth to 6 Months

Date:	Name:		Age:

List ALL feedings in 24 hour period (use the back as needed)
Time   Feeding/Food   Length of Breastfeeding OR Amount of Formula/Food

Goals Used to Score Diet—if goal is NOT met, check the box.	0–3 months	4–6 months
Exclusive breastfeeding for the first 6 months		
0–3 months: Breastfed, breast milk, or iron-fortified formula		
Solids introduced at appropriate age with use of a spoon		
Hours between breast or formula feedings: 0–2 mos.: 1½–3 hrs. 2–3 mos.: 2–4 hrs. 4–6 mos.: 3–4 hrs.		
Number of breast or formula feedings/24 hours: 0–2 mos.: 8–12 times 2–3 mos.: 6–10 times 4–6 mos.: 6–8 times		
No extra water given		
Mix formula according to directions		
Baby fed amount listed below for age: *Age Ounces of formula Age Ounces of formula* 1 mo. 14–28 ounces 4 mos. 27–39 ounces 2 mos. 23–34 ounces 5 mos. 27–45 ounces 3 mos. 25–40 ounces 6 mos. 30–50 ounces		
Total Checks: 2 or more, inadequate diet		

Optional Section:

# of wet diapers in 24-hour period?

# of stools in 24-hour period?

How do you know when your baby is hungry/full?

How do you hold or position your baby at feedings?

Are food safety precautions being followed (i.e., washing of hands and containers, appropriate storage of breast milk, formula, etc.)?

Nutrition Questionnaire for Children

1. How would you describe your child's appetite?

   ☐ Good
   ☐ Fair
   ☐ Poor

2. How many days does your family eat meals together per week?

3. How would you describe mealtimes with your child?

   ☐ Always pleasant
   ☐ Usually pleasant
   ☐ Sometimes pleasant
   ☐ Never pleasant

4. How many meals does your child eat per day? How many snacks?

5. Which of these foods did your child eat or drink last week? *(Check all that apply.)*

   Grains

   ☐ Bread   ☐ Noodles/pasta/rice
   ☐ Rolls   ☐ Tortillas
   ☐ Bagels   ☐ Crackers
   ☐ Muffins   ☐ Cereal/grits
   ☐ Other grains: _____

   Vegetables

   ☐ Corn   ☐ Greens (collard, spinach)
   ☐ Peas   ☐ Green salad
   ☐ Potatoes   ☐ Broccoli
   ☐ French fries   ☐ Green beans
   ☐ Tomatoes   ☐ Carrots
   ☐ Other vegetables: _____

Fruits

☐ Apples/juice   ☐ Bananas
☐ Oranges/juice   ☐ Pears
☐ Grapefruit/juice   ☐ Melon
☐ Grapes/juice   ☐ Peaches
☐ Other fruits/juice: _____

Milk and Other Dairy Products

☐ Whole milk   ☐ Yogurt
☐ Reduced-fat (2%) milk   ☐ Cheese
☐ Low-fat (1%) milk   ☐ Ice cream
☐ Fat-free (skim) milk   ☐ Flavored milk
☐ Other milk and dairy products: _____

Meat and Meat Alternatives

☐ Beef/hamburger   ☐ Sausage/bacon
☐ Pork   ☐ Peanut butter/nuts
☐ Chicken   ☐ Eggs
☐ Turkey   ☐ Dried beans
☐ Fish   ☐ Tofu
☐ Cold cuts
☐ Other meat and meat alternatives: _____

Fats and Sweets

☐ Cake/cupcakes   ☐ Doughnuts
☐ Pie   ☐ Candy
☐ Cookies   ☐ Fruit-flavored drinks
☐ Chips   ☐ Soft drinks
☐ Other fats and sweets: _____

Source: Story, M., Holt, K., & Sofka, D. (2000). *Bright Futures in Practice: Nutrition.* Arlington, VA: National Center for Education in Maternal and Child Health, Georgetown University.

6. If your child is 5 years old or younger, does he or she eat any of these foods? *(Check all that apply.)*

   ☐ Hot dogs   ☐ Popcorn
   ☐ Pretzels and chips   ☐ Marshmallows
   ☐ Raw celery or carrots   ☐ Round or hard
   ☐ Nuts and seeds   candy
   ☐ Raisins   ☐ Peanut butter
   ☐ Whole grapes

7. How much juice does your child drink per day? How much sweetened beverage (for example, fruit punch, and soft drinks) does your child drink per day?

8. Does your child take a bottle to bed at night or carry a bottle around during the day?

   ☐ Yes   ☐ No

9. What is the source of the water your child drinks? Sources include public, well, commercially bottled, and home system–processed water.

10. Do you have a working stove, oven, and refrigerator where you live?

    ☐ Yes   ☐ No

11. Were there any days last month when your family didn't have enough food to eat or enough money to buy food?

12. Did you participate in physical activity (for example, walking or riding a bike) in the past week? If yes, on how many days and for how long?

    ☐ Yes   ☐ No

13. Does your child spend more than 2 hours per day watching television and videotapes or playing computer games? If yes, how many hours per day?

    ☐ Yes   ☐ No

14. What concerns or questions do you have about feeding your child?

Appendix VI
Special Supplemental Nutrition Program for Women, Infants, and Children (WIC Program)

In 1972 Congress authorized the Special Supplemental Nutrition Program for Women, Infants, and Children (WIC).* WIC provides participants with specific nutritious supplemental foods and nutrition education, at no cost. WIC participants are eligible low-income persons who are determined by health professionals (physicians, nutritionists, nurses, and other officials) to be at "nutritional risk" because of inadequate nutrition, health care, or both. Federal funds are available to participating state health departments or comparable state agencies. Indian tribes, bands, groups, or their authorized representatives who are recognized by the Bureau of Indian Affairs (U.S. Department of Interior) or the appropriate area office of the Indian Health Service (U.S. Department of Health and Human Services) may also act as state agencies. These agencies distribute funds to the participating local agencies. The funds pay for supplemental foods for participants and pay specified administrative costs, including those of nutrition education.

ELIGIBILITY FOR THE PROGRAM

Pregnant, postpartum, and breastfeeding women and infants and children up to 5 years of age are eligible if they (1) meet the income standards (a state agency may either set a statewide income standard or allow local agencies to set their own); (2) are individually determined to be at nutritional risk and in need of the supplemental foods the program offers; and (3) live in an approved project area (if the state has a residency requirement) or belong to special population groups, such as migrant farm workers, Native Americans (Indians), or refugees.

---

*U.S. Public Law 94–105, Oct. 7, 1975.

FOODS INCLUDED IN THE WIC PROGRAM

The program provides nutritious food to breastfeeding mothers and allows infants up to 4 months of age to receive iron-fortified formula. Older infants, breastfed or not, (4 through 12 months) may receive formula, iron-fortified infant cereal, and fruit juices high in vitamin C. An infant may receive special therapeutic formula when it is prescribed by a physician for a specified medical condition. Participating women and children receive fortified milk and/or cheese; eggs; hot or cold cereals high in iron; fruit and vegetable juices high in vitamin C; and either peanut butter or dried beans or peas. WIC provides breastfeeding women with a food package to meet their extra nutritional needs, which may include carrots and tuna. Women and children with special dietary needs may receive a package containing cereal, juice, and special therapeutic formulas. For a participant to receive this package, a WIC-trained health professional must determine that the participant has a medical condition that precludes or restricts the use of conventional foods.

The state agency administering the program may use one or all of the following food delivery systems: (1) retail purchase, where participants use vouchers or checks to buy foods at local retail stores authorized by the state agency to accept WIC vouchers or checks; (2) home delivery, where the food is delivered to participants' homes; (3) direct distribution, where participants pick up the food from the warehouse or participants purchase food at a farmers market.

NUTRITION EDUCATION IN WIC

Nutrition education is available to parents or caregivers of infant and child participants, and whenever possible, to the child who participates. This nutrition education is designed to have a practical relationship to participants' nutritional needs, household situations, and cultural preferences and includes information on how participants can select food for themselves and their families. The goals of WIC nutrition education are to teach the relationship between proper nutritional risk to develop better food habits, and to prevent nutrition-related problems by showing participants how to best use their supplemental and other foods. The WIC program also encourages breastfeeding and counsels pregnant women on its nutritional advantages.

Appendix VII
Equipment and Play Materials
for Preschoolers

Equipment must be available in needed quantity and it must be varied according to children's needs. The following items* are suggested.

Balance boards

Balls   of various sizes and materials.

Barrels   for creeping through, for rolling in, and for imaginative play.

Bars   firmly fixed and at varied heights for hanging, swinging, turning.

Bats   paddles, mallets.

Batting tees   These should be adjustable; they may be made of galvanized pipe and pieces of old garden hose.

Bean bags

Benches   These must be sturdy but light enough for children to carry; they can be used for jumping, as inclined planes, and for vaulting.

Blocks, bricks, stones, and boards   for building and for carrying, lifting, pushing, and pulling.

Boards   These should be well-cured, smooth, and 6 to 8 inches wide; cleats underneath or hooks on the ends allow various attachments.

Bounce board   This may be purchased or constructed.

Boxes   Sturdy wooden boxes and large corrugated cardboard boxes such as those refrigerators come in.

Cargo nets (climbing nets)   These may be obtained from Army-Navy surplus stores or from regular supply sources; they are useful for a variety of climbing activities.

Climbing structures   Sturdy arrangements of metal tubing sometimes called towers, jungle gyms, and so on. The larger ones are permanent fixtures; smaller structures are portable but also must be very sturdy.

Flip-It Bowling Set   A useful device easily cared for; it may be purchased or constructed.

Hoops

*Source: Sinclair, C.B. (1973). *Movement of the Young Child Age Two to Six*. Columbus, OH: Merrill Publishing Co.

Jumping standards   These may be easily constructed and are now commercially available in suitable sizes.

Ladders   to be used vertically, horizontally, and inclined at various angles; hooks on the end provide stable fixation.

Logs   short and long; poles with smooth surfaces.

Mats   small and washable for individual use; larger mats for small group activities; pads of foam rubber may be used temporarily.

Obstacle course   A wide variety of materials may be used to involve jumping, running, climbing, and going over, under, and through.

Old bathtub   When appropriately set up is fine for water play.

Padded sawhorses, tables, and benches   may be used for vaulting and many tumbling activities instead of more expensive apparatus.

Parachute   may be obtained at Army-Navy surplus stores.

Pitchback net   may be purchased or constructed; enables one child to play throw and catch.

Pool   portable plastic pool for wading and shallow water play.

Portable metal stands   These are light enough for children to carry but well constructed; they may be utilized with boards and ladders to make ever-changing apparatus.

Reach and jump target   Strips of plastic graduated in length and suspended from a bar so that children may jump and reach to touch them.

Record player and records   readily available from many sources. Records selected should allow for creativity in movement.

Rhythm instruments   A sturdy drum is a must and should be used often by the teacher; rattles, drums, triangles, and many other instruments may be purchased or constructed.

Roller skates   These are not usual in nursery schools but may be used if facilities and space permit.

Rope ladder   One or more of these offer an interesting challenge and they are easily stored.

Ropes   Long ropes are useful for turning and as climbing equipment; they may be used on the ground to mark off areas to jump over, to define floor patterns, and so on. Short ropes for individual use may be used in countless ways.

Rugs   For outdoor use, a blanket or sheet of foam rubber may be used as a rug. Small woven rugs may be used as substitutes for mats.

Slides and swings   should be selected, located, and erected with professional advice.

Spades, rakes, shovels   are available in small sizes and should be of strong construction.

Spools   Large wooden spools are often discarded after utility construction; they should be weatherproofed and used for jumping, climbing, and building. They may also be rolled about the area.

Stairways   Five to seven steps should be provided for a realistic experience. Many children do not use stairways at home or school.

Stall bars   Ladder-like bars erected close to a wall; these take up little space and are excellent for indoor use.

Suspended balls   Good for hitting practice; require adequate space; should be pulled up after use.

Stools and tables   If strongly constructed, these may be used for many purposes, and old ones may be substituted for more expensive equipment.

Swinging bridge   made of rope and boards and suspended about head height.

Targets   Fixed or portable; these may vary widely in type—an open-frame, concentric circles painted on cloth or plastic, flags or traffic cones for markers, and many others.

Tires   Bicycle, car, and truck; tubes and casings.

Traffic cones   may be available without cost or can be easily constructed. They are useful as markers and goals and may also be used as supports for light objects.

Tree trunks and stumps   Wonderful for climbing, vaulting, jumping; they may be used as or converted into ships, horses, trucks, houses, and so on.

Trestles and sawbenches   may be used as supports for boards, ladders, and bridges. When constructed of wood the tops can be padded and used for vaulting and tumbling.

Tricycles and bicycles

Tunnels   Fabric and collapsible, concrete or ceramic.

Wagons, sleds, and wheelbarrows

Walking beam

Wands   Smooth wooden sticks, also may be made of metal; the wooden ones are strong and inexpensive.

Appendix VIII
Traditional Food-Based Menu Planning Approach—Meal Pattern for Lunches

	Minimum Quantities				Recommended Quantities
Food Components and Food Items	**Group I** Ages 1–2 Preschool	**Group II** Ages 3–4 Preschool	**Group III** Ages 5–8 Grades K–3	**Group IV** Ages 9 and Older Grades 4–12	**Group V** Ages 12 and Older Grades 7–12
Milk (as a beverage)	6 fl oz	6 fl oz	8 fl oz	8 fl oz	8 fl oz
Meat or Meat Alternate (quantity of the edible portion as served):					
Lean meat, poultry, or fish	1 oz	1 1/2 oz	1 1/2 oz	2 oz	3 oz
Alternate protein products*	1 oz	1 1/2 oz	1 1/2 oz	2 oz	3 oz
Cheese	1 oz	1 1/2 oz	1 1/2 oz	2 oz	3 oz
Large egg	1/2	3/4	3/4	1	1 1/2
Cooked dry beans or peas	1/4 c	3/8 c	3/8 c	1/2 c	3/4 c
Peanut butter or other nut or seed butters	2 Tbsp	3 Tbsp	3 Tbsp	4 Tbsp	6 Tbsp
Yogurt, plain or flavored, unsweetened or sweetened	4 oz or 1/2 c	6 oz or 3/4 c	6 oz or 3/4 c	8 oz or 1 c	12 oz or 1 1/2 c
The following may be used to meet no more than 50% of the requirement and must be used in combination with any of the above:					
Peanuts, soynuts, tree nuts, or seeds, as listed in program guidance, or an equivalent quantity of any combination of the above meat/meat alternate (1 oz of nuts/ seeds=1 oz of cooked lean meat, poultry, or fish)	1/2 oz = 50%	3/4 oz = 50%	3/4 oz = 50%	1 oz = 50%	1 1/2 oz = 50%
Vegetable or Fruit: 2 or more servings of vegetables, fruits, or both	1/2 c	1/2 c	1/2 c	3/4 c	3/4 c
Grains/Breads (servings per week): Must be enriched or whole grain. A serving is a slice of bread or an equivalent serving of biscuits, rolls, etc., or 1/2 cup of cooked rice, macaroni, noodles, other pasta products, or cereal grains	5 servings per week†— minimum of 1/2 serving per day	8 servings per week†— minimum of 1 serving per day	8 servings per week†— minimum of 1 serving per day	8 servings per week†— minimum of 1 serving per day	10 servings per week†— minimum of 1 serving per day

*Must meet the requirements of 7 CFR 210.

†For the purposes of this table, a week equals 5 days.

Appendix IX
Enhanced Food-Based Menu Planning Approach—Meal Pattern for Lunches

Food Components and Food Items	Minimum Requirements				Option for
	Ages 1–2	Preschool	Grades K–6	Grades 7–12	Grades K–3
Milk (as a beverage)	6 fl oz	6 fl oz	8 fl oz	8 fl oz	8 fl oz
Meat or Meat Alternate (quantity of the edible portion as served):					
Lean meat, poultry, or fish	1 oz	11/2 oz	2 oz	2 oz	11/2 oz
Alternate protein products*	1 oz	11/2 oz	2 oz	2 oz	11/2 oz
Cheese	1 oz	11/2 oz	2 oz	2 oz	11/2 oz
Large egg	1/2	3/4	1	1	3/4
Cooked dry beans or peas	1/4 c	3/8 c	1/2 c	1/2 c	3/8 c
Peanut butter or other nut or seed butters	2 Tbsp	3 Tbsp	4 Tbsp	4 Tbsp	3 Tbsp
Yogurt, plain or flavored, unsweetened or sweetened	4 oz or 1/2 c	6 oz or 3/4 c	8 oz or 1 c	8 oz or 1 c	6 oz or 3/4 c
The following may be used to meet no more than 50% of the requirement and must be used in combination with any of the above:					
Peanuts, soynuts, tree nuts, or seeds, as listed in program guidance, or an equivalent quantity of any combination of the above meat/meat alternate (1 oz of nuts/seeds=1 ounce of cooked lean meat, poultry, or fish)	1/2 oz = 50%	3/4 oz = 50%	1 oz = 50%	1 oz = 50%	3/4 oz = 50%
Vegetable or Fruit: 2 or more servings of vegetables, fruits, or both	1/2 c	1/2 c	3/4 c plus an extra 1/2 c over a week†	1 c	3/4 c
Grains/Breads (servings per week): Must be enriched or whole grain. A serving is a slice of bread or an equivalent serving of biscuits, rolls, etc., or 1/2 cup of cooked rice, macaroni, noodles, other pasta products, or cereal grains	5 servings per week†—minimum of 1/2 serving per day	8 servings per week†—minimum of 1 serving per day	12 servings per week†—minimum of 1 serving per day‡	15 servings per week†—minimum of 1 serving per day‡	10 servings per week†—minimum of 1 serving per day‡

*Must meet the requirements in Appendix A of 7 CFR 210.
†For the purposes of this table, a week equals 5 days.
‡Up to one grains/breads serving per day may be a dessert.

Appendix X
Minimum Calorie and Nutrient Levels for Enhanced Food-Based and NuMenus

| Nutrients and Energy Allowances | Minimum Requirements | | | |
| | Required | | | Optional |
	Preschool	Grades K–6	Grades 7–12	Grades K–3
Energy allowances (calories)	517	664	825	633
Total fat (as a percentage of actual total food energy)	1	1, 2	2	1, 2
Saturated fat (as a percentage of actual total food energy)	1	1, 3	3	1, 3
RDA for protein (g)	7	10	16	9
RDA for calcium (mg)	267	286	400	267
RDA for iron (mg)	3.3	3.5	4.5	3.3
RDA for vitamin A (RE)	150	224	300	200
RDA for vitamin C (mg)	14	15	18	15

[1] The Dietary Guidelines recommend that after 2 years of age ". . . children should gradually adopt a diet that, by about 5 years of age, contains no more than 30% of calories from fat."

[2] Not to exceed 30% over a school week

[3] Less than 10% over a school week

Appendix XI
National School Breakfast Program, Summer Food Service Program for Children, and Special Milk Program

THE SCHOOL BREAKFAST PROGRAM

Description of the program (http://www.fns.usda.gov/cnd/Breakfast/Default. htm): The School Breakfast Program (SBP) is a federally assisted meal program operating in schools and institutions. It provides nutritionally balanced, low-cost or free breakfasts to children each school day. The program was established under the Child Nutrition Act of 1966 to ensure that all children have access to a healthy breakfast at school to promote learning readiness and healthy eating behaviors. The School Breakfast Program is a federal entitlement program that provides states with cash assistance for nonprofit breakfast programs in schools and residential child-care institutions. It began as a pilot project in 1966, and was made permanent in 1975. It is administered at the federal level by the Food and Nutrition Service. State education agencies and local school food authorities administer the program at the local level in more than 72,000 schools and institutions.

Regulations require that all school meals meet the recommendations of the Dietary Guidelines for Americans. In addition, breakfasts must provide one-fourth of the daily-recommended levels for protein, calcium, iron, vitamin A, vitamin C, and calories.

Eligibility: Public schools or nonprofit private schools of high school grade or under, and residential child-care institutions are eligible to participate in the School Breakfast Program. Any child at a participating school may purchase a meal through the School Breakfast Program. However, children whose families meet income criteria may receive free or reduced-price breakfasts. Children from families with incomes at or below 130% of the federal poverty level are eligible for free meals. Those with incomes between 130% and 185% of the poverty level are eligible for reduced-price meals. (For the period July 1, 2001, through June 30, 2002,

130% of the poverty level is $22,945 for a family of four; 185% is $32,653.) Children from families over 185% of poverty pay full price, though their meals are still subsidized to some extent.

SUMMER FOOD SERVICE PROGRAM (SFSP) FOR CHILDREN

Description of program (http://www.fns.usda.gov/cnd/Summer/Default.htm): The Summer Food Service Program for Children was created by Congress in 1968. It is an entitlement program designed to provide funds for eligible sponsoring organizations to ensure that children in lower-income areas can continue to receive nutritious meals during long school vacations, when they do not have access to school lunch or breakfast. Nearly 14 million children depend on nutritious free and reduced-price meals and snacks at school for 9 months out of the year, only about 2 million receive the free meals provided by the SFSP during the summer months. This program provides meals and snacks for children who might otherwise go hungry and is often provided in conjunction with educational, developmental, and recreational activities. The program provides one-third of children's RDA for key nutrients.

The SFSP is the single largest federal resource available for local sponsors who want to combine a feeding program with a summer activity program. However, many schools and summer recreation programs are not aware that federal funds are available to provide free meals and snacks to children in needy areas during the summer months.

Eligibility: Children 18 and younger may receive free meals and snacks through SFSP. Meals and snacks are also available to persons with disabilities, over age 18, who participate in school programs for people who are mentally or physically disabled. The program may be sponsored by public or private nonprofit schools; units of local, municipal, county, tribal, or state government; residential camps or National Youth Sports Programs; and private nonprofit organizations to feed free meals and snacks to children 18 or younger. Potential sponsors must demonstrate that meal sites will meet either geographic or enrollment criteria. A site is "geographically eligible" if it is located in an area in which 50% of the children qualify for a free or reduced-price school meal. A site is "enrollment eligible" if 50% of the children enrolled can be documented to qualify for a free or reduced-price school meal (family income up to 185% of poverty). In addition, anyone attending a school program for people with disabilities, regardless of age, may also participate.

SPECIAL MILK PROGRAM

Description of program (http://www.fns.usda.gov/cnd/Milk/AboutMilk/faqs. htm): The Special Milk Program provides milk to children in schools, child-care institutions and eligible camps that do not participate in other federal child nutrition meal service programs. The program reimburses schools for the milk they serve.

Schools in the National School Lunch or School Breakfast Programs may also participate in the Special Milk Program to provide milk to children in half-day prekindergarten and kindergarten programs where children do not have access to the school meal programs.

Participating schools and institutions receive reimbursement from the U.S. Department of Agriculture (USDA) for each half pint of milk served. They must operate their milk programs on a nonprofit basis. They agree to use the federal reimbursement to reduce the selling price of milk to all children. Schools or institutions may choose pasteurized fluid types of unflavored or flavored whole milk, low-fat milk, skim milk, and cultured buttermilk that meet state and local standards. All milk should contain vitamins A and D at levels specified by the Food and Drug Administration.

The Federal reimbursement for each half-pint of milk sold to children in school year 2001–2002 is 14.5 cents. For children who receive their milk free, the USDA reimburses schools the net purchase price of the milk.

Eligibility: Any child at a participating school, kindergarten program, or eligible camp can get milk through the Special Milk Program. Children may buy milk or receive it free, depending on the school's choice of program options. When local school officials offer free milk under the program, any child from a family that meets income guidelines for free meals is eligible. Each child's family must apply annually for free milk eligibility.

Checklist of Foods and Preparation Methods for Menu Planning

Vegetables

Beans
  Fresh lima beans
    Raw
    Buttered
    Cooked with bacon or ham
    With tomatoes
Snap beans
  Raw
  With bacon or salt pork
  With crisp bacon chips
  With cream sauce
  With new potatoes
  With tomatoes
  With carrot circles
  In salad
Beets
  Buttered
  Harvard
  Cold sliced
  And lettuce salad

Broccoli*†
  Raw
  Buttered
  With lemon sauce
  With cheese sauce
  With cream sauce
Cabbage§
  With carrots, cooked
  Buttered
  Cole slaw
  Creamed
  In gelatin
  Raw wedge
  Salad with fruit or other
    vegetables
  With corned beef
  Sauerkraut
Carrots*
  Raw sticks, curls, wheels
  Baked

Cooked with celery
Cooked with peas
Creamed
Glazed
In gelatin (with fruit juice)
Mashed
Scalloped
And cabbage slaw
And raisin salad
Cauliflower†
  Raw
  With cheese sauce
  Buttered
  With cream sauce
  With peas
Celery
  Raw sticks
  Braised
  Buttered
  With carrots, cooked

*Rich in vitamin A.
†Rich in vitamin C.
‡Fair source of vitamin A.
§Fair source or vitamin C.

(continued)

Corn
  On ear
  Buttered
  Creamed
  With lima beans
  Popped
Cucumber
  Raw slices
  In salads
Eggplant
  Baked
  Scalloped
  With tomatoes
Green peas
  Buttered
  Creamed
  Scalloped
  With onion
  With bacon or ham
  Raw
Green pea pods (snow peas)
  Raw
  Sauteed
  Buttered
Lettuce
  Raw
  Shredded
  Wilted
  Combination salad
  Wedges
  Cooked
  Fried
  Creamed
Okra§
  Raw
  Boiled
  Buttered
  Stewed with tomato
Onions, green, yellow, white, dry
  Fried
  Raw

Boiled with peas
  In salad
Parsnips
  Buttered
  Browned
  Raw strips
Potatoes (white)§
  Raw
  With cheese sauce
  Baked
  Boiled and sprinkled with
      parsley and butter
  Browned in oven
  Creamed
  Pancakes
  Mashed
  Salad
  Scalloped
  Peeled baked
  Hash brown
  French fries
Pumpkin*
  Baked
  Mashed
  Cooked whole—cut lid and
      remove seeds and roast
Rutabagas§
  Raw
  Cubes
  Mashed
  Raw strips
Spinach/other greens*†
  Buttered
  Creamed
  Raw leaf
  With celery
  With hard-cooked eggs
  With cheese sauce
  With onions and bacon

Squash (summer)
  Raw
  Buttered
  With tomato
  Seasoned with bacon and/or
      onion
  Baked
Squash (winter)
  Raw sticks, curls, wheels
  Baked
  Mashed
  Cooked in shell
  Roast seeds
Sweet Potato*†
  Baked
  Mashed
  Scalloped with apple
  With marshmallows (rarely)
  Fried
  Buttered
Tomatoes†‡
  Baked
  Broiled
  Raw wedge
  Juice
  Scalloped
  Stewed
  Cold canned
  Sliced
  And okra
  And cucumber salad
  And lettuce salad
  Aspic
Turnips
  Buttered
  Mashed
  Scalloped
  Raw strips

*Rich in vitamin A.
†Rich in vitamin C.
‡Fair source of vitamin A.
§Fair source or vitamin C.

Fruits

Apple
  Applesauce
  Applesauce with cinnamon
      hearts or raisins
  Baked
  Brown Betty
  Fresh Wedge
  Pudding
  Snow
  Tapioca
  And raisin salad
  Fried
Apricot*
  In fruit cup
  Plain
  Stewed dry fruit
  Whip
  With cheese
Banana
  In fruit cup
  In gelatin
  In orange juice
  Pudding
  Sliced
  Snow
  Whole or half
  With milk
  Fried
Berries
  Plain
  With milk

Cantaloupe*†
  Balls
  In fruit cup
  Sliced
Cherries‡
  Plain
  Pudding
Grapefruit†
  Juice
  Salad
  Sections
Grapes (seedless)
  In gelatin
  Plain
Melons§
  Balls
  Cubes
  Fruit cup
  Sliced
Oranges†
  Betty
  Custard
  Juice
  Sections
  Wedges
  Wheel
Peach‡
  In gelatin
  Plain—sliced, half
  Salad
  Sauce

Snow
Stewed dry fruit
Tapioca
Pear
  Plain
  Stewed dry fruit
  Whip
  With cheese
  Sauce
  With other fruit
  Fried
Pineapple
  Crushed
  Cubes, plain
  In gelatin (cooked)‖
  With cabbage or carrot
Plum*
  Plain
Prunes‡
  Custard
  Snow
  Stewed
  Whipped
  With applesauce
Pumpkin*
  See vegetables
Raisins
  In bread or rice pudding
  Plain
  Stewed
  In salad

Meat

Beef
  American chop suey
  Beef-noodle casserole
  Beef and liver loaf*
  Ground beef patty
  Roast

Hot beef sandwich with gravy
Beef stew with vegetables
Cold sliced beef
Meatballs and spaghetti
Meatballs and vegetable
    casserole

Beef hash
Ground beef and macaroni
    casserole
Cold sliced beef sandwich
Meat sauce and spaghetti
Corned beef with cabbage

*Rich in vitamin A.
†Rich in vitamin C.
‡Fair source of vitamin A.
§Fair source or vitamin C.
‖ Gelatin will not become firm if fresh rather than cooked fruit is used.

(continued)

Beef stew with brown gravy over rice	Creamed ham and peas on toast	Ham sandwich
Beef stew with red gravy over noodles	Ham salad	Pork roast
		Lamb
Sloppy Joe	Ham and sweet potato* casserole	Lamb patty
Meat loaf with tomato gravy	Lean pork steak	Lamb meat loaf
Pork	Scalloped ham and potato	Lamb stew
Chop suey	Sliced baked ham	Roast leg of lamb
		Scalloped lamb

Poultry and Fish

Poultry	Baked turkey	Creamed fish with celery and peas
Stewed chicken with rice	Turkey hash	
Chicken and dumplings	Hot turkey sandwich with gravy	Salmon loaf
Chicken with noodles		Tuna fish salad
Chicken with vegetables	Cold sliced turkey sandwich	Tuna-noodle casserole
Creamed chicken	Turkey salad	Tuna boats
Smothered chicken	Fish	Salmon patty
Baked chicken	Baked fish fillet with creole seasoning	Baked fish sticks
Fried chicken		Fish flake balls
Chicken salad		

Other Meats

Strips	Liver with onions	Rice dressing with giblets
With gravy		

Meat Alternates

Cheese	Baked beans with ham seasoning	Eggs†
American cheese cubes or wedges		Baked egg and cheese
	Bean, rice, tomato, and cheese casserole	Baked egg and vegetable
Cheese and noodle or macaroni		Creamed egg and spinach
	Bean soup with ham	Egg à la king
Cheese, tomato, and macaroni	Red beans with ham	Goldenrod eggs
Cheeseburger	Lima beans with cheese	Hard-cooked eggs in tomato sauce
Cheese toast	Lima beans and cheese casserole	
Cheese and vegetables		Scrambled eggs
Cottage cheese with fruit	Lima beans with tomatoes, celery, and wieners	Scrambled eggs with cheese
American cheese sandwich		Stuffed deviled eggs
Beans	Pinto beans and wiener rings	Tofu††
Dried beans, peas, and peanut butter	Black-eyed peas with ham	

*Rich in vitamin A.
†Egg yolk is a fair source of vitamin A.
‡Fair source of vitamin A.
§Fair source or vitamin C.
††Not a replacement for protein source in the Child and Adult Care Food Program.

Breads, Sandwiches, and Cereals

Bread
  Plain
    Whole wheat
    Raisin
    Rye
    Biscuit
    Corn bread (pan or sticks)
    Corn spoon bread
  Hot
    Biscuits
    Corn bread
    Muffins
    Rolls
  Shapes
    Strips
    Squares
    Triangles
    Circles
    Animals
Sandwiches
  Butter
  Cheese

Meat
  Peanut butter
  Vegetable*‡
    Grated carrots and
      cabbage
    Sliced tomato/green
      pepper
  Cream cheese
Macaroni
  Buttered
  Bouillon
  Plain
  Salad
  With cheese
  With tomato sauce
  See beef list
Noodles
  Buttered
  Plain
  With sauce
  See meats

Rice (brown)
  Buttered
  Bouillon
  Pudding
    With raisins
    With cheese
    With chicken
Grits
  Buttered
  With ham
  With cheese
  Baked
Crackers
  Graham
  Whole grain
  With peanut butter
  With cheese
  With cream cheese

Other Foods (Use occasionally)

Cake (using whole-grain flour)
  Gingerbread
  Plain cake with fruits
Cookie (with whole-grain
    cereal)
  Gingersnap
  Oatmeal/raisin
  Peanut butter

Plain vanilla
  Molasses
Gelatin (unsweetened)
  Plain, add fruit juice
  Whipped, add fruit juice
  With fruit
Pudding
  Cornstarch

Vanilla with fruit
  Squash or pumpkin
Custard
  Bread pudding with raisins
  Egg
  Rice
Tapioca
  With raisins

*Rich in vitamin A.
†Rich in vitamin C.
‡Fair source of vitamin A.

Appendix XIII
Center Feeding Chart

CENTER FEEDING CHART

Date: _March 23_   Sample:

	Time: 9:15			
	John	Solids Milk	1/2 j 8 oz	1/4 j 6 oz.

Name	1st feeding Food prepared/eaten			2nd feeding Food prepared/eaten			3rd feeding Food prepared/eaten			4th feeding Food prepared/eaten		
Amy	Time: 9:40			Time: 1:10			Time:			Time:		
	formula cereal	8 oz 5 T	6 oz all	milk fruit meat	4 oz 4 T 2 T	all 2 T 1 T						
Cathie	Time: 9:30			Time: 11:36			Time: 3:15			Time:		
	juice cracker	4 oz 1	all	sandwich milk fruit	1/2 8 oz 1/2 jar	1/4 6 oz all	milk fruit	4 oz 1/2 jar	1 oz all			
Emmy	Time: 10:07			Time:			Time:			Time:		
	milk fruit	4 oz 1 jar	2 oz all									
Frances	Time: 10:05			Time: 12:37			Time: 3:04			Time:		
	cereal fruit	1 jar 1/2 jar	3/4 j. all	meat veg. milk	1 jar 1/2 jar 6 oz.	1/2 jar all all	juice	8 oz	6 oz			
Kerry	Time: 11:45			Time:			Time:			Time:		
	meat veg. fruit	1/2 jar 1/2 jar 1/2 jar	all	juice	4 oz.	all						
Leigh	Time: 12:30			Time: 2:45			Time:			Time:		
	banana milk	1 4 oz	2/3 3 oz	juice sandwich	8 oz 1/2	all						
Leslie	Time: 10:09			Time: 1:15			Time:			Time:		
	milk cereal	6 oz 2 T	3 oz ref.	juice sandwich	8 oz 1/2	all						
Munro	Time: 1:13			Time:			Time:			Time:		
	sandwich cheese fruit milk	slice 1 jar 8 oz	all all all									
Oliver	Time: 9:30			Time: 12:30			Time: 3:10			Time:		
	juice	4 oz	all	meat + veg. fruit milk	1 jar 1/2 jar 4 oz	all all all	milk	8 oz	all			

Source: Herbert-Jackson, E., O'Brien, M., Porterfield, J., and Risley, T. R. (1977). *The Infant Center.* Baltimore: University Park Press.

Appendix XIV
Notes for Parents of 3- to 18-Month-Old Infants

Parent Report   Date _____

Name _____ Leaving _____

Last fed: _____ Last slept from: _____ To: _____

Parent's instructions for today:

Medicines:

Give phone number if different from the one we have on file: _____

Center Report

Your baby slept from: Diapering

_____ to _____   _____   _____

_____ to _____   _____   _____

_____ to _____   _____   _____

_____ to _____   _____   _____

Your baby ate:

When   What

1st

2nd

3rd

4th

_____

Some of the activities your   Disposition:
baby participated in were:

Center Comments:

Source: St. Louis Community College at Florissant Valley, Child Development Center, 1988.

Appendix XV
Notes for Parents of 18- to 24-Month-Old Toddlers

Name: _____

Date: _____

Did your child sleep
well last night?

Yes _____ No _____

Is your child having a
hard morning?

Yes _____ No _____

Reason:

Give phone number if
different: _____

Special instructions for
today:

Food Intake

+ = good

1 = one serving

0 = nothing

Breakfast _____

Lunch _____

Snack _____

Sleeping

_____ to _____

_____ to _____

Extra Comments:

OLDER
TODDLERS

Diapering (bowel movements)

L = Loose

H = Hard

N = Normal

_____

_____

_____

Activities

Source: St. Louis Community College at Florissant Valley, Child Development Center, 1988.

Appendix XVI
Sample Agenda for Preplanning, Conducting, and Evaluating a Family Workshop

WORKSHOP AGENDA

Workshop Title
Show, Tell, and Taste Snacks: A Fun Way to Eat for Nutrition

Theme
Nutritious snacks

Purpose

- To promote family togetherness
- To increase parents' awareness of what their children eat
- To teach children to choose, make, and enjoy nutritious food and snacks
- To help families choose nutritious snacks
- To suggest that children keep a record of the snacks they eat
- To know the difference between nutritious snacks and those that are not

Advance Preparation
Three weeks before:

1. Clear meeting with principal.
2. Secure authorization for room use.
3. Secure room for babysitting facility.
4. Make arrangements for several babysitters—one on "standby" status.
5. Form committee to make arrangements for possible transportation for parents.
6. Set up food committee with chairman. Pass out food sign-up sheet.

Two weeks before:

1. Make invitations.
2. Remind parents of food items they signed up to bring for use as workshop material or refreshments.
3. Organize games (include extra one if time permits).
4. Prepare on paper physical arrangement of the room.

One week before:

1. Prepare name tags.
2. Prepare mixer activity.
3. Prepare evaluation form and box.
4. Organize material for workshop.
5. Check with food committee to see what items are still lacking.
6. Prepare and organize materials for snack kit.
7. Send invitations.

One day before:

1. Remind parents of meeting.
2. Check progress of food committee.
3. Remind babysitters of the date and time.
4. Check with transportation committee to verify rides for parents needing them.

Day of the meeting:

1. Set up tables and activity centers.
2. Put posters, name tags, handouts in place.

Mixer

Materials:

1. Poster of the Food Guide Pyramid
2. Paper plate with pictures depicting a balanced meal
3. Ten envelopes of food pictures
   a. Two envelopes of bread, cereal, rice, and pasta pictures
   b. Two envelopes of vegetable pictures
   c. Two envelopes of fruit pictures
   d. Two envelopes of milk, yogurt, and cheese pictures
   e. Two envelopes of meat, poultry, fish, dried beans, eggs, and nuts pictures
4. Ten plates

Activity

1. Each person receives a food envelope and a paper plate.
2. Each person must ask others for food items to place on his/her plate until a balanced meal is received.

NAME TAGS

Name tags are cut in the shape of a glass from orange construction paper (orange juice) or white construction paper (milk) with space for a name to be written in marker.

Milk

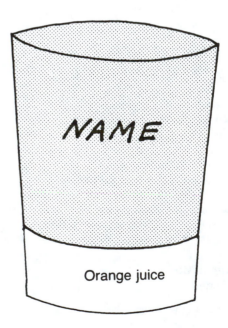

Orange juice

WORKSHOP SCHEDULE

Time	Activity	Technique	Resources	Person Responsible
12:45–12:55	Welcome	Name tags Mixer	Paper, markers, pins Paper plates, tape, food pictures	Janet Susan
12:55–1:05	Introduction of meeting purpose: Choosing nutritious snacks	Good nutrition is important. We can make nutritious food more interesting and fun to eat, especially snacks. This can be a family or child project.	Basic food groups posters	Donna
	Parents go to the six activity centers (see next section)	Explain each activity center. Look at the number on your name tag. Begin at that station and continue wherever your interest takes you.	Name tags Activity centers	Amanda
1:05–1:30	Activity centers			
	1. Peanut butter play dough	Follow recipe #1 in parent handout.	Peanut butter, dry milk, honey	Amanda
	2. Bugs on a log	Follow recipe #2 in parent handout.	Peanut butter, celery, raisins	Donna
	3. Peanut butter fruitwich	Follow recipe #3 in parent handout.	Crushed cereal, banana, peanut butter	Erma
	4. Fruit face and variations	Follow recipe #4 in parent handout.	Apple slices, raisins, pineapple chunks, shredded carrots, orange	Susan
	5. Decorated crackers	Follow recipe #5 in parent handout.	Crackers, cheese spread in a can	Katie
	6. Bread cut-outs	Follow recipe #6 in parent handout.	Whole-wheat bread, cookie cutters, cream cheese	Janet
1:30–1:45	Refreshments	Serve yourself juice; eat snacks prepared.	Fruit punch, bowl, cups	All
	Conclusion	Pass out evaluation sheet.	Pencils, parent handout	Katie

EVALUATION SHEET

We are interested in knowing whether you enjoyed our meeting this afternoon. Please put a check in the box below that best describes your feeling about the meeting. The space provided at the bottom of this page is for any suggestions you might have concerning our parent group meetings. We would be happy to hear from you, so feel free to comment!

Comments:

_____

_____

_____

_____

_____

RECIPES FOR SNACKS PREPARED AT ACTIVITY CENTERS

#1 Peanut Butter Play Dough
(meat and milk groups)
18 oz peanut butter
6 tbsp honey
Nonfat dry milk to right consistency
Cocoa (optional)

Mix together and form into shapes. Eat and enjoy!

#2 Bugs on a Log
(meat and fruit/vegetable groups)
Celery washed and cut into 4" lengths
Peanut butter
Raisins

Spread peanut butter in celery. Arrange 3 or 4 raisins on top of peanut butter.

#3 Peanut Butter Fruitwich
(fruit/vegetable and grain or meat groups)
Banana cut in half lengthwise
Peanut butter to spread on banana
Crushed cereal or nuts

Reassemble the bananas and roll in the crushed cereal or nuts. Slice in round if desired.

#4 Fruit Face
(fruit/vegetable group)
Apple, cut into quarters
Pineapple chunk
2 raisins
2 orange slices
1/2 c shredded carrot
Paper plate

Arrange 1/4 apple below center of plate for mouth. Put two apple quarters on either side for ears. A pineapple chunk in the middle becomes the nose. Use two raisins for eyes and two orange slices for eyebrows. Shredded carrots at the top make hair. Substitute any fruit and vegetables you like.

#5 Decorated Crackers
(grain and milk groups)
Whole-wheat or whole-grain crackers
Cheese in a can

Create designs, faces, or animals with the cheese on the crackers, or spread cream cheese on preshaped crackers.

#6 Bread Cut-Outs
(grain and milk groups)
Whole-wheat bread
Cheese from a can or cream cheese
Cookie cutters

Cut shapes from a slice of whole-wheat bread with cookie cutters. Decorate with cheese from a can, or spread cream cheese on the bread with a knife.

ADDITIONAL RECIPES TO TRY AT HOME

#7 Pudding Finger Paint
1 package pudding mix, cooked type
2 c milk
Waxed paper, large sheet

Cook pudding according to package directions. Pour a small amount (1/4 c) on the waxed paper. Make designs with fingers or spoon. Lick fingers as necessary. Eat remainder of "painting" with spoon.

#8 Sandwich Special
Cottage cheese and shredded carrots on whole-wheat raisin bread
Peanut or soy butter between apple rings
Honey butter (mix equal parts of honey and soft butter) between graham crackers (much better for a snack or dessert than cookies)
Peanut/soy butter or tomato slices on whole-wheat bread

#9 Banana Pops
Banana on a stick
Yogurt
Chopped nuts, coconut, or crushed cereal

Dip banana in yogurt, then roll in nuts, coconut, or granola. Freeze.

#10 Crunchy Bananas
Banana cut into 1" thick slices
Popsicle stick
Orange juice
Coconut, wheat germ, or chopped peanuts

Spear banana slices with stick, dip in juice, and roll in favorite topping.

#11 Banana Candle
Pineapple slice on a plate
Banana, peeled and cut in half
Maraschino cherry

Cut off ends of banana. Stand up the half banana in the pineapple ring. Put a cherry on top for the flame.

#12 Cheese Kabobs
Cubed cheese
Pretzel sticks
Fruit chunks, any variety

Thread cubes of cheese on pretzel sticks alternating with fruit.

#13 Cheese Balls
Cream cheese
Milk
Chopped peanuts

Soften cream cheese with a little milk; form into balls. Roll in chopped peanuts.

#14 Cheese Crunchies
Cheese cubes
Pretzel sticks
Wheat germ

Spear cheese cube with pretzel stick and roll in wheat germ.

#15 Finger Jello (Knox Blox)
7 envelopes unflavored gelatin (or 4 envelopes
    unflavored gelatin and 3 envelopes flavored)
4 c boiling fruit juice (or 4 c boiling water)

Mix and pour into a 13" × 9" pan. Chill until firm and cut into approximately 100 squares.

#16 Toad-in-a-Hole
1 slice of bread
1 Tbsp butter
1 egg

With a cookie cutter cut out a circle in the center of the bread. Melt butter in pan and brown bread on both sides. Break an egg in the hole. Cook covered until the egg doesn't jiggle.

#17 Bunny Salad
1 lettuce leaf
1 canned pear half
4 orange sections
1 maraschino cherry cut into 6 slices (or substitute
    pieces of apple or tomato for the cherry)

Put the lettuce leaf on the table. Put the pear half cut-side down on the lettuce leaf. Add orange sections for ears. Use cherry or apple or tomato slices for eyes, nose, mouth, and inside of ears.

#18 Mellow Yellow
2 slices of bread, buttered
1 slice of cheese between the bread slices
1 tbsp butter melted in a pan

Brown bread on both sides. Cut into triangles and share with a friend.

#19 Purple Cow
1/2 c 100% grape juice
1/2 c milk
2 scoops vanilla ice cream

Add grape juice, milk, and ice cream to blender container.
Blend on medium speed until smooth.
Drink.

#20 Banana Smoothie*
2 ripe bananas peeled and cut into chunks
1 c frozen unsweetened strawberries
8 oz carton vanilla low-fat yogurt
3/4 c milk

Place banana chunks, strawberries, yogurt, milk into blender.
Blend at high speed for 1 min.
Pour into glass and enjoy.

#21 Pancake Peanut Butter Taco*
Pancakes, 4" diameter
1 c peanut butter
2 c mashed bananas

Prepare pancakes using pancake mix or use frozen prepared pancakes.
Mash bananas in mixer.
Mix peanut butter and mashed bananas together.
Place 3-Tbsp scoops of mixture in each pancake.
Fold pancake over mixture and eat.

#22 Raspberry-Banana Soy Shake*
2 c soy milk
2 c fresh raspberries
2 bananas sliced
1/4 c low-fat plain yogurt
1/4 tsp ground nutmeg

Mix soy milk, fruit, and yogurt in blender until smooth.

#23 Tofu Berry Shake*
1 c pineapple juice
1 banana
1/2 c silken tofu (1/2 block, 5 oz)
1/2 c fresh or frozen strawberries
1/2 tsp vanilla
1/4 c sugar

Combine all ingredients in a blender and mix until smooth.

#24 Strawberry Banana Shake*
1/2 c frozen or fresh strawberries
1/2 banana sliced
1/2 c orange juice
1/4 c low-fat plain yogurt

Combine all ingredients in blender and mix until smooth.

#25 Watermelon Ice*
1 c cubed watermelon
1/2 c crushed ice
Juice squeezed from 1 lime

Put ice, melon, and juice in blender and mix.

#26 Cinnamon Apple Roll Wrap*

Tortillas, flour, 7" diameter
2 c unsweetened applesauce
Low-fat cheddar cheese
2 1/2 Tbsp cinnamon, ground
2 1/2 Tbsp sugar

Mix cinnamon and sugar.
Spread 1/4 c applesauce over tortilla.
Sprinkle 2 tsp cinnamon over applesauce.
Top with 1/4 c of cheddar cheese.
Wrap each tortilla and heat in microwave until cheese melts.

SNACKS

The following list is a list of simple, economical, and nutritious snack ideas you may find practical. Remember, to make snacks more tempting have them readily accessible and attractive for eyecatching appeal.

Milk Group
Flavored milk drink—1/2 c milk with 1/2 c any fruit juice
Cheese cubes
Ice cream

---

*Recipes reprinted with permission from The American School Food Service Association Your Child Nutrition eSource at http://www.asfsa.org.

Meat Group
Sunflower seeds, pumpkin seeds
Toasted soybeans
Assorted nuts
Peanut butter
Peanut butter balls rolled in sesame seeds
Beef jerky
Eggs sliced with pickle
Walnut, pecan halves with soft cheese spread as
    filling

Fruits and Vegetables
Using any fresh fruit or vegetable, experiment with
imaginative shapes (minted or dilled cucumbers,
radish fans, celery branches, pepper strips, carrot
curls, or cauliflower buds).

Make fruit juice by rolling unpeeled orange between hands until soft; insert straw.

Cut apples into small wedges and place on tooth-
pick with raisins.

Freeze orange juice on sticks in ice cube trays to
make sunshine pops.

Grains
Chow mein noodles
Crackers—use cheese and whole-grain varieties
Unsugared, ready-to-eat cereal
Taco shells (broken into chips)

Glossary

Acquired immunodeficiency syndrome (AIDS) Used to describe someone who is HIV positive and has CD4 count below 200 (CD4's are the cells that protect your body from infection, a healthy adult has a CD4 count of about 500–1200) or the presence of one or more opportunistic infections (infections that the human body normally fights off easily).

Amino acid Organic molecule containing carbon, hydrogen, oxygen, and nitrogen; the structural unit of protein; contains an amino group (–NH2) and a carboxyl or acidic group (–COOH).

Asthma A chronic inflammatory disease of the airways resulting from interactions among inflammatory cells, mediators, and other airway cells and tissues. Common symptoms include episodic or chronic wheeze, cough, and breathlessness.

B vitamins Group of water-soluble vitamins originally considered to be a single essential factor and now known to consist of eight separate vitamins.

Bag lunch Simple foods packed in a bag. A spoon may be added for eating some foods, but most foods should be finger foods.

Buffet style Allows children to take a plate, flatware, and food from a serving table with little or no assistance.

Cafeteria style In *cafeteria style* service, food, flatware, and plates are placed on a serving tray. A server portions and places food on the plate or tray. Some items may be self-selected.

Cholesterol A waxy substance found in all body tissues of humans and animals. All animal foods contain cholesterol; however, fatty plant foods like peanuts or avocados do not.

Cultural The transmission of social information from generation to generation, such as behavior, manners, artistic, and intellectual works.

Diabetes A group of diseases characterized by high levels of blood glucose resulting from defects in insulin secretion, insulin action, or both.

Dietary Reference Intakes (DRIs) DRI is a generic term that includes tools or standards used to evaluate nutrients in the diet, especially for groups such as day-care centers, group homes, or schools.

Disaccharide Carbohydrate that breaks down to two monosaccharide molecules during digestion. Examples are sucrose, maltose, and lactose.

Enzyme Proteins that catalyze reactions in the body. The names of enzymes frequently end with the suffix *-ase,* such as sucrase, the enzyme that effects the breakdown of sucrose.

Ethnic Of or relating to a sizable group of people sharing a common and distinctive racial, national, religious, linguistic, or cultural heritage.

Failure-to-thrive When a child's growth falls below reference standards for weight and height during the first three years. This growth failure may also be combined with a small head circumference.

Family style In *family style* food service, all children sit at a table, which has been prepared with individual plates and flatware. Food is placed on the table in serving bowls and is passed. Children help themselves from serving bowls with the assistance of the teacher.

Fiber (dietary)   Generic term that includes those plant constituents, mostly carbohydrates, that are not digestible by humans.

Gastroesophageal reflux disease (GERD)   Persistent spitting up or regurgitation combined with growth failure and/or other complications.

Gastroesophageal reflux (GER)   Spitting up, or regurgitation, is the return of small amounts of food during or immediately after eating.

Heme iron   Dietary iron derived from animal foods such as beef, poultry, and fish.

Human immunodeficiency virus (HIV)   An infection that attacks and wears down the immune system resulting in increased sensitivity to infection. HIV is transmitted primarily by exposure to contaminated body fluids, especially blood and semen, however, most children are infected through perinatal transmission.

Hydrogenation   The controlled addition of hydrogen to an unsaturated fatty acid. This process changes the melting point, thus producing solid fats from oils, depending on the extent of hydrogenation.

Hypercarotenemia   *Hypercarotenemia* is caused by very large intakes of beta-carotene resulting in yellow-orange pigmentation of the skin. This condition is not harmful but may be seen in children who consume large amounts of carrots.

Juvenile-onset diabetes   Currently referred to as Type 1 diabetes, characterized by an inability to produce the hormone insulin due to damage caused by the body's own immune system. This type of diabetes is most often seen in children and young adults and requires the use of insulin injections to survive.

Kilocalorie   The amount of heat required to raise 1 kg of water (at 1 atmosphere of pressure) 1 centigrade degree; same as a calorie.

Lead poisoning   Vulnerable individuals can be exposed to a toxic amount of the metal, lead, and experience a detrimental effect on almost all body systems including the central nervous system, kidneys, and reproductive system. Low levels of exposure can result in decreased cognition, while higher levels can result in coma or death.

Lipids   Organic compounds composed of carbon, hydrogen, and oxygen and generally immiscible with water, fats, or fat-like substances.

Lipoprotein   Compound composed of a lipid and a protein.

Macrominerals   Minerals present in the body in relatively large amounts.

Microminerals   Minerals present in the body in relatively small amounts; also called trace elements.

Modified family style   A *modified family style* may be used with a group of children new to the center. Only one or two items would be placed in serving bowls, and the teacher would place other foods on the plates.

Monosaccharide   Carbohydrate in its simplest form. Examples are fructose, glucose, and galactose.

Monounsaturated fatty acid   Fatty acid containing one double bond in its carbon chain.

Nutrient-dense foods   Foods that contain relatively high amounts of essential dietary factors required for growth and maintenance of the body, compared to the total calories.

Nutrients   Substances found in food that must be supplied to the body to ensure proper growth, maintenance, and repair.

Nutrition   The processes by which food is consumed, digested, absorbed, and transported. In general, nutrition is the science of food and how it is used by the body to achieve growth and health.

Obesity   Condition of being 20% or more above desirable or standard weight.

Overweight   Body weight 10% above desirable or standard weight.

Phytochemicals   Chemicals found in plants (fruits and vegetables) that may reduce the risks associated with heart disease, cancer, osteoporosis, and other chronic diseases in people who consume them regularly.

Picnic style   A meal usually eaten at a picnic table or on the ground out-of-doors. This style has been used indoors.

Polysaccharide   Complex carbohydrate molecule often consisting of 10,000 or more monosaccharides.

Polyunsaturated fatty acid (PUFA)   Fatty acid with two or more double bonds in its carbon chain; present in large amounts in plant oils and liquid at room temperature.

Prevalence   The widespread presence or extensiveness of an occurrence. When referring to health prevalence rates it measures current sickness in a population at a particular time or over a period of time.

Saturated When referring to fat, saturated means solid at room temperature because the carbon chains are completely filled with hydrogen.

Saturated fatty acid Fatty acid in which the carbon chains are filled with hydrogen; present in large amounts in animal fats and usually solid at room temperature.

Trans fatty acids Created when unsaturated fats (liquid) are manipulated to become solid by adding hydrogen to the carbon bonds.

Unsaturated When referring to a type of fat, unsaturated means a fat that is liquid at room temperature, because the carbon chains are not completely filled with hydrogen.

Index

Absorbic acid. *See* Vitamin C
Academic skills approach, 272
Acceptable macronutrient distribution range (AMDR), 131
Acesulfame potassium, 13
Acetic acid, 188
Acquired immunodeficiency syndrome (AIDS), 69
Activity pyramid, 61
Added sugars, 14
Addition and subtraction (lesson plan), 296
Adequate intake (AI), 57
Adult onset diabetes, 66
African Americans, 6
Age. *See* Life stages
AI, 57
AIDS, 69
Alcohol, 36
Allergies. *See* Food allergies
Alternate menu planning approach, 234
AMDR, 131
American Dietetic Association, 110
American Dietetics Association, 218
Amino acids, 15–16
Android obesity, 39–40
Anemia, 31, 67, 154
Anencephaly, 26
Anorexia nervosa, 218–219
Antioxidants, 22
Asian Americans, 6–7
Aspartame, 13
Assisted NuMenus, 234

Assisted nutrient menu planning (Assisted NuMenus), 234
Asthma, 70–71
Auditory discrimination and memory (lesson plan), 294

B vitamins, 23, 25
Baby bottle tooth decay, 112
Bad cholesterol, 19
Bag lunch, 246
Bereiter-Englemann academically oriented preschool program, 272
Beta-carotene, 24
Biotin, 23
Birth to 12 months. *See* Infant
BMI, 37–38, 60–64
BMI-for-age charts, 62–64
BMI growth charts, 167–170
Body fat, 169
Body image, 216
Body mass index (BMI), 37–38, 60–64
Bottle feeding, 99–100, 101
Bottle warming, 99
Bottled *vs.* tap water, 34
Breast milk substitutes, 96
Breast pump, 89, 91
Breastfeeding
    advantages, 91–92, 108
    breast milk substitutes, 96–98
    breast pump, 89, 91
    care/handling of milk, 92–93

DATE DUE

NOV 16 2005		
DEC 07 2005		
DEC 05 2006		
MAY 15 2008		
APR 23 2008		
DEC 12 2008		

GAYLORD   PRINTED IN U.S.A.